THE EVOLUTION OF TRANSNATIONAL RULE-MAKERS THROUGH CRISES

In recent years, transnational private rule-makers have emerged and multiplied. In this book, experts from various academic disciplines offer empirically grounded case studies and theoretical insights into the evolution and resilience of these bodies through crises. Transnational private rule-makers display considerable flexibility if compared to public institutions both in exercising their rule-making functions and in adapting and transforming in light of endogenous or exogenous crisis events calling for change. The contributors identify such events and reflect on their impact on transnational private rule-makers. This edited volume covers important areas of global production and finance that are associated with private rule-making and delves into procedural, substantive, and practical elements of private rule-making processes. At a policy level, the book provides comparisons among practices of private bodies in various areas, allowing for important lessons to be drawn for all public and private stakeholders active in, or affected by, private and public rule-making. This title is Open Access.

Panagiotis Delimatsis is Professor of EU and International Economic Law and Director of the Tilburg Law and Economics Center (TILEC) at Tilburg University.

Stephanie Bijlmakers is Assistant Professor of Transnational Private Regulation and Governance at Tilburg University.

M. Konrad Borowicz is Assistant Professor of Transnational Financial Regulation and Research Coordinator of TILEC at Tilburg University.

The Evolution of Transnational Rule-Makers through Crises

Edited by

PANAGIOTIS DELIMATSIS
Tilburg University

STEPHANIE BIJLMAKERS
Tilburg University

M. KONRAD BOROWICZ
Tilburg University

CAMBRIDGE
UNIVERSITY PRESS

CAMBRIDGE
UNIVERSITY PRESS

Shaftesbury Road, Cambridge CB2 8EA, United Kingdom

One Liberty Plaza, 20th Floor, New York, NY 10006, USA

477 Williamstown Road, Port Melbourne, VIC 3207, Australia

314–321, 3rd Floor, Plot 3, Splendor Forum, Jasola District Centre, New Delhi – 110025, India

103 Penang Road, #05–06/07, Visioncrest Commercial, Singapore 238467

Cambridge University Press is part of Cambridge University Press & Assessment, a department of the University of Cambridge.

We share the University's mission to contribute to society through the pursuit of education, learning and research at the highest international levels of excellence.

www.cambridge.org
Information on this title: www.cambridge.org/9781009329361

DOI: 10.1017/9781009329408

First published 2023

A catalogue record for this publication is available from the British Library.

A Cataloging-in-Publication data record for this book is available from the Library of Congress.

ISBN 978-1-009-32936-1 Hardback

Contents

Figures

Tables

Contributors

Abdel fattah Alshadafan PhD Candidate at the Technical University of Munich, Germany

Justus Baron Senior Research Associate at the Center on Law, Business, and Economics, Northwestern University Pritzker School of Law, United States

Rosalba Belmonte Research Fellow in Political Sociology at Tuscia University, Italy

Stephanie Bijlmakers Assistant Professor of Transnational Private Regulation and Governance at Tilburg University, the Netherlands

M. Konrad Borowicz Assistant Professor of Transnational Financial Regulation and Research Coordinator of the Tilburg Law and Economics Center (TILEC) at Tilburg University, the Netherlands

Tim Büthe Professor and Chair for International Relations, Hochschule für Politik at the Technical University of Munich (TUM), TUM School of Social Science & Technology, and TUM School of Management, Germany; Technology Policy Fellow, Duke University, United States

Fabrizio Cafaggi Judge at the Italian Council of State, Italy

Philip G. Cerny Professor Emeritus of Politics and Global Affairs at the University of Manchester, United Kingdom, and Rutgers University, United States

Panagiotis Delimatsis Professor of EU and International Economic Law and Director of the Tilburg Law and Economics Center (TILEC) at Tilburg University, the Netherlands

Jimmy Donaghey Professor of Human Resource Management at the University of Southern Australia Business School, Australia

Tetty Havinga Fellow in Sociology of Law at Radboud University Nijmegen, the Netherlands

Olia Kanevskaia Assistant Professor of European Economic Law and Technology at Utrecht University, the Netherlands

Margarita Nieves-Zárate PhD Candidate at the University of Groningen, the Netherlands

Matteo Ortino Associate Professor of Economic Law at the University of Verona, Italy

Enrico Partiti Group Senior Legal Counsel - Sustainable Finance at Triodos Bank NV, the Netherlands

Daniel R. Quiroga-Villamarín PhD Candidate and Researcher at the Graduate Institute of International and Development Studies in Geneva, Switzerland

Juliane Reinecke Professor of Management Studies at Saïd Business School, University of Oxford, United Kingdom

Rebecca Schmidt Postdoctoral Researcher at the University of Oslo, Norway

Slobodan Tomic Lecturer in Public Management and Administration at the University of York, United Kingdom

Paul Verbruggen Professor of Private Law at Tilburg University, the Netherlands

Pierre-Hugues Verdier Professor of Law and Director of Graduate Studies, University of Virginia School of Law, United States

Jan Wouters Professor of International Law and International Organisations and Jean Monnet Chair at KU Leuven, Belgium

Abbreviations

3GPP	3rd Generation Partnership Project
AAP	alternative approval process
AB	accreditation body
AFi	Accountability Framework initiative
AI	artificial intelligence
ALF-CIO	American Federation of Labor and Congress of Industrial Organizations
ANSI	American National Standards Institute
API	American Petroleum Institute
ARRC	Alternative Reference Rates Committee
ASA	American Standards Association
ASP	audit service providers
BBA	British Bankers Association
BCBS	Basel Committee on Banking Supervision
BIS	Bank for International Settlements
BRI	Belt and Road Initiative
BSCI	Business Social Compliance Initiative
BSEE	Bureau for Safety and Environmental Enforcement
CAC	Codex Alimentarius Commission
CACs	collective action clauses
CAS	Court of Arbitration for Sport
CCP	central counterparties
CCQ	Code Compliance Questionnaire
CDS	credit default swap
CFTC	Commodities Futures and Trading Commission
CGF	Consumer Goods Forum
CJEU	Court of Justice of the EU
COPOLCO	ISO Committee on Consumer Policy

COS	Center for Offshore Safety
CSR	corporate social responsibility
DEVCO	ISO Committee on Developing Country Matters
DEVPRO	ISO Programme for Developing Countries
DSSI	Debt Service Suspension Initiative
DWH	Deepwater Horizon
ECJ	European Court of Justice
ECOSOC	UN Economic and Social Council
EU	European Union
FAO	Food and Agriculture Organization
FCA	Financial Conduct Authority
FRBNY	Federal Reserve Bank of New York
FSA	Financial Services Authority
FSB	Financial Stability Board
FSC	Food Stewardship Council
FSF	Financial Stability Forum
FSOC	Financial Stability Oversight Council
GAP	Global Practices for Agriculture, manufacturing, and distribution
GDPR	General Data Protection Regulation
GFC	global financial crisis
GFSI	Global Food Safety Initiative
GSTC	Global Sustainable Tourism Council
GUF	Global Union Federation
HACCP	hazard analysis and critical control points
HRDD	human rights due diligence
IBA	ICE Benchmark Administration
ICE	Intercontinental Exchange
ICMA	International Capital Market Association
ICT	information and communications technology
IEC	International Electrotechnical Commission
IEEE	Institute of Electrical and Electronics Engineers
IETF	Internet Engineering Task Force
IIF	Institute of International Finance
ILO	International Labour Organization
IMF	International Monetary Fund
IOC	International Olympic Committee
IOSCO	International Organization of Securities Commissions
IPMA	International Primary Market Association
ISDA	International Swaps and Derivatives Association
ISEAL	International Social and Environmental Accreditation and Labelling Alliance

ISMA	International Securities Markets Association
ISO	International Organization for Standardization
ISSB	international standard-setting body
ITA	Independent Testing Authority
ITC	International Trade Center
ITF	International Task Force on Harmonization and Equivalence in Organic Agriculture
ITU	International Telecommunications Union
ITU-D	ITU-Telecommunication Development Sector
ITU-R	ITU-Radiocommunication Sector
ITU-T	ITU-Telecommunication Standardization Sector
LIBOR	London Interbank Offered Rate
MA	master agreement
MarAD	US Maritime Administration
MMS	Minerals Management Service
MNC	multinational corporation
MODU	mobile offshore drilling units
MSC	Marine Stewardship Council
NADO	National Anti-Doping Organization
NAMA	non-agricultural market access
NCP	national contact point
NGO	nongovernmental organization
NTMs	non-tariff measures
OECD	Organisation for Economic Co-operation and Development
OTC	over-the-counter
PEFC	Programme for the Endorsement of Forest Certification
R&D	research and development
RA	Radiocommunication Assembly
RADO	Regional Anti-Doping Organization
RCAP	Regulatory Consistency Assessment Program
RMG	ready-made garment
RSPO	Roundtable on Sustainable Palm Oil
SDO	Standards development organization
SDRM	Sovereign Debt Restructuring Mechanism
SEMP	Safety and Environmental Management Plan
SOFR	secured overnight financial rate
SSB	standard-setting body
SSO	standard-setting organization
TAP	traditional approval process
TBT	Agreement on Technical Barriers to Trade

TCP/IP	Transmission Control Protocol/Internet Protocol
TFEU	Treaty on the Functioning of the EU
TPR	transnational private regulation
TR	trade repositories
TSAG	Telecommunication Standardization Advisory Group
UN	United Nations
UNCTAD	UN Conference on Trade and Development
UNEP	UN Environment Programme
UNGP	UN Guiding Principles on Business and Human Rights
UNIDO	UN Industrial Development Organization
VEA	voluntary economic activism
VSS	voluntary sustainability standards
WADA	World Anti-Doping Agency
WTDC	World Telecommunication Development Conference
WTO	World Trade Organization
WTSA	World Telecommunication Standardization Assembly

Acknowledgements

The contributions included in this edited volume were presented at an international multidisciplinary online conference held on 3-4 December 2020 on the topic 'The evolution of transnational private rule-makers: Understanding drivers and dynamics'. This conference was organized by the Tilburg Law and Economics Center (TILEC), a Center of Excellence at Tilburg University.

The event marked the completion of the first two years of a 5-year research project, led by Panagiotis Delimatsis, on 'The Resilience and Evolution of Economic Activism and the Role of Law' (REVEAL) – that received funding from the European Research Council (ERC) under the European Union's Horizon 2020 research and innovation programme (ERCCoG – Grant Agreement No 725798).

The conference and this edited volume would not have been possible without the support of many people. We would like to thank Enrico Partiti, who played a pivotal role in co-organizing the conference and bringing people and ideas together in the early stages of preparing this volume. For his intellectual engagement, collegiality, and advice, we are grateful to him. We would like to thank the contributors for their time and expertise dedicated to our project, and their hard work to deliver this volume in time. Your continued commitment and cooperation throughout the Covid-19 pandemic, which posed challenges of all sorts, is greatly appreciated.

We would like to thank the three anonymous reviewers for their constructive and valuable comments, and Finola O' Sullivan, Tom Randall, Marianne Nield, Robert Judkins and their colleagues at Cambridge University Press, for their professionalism, support and timely responses throughout the publication process.

We are thankful to the Tilburg University Library for their generous financial contribution, making it possible to publish this volume Open Access.

We would like to dedicate this book to the TILEC community.

Panagiotis Delimatsis, Stephanie Bijlmakers, and M. Konrad Borowicz

Tilburg, December 2022

Introduction

How Private Rule-Makers Evolve through Crises

Panagiotis Delimatsis, Stephanie Bijlmakers, and M. Konrad Borowicz

I.1 INTRODUCTION

Transnational private regulation (TPR) is gradually expanding beyond regulatory areas traditionally associated with private rules such as technical standardization, finance in domains such as trade in derivatives and payment systems, or the field of sports. Private rules are increasingly encroaching upon areas traditionally considered as the preserve of State regulation such as sustainability, food safety, and human rights. The relative importance of private regulation varies across domains. In some instances, such as in the domain of sustainability, or food safety, private regulators fiercely compete for acceptance and uptake by the market and the State. In fields such as finance, on the other hand, private regulation is at times the preserve of a strong "monopolist" wielding considerable power and influence.

The main reason for private bodies' success in the acquisition and consolidation of their regulatory influence lies in their epistemic knowledge that endows them with the capacity to design rules that are complementary to (and, in extreme cases, substitutes for) public rules at the national, regional, and transnational level. This edited volume acknowledges this fundamental driver while shifting the focus of studies of transnational private regulation to its distinctive organizational features,[1] which, crucially for the purposes of this volume, are activated and leveraged around crises.

Transnational rule-makers display considerable flexibility if compared to public institutions both in exercising their rule-making functions and adapting and transforming in light of endogenous or exogenous events calling for change. Private bodies can easily include broad multi-stakeholder constituencies in rule-making processes and experiment with creative organizational forms and enforcement

[1] See F. Cafaggi, A Comparative Analysis of Transnational Private Regulation: Legitimacy, Quality, Effectiveness and Enforcement, EUI Department of Law Research Paper No. 2014/145.

mechanisms. These may subsequently be institutionalized and incorporated in public frameworks, which further testifies to the success of transnational private regulation.

Organizational forms, procedural rules, informal decision-making processes of transnational private rule-makers, as well as rule-making outcomes and forms appeared and evolved over time as a response to pressures and demands from within and outside these organizations. In particular, crucial events in their regulatory environment – such as a financial crisis, a product safety scandal, a large-scale manufacturing or production failure, or a pandemic – reinforce existing incentives and rationales (or create new ones) for private regulators to internalize the need for change. Arguably, domains of private rule-making such as technical standardization or forms of private ordering in the financial sector evolved relatively insulated from the demands and influence of public authority. Other private regulators seem intimately intertwined with, and even dependent on, public rules and thus extremely sensitive and receptive to changes – be it current or prospective – in regulatory environments, enforcement practices of regulatory authorities, and court rulings.

Private regulatory bodies that seek to persuade various stakeholders about the value of their rules do that by acquiring and maintaining legitimacy. Private standard-setters adapt their rules and procedures to meet demands for legitimacy and accountability from both public authority at various regulatory levels and different stakeholder groups. Change and evolution of private rule-makers improves input and output legitimacy, solves transnational collective action problems, and provides mechanisms through which private regulators are held accountable. On occasions, however, private regulators are also motivated by a need to maintain their operations, protect the interests of their members or a subset of their membership, and pursue other institutional goals to preserve the status quo. On other occasions, private regulators coevolve, as a result of their interaction with other private regulators within the ever-changing environment they collectively create. The evolution of private regulators through critical junctures may occur for several reasons other than a pure instinct for survival, including to defuse internal opposition, to sideline specific interest groups to the benefit of others, perhaps even to hollow out public rules.

Crises may be multifaceted, complex events of a varying intensity and duration. The negative externalities they generate for society often cause States to struggle to address the consequences, whereas private forces, which may have caused, in part, such crises, continue to regulate economic activity; frequently, in an ever-assertive manner. This type of "free riding" (in that private bodies benefit from increased legitimacy without internalizing the costs of, first, acquisition of this legitimacy and, second, regulatory disasters with substantial financial, health-related, or other consequences), is not a new phenomenon. What is new, however, is that private bodies aggressively seek more power in the immediate aftermath of a crisis event, taking advantage of a crisis-struck State. That is the central hypothesis of the research project Resilience and Evolution of Economic Activism and the Role of Law (REVEAL), which inspired this volume.

Against this backdrop, the objective of this edited volume is to explore the fundamental role of transnational private rule-makers in the regulation of global production and finance, thereby furthering our knowledge of the organizational and contextual features and other characteristics contributing to the flexibility, adaptability, and – ultimately – resilience of transnational private rule-making. More specifically, in this volume, we aim to cast light over the inherently dynamic and evolutionary nature of transnational private regulation when regulatory failures, crises, and critical turning points arise. The reason for choosing this approach is that empirically grounded accounts foregrounding flexibility, evolution, and the associated resilience of transnational private regulators remain scant in legal but also broader regulatory scholarship. Structures, characteristics, internal mechanics, rules, and behavior of rule-making participants and the overarching ecology of private regulation remain systematically underdeveloped in current legal research. The lack of a systematic empirical study of their origin and evolution is striking and in direct contrast to the ever-increasing role such bodies acquired in global governance. However, the perspective of evolution and dynamism in relation to the resilience, effectiveness, and legitimacy of private rule-makers offers a new viewpoint to look into the establishment and development of transnational private regulation, its consolidation as a key staple of global governance, and its impact on the smooth functioning of economic activity.

I.2 THE COMPLEXITY OF DELINEATING THE CONTOURS OF CRISES

At present, other than the distinction between natural and man-made causations,[2] there is no unequivocal consensus regarding the contours of crisis as a scholarly concept or its normative and prescriptive orientation.[3] We see crisis as a value-laden concept that attempts to capture low-probability yet high-impact events that threaten the very survival of an organization and thus create fertile ground for rapid decisions. Its cause, effect on the organization itself and its stakeholders, and means of resolution are ambiguous. In addition, crises are accompanied by a relatively shared belief that decisions must be taken rapidly due to the significance and impact of the events occurred.[4]

[2] See U. Rosenthal and A. Kouzmin, Globalizing an Agenda for Contingencies and Crisis Management: An Editorial Statement (1993) 1:1 *Journal of Contingencies and Crisis Management*, 1.

[3] See T. Williams et al., Organizational Response to Adversity: Fusing Crisis Management and Resilience Research Streams (2017) 11:2 *Academy of Management Annals*, 733, at 734.

[4] See C. M. Pearson and J. A. Clair, Reframing Crisis Management (1998) 23:1 *Academy of Management Review* 59, at 60.

Crises are extraordinary, erratic events that are perceived as a threat against the core values or life-sustaining functions of a given system, thereby revealing the weaknesses of regular structures and the lack of contingency planning in an organization.[5] Thus, rarity, irregularity, and low likelihood are key traits of crisis events, calling for swift crisis management to allow for recovery. Crises constitute critical junctures that may result in distinct trajectories of change: chain reaction leading to collapse and extinction, transformation for the better, or recovery and rebirth under a renewed framework and context.[6] In that sense, crises are test-beds for effective crisis management and its potential for recovery and readjustment.[7]

A crisis can be instant or grow gradually, notably if it is internal (for instance, a growing sense of delegitimization within an organization). It can often be the result of a regulatory disaster, that is, a catastrophic event or series of events, which are caused, at least in part, by a failure in the design or the operation of the regulatory regime put in place to prevent its occurrence. In this regard, the ensuing crisis will be the result of sometimes unintended and unpredictable consequences of the system's mechanics and its interactions with other systems. In that sense, a regulatory disaster may be deemed as one of fundamental nature, capable of changing ultimately the regulatory approach in a given sector and thus of transforming private activity and its interaction with public regulation. On the other hand, when a crisis unfolds (which is a matter of subjective perception), it is considered that intervention may still limit the effects of an emerging or escalating event. No (timely) intervention may then lead to a disaster.

Much of the organization scholarship focuses on crisis management. Crisis management comprises processes for identification, assessment, and tackling of a crisis before, during, or after it has happened. Relevant scholarship examines under which conditions an organization or system can return to normal functioning after a disruption.[8] Crisis management goes beyond technical containment to control conflicts at the managerial or broader organizational and institutional level, thereby raising issues of power, trust, or legitimacy. Indeed, one could view as crises events that have unprecedented effects within an organization; for instance, events that bring about previously unanticipated internal mobilization, discussions, protests, even boycotts or departures from a given organization altogether.[9] In that

[5] See D. Smith, Crisis Management: Practice in Search of a Paradigm, in *Key Readings in Crisis Management: Systems and Structures for Prevention and Recovery* (D. Smith and D. Elliott eds., 2006).

[6] See the contribution by P. Delimatsis, "The Resilience of Private Authority in Times of Crisis" in this volume (Chapter 1).

[7] See also A. Carmeli and J. Schaubroeck, Organisational Crisis-Preparedness: The Importance of Learning from Failures (2008) 41 *Long Range Planning* 177, at 179.

[8] See C. Roux-Dufort and C. Lalonde, Editorial: Exploring the Theoretical Foundations of Crisis Management (2013) 21:1 *Journal of Contingencies and Crisis Management* 1.

[9] Cf. Williams et al., *supra* note 3, at 739.

respect, crises call for critical decision-making under conditions of uncertainty and time pressure.[10]

Analytically, we also find it useful to distinguish crises as one-off events and crises as a process that gradually grows to challenge the fundamental attributes, mechanics, and managerial acumen of a given organization, thereby exposing ill-structured systems. The problem with viewing a crisis as a one-off event is that it may neglect how crises are produced in the first place, thereby shifting responsibility outside a given system due to the unpredictability of the crisis event. In contrast, by viewing crises as a process, we can capture the often-observed phenomenon of an incubation period preceding a crisis.[11] Conceptualizing crises as a process helps overcome the problem of responsibility-shifting because it focuses on the need to fully capture the dynamics of crisis-fostering landscapes and factors of organizational degeneration as a process that entails repeated interaction and responses by the various actors involved that are dispersed over time and space.[12]

A fundamental finding of theories that view crises as a process is that even otherwise run-of-the-mill events can accumulate and evolve into substantial triggering events, notably due to mistaken assumptions, information asymmetries and overall complexity, organisational culture that misses or misinterprets critical signals, and unjustified optimism.[13] Crucially, an as-a-process conceptualization of crises diminishes the element of unpredictability. In other words, certain crises of this type may be anticipated and handled.[14] Depending on the context, crises may be generated by small disturbances that were overlooked. Therefore, such disturbances should be encouraged, as they increase the adaptive capacity of the organization or system and its ability to innovate, self-learn, and share upward flows of information.[15]

In addition, we argue that considering crises that bring organizations to the brink of collapse as either exogenous shocks or internal deficiencies may be too reductive of an approach. In practice, change will often be instigated by a blend of internal

[10] See J. Wolbers, S. Kuipers, and A. Boin, A Systematic Review of 20 Years of Crisis and Disaster Research: Trends and Progress (2021) 12 *Risk, Hazards and Crisis in Public Policy*, 374, at 375.

[11] So-called creeping crises are threats to widely shared societal values or life-sustaining systems that evolve over time and space and is foreshadowed by precursor events, subject to varying degrees of political and/or societal attention, and in part or insufficiently addressed by authorities: See A. Boin, M. Ekengren, and M. Rhinard, Hiding in Plain Sight: Conceptualizing the Creeping Crisis (2020) 11:2 *Risk, Hazards and Crisis in Public Policy*, 116, at 122.

[12] Cf. Roux-Dufort, Delving into the Roots of Crises: The Genealogy of Surprise, in *The Handbook of International Crisis Communication Research* (A. Schwarz, M. Seeger, and C. Auer eds., 2016), 24.

[13] See the seminar work by B. Turner, Organizational and Interorganizational Development of Disasters (1976) 21:3 *Administrative Science Quarterly* 378.

[14] Gundel calls such crises "conventional." He goes on to identify another three types of crisis: unexpected, intractable, and fundamental: See S. Gundel, Towards a New Typology of Crises (2005) 13:3 *Journal of Contingencies and Crisis Management* 106, at 110.

[15] See R. Biggs et al., Toward Principles for Enhancing the Resilience of Ecosystem Services (2012) 37 *Annual Review of Environment and Resources* 421.

processes and exogenous forces as they interact with the organization, its stakeholders, and the surrounding environment, causing a shift of state by bringing a system of reduced resilience into a tipping point.[16] Following this line of thought allows us to scrutinize both the nature of the crisis and the system that it affects by exploring the origin, evolution, reaction, and adaptation of a given organization before, during, and after a triggering event.

Overall, we believe that, by putting crises at the heart of this volume we capture moments in an institutional setting where we can observe strategies, values, rules and their enforcement, learning by doing, mutability, diffusion patterns and understanding of interdependence, and institutional memory (and the factors for deviating therefrom) with a view to offering robust explanations as to how and why certain institutions survive through fire and water.

I.3 CRISES AND THEIR INTERACTION WITH THE QUEST FOR ORGANIZATIONAL RESILIENCE

Just as recovery cannot exist without a preceding crisis, resilience presupposes a disturbance that instigates a moment of stress, and which is surmounted after the organism or system demonstrates certain resilience-causing traits. Throughout this volume, the institutional setup of a system (for instance, the actor constellations and conflict dynamics in the previous period) is a significant variable. While crises are potentially devastating moments that put a spotlight on any deficiency in the design and activities of an organizational system and therefore put the resilience of an organization to the test, they will also most likely offer opportunities for certain actors (willing to be) involved in their management and leadership.

More generally, external triggering points that challenge the institutional status quo; question the legitimacy, practices, and mechanics of a given organisation; and call for urgent introspection, action, and radical institutional reform challenge the resilience of that institution. Over time, as institutions grow in prominence and legitimacy gaps emerge, contestation internally and externally increases. Often, delegitimation is the result of internal conflicts that intentionally challenge, through discursive and behavioral practices, the adequacy of the status quo. In those instances, we refer to critical junctures and how institutions internalize them.

As a concept, resilience is strongly associated with crises, as it entails a process of adaptation, improvisation to find responses to shocks, and recovery. Notably, if we view crises as a dynamic process that evolves over time, then resilience and crises are two closely interrelated concepts with similar characteristics. The dynamism of resilience is an inherent trait thereof; indeed, it cannot be otherwise. The resilience of organizations is constantly tested by triggering events that bring about adversity.

[16] See M. Scheffer et al., Catastrophic Shifts in Ecosystems (2001) 413 *Nature* 591.

Resilience is a heavy-laden yet malleable concept that permeates various scientific disciplines, issue areas, and even discussions in the public discourse.[17] When talking about resilience, discussions evolve around resilient society, network systems, financial institutions, or ideas. Often, resilience is presented as an outcome but also as a process. In all cases, resilience is typically mentioned in a positive manner and is associated with and viewed under the prism of risks or shocks, which often will be exogenous to the subject; yet such shocks can very well result from internal conflicts and system dynamics, jeopardizing the existence or survival of the subject, at least in its previous form.[18]

Resilience should not be confounded with sustainability: for a system to achieve the latter, resilience is a necessary but insufficient condition. Resilience enhances perseverance, functioning, and reliability of an organization against events that challenge its existence. Resilience can be a set of traits present in an organization in order to avoid adversity. These would include resources and energy to grow – a flexible structure but also complexity and heterogeneity to maintain maturity.[19] However, resilience can also relate to a set of traits that allow an organization or system to overcome adversity either by recovering or, crucially, by reaching a new state of equilibrium. These traits would entail low connectivity to decrease vulnerability of a system; information flow through feedback loops; the ability to improvise and reorient, for instance, through emergent leadership; or the learning of new behaviors and organizational patterns. As a consequence, then, resilience should be deemed as including pre-adversity organizational capabilities, capabilities of in-crisis organization and adjustment, and post-crisis resilient responses.[20] Still, past resilience may only to a limited extent allow predicting future resilience, as, conceptually, resilience implies the ability to navigate new and potentially different challenges.

Finally, there is also a dark side to resilience, which is often neglected.[21] Resilience may also mean resistance to change, inability to learn and adapt, and lack of flexibility and transformational capacity. Resilience then has a flip side, which relates to the vulnerability of a given organization: while being resilient suggests the existence of a successful mechanism to address adversity, a near disaster also brings to the fore the importance of identifying how prone an institution can be to similar perilous situations and how important future caution with respect to mitigating potential risks can be.

[17] See J. Walker and M. Cooper, Genealogies of Resilience: From Systems Ecology to the Political Economy of Crisis Adaptation (2011) 42:2 *Security Dialogue* 143.

[18] See C. S. Holling, Resilience and Stability of Ecological Systems (1973) 4 *Annual Review of Ecology and Systematics* 1, at 17.

[19] See B. Fath; C. Dean and H. Katzmair, Navigating the Adaptive Cycle: An Approach to Managing the Resilience of Social Systems (2015) 20:2 *Ecology and Society* 24.

[20] Cf. Williams et al., *supra* note 3, at 742.

[21] Ibid., at 756.

I.4 A MULTIDISCIPLINARY INQUIRY INTO TRANSNATIONAL RULE-MAKING THROUGH CRISES

This edited volume is a multidisciplinary inquiry into the dynamics of transnational private rule-making, an empirically under-researched yet fundamental component of global governance. We believe that directing our attention toward these evolutionary forces, their impact on the goals pursued by transnational private regulators, as well as on the implications for targets and beneficiaries of their rules will contribute to shedding new light on the mechanics and dynamics of resilience of private regulation and its implications.

It will also allow us to evaluate from a new perspective the relation between public and private authority and, in particular, the capacity and limitations of the former to effectively enroll, steer, and influence the latter. Finally, this edited volume tackles organizational resilience and crisis management together, which, quite paradoxically, is rare in the relevant literature in management and organization studies and much less in the legal and political science literature. The volume therefore aspires to inform legal and regulatory debates about input and output legitimacy of transnational private rule-makers, as well as various strands of literature concerned with the interplay between public and private rules and public steering of transnational regulators, with a distinct focus on the role of crisis events.

The mix of selected contributors is particularly fitting to tackle these issues. We have invited scholars from various fields of law, financial regulation, economics, management, international relations, and public policy. Contributors were carefully selected to include both renowned experts in various key domains intersecting with transnational private regulation and younger, emerging scholars with a genuine willingness to delve into the dynamics and evolution of transnational private rule-making and the impact of crises on institutional dynamics, both conceptually and empirically.

Contributions to this volume take a careful look at the evolutionary dynamics of transnational private rule-making in selected issue areas. Other than the conceptual and theoretical contributions that set the scene, most contributions take the form of a case study–based inquiry into specific private bodies, with two case studies covering a public and a hybrid body to offer fitting comparisons. Previous crises-related scholarship has shown the adequacy of such method in advancing research in this field. The regulatory domains covered by the case studies include rule-making in financial domains of debt restructuring, decentralized financial institutions, and financial benchmarks. They also include case studies tackling product standardization in the areas of food safety, sustainable production, technical standards set by the International Organization for Standardization (ISO), the International Telecommunication Union (ITU) and Information and Communication Technology (ICT) bodies, and sectoral self-regulation in the oil industry as well as sport-related bodies. Through this exercise, we can identify distinct evolutionary trends in transnational private regulation. Do private regulators manage to design effective solutions under the pressure of various stakeholders and critical events? How do private regulators respond to legitimacy and accountability demands from different constituencies? Do crises and regulatory failures contribute to bring back rule-making competences to public authority or rather contribute to further expand the competences of private regulators? What variations between these bodies, their relations with public authority, and other contextual elements can explain different outcomes?

This edited volume does not aim to look into accountability or legitimacy in the abstract. Rather, through the various contributions included in this book, we approach the evolution and change of private organizations as a means to build legitimacy gradually and maintain relevance or even achieve dominance in the field in which those organizations are active. Although we do not consider as necessary to conceptualize legitimacy or accountability, certain contributions tackle legitimacy in that they identify events within a given organization that may have created a composite legitimacy crisis. Nevertheless, and arguably more fundamentally than this, we view such events as yet another possibility to properly explore the role of crises in the evolution of institutions.

While claiming to be anything but exhaustive, the proposed edited volume represents a balanced account that foregrounds the importance of a dynamic and evolutionary perspective in analyzing and understanding transnational private regulation. The volume aims to offer to our readership a nuanced understanding of the role of critical events and crises on the operation of private regulatory bodies and their relations with State actors, while also touching upon the allocation of regulatory powers between public and private authority. It will also encourage further empirical and evolutionary accounts of transnational private regulation, a crucial rule-making domain that enables and determines the fate and pace of transnational economic activity and intersects with fundamental public objectives.

1.5 THE DIFFERENT FACETS OF RESILIENCE AND EVOLUTION OF PRIVATE RULEMAKING

This edited volume investigates the relentless evolution, mutability, and crisis-absorbing capacity of transnational private regulators and standard-setters from various disciplinary perspectives. The contributions included in this volume intend to provide a thorough account of the dynamic evolution of transnational private regulators and their output in relation to critical events in their regulatory environment. The contributors were requested to identify the external regulatory dynamics and drivers for change, including crises; the interactions with, or requests from, public authority, rules, and legal regimes at various regulatory levels (i.e., international, regional, national, sub-national, and other private regimes); as well as the heterogeneity and internal organizational dynamics within these organizations.

Contributors were then invited to reflect on the impact of these features on the evolution of transnational private rule-makers and their resilience.

In this respect, contributors reflected on certain propositions that we made in the REVEAL project regarding private rule-makers: for instance, that private regulators in the domains under review have a crisis-absorbing capacity owing to their organizational heterogeneity and flexibility or that, through their inertia in the aftermath of crisis events that may be attributed to path dependencies, behavioral biases or capture, public regulators, and supervisors of private rule-makers facilitate the continuous dominance of private rule-making. In terms of the resilience-related inquiry of private authority in this book, contributors also had to reflect on the role that the promulgation of (voluntary) standards exerts in the continuous dominance of private rule-making bodies. In other words, does expeditious diffusion of (new) ideas and lobbying for the wisdom and necessity of private action pay off vis-à-vis public authority.

The book covers the most important areas that are associated with private rule-making (product/manufacturing, financial regulation, sports, professional self-regulation). In addition, it delves into procedural, substantive, and practical elements of private rule-making processes that would otherwise be unobservable without a close empirical lens, covering both institutional and contextual features. At a policy level, the volume calls for comparisons among practices of private bodies in various areas, allowing for important lessons to be drawn for all stakeholders (public or private) active in, or affected by, private and public rule-making. In more general terms, the comprehensive approach adopted allows for a more informed study of areas that have been rarely included in legal books, including business and management studies insights, various layers of governance, or innovation law and economics.

The book is divided into five parts. In Part I, Panagiotis Delimatsis, Rosalba Belmonte with Philip Cerny, and Jan Wouters set the scene. Delimatsis (Chapter 1) provides a conceptual and theoretical framework concerning the resilience-related features of transnational private regulators, based on the role of private standard-setting after a crisis as a power-maximization device. Private bodies take advantage of the procrastination of the State, grow stronger, and become more assertive in norm-creation, overriding and even substituting for State powers. Regulatory disasters leave them intact. Rather, such crises constitute opportunities to accumulate knowledge and develop the capacity to expect the unexpected and absorb it. Free from organizational hierarchies and formal accountability structures and scrutiny, private bodies enhance their collective memory and identity and eventually grow stronger out of episodes and shocks, perpetuating their regulatory dominance.

Cerny and Belmonte (Chapter 2) situate Delimatsis' framework in the context of international relations (IR) theory, which, since the study of IR formally began at the University of Wales, Aberystwyth, in 1919, has been dominated by the presumption that world politics is at its core a system of states. They argue that this way of conceiving world politics was (a) always problematic and challengeable and (b) time-bound and increasingly anachronistic. In the twenty-first century, world politics is becoming increasingly multi-nodal and characterised by heterarchy – the predominance of cross-cutting sectoral mini- and meso-hierarchies above, below, and cutting across states. These heterarchical institutions and processes are characterized by increasing autonomy and special interest capture. In this context, states are becoming "reactive states" as state capacity is eroded. Their capacity may not have been eroded equally in all domains, as different sectors at various levels and organizational structures play differentially powerful roles in this process. Therefore, it is important to examine the evolution and resilience of transnational private regulation across sectors.

Jan Wouters (Chapter 3) studies the interplay between public and private authority while zooming in on the dynamics of standard-setting through a case study of the growing (security) concerns for regulatory capture in the critical standard-setting domain of international telecommunications within the ITU. Wouters sheds light on the regulatory battles currently waging within the ITU; Chinese delegations, including Huawei and state-owned enterprises, have a strong presence and participate actively within the ITU's study groups that develop the technical basis for ITU agreements, standards, and reports. China and its companies team up to exert (normative) influence by submitting proposals and seeking acceptance of new international standards on various topics. Wouters views a need to better safeguard democratic legitimacy and accountability of transnational rule-makers both ex ante and ex post through forms of recognition and a need for stronger scrutiny of these regulatory processes from a human rights point of view.

Part II deals with evolution and resilience in finance and banking.

In his chapter discussing the resilience of the Institute for International Finance (IIF), a lobbying group for private creditors of sovereign debt, M. Konrad Borowicz (Chapter 4) highlights the role of standard-setting as a strategy of organizational resilience. In the IIF's case, the success of the strategy, most recently highlighted by the IIF's role in the immediate aftermath of the COVID-19 crisis and its possible impact on the solvency of sovereign debtors, is attributed to a combination of endogenous and exogenous factors. On the endogenous side, enterprising management capable of anticipating opportunities for developing and promoting standards, forming alliances, and attracting new members all contributed to the IIF's success. On the exogenous side, the success of the IIF's standardization efforts is attributed to the failure of transnational public bodies, such as the IMF, to establish an alternative framework for sovereign debt resolution.

Path dependencies and capture may affect different public regulators differently. Pierre-Hugues Verdier (Chapter 5) attributes the somewhat unexpected shift of the equilibrium between public and private authority toward the former in the case of the LIBOR scandal to the involvement of a particular set of agents – namely prosecutors and the enforcement arm, the United States Commodities Futures Trading Commission. As Verdier notes, priorities and incentives of these public actors differ substantially from those of public actors active in prudential banking regulation traditionally involved in overseeing private standard-setting in the banking industry allowing for less deference to private ordering.

The proactive activities of private regulators stand in stark contrast to the activities of public regulators, which tend to be reactive. The protracted negotiations of the reformed Basel package described by Matteo Ortino (Chapter 6) are a case in point, providing further support for the claims made in the framing chapter about states becoming reactive actors in world politics and global governance. In his chapter, through a legal and political economy perspective, Ortino offers a fitting comparison of transnational private regulation with the study of a public body, the Basel Committee on Banking Supervision, and its own strategies for resilience in the face of repeated regulatory failures to which it has contributed. His analysis suggests that even when states do react, they find it difficult to overcome the path dependence and capture that have characterized rule-making in the area of banking for decades.

In Part III, the edited volume turns to the evolution and resilience of private regimes in the domains of sustainability and food safety.

Enrico Partiti (Chapter 7) shows that prospective legislation on mandatory human rights due diligence (HRDD) profoundly affects rules and approaches of voluntary sustainability standards (VSS). This chapter adopts a comparative perspective to analyze the adaptations and transformations of some of the most relevant multi-stakeholder and industry-driven initiatives across domains covered by VSS to this change in (regulatory) context. The domain of VSS is characterized by NGO pressure, a declining trust in voluntary certification, and a lack of a binding international framework, which has resulted in considerable institutional emergence and proliferation of rather heterogeneous private standards.

In his chapter, Partiti illustrates how for private schemes, the forthcoming HRDD legislation can be viewed as an organizational crisis, creating both opportunities to consolidate their regulatory prerogatives and a threat of losing in relevance to other risk management tools and (firm-level) initiatives. VSS have demonstrated a capacity to expand the application of key requirements to non-certified volumes and firms, and their activities to new non-regulatory domains, which attests to their resilience. The relationship of complementarity between VSS and public regulation is refined as the former aligns its standards and approaches to the emerging HRDD requirements set by the latter. According to Partiti, "this could be seen as an instance where public authority has been capable, if partially, to get a handle on economic private activism."

Juliane Reinecke and Jimmy Donaghey (Chapter 8) investigate how one of the largest industrial incidents of modern time, the Rana Plaza building complex collapse, triggered the emergence and development of the Bangladesh Accord for Building and Fire Safety (Accord), a transnational private regime for collective action around workers' safety in Bangladesh. This Accord was created as a legally binding agreement between unions and over 200 companies to end the series of deadly accidents in the Bangladesh garment sector. The authors investigate the collective action approach driving this initiative and how the crisis nature of Rana Plaza for brands sourcing from Bangladesh played a role in shaping it. This study highlights certain institutional conditions and operational principles that were at the Accord's foundation, which prompted its efficacy as a governance mechanism.

While the Accord was successful in certain aspects, as demonstrated by improvements in worker safety and the reduction of workplace accidents, the exclusion of Bangladeshi employers from the Accord's governance structures, while being subject to and affected by its operations, generated resentment and opposition over time. The dynamics of contestation about the Accord's actions, which were highly political, eventually contributed to its termination. The actions by the State, through the Bangladeshi court system, brought the Accord to a premature end. This case study provides an instance of public authority overriding and reasserting rule-making competences from a private initiative.

Finally, Tetty Havinga and Paul Verbruggen (Chapter 9) analyze the evolution of the Global Food Safety Initiative (GFSI), a focal industry-driven meta-regulator for food safety, in connection to external criticism that over time was raised about its legitimacy. From a relatively limited retailer-led initiative in 2000, GFSI evolved into a leading and influential actor in the field of global food safety. The authors discuss the transitions in the GFSI's governance structure, its activities, and its framing as perceived through the lens of legitimacy. The authors argue that GFSI has evolved via processes of pluralization of its constituents, increased transparency, ratcheting up of food standards' quality, and globalization of its benchmarking activities. They find that many of these changes can be interpreted as a response to crises, defined as fundamental objections and doubts voiced by external actors against GFSI or the practice of food certification more generally. This chapter illustrates how the GFSI through its responses and meeting (deep-rooted) legitimacy challenges during crisis moments has demonstrated its potential for adaptation, nourishing its resilience and dominance.

Part IV moves to the assessment of evolution and adaptation of private regulators in sector-specific regimes.

In the aftermath of the Deepwater Horizon oil spill, Margarita Nieves-Zárate (Chapter 10) zooms in on the American Petroleum Institute (API), the United States trade association of oil and natural gas industry, and how public regulators reacted to a changed approach by the sectoral organization in regulating offshore activities. The Deepwater Horizon (DWH) oil spill in April 2010 caused serious environmental damage in the Gulf of Mexico. According to the author, this disaster originated a "regulatory crisis," an episode of disorder and uncertainty during which the regulatory regime to prevent accidents and marine pollution from offshore oil and gas operations in the United States was questioned. The API was under pressure to change in face of criticism about its role in influencing public policy and the reliance of the federal regulator on its standards, which did not reflect "best industry practises." The API demonstrated its resilience through an organizational response that allowed it to adapt to the post-DWH oil spill era: the creation of the Center for Offshore Safety (COS).

The Bureau for Safety and Environmental Enforcement (BSEE) had adopted new safety regulation making safety and environmental management systems (SEMS) programs mandatory (amended in 2013) after the disaster. The BSEE introduced a co-regulatory scheme to its SEMS regulation and responded to API's change by approving the COS, giving it a formal role in the implementation of this regulation. In 2015, COS became the first and only accreditation body thus far to assess and accredit audit service providers (ASPs) that audit SEMS programs. The author argues that certain gaps in transparency and regulatory practices may undermine the effectiveness of the new co-regulatory scheme. An important finding is that the API increased its influence in offshore oil and gas regulation in the United States as a rule-maker and supervisor. According to Nieves-Zárate, the reorganization of the API after the DWH accident provides an example of the perpetuation of private regulatory power.

Certain types of private regimes enjoy considerable leeway in handling legitimacy pressures. This is the case when stakeholders have neither formal "voice" nor exit options, as was the case with the hybrid global anti-doping regime analyzed by Slobodan Tomic and Rebecca Schmidt (Chapter 11). Such political economy conditions allow regulatory regimes to direct legitimacy pressures toward solutions that do not structurally diminish their power over the other actors in the regime and stakeholders. Tomic and Schmidt assess the specificities of the hybrid anti-doping regime and the evolving accountability arrangements it established following its repeated failures to ensure doping-free sports. A culmination of this failure was the 2015 Russian doping scandal in which it was exposed that Russian state authorities had been operating a large-scale doping scheme over several years. Tomic and Schmidt analyze how the accountability arrangements of the global anti-doping regime evolved since its creation in 1999, looking into its formal structures as well as the changes surrounding the actors' understanding of accountability caused by legitimacy pressures.

The authors identify varying degrees of accountability reactions after the outbreak of the Russian doping scandal across five different accountability dimensions. The transparency response seemed especially strong and less threatening to an organization's power than other accountability responses. Some institutionalization of the regime's accountability framework occurred after the scandal, with variation in degree across different tiers. This was after the regime had deflected pressures for change and resisted major reform of this kind prior to the 2015 Russian doping scandal. The severity of this crisis is considered to have played a role in catalyzing this institutional change. According to Tomic and Schmidt, legitimacy pressures can catalyze institutionalization, even in the most unfavorable structural environment. "The extent of accountability demonstration will be shaped by power struggles, and where the prior structure accords one governing actor the position of supreme authority, the accountability institutionalisation will be most pronounced in the 'lower tiers' of the system."

The assessment of evolution and adaptation of private regulators in sector-specific regimes in Part IV also reveals that we have much to learn from the long histories of "pre-neoliberal" non-state transnational regulation and standardization. Daniel Quiroga-Villamarín (Chapter 12) provides a fitting historical international law perspective into the development and evolution of transnational private regulation, showing how power struggles and blurring of the public–private divide were already well visible during the development of global standards for containerized shipping in the 1950s. The rise of containerized maritime trade was a revolution that occurred across several decades and regions of the globe and can only be understood against the backdrop of the crisis and collapse of this previous regulatory imagination of world ports. The vigorous competition between private and public actors to set standards for the industry within ISO (and beyond) suggests that the dynamic described in the framing chapter may not be new at all. Instead, as Quiroga-Villamarín suggests, as we are entering an era of "Private Ordering 2.0," it might be helpful to unearth the blueprints of previous hybrid regulatory constellations that preceded the age of the "territorial" and "public" nation-state.

Resilience in the domain of technical standardisation is discussed in Part V. Stephanie Bijlmakers (Chapter 13) examines empirically how ISO, a hybrid standard setting body, has evolved and increased its resilience throughout its seventy-five-year existence in relation to crisis. It departs from the assumption that ISO's evolution can be explained in relation to its ability to respond to dynamics and challenges that identify distinct shifts in regulatory paradigms within ISO. Bijlmakers builds on Delimatsis' contribution and tests some of its claims against the empirical findings. She illuminates important traits of ISO that confer resilience onto the organization today, how ISO has acquired or built these qualities in connection to crisis moments in the past, and their cultivation over time. Bijlmakers affirms that ISO derives strength from its standard-setting capacity and flexibility, having demonstrated an ability to promulgate rapidly their voluntary standards and to ensure their underlying potential and qualities, expanding its influence in existing and new domains of standard setting, also in relation to the state. ISO's institutional structure and its complexity, and its continued adherence to the governance principles founding it, also confer strength onto ISO. ISO's ability to resist pressures to enact changes to its governance principles, and its business model, attests to its resilience. Bijlmakers provides an illustrative example of how a standard-setting body over the decades through strategies and meeting challenges during crisis moments has managed to increasingly grow in strength and influence.

Through an empirical quantitative analysis, Justus Baron and Olia Kanevskaia (Chapter 14) study the evolution of ICT standard-setting processes. Their focus is the current dynamics and tensions over undue Chinese influence in standards development organizations (SDOs) developing international ICT standards. The acquisition by Chinese companies, and especially Huawei, of leadership positions within these international ICT SDOs risks their processes becoming partisan toward China's commercial and political strategic interests. Current dynamics challenge well-established institutional principles that safeguard the neutrality and independence of the deliberation processes within these SDOs, creating a "moment of stress" for SDO governance. The authors present empirical evidence of Chinese and Huawei's increased participation in four prominent ICT SDOs (ITU, 3GPP, IEEE, IETF).

Baron and Kanevskaia demonstrate how committee leadership appointments and the expected conduct of individuals holding critical positions are key mechanisms to ensure resilience to political and commercial pressures in standard-setting. They distinguish between four different institutional models of SDOs and examine their ability to safeguard the integrity and independence of standard-setting procedures by how individuals are selected to critical leadership positions. While the four global ICT SDOs have different approaches to the legitimacy of SDO leadership, each contributing checks and balances, they are similar in that leadership appointments are mainly determined by certain requirements of expertise and experience. The authors argue that these requirements demonstrate a strong culture of individual independence and meritocracy that functions outside the SDOs' organizational hierarchy or State-driven processes.

Tim Büthe and Abdel fattah Alshadafan (Chapter 15) examine the history of the International Electrotechnical Commission (IEC). Over the course of its 115-year history, this SDO has faced numerous different challenges to its role and legitimacy as the preeminent global body for developing standards for an ever-broader range of electro-technologies. Büthe and Alshadafan examine how the IEC has responded to those challenges, employing an original theoretical framework that emphasizes its capacity and capability for autonomous pursuit of the organization's institutional self-interest, its embeddedness among stakeholders, and the skill and ambition of the organization's leadership.

Büthe and Alshadafan show that these characteristics have allowed the IEC to respond resiliently to numerous changes in electro-technologies, the rise of possible competitor SDOs, and the growing importance of the Global South for the legitimacy and effectiveness of global governance. In all of these episodes, the IEC exhibited adaptability while keeping its essential, defining attributes intact. Far more challenging has been addressing legitimacy concerns due to the marginalization of consumer interests and alleviating the gender imbalance in IEC standard-setting.

The Epilogue by Fabrizio Cafaggi (Chapter 16) offering several insightful remarks and suggestions regarding how we view resilience in the light of crises as well as various avenues for future research concludes this volume on international standardization. Although this volume improves our understanding of the importance of standard-setting – be it publicly, privately, or hybrid driven – and the processes used, it also advocates for more comprehensive research efforts that would allow for testing certain hypotheses and assumptions that are – sometimes light-heartedly – made with respect to the mechanics, dynamics, and evolution of actors and values in the standard-setting ecology.

PART I

Global Governance and Politics

1

The Resilience of Private Authority in Times of Crisis

Panagiotis Delimatsis[*]

1.1 INTRODUCTION

Private regulatory bodies, including trade associations of professionals and companies such as banks or big manufacturers, have been part and parcel of the neoliberal orthodoxy premised on the concepts of market competition and an increasingly limited role for the State.[1] Largely unleashed to determine their fate, such close-knit groups have shaped the trajectory of neoliberal globalization.[2] Yet all governance modes can be vulnerable to specific kinds of failures due to their innate weaknesses in different problem contexts.[3] Reliance on private expertise has not prevented regulatory disasters (that is, events of varying scale and scope resulting from the – often unintended and unforeseen – consequences of the design or operation of a regulatory system and its interactions with other systems) in finance and manufacturing from occurring.[4] Despite the ever-increasing powers that are transferred to such private actors, existing theories fail to explain satisfactorily

* This research has received funding from the European Research Council (ERC) under the Horizon 2020 research and innovation program (Consolidator Grant Agreement No ERC-2016-CoG 725798). Comments by Fabrizio Cafaggi, Enrico Partiti, Stephanie Bijlmakers, Konrad Borowicz, and participants at the TILEC Workshop on "The Resilience of Private Collective Action in Finance and Manufacturing: Theoretical Challenges" in November 2019, the Biennial Conference of the American Society of International Law in February 2020, and the ERC conference on "The Evolution of Transnational Private Rule-Makers" in November 2020. Remaining errors are the author's alone.

1 See C. Donnelly, *Delegation of Governmental Power to Private Parties: A Comparative Perspective* (2007).

2 See P. Cerny, Embedding Neoliberalism: The Evolution of a Hegemonic Paradigm (2008) 2:1 *Journal of International Trade and Diplomacy* 1, at 32.

3 See also M. Howlett and M. Ramesh, The Two Orders of Governance Failure: Design Mismatches and Policy Capacity Issues in Modern Governance (2014) 33:4 *Policy and Society* 317.

4 See J. Black, Learning from Regulatory Disasters (2014) 10:3 *Policy Quarterly* 3.

why their dominance remains largely unaffected by regulatory disasters that they partly cause.[5]

Against this backdrop, this chapter argues that crisis events or other unfortunate regulatory disasters appear to empower such private-driven forces or generate new ones, whereas existing public checks and balances fail to pursue their initial objective. In this regard, we introduce the concept of "free riding of private ordering" to describe this phenomenon and expose this mismatch between costs and benefits of regulatory legitimacy transfer. We believe that this phenomenon is particularly visible in two critical areas of economic activity: manufacturing and finance.

Arguably, we currently witness early signs of a transition from a constellation whereby private bodies serve a role assigned to them by the State (reactive mode) toward a convention whereby private forces create rules that regulate economic activity more assertively, without being affected by regulatory disasters; rather, such crises constitute opportunities to accumulate knowledge and develop the capacity to expect the unexpected, absorb it, and grow (reactive mode). Our main claim is that the continued dominance of private authority through crisis events is premised on the core rule-making activities that such private bodies undertake. The most important of them is the continuous promulgation of voluntary standards that are rapidly prepared, adopted, and diffused to preempt rules by public rule-making competitors. Because of the voluntary nature of the standards but also the underlying potential and properties that allow for grabbing authority located elsewhere, we further introduce the concept of "voluntary economic activism" (VEA). Overall, our objective is to set the foundations for a theory that explains crisis-proof private authority.

The remainder of the chapter proceeds as follows. We draw from the resilience theory in Section 1.2 to unravel the phenomenon of the resilience of private collective action, using examples from the world of finance and manufacturing. We underscore the importance of malleability, flexibility, mutability, and heterogeneity as foundational traits of organizational continuity but also how the role of crises (and crisis management) has been largely neglected in the private governance scholarship. Section 1.3 complements the largely theoretical analysis of organizational resilience by discussing the essential features of the transition we arguably witness regarding the empowerment of private collective action, that is, from a reactive toward a proactive role of private regulatory bodies seeking more authority. Importantly, it describes the contours of a new theory of private collective action. Based on the analysis offered, Section 1.4 sets the foundations for studying the transition to a new era of private ordering and underscores the importance of further

[5] See also V. Schmidt and M. Thatcher, Theorizing Ideational Continuity: The Resilience of Neo-liberal Ideas in Europe, in *Resilient Liberalism in Europe's Political Economy* (V. Schmidt and M. Thatcher eds., 2013), 1, at 13.

research to test the new theory put forward and the hypotheses associated with it. Section 1.5 concludes.

1.2 THE RESILIENCE OF PRIVATE COLLECTIVE ACTION

1.2.1 *What Makes a System Resilient? Insights from Ecosystems Theory*

Resilience is the ability of recovery to the state of equilibrium that a subject would have depending on the risk management strategy it will employ. Resilience in ecosystems can relate to efficiency, control, constancy, or predictability (coined "engineering resilience"). In such, rather static, ecosystems, because uncertainty is low, the focus is on optimal performance. However, resilience can also relate to persistence, adaptiveness, fungibility, variability, and unpredictability (coined "ecosystem resilience"). In dynamic ecosystems, variability and novelty result in high uncertainty. As the latter form of resilience focuses on the interplay between stabilizing and destabilizing properties of a given system, it appears to be the most useful for developing sustainable social orders.[6]

Resilience would emphasize the capacity to absorb stress and reorganize after the occurrence of a disturbance that upsets the equilibrium; thus, it presupposes a phase of growth and accumulation, followed by a phase of reorganization and renewal; a resilient system would survive successfully through these four phases.[7] Perturbations can lead to a critical point ("a tipping point") of such a disruptive nature that triggers a paradigm shift, thereby creating a new equilibrium, allowing for the continuation of the system. The occurrence of a tipping point is typically evidenced by the delay of recovery or by the fact that a system has become more vulnerable or fragile to small changes, resulting in critical transitions.[8] The transition is nonlinear and the new equilibrium reached is not necessarily better or worse.

Resilience would entail flexibility rather than rigidity and persistence rather than collapse.[9] Overall, it appears that systems are more resilient when they are moderately connected while maintaining high levels of heterogeneity.[10] More generally, a system, subject, institution, or idea is resilient when it can weather episodic or

6 See C. S. Holling and L. H. Gunderson, Resilience and Adaptive Cycles, in *Panarchy: Understanding Transformations in Human and Natural Systems* (L. H. Gunderson and C. S. Holling eds., 2002), 25, at 27–28.

7 See C. S. Holling, Understanding the Complexity of Economic, Ecological, and Social Systems (2001) 4 *Ecosystems* 390, at 393ff.

8 See Y. Li et al, An Analysis of Power Law Distributions and Tipping Points during the Global Financial Crisis (2018) 13:1 *Annals of Actuarial Science* 80, at 85.

9 See J. Ruhl, General Design Principles for Resilience and Adaptive Capacity in Legal Systems: With Applications to Climate Change Adaptation (2011) 89 *North Carolina Law Review* 1373, at 1389.

10 See R. Biggs et al, Toward Principles for Enhancing the Resilience of Ecosystem Services (2012) 37 *Annual Review of Environment and Resources* 421, at 429.

gradual change and emerge closely resembling its former state and functionality after a disturbance.[11] Such a process of demonstrating adaptability may entail the change of resilience strategies without changing the fundamental attributes of a given system.[12] This reemergence of a given system into a feasible alternative status would also be efficient from an economic viewpoint.[13]

When applying these theoretical insights to private regulation regimes, we observe that a man-made system like a regulatory system can show its resilience by internalizing any succession of regulatory and governance paradigms (growth and accumulation). This can eventually lead to new constructs of alternative governance (reorganization and renewal), provided that the characteristics of the previous regime remain largely intact. Resilient private systems cannot survive without the idea that underlies them being resilient to shocks. Ideas can show resilience through adaptive processes of metamorphosis (old ideas returning in new guises), absorption (of seemingly contradictory ideas), and hybridization (adaptability in different contexts).[14] This approach would emphasize the heterogeneous and inclusive nature of ideas that aspire to be (or have been) resilient, as long as a connecting factor, even if only loose and remote, could bring them together. This coalescence can be the result of centripetal forces but many times will result from active inclusion management of a strategic nature.[15]

1.2.2 *The Rise of Private Collective Action to Authority as a Manifestation of Neoliberalism*

Much of the governance carried out in the last thirty years has been indirect, delivered via several private rule-making bodies acting as governance intermediaries, be it trade associations; professional bodies; private contractors delivering public services such as transport, health, security, or education; or associations of firms to which the State delegated a given task.[16] The retrenchment of the State that fitted

[11] See S. Kaufman, Complex Systems, Anticipation, and Collaborative Planning for Resilience, in *Collaborative Resilience: Moving through Crisis to Opportunity* (B. Goldstein ed., 2012), 61, at 65; also C. Folke, Resilience: The Emergence of a Perspective for Social-Ecological Systems Analyses (2006) 16:3 *Global Environmental Change* 253.

[12] See B. Fath, C. Dean, and H. Katzmair, Navigating the Adaptive Cycle: An Approach to Managing the Resilience of Social Systems (2015) 20:2 *Ecology and Society* 24.

[13] See O. Williamson, Economic Organization: The Case for Candor (1996) 21:1 *The Academy of Management Review* 48, at 53.

[14] See V. Schmidt and M. Thatcher, Why Are Neoliberal Ideas So Resilient in Europe's Political Economy? (2014) 8:3 *Critical Policy Studies* 340, at 341.

[15] See C. Ansell et al., Understanding Inclusion in Collaborative Governance: A Mixed Methods Approach (2020) 39:4 *Policy and Society* 570.

[16] See K. Abbott, P. Genschel, D. Snidal, and B. Zangl, Two Logics of Indirect Governance: Delegation and Orchestration (2015) 46 *British Journal of Political Science* 719; also S. Shapiro, Outsourcing Government Regulation (2003) *Duke Law Journal* 389; and E. P. Stringham, *Private Governance: Creating Order in Economic and Social Life* (2015).

the neoliberal ideological framework proved fertile ground for this development, allowing for market-led governance and the gradual introduction of self-correcting processes, eventually leading to a reconfiguration of the role of the State.[17]

Privatization and deregulation of monopolies and later public authority was the inevitable consequence of the coalescence between the economic and the political. Economics (notably the Chicago School and the Law and Economics movement)[18] came to corroborate and justify such a constellation early on by finding that public goods such as regulations can be produced by non-state actors[19] or demonstrating how the use of nonlegal mechanisms such as informal rules and social norms can bring about efficient outcomes in the marketplace.[20]

These developments would pave the way for the ultimate decoupling of the regulatory function from the executive function. Regulation would merely shift "penholders" to become the very responsibility of the regulatees (often experts in a highly technical and complex field).[21] Proponents of market-led governance and self-regulation would advocate that a bottom-up approach to authority is more apposite due to expertise and insider knowledge that only the professionals possess.[22]

Various resilience-related attributes mentioned above can be identified in the modus operandi of private regulators: malleability, flexibility, and relatively low costs have defined the resilience of private regulators and the ideas they advocate.[23] Private bodies can draft and review rules more swiftly and flexibly than any public authority.[24] Norm-making groups can also adapt more quickly in the wake of exogenous shocks, thereby demonstrating their transformative capacity and mutability traits.[25] Furthermore, with the proliferation of technological advances that facilitated global exchange of ideas and commercial transactions, new layers of regulation at the national but also the international level would emerge, allowing

[17] See P. Kjaer, Law and Order within and Beyond National Configurations, in *The Financial Crisis in Constitutional Perspective: The Dark Side of Functional Differentiation* (P. F. Kjaer et al. eds., 2011), 395, at 418.

[18] See P. Mirowski and D. Plehwe (eds.), *The Road to Mont Pélerin: The Making of the Neoliberal Thought Collective* (2009).

[19] See R. Coase, The Lighthouse in Economics (1974) 17:2 *Journal of Law and Economics* 357; and E. Ostrom, *Governing the Commons: The Evolution of Institutions for Collective Action* (1990).

[20] See R. Ellickson, *Order without Law: How Neighbours Settle Disputes* (1991).

[21] See also D. Levi-Faur, The Global Diffusion of Regulatory Capitalism (2005) 598:1 *Annals of the American Academy of Political and Social Science* 12.

[22] Cf. C. Cutler et al. (eds.), *Private Authority and International Affairs* (1999).

[23] See K. Abbott and B. Faude, Choosing Low-Cost Institutions in Global Governance (2021) 13 *International Theory* 397.

[24] See also J. Basedow, The State's Private Law and the Economy: Commercial Law as an Amalgam of Public and Private Rule-Making (2008) 56:3 *American Journal of Comparative Law* 703.

[25] See also R. Ellickson, The Market for Social Norms (2001) 3:1 *American Law and Economics Review* 1, at 22.

for the creation of co-regulatory constellations and other types of partnership between the private and the public.[26]

The evolution of private regulation can be attributed to early successes of self-regulatory patterns. In other words, self-regulation is directly associated with the phenomenon of private regulation in that the former established solid foundations for the evolution of the latter. In turn, the very foundation of self-regulation (and, a fortiori, private regulatory power) is the legal principle of private autonomy, going back as early as the Roman times.[27] Self-regulation entails an explicit or tacit transfer of authority to private bodies, which allows them to delineate a sphere of expertise,[28] establish conditions for membership, limit competition for the excluded nonmembers (either because they objectively do not qualify or because the incumbents want to maximize their rents), and impose deontological rules of conduct on the regulatees.[29] Self-regulation further entails monitoring of compliance with such rules and instituting enforcement mechanisms based on the deterring impact of potential exclusion, transforming compliance into a "normative demand."[30]

Private bodies have been key pillars of contemporary regulatory governance.[31] The emergence of private regulatory regimes has often been the result of a well-functioning, self-contained ecosystem, whereas in other cases it can be enlisted as part of experimental regulatory governance.[32] In this respect, professional associations are a good example. Certain associations gained immunity from public interference decades or even centuries ago and established normative principles of professional elitism.[33] These principles are meant to regulate access and pursuit of a given profession in the public interest: they are set out to ensure high levels of consumer protection and service quality. However, other than protecting public interest objectives, professional associations should also protect the interests of their members. This dual mission may lead to undesirable conflicts of interest.[34]

[26] See also I. Ayres and J. Braithwaite, *Responsive Regulation: Transcending the Deregulation Debate* (1992); and N. Gunningham and P. Grabosky, *Smart Regulation* (1998).

[27] See L. Fuller, Consideration and Form (1941) 41:5 *Columbia Law Review* 799, at 806–807.

[28] See J. Black, Constitutionalising Self-Regulation (1996) 59:1 *Modern Law Review* 24, at 27.

[29] See also C. Coglianese and E. Mendelson, Meta-Regulation and Self-Regulation, in *The Oxford Handbook of Regulation* (R. Baldwin et al. eds., 2010), 146, at 146.

[30] See M. Auer, The Anti-network: A Comment on Annelise Riles (2008) 56 *American Journal of Comparative Law* 631, at 636–637.

[31] We adopt here a function-driven definition: Regulatory governance is the organized attempt to manage risks or behavior to achieve a publicly stated objective or set of objectives. See also Black, *supra* note 4.

[32] Cf. G. de Búrca, R. Keohane, and C. Sabel, Global Experimentalist Governance (2014) 44:3 *British Journal of Political Science* 477.

[33] See R. Suddaby et al., Transnational Regulation of Professional Services: Governance Dynamics of Field Level Organizational Change (2007) 32 *Accounting, Organizations and Society* 333.

[34] See H. McVea, Predators and the Public Interest: "The Big Four" and Multidisciplinary Practices (2002) 65:6 *Modern Law Review* 811.

Additionally, there is always the danger of regulatory capture from within,[35] as special interests are well-organized and homogeneous.

The concerns described above may become even more serious, as monitoring and harnessing the behavior of private bodies becomes more complex once private regulation of a given economic activity becomes borderless at the transnational level.[36] An interesting feature of these regimes is that procedural requirements become essential due to their reach and type of addressees, impact, and increased level of regulatory tasks that they have.[37] Issues of jurisdiction and conflict surface, and, quite interestingly, their complexity nourishes the evolution of transnational regulation, post-national legal authority and private ordering.

Similar concerns apply to co-regulatory constellations. Co-regulation or cooperative regulation in several sectors of the economy is a form of regulation that goes beyond the coercion that State authority can exert. In theory, co-regulatory approaches allow self-regulation, private regulation, and state regulation to come together with a view to optimizing regulatory performance and more efficiently addressing market failures and certain malfunctions.

As a rule, rule-making within such bodies is highly political. Internal politicization can often turn into a battle for internal dominance, which requires an investment of sometimes substantial financial resources and effective representation.[38] However, toward the external addressees, a persistent problem has been the high level of immunity from liability that private bodies largely enjoy. Immunity for some is the result of theories of corporation and liberalism that have dominated economic activity over the years. In such a framework, liability becomes an abstraction, scattered in the private regulatory sphere.

1.2.3 *The European Example of Private Governance*

In the history of European economic integration, the involvement of the private sector is well documented.[39] The contribution of private authority proved a key ingredient of European integration, in line with the neofunctionalist approach that essentially characterized much of the evolution of European rapprochement, as exemplified by the New Approach in mid-1980s, the controversial Lisbon strategy

35 See G. Stigler, The Theory of Economic Regulation (1971) 2 *Bell Journal of Economics* 3; also R. Posner, Theories of Economic Regulation (1974) 5 *Bell Journal of Economics* 335.

36 See also G: Teubner, Global Bukowina: Legal Pluralism in the World Society, in *Global Law without a State* (G. Teubner ed., 1996), 1, at 3.

37 See F. Cafaggi, New Foundations of Transnational Private Regulation (2011) 38:1 *Journal of Law and Society* 20.

38 See W. Mattli and T. Büthe, *The New Global Rulers: The Privatization of Regulation in the World Economy* (2011), at 12.

39 For a critique, see G. Majone, *Rethinking the Union of Europe Post-crisis: Has Integration Gone Too Far?* (2014), at 149ff; also *Private Regulation and Enforcement in the EU* (M. de Cock Buning and L. Senden, eds., 2020).

and the better regulation initiative at the beginning of the twenty-first century, but also the more recent Europe 2020 flagship initiative. The accumulated technical expertise in private bodies and the adoption of a less top-down regulatory approach rendered their involvement inevitable. The contribution of the "depoliticization" desire and the spread of non-majoritarian regulatory agencies that characterized European integration was equally important.[40] In this landscape, private regulators have been to date among the most transformative and motivating forces of economic activity in Europe and an essential component of the EU legal order.[41]

The Court of Justice of the European Union (CJEU) also played an important role in the creation of a neoliberal normative model for the regulation of markets within the EU. Such a model was based on promoting competition and cross-border market liberalization, thereby giving greater leverage to markets to the detriment of States. The Court adopted a rather agnostic approach as to legal forms and regulatory institutions thereby eroding the role of the State as a monopoly supplier of regulation.[42] The next step taken by the Court would be to consider private conduct as a potential trigger of violation of the fundamental freedoms, allowing other private parties to challenge such contact, coined as the infamous "horizontal direct effect" of the fundamental freedoms. This adoption of a functional approach to authority was decisive: while the Court's stance strengthened the European rule of law, it also legitimized authority that was previously elusive and internal to the private parties at issue.

Enrolling private actors in the regulatory process has then been a manifestation of so-called Europeanization, a term aiming to capture the influence of EU law on national practice but also a method that aims to cater for the lack of accountability and legitimacy of European institutions, as it brings to the fore more participatory forms of governance and rule-making.[43] However, this process carries with it several risks as noted earlier; identifying and addressing such risks may become less straightforward once the activities by private actors transcend national borders.[44]

From European integration to domestic politics to the development of the global economy, technocracy has flourished within the ebb and flow of European politics, thereby shaping, harnessing, and monitoring economic behavior. In recent times, the intermingling of technocracy and politics[45] may have contributed to the rise of

[40] See M. Moran, The Rise of the Regulatory State, in *The Oxford Handbook of Business and Government* (D. Coen and W. Grant eds., 2010), 383, at 393.

[41] See H. Schepel, *The Constitution of Private Governance: Product Standards in the Regulation of Integrating Markets* (2005).

[42] Cf. G. Davies, Tough Love in the Internal Market, in *The Internal Market and the Future of European Integration: Essays in Honour of Laurence W. Gormley* (F. Amtenbrink et al. eds., 2019), at 15.

[43] Cf. S. Weatherill, *Law and Values in the European Union* (2016), at 105.

[44] See C. Joerges, Integration through De-legalisation (2008) 33 *European Law Review* 291.

[45] Cf. N. Fligstein and A. Stone Sweet, Constructing Polities and Markets: An Institutionalist Account of European Integration (2002) 107 *American Journal of Sociology* 1206.

populism and the antiestablishment movement.[46] In Europe and beyond, transnational (that is, increasingly international, but non-State-centered) private standard-setting became the norm in central areas of economic activity, including financial services and manufacturing. It is in these two areas of economic activity in particular that global interdependence increasingly manifests itself.

1.2.4 *Resilience and Crises*

Exogenous shocks such as financial crises, technological disasters, or a pandemic increase the likelihood of non-incremental institutional change at the global level.[47] Every crisis brings with it urgent calls for a new regulatory paradigm in dealing with a certain area, be it food safety, technology and its use, finance, or accountancy services. Although the global financial crisis of 2008 has thrust policy-making failures into the limelight, such regulatory disasters have been diachronic, albeit with a varying degree of specific configuration, probability (ex ante) and casualties (ex post).[48]

The current scholarship appears to suggest that the State (previously a monopoly regulator) has been transformed into the orchestrator of private regulatory activity. In this setting, the State, via soft influence and other voluntary means, enlists the third party (here, a non-State body) through material or ideational support and nudges it toward governance goals that align to the State's.[49] Such enrollment may be beneficial for both sides: whereas the State economizes on resources, the private body at issue increases its legitimacy as the prime collaborator of the State in a given issue area.[50] Other theories focus on the delegation relationship, suggesting that agency-related challenges shall be resolved by the State as the last resort and ultimate commander; for instance, information asymmetries shall be addressed via transparency-related legislation or disclosure requirements for financial institutions.

If one attempts to apply these theories into practice, it would expect a new era of significant State intervention in case of misuse of delegation or deviation from the pursuit of public policy objectives, thereby upending conventional wisdom about self-regulation and private authority.[51] Arguably, the great return of the State has not really happened as of yet.[52]

46 See I. Colantone and P. Stanig, The Surge of Economic Nationalism in Western Europe (2019) 33:4 *Journal of Economic Perspectives* 128.

47 R. B. Collier and D. Collier, *Shaping the Political Arena: Critical Junctures, the Labor Movement and Regime Dynamics in Latin America* (1991).

48 See C. Reinhart and K. Rogoff, *This Time Is Different: Eight Centuries of Financial Folly* (2011).

49 See K. Abbott, P. Genschel, D. Snidal, and B. Zangl (eds.), *International Organizations as Orchestrators* (2015).

50 See J. Braithwaite and P. Drahos, *Global Business Regulation* (2000).

51 The Growth of the State – Leviathan Stirs Again, *The Economist*, January 21, 2010.

52 See C. Crouch, *The Strange Non-death of Neo-liberalism* (2011).

This reveals the need for more theoretical and empirical work on the mechanics of the transformative, motivating, adaptive, and reinvigorating forces of private economic regulation. We suggest that particular focus shall be given to finance and manufacturing, where striking levels of resilience with obvious consumer welfare implications are particularly discernible. Several scholars have previously pinpointed the various conflicts of interest that permeate private regulation, from credit rating agencies[53] to professional associations,[54] label accreditation bodies,[55] and ICT private standard-setters.[56] However, in these two areas, private collective action has dominated the field, taking a largely unchallenged pole position despite crisis events.

In addition, in both issue areas, private regulatory activity was translated into an important degree of constitutionalization (which suggests an effort to increase legitimacy but is also indicative of a higher degree of institutional complexity), although this characteristic did not render it crisis-proof. For these reasons, the two fields identified are significant test-beds for the theoretical background of institutional resilience and the role of crises described above.

In what follows, we briefly identify certain illustrative examples. Our modest intention is to instigate further research in the two important issue areas of private standard-setting through the conceptual lens proposed in this chapter, rather than exhaustively present them and confirm our hypotheses.

1.2.4.1 Finance

Private rule-making in finance has flourished in the last three decades, notably after the creation of significant transnational organizations that were established to ensure that capital account liberalization and financial openness would not disturb global financial stability.[57] Finance is an important area for our purposes, as it not only exemplifies the problem of domestic enforcement in a global economic

[53] See A. Johnston, Corporate Governance Is the Problem, Not the Solution: A Critical Appraisal of the European Regulation on Credit Rating Agencies (2011) 11:2 *Journal of Corporate Law Studies* 395.

[54] See P. Delimatsis, The Future of Transnational Self-Regulation: Enforcement and Compliance in Professional Services (2017) 40:1 *Hastings International and Comparative Law Review* 1.

[55] See A. Marx et al. (eds.), *Private Standards and Global Governance: Economic, Legal and Political Perspectives* (2012).

[56] See P. Delimatsis, O. Kanevskaia, and Z. Verghese, Strategic Behavior in Standards Development Organizations in Times of Crisis: The Case of IEEE (2021) 29:1 *Texas Intellectual Property Law Journal* 127.

[57] See P-H. Verdier, The Political Economy of International Financial Regulation (2013) 88 *Indiana Law Journal* 1405.

environment but also the fluidity of authority, whereby public and private regulators and enforcers interact.[58]

In the aftermath of important privatization efforts in the 1980s, financialization became the hallmark of the neoliberal new world order.[59] Financial services regulation was routinely discussed in international fora where State regulators were absent or simple observers. New rules would be the outcome of joint legal engineering between bankers and independent national central banks in London, New York, or Basel. Many of these rules were initially established as voluntary benchmarks, indeed, as suggestions that a group of like-minded financiers brought forward.[60] However, they soon became either important benchmarks that companies or financial institutions could not ignore or even mandatory technical requirements referenced in State laws, thereby determining market access to global markets.[61]

Two examples from the world of finance are telling for the resilience of financial private rule-making despite crisis events; both relate to the mortgage markets: in the immediate aftermath of the subprime crisis and amidst protests against banking practices, only one small community bank, Abacus, with assets of $282 million – that is a hundredth of 1 percent of the assets of Bank of America – was brought to trial for mortgage fraud in the United States. Securitization, created by lawyers[62] and once lauded as a source of resilience and stability for financial institutions, continues to be a problem that governments appear to be scratching nothing more than the surface by instituting simple, transparent, and standardized (STS) frameworks.[63]

The second example relates to the scandalous manipulation of the infamous London Interbank Offered Rate or "LIBOR," the most important inter-bank interest rate globally that determines the price of multiple financial instruments and contracts, worth hundreds of trillions of dollars. LIBOR used to be administered by the British Bankers Association (BBA), calculated by Thomson Reuters based on data submitted by major London banks.[64] The BBA is a private organization. It is the leading trade association for the UK banking sector but has a global reach with 200 member banks established in over 50 countries. BBA represents over 80 percent of global systemically important banks. The use of LIBOR has been pervasive:

[58] See Pierre-Hugues Verdier's contribution in this volume, "Resilience and Change in Private Standard-Setting: The Case of LIBOR" (Chapter 5).

[59] See G. Krippner, *Capitalizing on Crisis: The Political Origins of the Rise of Finance* (2011).

[60] See P. Tucker, *Unelected Power: The Quest for Legitimacy in Central Banking and the Regulatory State* (2018).

[61] See P. Delimatsis, Financial Innovation and Prudential Regulation: The New Basel III Rules (2012) 46:6 *Journal of World Trade* 1309.

[62] See T. Frankel, The Law of Cross-Border Securitization: Lex Juris (2002) 12 *Duke Journal of Comparative and International Law* 475.

[63] See also S. Schwarcz, Securitization Ten Years after the Financial Crisis: An Overview (2018) 37 *Review of Banking and Financial Law* 757.

[64] See also Bangsters – How Britain's Rate-Fixing Scandal Might Spread – and What to Do about It, *The Economist*, July 7, 2012. See also Pierre-Hugues Verdier's contribution in this volume, "Resilience and Change in Private Standard-Setting: The Case of LIBOR" (Chapter 5).

mortgages, student loans, financial derivatives, and other financial products use LIBOR as a reference rate, suggesting that any interference with this benchmark can have negative financial consequences for millions of people.

Revelations about extensive rigging unleashed when evidence was adduced about banks falsely inflating or deflating their rates to profit from trades.[65] In the aftermath of the scandal, the Financial Services Authority recommended the transfer of LIBOR oversight and governance away from the BBA.[66] The Financial Conduct Authority (FCA), the offspring of the recent financial reform in the United Kingdom, guaranteed the overall success of the process of transferring the LIBOR administrator. The call for tender resulted in the transfer in 2013 of the LIBOR administration from BBA to the NYSE Euronext Rate Administration Ltd., a UK-based company licensed by the FCA.[67]

Thus, despite the admitted failure of LIBOR oversight by the BBA, which is a private body, LIBOR oversight was entrusted, against all odds, to another private body, NYSE Euronext. NYSE Euronext is a Delaware corporation, although the actual headquarters are in New York. NYSE Euronext was acquired by the Intercontinental Exchange (ICE), an energy-related commodities trading company, in 2012. The ICE Benchmark Administration (IBA) is currently the de facto administrator of LIBOR.[68] An oversight committee composed of nineteen members oversees IBA. Crucially, only three members of this committee are representatives of regulators: the Bank of England, the National Bank of Switzerland, and the US Federal Reserve. These three representatives merely have an observer status.

An inherent finance-related peculiarity for any regulator is that most financial information is produced privately. Consider, for instance, the mechanics of credit ratings. Credit rating agencies were heavily criticized in the aftermath of the financial crisis and regulations on both sides of the Atlantic attempted to tame conflicts of interest and other governance issues. That aside, however, any public intervention may be unable to introduce mechanisms to substitute for such information produced privately. Likewise, in the case of benchmarks, the participating financial institutions in the calculation of LIBOR possessed private (sometimes constructed) information, which served to standardize and synchronize the

65 See The Rotten Heart of Finance, *The Economist*, July 7, 2012.

66 Financial Services Authority (FSA), The Wheatley Review of LIBOR: final report (hereinafter the "Wheatley Review"), September 2012.

67 See The Hogg Tendering Advisory Committee Announces that NYSE Euronext Is to Be the New LIBOR administrator, Press Release of July 9, 2013, www.gov.uk/government/groups/hogg-tendering-committee-for-libor.

68 Recently, the UK Financial Conduct Authority announced that LIBOR will be replaced by the end of 2021 with a system of Overnight Financing, Risk-Free Rates which will be administered by the Bank of England. See also A. Schrimpf and V. Sushko, Beyond LIBOR: A Primer on the New Reference Rates (2019) *BIS Quarterly Review* 29; and LIBOR Is Due to Die in 2021. Hurry up and Drop It, Say Regulators, *The Economist*, June 8, 2019. However, new financial contracts maturing after the end of 2021 continue to reference LIBOR.

otherwise uncoordinated actions of public and private actors by offering a common code.[69] Despite their integrity and credibility being shaken during the crisis, the channels of financial information largely remain private.

Often, efforts for dominance and intensive lobbying by private bodies lead to strengthening of their regulatory power. For instance, the International Swaps and Derivatives Association (ISDA), a transnational coalition of banks with a crucial role in the over-the-counter (OTC) derivatives market, has managed to maintain and even strengthen the role that its successive Master Agreements have played in OTC transactions. One successful action was to codify the contractual language used by market actors into a Master Agreement (MA), thereby minimizing transaction costs.[70]

Another, more important, victory for ISDA was to successfully lobby for ISDA's netting rules so that ISDA members are able to net out their positions before the imposition of the judicial stay that would occur in ordinary bankruptcy proceedings. The justification given was that any other solution may increase systemic risk.[71] However, the financial crisis showed that such favouritism – unavailable to other creditors – weakens the incentives of derivatives counterparties for market discipline, as they do not need to cater to counterparty solvency, as the cases of AIG, Bear Sterns, and Lehman suggested.[72] Despite its role in the financial crisis, ISDA remained the private regulator par excellence in global derivatives contracts: it collaborated with the eighteen largest banks and the FSB for the adoption of the Resolution Stay Protocol, which is yet another indication of the regulatory role that ISDA plays in the derivatives market via its MA.

However, and crucially for our purposes, ISDA managed to remain relevant in the post-crisis landscape by adopting an adaptation strategy that focused on more intensive and swift standardization of key contractual terms for credit default swaps (CDS) and other trading terms for other types of products and processes such as interest rate swaps. Furthermore, through the creation of the CDS determination committees (DC), ISDA has also become the de facto arbiter of credit event questions globally. After the controversy this governance issue sparked, in 2018, ISDA transferred the role of credit derivatives DC secretary to DC administration services, Inc. (DCAS). However, although ISDA no longer participates in the DC

69 See B. Carruthers, Financialization and the Institutional Foundations of the New Capitalism (2015) 13:2 *Socio-Economic Review* 379, at 386.

70 See J. Braithwaite, Standard Form Contracts as Transnational Law: Evidence from the Derivatives Markets (2012) 75 *Modern Law Review* 779.

71 See K. Borowicz, Contracts as Regulation: The ISDA Master Agreement (2021) 16:1 *Capital Markets Law Journal* 72, at 85.

72 See M. Roe, The Derivatives Market's Payment Priorities as Financial Crisis Accelerator (2011) 63 *Stanford Law Review* 539.

process, DCAS is a Delaware-incorporated subsidiary of ISDA.[73] In addition, it appears that DCs continue favoring the seller side in the composition of committees, even if a supermajority if required.

If anything, the examples mentioned above exemplify the resilience of private regulatory bodies overtime and the existing difficulties for financial regulators, be it public- or private-driven, to move toward a paradigm shift despite the significant losses from the most recent financial crisis. The inherent complexity of a given industry certainly plays a crucial role in the type, timing, and determination of public intervention. Financial regulators must make regulatory and supervisory choices, as the "human factor" and personal judgment can have far-reaching repercussions on financial institutions. As regulators are risk-averse, complexity of a given industry can lead to limited intervention.

1.2.4.2 Manufacturing

Similar instances can be traced in manufacturing, whereby the proliferation of private standard-setters has grown at a rapid pace in the last three decades. Product safety became the prerogative of private bodies (companies and associations thereof) that have proactively sought participation and influence in setting standards and confirming compliance therewith.[74] Some of these private bodies, such as the ISEAL Alliance, have built coalitions to also assume a meta-governance role in that they develop codes that govern the conduct of private standard-setters such as the Forest Stewardship Council (FSC) or the Marine Stewardship Council (MSC).[75]

Private meta-governance initiatives in areas such as fair labor (the Joint Initiative on Corporate Accountability and Workers' Rights or JO-IN), sustainable tourism (the Global Sustainable Tourism Council or GSTC), or organic agriculture (the International Task Force on Harmonization and Equivalence in Organic Agriculture or ITF) and environmental labelling (ISEAL) have gained significant traction in the last two decades.[76] In practice, however, it is not always easy to distinguish the benign intentions from a strategy of growing dominance that allows occupying the relevant field of meta-governance.[77]

[73] See ISDA, ISDA Transfers Determinations Committees Secretary Role to New Independently Managed Company, October 12, 2018, www.isda.org/a/P6dEE/DCAS-Appointed-DC-Secretary-final.pdf.

[74] See J. Doh and T. Guay, Corporate Social Responsibility, Public Policy, and NGO Activism in Europe and the United States: An Institutional Stakeholder Perspective 43:1 (2006) *Journal of Management Studies* 47.

[75] See also S. Bernstein and H. van der Ven, Best Practices in Global Governance (2017) 43:3 *Review of International Studies* 534.

[76] See B. Derkx and P. Glasbergen, Elaborating Global Private Meta-governance: An Inventory in the Realm of Voluntary Sustainability Standards (2014) 27 *Global Environmental Change* 41.

[77] See A. Loconto and E. Fouilleu, Politics of Private Regulation: ISEAL and the Shaping of Transnational Sustainability Governance (2014) 8 *Regulation and Governance* 166.

The proliferation of private schemes setting voluntary food safety standards is a recent phenomenon that can be traced back to previous food crises that grew out of consumer wariness of food quality and safety.[78] As quality and safety became more important and NGOs calling for increased responsibility and accountability by retailers became stronger and more vocal,[79] the emergence of such schemes that expand the scope of self-regulation was inevitable.[80] Additional reasons for such emergence were the increased awareness of the importance of brand protection, the need to minimize reputational costs,[81] the possibility for the creation of new markets for certified products,[82] the growing outsourcing and the global diffusion of the production by supply chains that call for better monitoring, and, a fortiori, standardization as a logical step once best practices at the upstream level that streamline processes have identified.

Voluntary sustainability standards (VSS) specify requirements that producers, traders, manufacturers, retailers, and, increasingly, service suppliers (such as the standards created by the Global Sustainable Tourism Council) may be asked to meet. Such standards may relate to a particular aspect of the production process or be otherwise concerned with various stages until the product reaches the consumer.[83]

VSS schemes differ on three dimensions: on governance (including the governance arrangements and actors involved, the regulatory mechanisms, and the strategies in place), on the content of standards (social and/or environmental), and the market coverage and potential for growth.[84] Such schemes have come to the forefront not only because of the breadth of areas that they cover (such as forest management, agriculture, or mining) and the novelty of the criteria they highlight (ranging from social issues to greenhouse gas emissions to the protection of biodiversity) but also because of their organizational resourcefulness and the institutional breakthroughs that they allegedly advance: bottom-up and inclusive, participatory platforms that sometimes bring together State actors, NGOs, trade

78 See Havinga and Verbruggen's contribution in this volume, "The Evolution of the Global Food Safety Initiative: The Dynamics of the Legitimacy of a Transnational Private Rule-Maker" (Chapter 9).

79 Cf. C. Rhodes, Democratic Business Ethics: Volkswagen's Emissions Scandal and the Disruption of Corporate Sovereignty (2016) 37:10 *Organization Studies* 1501, at 1513.

80 See D. P. Baron, Morally Motivated Self-Regulation (2010) 100 *American Economic Review* 1299.

81 See Y. Chen and X. Hua, Competition, Product Safety, and Product Liability (2017) 33:2 *Journal of Law, Economics and Organization* 237.

82 See T. Bartley, Certification as a Mode of Social Regulation, in *Handbook on the Politics of Regulation* (D. Levi-Faur, ed., 2011), at 441.

83 *See* P. Delimatsis, Sustainable Standard-Setting, Climate Change and the TBT Agreement, in *Research Handbook on Climate Change and Trade Law* (P. Delimatsis ed., 2016), 148, at 152.

84 See E. Lambin and T. Thorlakson, Sustainability Standards: Interactions between Private Actors, Civil Society, and Governments (2018) 43 *Annual Review of Environment and Resources* 369.

unions, corporations, and private parties; experimental governance methods; benchmarking and continuous impact assessment reviews.

However, food-related crises were not prevented from occurring. From the mad-cow/BSE disease to the food and mouth disease to the horsemeat scandal, crises have shaped the VSS landscape and called for regular changes in the rules of the game. When reviewing more recent crises, the State may maintain oversight, but it remains unclear as to how much control and effective supervision the public authorities actually exercise, as the private regulatory landscape becomes increasingly convoluted and multifaceted (often with retailers playing a dubious role in production, standard-setting, and certification)[85] and by implication contests the State legitimacy and ability to regulate food safety.[86]

1.2.5 *The Role of Crises, Regulatory Disasters, and Tipping Points in Challenging Resilience*

Exogenous crises (but also internal heated situations such as intra-institutional conflicts or inter-institutional pluralism and ensuing competition)[87] that amount to tipping points are opportunities for organisms and systems to test and demonstrate their resilience. A crisis brings disorder with it: it is a moment of – often severe – mutation that leads to a rapid and intense oscillation of a given process or system. It typically is a moment at the interstices of regularity in that it follows the business-as-usual process and time period. Such a critical moment is expected, depending on its severity, to allow for recovery or the establishment of a new status quo. However, it may lead to disruption and the collapse of the system as well, depending on the system's resilience and internal dynamics.[88] For the final repercussions of such a critical moment, whether the crisis is endogenous or exogenous is critical. An endogenous critical juncture may follow from an exogenous episode that shakes and raises doubts about the fundamentals, object, and purpose of a given system due to new ideas, revelations about the functioning of the system in a previous period or other new information that calls for a reorientation of the system as a whole.[89]

A crisis is not necessarily a moment of decline for a particular system. Crises can be of a varying magnitude, thereby affecting the choice of the moment of

[85] See S. Henson and J. Humphrey, Private Standards in Global Agri-food Chains, in Marx et al., *supra* note 55, at 98.

[86] See T. Havinga et al. (eds.), *The Changing Landscape of Food Governance: Public and Private Encounters* (2015).

[87] See A. Marx and J. Wouters, Competition and Cooperation in the Market of Voluntary Sustainability Standards, in *The Law, Economics and Politics of International Standardization* (P. Delimatsis ed., 2015).

[88] See A. Rinscheid et al., Why Do Junctures Become Critical? Political Discourse, Agency, and Joint Belief Shifts in Comparative Perspective, in *Regulation and Governance* (2019).

[89] See B. Cashore et al., *Governing Through Markets: Forest Certification and the Emergence of Non-State Authority* (2004), 219ff.

intervention against the disturbance. In that case, internal dynamics and past behavior is a significant variable. Organization studies have identified several characteristics and safeguards that institutions may have to ensure the continuation and recovery of a given system in times of uncertainty. For instance, an important feature of such a system would be its intrinsic value for those attached to it. The more established a system is the lower transaction costs will be (e.g., those relating to enforcement of private norms).[90] The possibilities that members have to raise their voice and be part of a potential way out of the crisis is another significant variable.[91] Another feature relates to the cultural construction of the institutional preferences in a given system, which may allow taking advantage of an uncertain situation to promote reform and even normative change strategically.[92] Docility of the actors involved and the system as a whole is also an important trait allowing for the continuous fitness of a given system.[93]

Whereas actions, decisions, or omissions of individuals may play a decisive role for a crisis to occur, the organizational context where individuals and systems interact and affect each other is important.[94] Individual responsibility and behavioral bias may be significant in all parts of a failing regulatory chain.[95] However, focusing on individuals alone may lead to drawing only incomplete lessons from a crisis. Often, inadequate training and skills of senior staff; incentive-related challenges that do not align with the goals of the regulatory system at issue; poor leadership and oversight management; and lack of or inefficient internal communication and coordination channels within and among the relevant stakeholders in the system, including in the vertical axis regulator-regulatee, are common causes that lead to regulatory disasters.[96]

Regulatory disasters and crises are quite significant in understanding institutional dynamics and resilience-related strategies. Yet events of lower scale can also bring about disruptive changes within institutions in the medium run and therefore are worth examining if we are to describe a more comprehensive picture of the complex private standard-setting ecology in manufacturing and finance. Thus, depending on the institutional and organizational context, certain turning points within

[90] See A. Aviram, Forces Shaping the Evolution of Private Legal Systems, in *Law, Economics and Evolutionary Theory* (P. Zumbansen and G.-P. Calliess, eds., 2011), at 187.

[91] Cf. A Hirschman, *Exit, Voice and Loyalty: Responses to Decline in Firms, Organizations and States* (1970).

[92] See G. Capoccia, Critical Junctures and Institutional Change, in *Advances in Comparative-Historical Analysis* (J. Mahoney and K. Thelen eds., 2015), at 147.

[93] See H. Simon, Organizations and Markets (1991) 5:2 *Journal of Economic Perspectives* 25, at 35.

[94] Also J. Reinecke et al., The Emergence of a Standards Market: Multiplicity of Sustainability in the Global Coffee Industry (1991) 33 *Organization Studies* 613 .

[95] Cf. R. Deeg and M. O'Sullivan, The Political Economy of Global Finance Capital (2009) 61:4 *World Politics* 731.

[96] See B. Hutter and S. Lloyd-Bostock, *Regulatory Crisis: Negotiating the Consequences of Risk, Disasters and Crises* (2017).

organizations are decisive moments to test adaptability and change, including regime interaction and disruptions due to State-driven actions.

1.3 FREE RIDING OF PRIVATE ORDERING

1.3.1 *The Initial Rise to Authority*

The retrenchment of public authority in recent times is inextricably associated with the ideational continuity and appeal of neoliberalism. Free trade, competition, liberalization, and laissez-faire are essential features of a neoliberal dogma, mediated through law,[97] which increasingly limits the powers of the State. The latter may focus on greater social obligations, in line with the ordo-liberal ideas that strive for a strong role of the State in certain areas and otherwise a facilitative function when it comes to market governance. As described earlier, this results in the failure of the State to get a handle on private rule-making bodies, also due to intermittent crises and unpredictable episodes, which keep the public-driven entities busy with remedying the consequences of such events. Arguably, this creates ideal conditions for opportunism by private rule-making bodies. In practice, a crisis event allows private bodies to consolidate their autonomy and move forward with proactive usurpation of regulatory power.

Crises, unfortunate regulatory disasters, and broader institutional changes in a given organizational ecology are the triggering points that empower such private-driven forces or generate new ones, whereas existing checks and balances and a rigid approach toward the enforcement of rule of law fail their initial purpose. Such private-driven forces are virtually uncontrollable vis-à-vis their alleged principals, the States. The initial delegation mandate of powers or the enhanced oversight-related responsibilities that the State may have in theory are not sufficient to reverse such a situation. Potential cooperation with the State is not the outcome of orchestration by the State whereby governmental actors steer interactions to improve regulatory performance. After all, orchestration at the transnational level is difficult and costly;[98] rather, it arguably is yet another expression of a strategy to increase the *terrain occupé* of private authority. That moment of increasing authority would occur in the wake of intermittent crises when the possibility for opportunism is at its highest, as the State and public-driven entities are in their most vulnerable phase, busy with alleviating the negative impact of such crises.

[97] Cf. D. Singh Grewal and J. Purdy, Introduction: Law and Neoliberalism (2014) 77:4 *Law and Contemporary Problems* 1, at 9.

[98] B. Eberlein et al., Transnational Business Governance Interactions: Conceptualisation and Framework for Analysis (2014) 8:1 *Regulation and Governance* 1; also K. Abbott and D. Snidal, Strengthening International Regulation through Transnational New Governance: Overcoming the Orchestration Deficit (2009) 42:2 *Vanderbilt Journal of Transnational Law* 501.

When delegation of regulatory power backfires, the State takes most of the blame in the public opinion[99] and acts through extreme instruments such as bailouts or the enforcement of import bans. However, in the meantime, a peculiar organizational progeny evolves apace "in the shadow of the State,"[100] detached from political constraints, which is difficult for the State (in its capacity as principal) to reverse due to substantial network effects that accompany the creation of new governance structures, coordination challenges among their overseers (principals),[101] political interferences that call for a light-touch regulatory and supervisory approach,[102] or cognitive constraints that the regulators face and that lead them to inferences that are often skewed by systematic information processing biases.[103] The fact that such public regulatory and supervisory authorities enjoy policy and bureaucratic autonomy exacerbates such phenomena,[104] as such independence is contained by ideological, operational, and communicative factors.[105]

We term the underlying phenomenon "free riding of private ordering" and are interested in the evolutionary process that nourishes private authority in finance and manufacturing activities. Arguably, the use of this theoretical construct has sufficient analytical power to cast new light upon the social processes of authority transformation described in this chapter rather than being a mere example of a trend that it seeks to explain.

Free riding refers to an individual or group that benefits from group actions without bearing the corresponding share of the costs incurred by the group or without contributing any efforts or sources to the beneficial group actions. Typically, free riding is discussed in the political theory but also the trade policy literature to explain intrinsic motivations of political or social groups in influencing (trade) policy formulation.[106] The pioneering work in this field is by Mancur Olson, who revised the prevailing theory at the time, which would preach the virtues of very large groups, to instead suggest that small group size allows for better coordination and more optimal outcomes.[107]

99 See J. Black, Guest Editorial: Rebuilding the Credibility of Markets and Regulators (2009) 3:1 *Law and Financial Markets Review* 1.

100 Cf. T. Johnson, *Organizational Progeny: Why Governments Are Losing Control over the Proliferating Structures of Global Governance* (2014).

101 See W. Mattli and J. Seddon, The Power of the Penholder: The Missing Politics in Global Regulatory Governance Analysis, in Delimatsis, *supra* note 87.

102 See Hutter and Lloyd-Bostock, *supra* note 96, at 48ff.

103 Cf. H. Simon, Rational Decision Making in Business Organizations (1979) 69:4 *American Economic Review* 493, at 503.

104 See T. Bach et al., The Role of Agencies in Policy-Making (2012) 31:3 *Policy and Society* 183, at 185.

105 See R. Baldwin and J. Black, Driving Priorities in Risk-Based Regulation: What's the Problem? (2016) 43:4 *Journal of Law and Society* 565; also R. Baldwin and J. Black, Really Responsive Regulation (2008) 71:1 *Modern Law Review* 59.

106 See P. Fontaine, Free Riding (2014) 36:3 *Journal of the History of Economic Thought* 359.

107 See M. Olson, *The Logic of Collective Action: Public Goods and the Theory of Groups* (1965).

The concept of free riding and its features relating to the enjoyment of the benefits of collective action without incurring the costs is particularly appealing for our purposes. We argue that, in the two areas of manufacturing and finance that we study, such free riding has been reactive for the most part. More specifically, it is the result of a process whereby, at the initial stage, private bodies respond favorably to calls for assistance conveyed by the State; these could entail, among others, the creation of hybrid partnerships or engaging in co-regulation.[108] One example among many is the private and hybrid European governance fervor that followed the European Commission's White Paper on Governance in 2001 – itself a reaction to a regulatory disaster at the time.

For our purposes and according to the vernacular we use here, free-riding has occurred in that private bodies benefited from increased legitimacy without however internalizing the costs of, first, acquiring this legitimacy and, second, regulatory disasters with substantial financial consequences for taxpayers. Typically, in such situations, the State will bear virtually all costs associated with this occurrence (a result of moral hazard that agency creates). This free-riding is even more astonishing if one considers that private bodies are also responsible – at least in part – for such catastrophic events.

1.3.2 *The Transition to Proactive Free-Riding*

As exogenous crises disturb the balance of distribution of authority to public and private actors, it appears that significant power shifts with potentially long-standing effects take place. We submit that, in recent times, we witness a transition from a phase of reactive free-riding, that is, a process where private bodies were offered authority by the State, toward a phase where private bodies actively seek and claim authority by a worn-out State that is occupied with addressing the effects of a crisis within the society. We argue that proactive free-riding has become a growing empirical phenomenon, which emerges out of several decades of bounded rationality, untested theories of uncontested technical superiority, the ideational flexibility of neoliberal rhetoric, and an increasingly globalized – and stateless – economic activity that domestic laws fail to regulate due to their non-extraterritorial application.

Proactive free riding is VEA's very manifestation at the transnational level. The success of proactive free riding derives from the core rule-making activities that such private bodies undertake, notably the continuous promulgation of voluntary standards that are promptly prepared, adopted, and diffused to preempt rules by public rule-making competitors and thus ensure increased authority and continuous

[108] See C. Chinkin, Monism and Dualism: The Impact of Private Authority on the Dichotomy between National and International Law, in *New Perspectives on the Divide between National and International Law* (J. Nijman and A. Nollkaemper eds., 2007), 134, at 135.

dominance.[109] Paradoxically enough, this phenomenon is particularly manifested and appears to grow stronger in the wake of regulatory failures and even disasters that raise doubts against the adequacy of the regulatory philosophy in a given field and the aptitude and fitness for purpose of private authority.[110] Against all odds, reclaiming authority in that material time comes at a relatively low cost.

More and more, private bodies take advantage of the procrastination of the State, grow stronger, and create norms more assertively in a strategic manner, overriding and even substituting for State powers. Regulatory disasters leave them intact. Rather, such crises constitute opportunities to accumulate wisdom and develop the capacity to expect the unexpected, absorb it, and grow.[111] Absent organizational hierarchies, formal accountability structures, scrutiny, pressure, and obligation, private bodies enhance their collective memory and identity and eventually use a critical shock to become grow stronger.[112]

Proactive free riding results from a lengthy process of volatility and shifting authority in complex regulatory areas where complex adaptive organizations are present. Private power accumulation is a continuous process that starts with the delegation (explicit or tacit) of power and thus the transfer of legitimacy to a private body. Thereon, through rule-making and intensive drafting of standards, the private body accumulates knowledge and builds trust toward its addressees as a reliable interlocutor.

Crucially, whereas the values and objectives of a complex adaptive system of this type are aligned, the characteristics and motivations of the group as a whole are not necessarily homogenous. Rather than this being an inhibitory factor, heterogeneity allows a particular group to overcome distress and adversity, thereby enhancing its resilience. In line with the discussion above relating to and the lessons drawn by the study of resilience of ecosystems,[113] diversity and heterogeneity are important traits for any group that aspires to harness its complexity for its benefit and establish solid foundations for exercising such authority over the long run.[114] Such traits appear to equip a given group with sufficient flexibility to be shielded from internal challenges

[109] Cf. A. Héritier and S. Eckert, New Modes of Governance in the Shadow of Hierarchy: Self-Regulation by Industry in Europe (2008) 28 *Journal of Public Policy* 113.

[110] See also N. Arnold, Accountability in Transnational Governance: The Partial Organization of Voluntary Sustainability Standards in Long-Term Account-Giving (2022) 16 *Regulation and Governance* 375 .

[111] See C. Folke et al., Adaptive Governance of Social-Ecological Systems (2005) 30 *Annual Review of Environment and Resources* 441.

[112] See B. Goldstein (2009), Resilience to Surprises through Communicative Planning (2009) 14:2 *Ecology and Society* 33.

[113] See *supra* Section 1.2.1.

[114] See R. Axelrod and M. Cohen, *Harnessing Complexity: Organizational Implications of a Scientific Frontier* (2000), at 32ff.

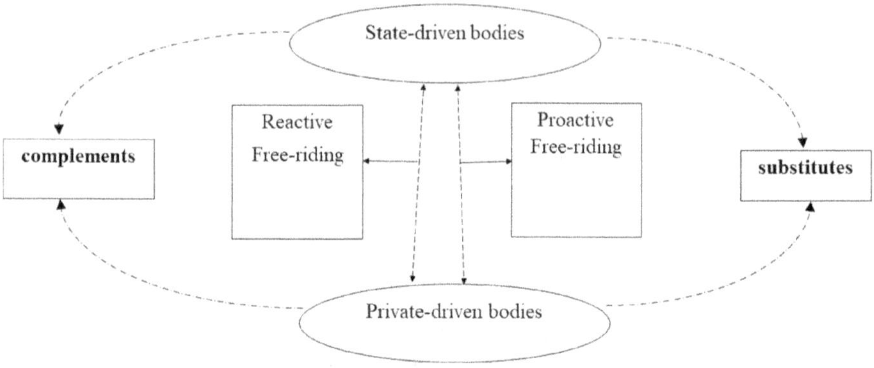

FIGURE 1.1. The evolution of free riding on authority

of due process and balance of interests and external attacks of arbitrariness and lack of legitimacy.[115]

In a given turning moment, the critical transition occurs: the private rule-making body overrides State power and reigns over a regulatory field, thereby slowly creating a new hierarchy; in other words, a different equilibrium and stable state of authority in a system.[116]

Much of proactive free riding is detached from any particular territory. Such free riding is led by powerful transnational elites that reinforce their independent norm-creating authority and expand the group of these norms' addressees,[117] gradually moving into the creation of legal authority and the production of authoritative collective action. In this emerging constellation, the State and the private bodies are no longer complements but rather substitutes (Figure 1.1).

How can one explain the mismatch between the expectations vis-à-vis public supervisory authorities and their lack of action? First, as we argued earlier, it appears that path dependencies and the irreversibility of delegation weakens their leverage. Supervisory authorities often make irrational decisions and adopt similarly irrational processes in their supervisory tasks. Additionally, cognitive biases developed during the interaction with the regulatee negatively affect the enforcement of existing laws and the appetite for decisive and timely action.[118] It has been argued that such inaction may be the result of cultural capture, that is, the interaction of supervisors with interest groups that increases industry influence through certain

[115] See C. Fiedler, M. Larrain, and J. Prüfer, Membership, Governance and Lobbying in Standard-Setting Organizations, TILEC Discussion Paper No. 2018-42.

[116] For a stylized illustration of institutional dynamics, see M. Janssen, The Future of Surprises, in Gunderson and Holling, *supra* note 7, 241, at 250.

[117] See C. Brölmann, Deterritorialization in International Law: Moving Away from the Divide Between National and International Law, in Nijman and Nollkaemper, *supra* note 108.

[118] C. Needham, Listening to Cassandra: The Difficulty of Recognizing Risks and Taking Action (2010) 78 *Fordham Law Review* 2347.

mechanisms.[119] Second, on the brink of a crisis, regulators and supervisors are occupied with reflecting on how to address and lessen the effects of the crisis. Eventually, stricter regulations that follow are frivolously enforced or the regulators have recourse to cosmetic changes, a type of indulgent regulation that allows for the maintenance of a system that turns random disruptive advantage to lasting advantage for private bodies.[120]

1.4 AN EMERGING AGENDA TOWARD A NEW THEORY OF PRIVATE COLLECTIVE ACTION

Driven by globalization, the ambitious progeny of transnational VEA seems to be in need of harnessing in the sectors discussed above and under certain circumstances. To do so, revisiting existing theories of private collective action, including the concepts, actors, and processes of private governance in finance and manufacturing in the light of what preceded, offers an exciting vista of the contemporary regulatory landscape in finance and manufacturing. To do so, however, meticulous empirical, longitudinal studies are an important prerequisite for any intervention with an ecosystem that has shown its resilience in multiple occasions.[121] Such studies need to be balanced and contextualized; VEA encompasses not only the type of free riding described earlier but also some of the most creative forces of private nature and rule ingenuity (think of codes of conduct, bylaws, guidelines and recommendations, performance and design standards, and other persuasion-based instruments) for centuries now.

Based on insights by complexity and resilience theories as well as law and economics and behavioral sciences, our analysis above suggests that certain properties need to be present for a system to reach the tempting stage of proactive free riding: such private rule-making bodies must have at least four types of different capacities: to grow, develop, survive, and renew. Thus, the system at stake should display a certain level of internal energy for activation, that is, available resources, information (for instance, feedback loops), and entrepreneurial and innovative leadership to start growing and invest in structure-building, notably a constellation that is relatively straightforward (for the capacities of the system) to scale. The latter will be the result of experimentation, stable network connections, internal trust-building, and dependencies: all of them important ingredients for the system's stable foundations.

[119] See J. Kwak, Cultural Capture and the Financial Crisis, in *Preventing Regulatory Capture: Special Interest Influence and How to Limit It* (D. Carpenter and D. Moss, eds., 2014), 71.

[120] See also J. Black, Paradoxes and Failures: The "New Governance" Techniques and the Financial Crisis (2012) 75:6 *Modern Law Review* 1037, at 1048.

[121] Cf. M. Jacobides, C. Cennamo, and A. Gawer, Towards a Theory of Ecosystems (2018) 39 *Strategic Management Journal* 2255.

Furthermore, in order to develop further, the system should be sufficiently self-organized to store information and capital that was acquired in the phase of growth with a view to strengthening its qualitative indicators. The system would also be keen to continued development, which may be crucial for persisting through a crisis event. In the wake of a crisis event (which is inevitable although its scale is unknown ex ante), a system would need to improvise to maintain vital functions. The previous accumulation of resources and innate characteristics of the system structure will allow for leadership (both existing and emergent) to invest effort for the survival of the system, leading to new knowledge, new forms of adaptive capacity, and, ultimately, resilience.

At this stage, modularity (the low levels of interdependence among components, which can still maintain a system's collective memory); diversity and heterogeneity (in function, in order to allow for leadership to emerge if needed, and in responses, to allow for short-notice varying action); as well as the ability for effective communication, information intermediation, and swift but robust decisions (such as new creation of standards and organizational rules) increases the likelihood of survival through crises. The subsequent renewal phase may lead to a reorientation of the system, drawing on lessons taken.[122]

It is exactly the moment that proactive free-riding may take place, which, however, depends on several variables, including the strength and determination of the private body when adopting new or modifying existing standards in an expedited manner as well as the strength and determination of the overseer to act upon a crisis event. In practice, one often gets the impression that rational public regulators, overseers, and even judges, constrained by political conditions and boundaries (including demands for swift action by an aroused public), massive uncertainty, bounded rationality and path dependencies, but also awareness of their own ignorance, hand the reins to private parties and hope for the best too often too easily.

Admittedly, the complexity of the two issue areas of finance and product safety we identified earlier does not help paint a candid image of the internal dynamics and the relational fabric of social interactions among the different actors and stakeholders. Both modern finance and food or technological product safety entail some of the most complex dynamics, structures and patterns, and interactive processes. However, whereas private regulatory entities, many times acting in unchartered waters full of uncertainty and risks, fail in their mission, the State and its public agents will rarely exercise coercion vis-à-vis private regulatory bodies and even less reclaim authority to protect the public interest.[123] Sometimes, these bodies will struggle to survive and eventually may disappear. However, if such bodies dissolve or lose part of their authority, it is not because of State intervention but rather

[122] See Fath et al., *supra* note 12.

[123] See M. Feintuck, Regulatory Rationales beyond the Economic: In Search of the Public Interest, in Baldwin et al. *supra* note 29.

because they lose in relevance, as new, typically private-driven, contesters emerge, many times internally, with a view to regaining strength.[124]

The new type of VEA that we witness is quite anarchic as much as it is conservative. Just like every evolving entity, its current preferences, structures, mechanics, and methods bear similarities with previous iterations of rule-making activity. However, it also displays innovative characteristics that nourish its resilience and dominance. Low connectivity, high diversity, and possibilities for collaborative learning, as well as strategies of system innovation, smoothened transition, and identity building are important attributes that render private regulatory bodies stable.[125]

The standard-setting activities of these bodies active in the areas of manufacturing and finance are directly related to crises of varying scales that may even lead to regulatory disasters. Safety and innovation in technology-laden products or financial instruments heavily rely on the smooth functioning and stability of such bodies. Arguably, whereas delegation of power contributes to their empowerment, crises allow them to capitalize on certain tipping points that strengthen their status and influence. While existing literature describes the dynamics among standard-setters, it fails to shed light on the possibility for a commonality of mind among actors in a given private regulatory body (or a group thereof) to exploit the weaknesses of the State at times of crisis. Yet it is quite striking that, in these complex ecosystems, periods of crisis were almost immediately followed by intensive, fast periods of expedited standard-setting by private bodies, thereby enlarging the breadth and reach of their output, which would typically come in the form of standards. This new form of antagonistic private ordering deserves closer attention and research, as it may allow for opening the black box of economic governance and the evolution of contemporary private collective action.

1.5 CONCLUSION

In what preceded, this contribution offered the contours of a new conceptualization of the resilience of private authority, particularly in the aftermath of crises. It argued that existing theories of delegation, orchestration, and private collective action fail to explain satisfactorily the survival of certain private regulatory bodies, notably in the fields of finance and product safety. Rather, the resilience of such bodies needs an alternative explanation that portrays more accurately the innate characteristics, mechanics, and dynamics of certain private bodies active in the regulation and governance of economic activity. In stressing the centrality of the role, the effects of,

[124] Cf. J. Morse and R. Keohane, Contested multilateralism (2014) 9 *Review of International Organizations* 385.

[125] Cf. A. Haldane and R. May, Systemic Risk in Banking Ecosystems (2011) 469 *Nature* 351; and C. Freeman and C. Perez, Structural Crisis of Adjustment, Business Cycles and Investment Behaviour, in *Technical Change and Economic Theory* (G. Dosi et al. eds., 1988).

and the reactions to crisis events, that is, tipping points that call for a paradigm shift in regulatory patterns and modi operandi, the above analysis aspires to recalibrate the study of private governance. The empirical study of crisis events, we argue, is key in understanding the resilience of private governance and may allow unraveling the reasons for an ever-increasing transfer of power to private regulatory bodies. Crucially, the chapter described the contours of a new theory of proactive free riding of private regulatory forces that use regulatory episodes as catalysts for gaining more regulatory power to the detriment of the State.

We hypothesized that the secret for the success of such free riding activity lies at two core features of resilient systems: the first relates to heterogeneity in membership, sources, and crisis responses – conflicting interests that manage to identify common denominators that allow things to keep going for the common (private) good; and the second relates to the core standard-setting activities of such private bodies and the rapidity with which such activities occur in the wake of a regulatory catastrophe in the field of finance or manufacturing and product safety. In that respect, we introduced VEA, yet another strategic effort by private bodies to maintain and increase the *terrain occupé* of their regulatory power by means of promulgation of voluntary but forceful standards.

2

Between Public and Private

Heterarchy in an Age of Intangibles and Financialization

Philip G. Cerny and Rosalba Belmonte

2.1 INTRODUCTION

In the twenty-first century, world politics is becoming increasingly multi-nodal and characterized by heterarchy, namely the predominance of cross-cutting sectoral mini- and meso-hierarchies above, below, and cutting across states.

In this context, states are becoming "reactive states" as their capacity for "pro-active" policymaking and implementation are eroded. This process is leading to an uneven spectrum of market/hierarchy or public/private de facto policymaking processes and diverse types of "capture" between a range of private actors and meso- and micro-hierarchies, institutions, and processes. The result is the decreasing capacity of macro-states to control both domestic and transnational political/economic processes. At the same time, global regulation is increasingly fragmented, whipsawed between transnational and subnational private special interest groups, leading to potential crises at a complex range of nodes and levels.

The core of this process is the triangulation of (a) the "disaggregated state,"[1] (b) fragmented global governance and "regime complexes,"[2] and (c) "sectoral (or functional) differentiation" in the international political economy.[3] Functional differentiation, which is organized around economic sectors with different "asset structures,"[4] increasingly cuts across state borders, enmeshing both state and non-state structures and actors in what have been called "third-level games" – political, economic, and social – that transform the nature of the state itself. What new forms

[1] A. M. Slaughter, A *New World Order* (2004).

[2] K. J. Alter and K. Raustiala, The Rise of International Regime Complexity (2018) 14 *Annual Review of Law and Social Science* 2, at 21.

[3] P. G. Cerny, Functional Differentiation, Globalisation and the New Transnational Neopluralism, in *Bringing Sociology into International Relations: World Politics as Differentiation Theory* (A. Mathias, Ba. Buzan, and M. Zurn eds., , 2013), 205–227.

[4] O. E. Williamson, *Markets and Hierarchies* (1975); O. E. Williamson, *The Economic Institutions of Capitalism* (1985).

of functional differentiation might evolve at global/transnational levels? Global governance (the transnational "political sector")? Domination by a transnational capitalist class or global markets (the transnational "economic sector")? Global civil society – or an amorphous "neomedievalism" or "durable disorder"?[5]

It can be argued that economic factors came to be the most significant variable in the consolidation of nation-states. The first industrial revolution transformed the United Kingdom into the first economic superpower. This led other protostates to consolidate in competition with other emerging states on both levels, especially in Europe, where the nation-state system developed and spread its organizational model internationally through innovation, trade, and empire.[6] More important historically, however, was the second industrial revolution, in which the combination of the consolidation of nation-states and the large factory system in a range of cutting-edge industries led to new forms of international competition.

These developments, both market-based and monopolistic/oligopolistic, gave rise to hierarchically organized state-economic complexes and, indeed, to social and institutional reorganization along the interacting lines of capitalist hierarchies and Weberian bureaucratization. The state, therefore, has nevertheless been seen as centripetal in the evolution of economic and socio-political life[7]. This conceptualization of the state has been dominated not only by empirical state-building processes themselves but also by the perception among mass publics that states, despite their disadvantages, are normatively the best way to organize political life. Furthermore, state-building has long been associated at least since the Enlightenment with notions of progress and modernity, whether liberal, capitalist, or socialist. Debates about the relations between business and politics have centered on this problematic.[8] In the twenty-first-century world, however, the capacity of states to effectively regulate the world political economy is being eroded from above, below, and cutting across borders. Regulatory authorities are increasingly characterized by private sector–dominated institutions and processes, especially in the financial sector.

2.1.1 *Beyond State-Centrism: The Dialectic of Globalization and Fragmentation*

A range of diverse governance processes are increasingly integrated into complex, heterogenous ways to other interactive, overlapping, and/or competing processes

5 P. G. Cerny, Neomedievalism, Civil War and the New Security Dilemma: Globalisation as Durable Disorder (1998) 1 *Civil Wars* 1, at 36–64.

6 P. Kennedy, *The Rise and Fall of the Great Powers* (1988).

7 P. Birnbaum, *La logique de l'État* (1982).

8 P. G. Cerny, *The Changing Architecture of Politics: Structure, Agency and the Future of the State* (1990).

and institutions – what we elsewhere call "heterarchy."[9] Furthermore, globalization itself is all too often perceived to be a structurally homogenizing process, requiring new forms of intergovernmental cooperation or global governance. Dimensions of homogenization are said to include economic globalization, the ideological hegemony of neoliberalism,[10] socio-cultural convergence, technological innovation and change, liberal internationalism and global governance, and the emergence of a particular kind of so-called flat world.[11] Normative calls for a world state follow this logic – so-called global governance.

Therefore, in a world that is increasingly characterized by complex interdependence, states, domestic political systems, and public policymaking are vulnerable to cross-cutting and intersecting independent variables they cannot control. In the structural environment of the third (and/or fourth) industrial revolution(s),[12] and the complex forces undermining neoliberal globalization and the state, whether ideological, social, or material, there is also a trend toward developing diverse forms of neoliberalism from the quasi-democratic to the authoritarian.[13]

This structural transformation revolves around the interaction of fundamental technological transformations and the interrelationships of business and politics in an ever-evolving dialectic of globalization and fragmentation.[14] These transformations involve a wide range of economic processes that include information and communications technologies (ICT), new forms of research and development (R&D), the shift of investment from expensive and hierarchical production processes to profit-making through distribution and the embedding of a consumer culture, artificial intelligence, digitalization, the advent of Big Data, the increasing use of algorithms,[15] robotics, the growing vulnerability of labor processes and their replacement by flexibilization of diverse kinds,[16] and the transformation of finance to "financial alchemy," including increasing dependence on debt and leverage or credit. The businesses that adapt successfully to these changes are crucial in shaping the relations between business and the "reactive state."

[9] R. Belmonte and P. G. Cerny Heterarchy: Toward Paradigm Shift in World Politics (2021) 14 *Journal of Political Power* 1.

[10] P. G. Cerny, *From Theory to Practice: The Paradox of Neoliberal Hegemony in 21st Century World Politics*, in *Theory as Ideology in International Relations: The Politics of Knowledge* (B. Martill and S. Schindler eds., 2020), 140–164.

[11] T. L. Friedman, *The World Is Flat: A Brief History of the 21st Century* (2005).

[12] J. Rifkin, *The Third Industrial Revolution: How Lateral Power Is Transforming Energy, the Economy, and the World* (2011); K. Schwab, *The Fourth Industrial Revolution* (2016); J. Haskel and S. Westlake, *Capitalism without Capital: The Rise of the Intangible Economy* (2018).

[13] Cerny, *supra* note 10.

[14] P. G. Cerny and A. Prichard, The New Anarchy: Globalisation and Fragmentation in 21st Century World Politics 2017 13 *Journal of International Political Theory* 3, at 378–394.

[15] D. Gritsenko and M. Wood, Algorithmic Governance: A Modes of Governance Approach (2020) *Regulation and Governance*, doi:10.1111/rego.12367.

[16] L. Gratton, *The Shift: The Future of Work Is Already Here* (2011).

Political agency is therefore no longer defined by interest groups seeking out the levers of state power, because these levers are seen to be largely impotent or politically suspect.[17] Related to this turn from the state is "deterritorialization" or the "poverty of territorialism."[18] Structural homogeneity between state and society in specific geographical/territorial locations, crucial to the unitary coherence of the nation-state, is being undermined by cross-border linkages.[19] In particular, the kind of strong, secure borders that are supposed to characterize the sovereign nation-state are becoming impossibly porous and in many cases more analogous to fluid, premodern "frontiers."[20] The increasing complexity of this system raises questions about whether this complexity will lead to endemic conflict or a "durable disorder" in which key actors are engaged in various forms of "brokerage" to smooth over the underlying dysfunctionality of the system.

One way to conceptualize these processes is thinking of them in terms of the kind of ongoing process that Rosenau calls "fragmegration"[21] – the dialectic of globalization and fragmentation in a "postinternationalist" world. The European Union, for example, is in continual structural quasi-crisis, trying to deal centrally with plural tensions between the local and the transnational dimensions. Indeed, the United States has always been characterized by internal socioeconomic division.[22] Furthermore, austerity and the erosion of the rights of labor are undermining the mid-twentieth-century social contract on which the welfare state and liberal democracy have been based.[23] Political leaders in unstable states are either engaged in attempting to restore authoritarian repression, as in Russia, China, Egypt, and Turkey, or are ensnared in the breakdown of the political system, as in Brazil, Venezuela, and a range of African countries, leading the emergence of quasi-authoritarian populism, including what has been called "personalist autocracy."[24]

Rationalities of marginal utility have transformed statehood itself into a marketizing, commodifying process[25]. Furthermore, the state has itself become a promoter

[17] J. Holloway, *Change the World without Taking Power: The Meaning of Revolution Today* (2002).

[18] A. Faludi, *The Poverty of Territorialism: A Neo-Medieval View of Europe and European Planning* (2018).

[19] J. A. Scholte, *Globalization: A Critical Introduction* (2000).

[20] P. De Wilde et al. (eds.), *The Struggle over Borders: Cosmopolitanism and Communitarianism* (2019).

[21] J. Rosenau, The Governance of Fragmegration: Neither a World Republic Nor a Global Interstate System, paper presented at the World Congress of the International Political Science Association, Quebec City, August 1–5, 1990.

[22] C. Woodward, *American Nations: A History of the Eleven Rival Regional Cultures of North America* (2011).

[23] M. Blyth, *Austerity: The History of a Dangerous Idea* (2013).

[24] T. Frye, Russia's Weak Strongman: The Perilous Bargains That Keep Putin in Power (May 23, 2021) *Foreign Affairs*, www.foreignaffairs.com/articles/russia-fsu/2021-04-01/vladimir-putin-russias-weak-strongman.

[25] Cerny, *supra* note 10.

of financialization rather than welfare or social democracy, prompting the financialization of society itself – replacing decommodifying welfare and public services through austerity and undermining the potential for what has been called the "entrepreneurial state" concerned with providing public goods.[26] Nevertheless, the state continues to be the primary provider of welfare programs, and finance cannot do without it either, for a host of public goods rely on finance for credit.

Actors develop and maintain particular institutions and structures over time. Society and polity shape our interactions through people and material processes that connect them.[27] They take place through our interactions with the computers, logistics, and groups of people "next" to us in an increasingly intangible world of "capitalism without capital."[28] The process is itself nonlinear and causally complex.[29] For example, actors and political processes can only react to price changes that are independently produced by market and institutional transactions, many of which are increasingly automated, and certain sectors like communications and social media require further regulation. What governance levels would be necessary for such regulation? Would it be effective? The United States and the European Union are dealing with this question through different and contrasting approaches, with the European Union paradoxically taking a more comprehensive and centralized approach with one main regulator, whereas the United States has maintained its divided regulatory system among a range of sectorally specific regulatory bodies.

Furthermore, actors' social positioning shapes their range of possible responses to material processes in multi-nodal fashion[30]. For example, information and communications technologies that circle the globe also create the potential for backlashes of diverse kinds as awareness of global-level problems, inequalities, and instabilities spreads through our everyday practices. Indeed, business actors are sometimes not only captured by preexisting state-based structures and practices but paradoxically also see them as valid reactions to globalization and transnationalization – what Bohas and Morley call

[26] Y. Tiberghien, *Entrepreneurial States: Reforming Corporate Governance in France, Japan, and Korea* (2007); F. Block and M. R. Keller, *State of Innovation: The U.S. Government's Role in Technology Innovation* (2011); M. Mazzucato, *The Entrepreneurial State: Debunking Public vs. Private Sector Myths* (2013); A. Herman, *Freedom's Forge: How American Business Produced Victory in World War II* (2012).

[27] N. Srnicek, Representing Complexity: The Material Construction of World Politics, PhD thesis, London School of Economics and Political Science, 2013; D. H. Coole and S. Frost, *New Materialisms: Ontology, Agency, and Politics* (2010).

[28] Haskel and Westlake, *supra* note 12.

[29] P. T. Jackson and D. H. Nexon, Relations before States: Substance, Process and the Study of World Politics (1999) 5:3 *European Journal of International Relations* 291; E. Cudworth and S. Hobden, *Posthuman International Relations: Complexity, Ecologism and Global Politics* (2011); A. Prichard, Collective Intentionality, Complex Pluralism and the Problem of Anarchy (2017) 13 *Journal of International Political Theory* 3, at 360–377.

[30] P. G. Cerny, Multi-nodal Politics: Globalisation Is What Actors Make of It (2009) 35:2 *Review of International Studies* 421.

an "anomic mindset."[31] The dialectic of globalization and fragmentation thus decenters the state itself by placing it alongside and competing with other social and economic groups and organizations – rather than above the social and below the international.[32] Strategic actors are able to mobilize resources, ideologies and mindsets, and knowledge to take advantage of the constraints and opportunities and to pursue their interests. This has led to the consolidation of a range of "extra-state authorities"[33] and regime complexes across a range of institutions and processes including "low-capacity states," fragmented global governance and oligopolistic, sectorally differentiated quasi-corporatist policymaking and regulatory and policy implementation processes.

These embed the "privileged position of business"[34] and transnationally powerful interest groups, including intangible sectors such as ICT,[35] banking, and finance, etc., as well as transnational corporations, supply chains, and other linkages transcending and undermining state territorial and economic boundaries. States themselves have sought to benefit from these transformations by sponsoring the competitiveness of domestically located firms, leading to transnational oligopolization and rent-seeking.[36] Paradoxically, the state is not shrinking in size, but the "macro-state" is less and less structurally dominant and bureaucratically effective in the face of these meso-state, micro-state, and trans-state apparatuses.

Crucial in this restructuration process are a range of private sector–dominated regulatory agencies. For example, in the derivatives market – the "world's biggest

[31] A. Bohas and M. Morley, Revealing the Anomic Mindset: Discontent of International Managers and Their Detours on the Pathway toward the Development of a Global Mindset, Academy of Management Annual Meeting Proceedings (2020), DOI:10.5465/AMBPP.2020.20240abstract.

[32] Prichard, *supra* note 28.

[33] R. Belmonte, Political power in a heterarchical world. A categorization of Extra-state authorities, in Heterarchy in world politics (P.G. Cerny eds, 2022), 80–92.

[34] C. E. Lindblom, *Politics and Markets: The World's Political-Economic Systems* (1977); C. E. Lindblom, *The Market System: What It Is, How It Works, and What to Make of It* (2001).

[35] F. Fukuyama et al., How to Save Democracy from Technology: Ending Big Tech's Information Monopoly (2021) 100 (January/February) *Foreign Affairs* 98; P. Delimatsis, The Resilience of Private Authority in Times of Crisis: A Theory of Free-Riding of Private Ordering, The Evolution of Transnational Private Rule-Makers: Understanding Drivers and Dynamics, Conference at Tilburg University, Tilburg Law and Economics Centre (TILEC) December 3–4, 2021. See S. Bijlmakers, The International Organisation for Standardisation: A 75-year Journey towards Organisational resilience, The Evolution of Transnational Private Rule-Makers: Understanding Drivers and Dynamics, Conference at Tilburg University, Tilburg Law and Economics Centre (TILEC) December 3–4, 2021; P. Hugues Verdier, Resilience and Change in Private Standard-Setting: The Case of LIBOR, The Evolution of Transnational Private Rule-Makers: Understanding Drivers and Dynamics, Conference at Tilburg University, Tilburg Law and Economics Centre (TILEC) December 3–4, 2021; and J. Reinecke, The Politics of Collaborative Governance in Global Supply Chains: Power and Pushback in the Bangladesh Accord, The Evolution of Transnational Private Rule-Makers: Understanding Drivers and Dynamics, Conference at Tilburg University, Tilburg Law and Economics Centre (TILEC) December 3–4, 2021.

[36] P. G. Cerny, Paradoxes of the Competition State: The Dynamics of Political Globalization (1997) 32:2 *Government and Opposition* 251.

market" – regulation is provided by such bodies as the International Swaps and Derivatives Association (ISDA), central counterparties (CCPs), trade repositories (TRs), and other bodies dominated by "dealer banks" (the G16), which do not constrain speculative trading, ignoring "calls for bans on derivatives products that were particularly associated with destabilizing speculative trading such as 'unattached' (or 'naked') CDS contracts [credit default swaps] in which the purchaser does not hold the underlying bond to which the contract is linked."[37] In other words, the only form of regulation that it is possible to institutionalize is dominated by private sector firms and actors. Recent history suggests that the development of an effective global governance structure as a way to reorganize world politics is increasingly unlikely, even moving in the opposite direction.[38] Biermann et al.[39] refer to the "fragmentation of global governance architectures" as the dominant trend in the twenty-first century.

In this context, the globalization/fragmentation dialectic opens up those processes to precisely the kind of special interests that have been identified in the long-standing critical domestic interest group, elitist, corporatist, and neopluralist literature of the twentieth century[40]. And the proliferating literature on multinational corporations and transnational production chains, the advances of information and communications technologies, and, in particular, the power of quasi-globalized financial markets and institutions[41] demonstrates that global governance itself can be even more vulnerable to whipsawing, bypassing, capture and manipulation, even corruption, than the traditional domestic public policy sphere. Lindblom[42] refers to this as "the privileged position of business".

At the core of these processes, furthermore, is the hybridization of the public and the private. Key actors – the more powerful economic interest groups, state actors in particular issue areas, certain NGOs, etc. – have differing and sometimes conflicting interests. In this heterarchical political process, actors depend upon the capacities of real-world, cross-cutting "interest" groups – including both "sectional" (or "material interest") and "value" groups,[43] civil society groups, NGOs, and social movements – to manipulate constraints, to identify and take advantage of opportunities, and to

37 The definitive source here is E. Helleiner, S. Pagliari, and I. Spagna (eds.), *Governing the World's Greatest Market: The Politics of Derivatives Regulation after the 2008 Crisis* (2018); the quote is from p. 7, but this theme dominates all the subsequent chapters about specific derivatives markets.

38 P. G. Cerny, The Limits of Global Governance: Transnational Neopluralism in a Complex World, in *Partnerships in International Policymaking: Civil Society and Public Institutions in European and Global Affairs* (R. Marchetti ed., 2016), 31–47.

39 F. Biermann (ed.), *International Organizations in Global Environmental Governance* (2009).

40 P. G. Cerny, *Rethinking World Politics: A Theory of Transnational Neopluralism* (2010).

41 P. G. Cerny, Rethinking Financial Regulation: Risk, Club Goods and Regulatory Fatigue, in *Handbook of the International Political Economy of Monetary Relations* (T. Oatley and W. Kindred Winecoff eds., 2014), 343–363.

42 Lindblom, *supra* note 33.

43 V. O. Key Jr., *Politics, Parties, and Pressure Groups* (1953).

shape new directions through processes of competition, coalition-building, "forum shopping," or "venue shopping" and the like. What is new, however, are the rapidly evolving transnational linkages among groups in a growing range of overlapping transnational webs of power. The most important movers and shakers are no longer simply domestic political forces, institutions, and processes but transnationalizing ones: whether in terms of economic interdependence; social interconnections, migration, the movement of people, and transnational awareness through world communications and social media; relationships of violence and force (including terrorism); "transgovernmental networks" cutting across governments themselves; problem-solving "epistemic communities";[44] technological change from the Internet to a growing variety of human activities; ideological conflict and competition; and a whole range of other deep trends.

Governance itself is therefore being transformed into a "polycentric" or "multinucleated" global political system operating within the same geographical space – and/or overlapping spaces – in ways analogous to the emergence of coexisting and overlapping functional authorities in metropolitan areas and subnational regions.[45] In the economic sphere, post-Fordist forms of production based on flexibilization have transformed "techniques of industry," labor markets, finance, and the like, thus leading to a "capitalism without capital."[46] The particular shape a transformed international system is likely to take will be determined primarily by whether particular sets of groups[47] that are able to exploit the structural resources or political opportunity structures available to them take advantage most effectively in a period of structural flux.

Key sets of groups that have in the past been closely bound up with the territorial nation-state and state actors themselves are increasingly captured instead by transnational sectors. These actors do not merely set state agencies and international regimes against each other – a process sometimes called "venue shopping," "forum

[44] P. Haas, Knowledge, Power, and International Policy Coordination (1992) 46 *International Organization* 1.

[45] V. Ostrom et al., The Organization of Government in Metropolitan Areas: A Theoretical Inquiry (1961) 55:3 *American Political Science Review* 831. P. Delimatsis, The Resilience of Private Authority in Times of Crisis: A Theory of Free-Riding of Private Ordering, The Evolution of Transnational Private Rule-Makers: Understanding Drivers and Dynamics (Conference at Tilburg University, Tilburg Law and Economics Centre (TILEC) December 3–4, 2021). See O. Kanevskaia, and J. Baron, Global Rivalry over the Leadership in ICT Standardisation: SDO Governance Amid Changing Patterns of Participation, The Evolution of Transnational Private Rule-Makers: Understanding Drivers and Dynamics (Conference at Tilburg University, Tilburg Law and Economics Centre (TILEC) December 3–4, 2021.

[46] Haskel and Westlake, *supra* note 12; C. B. Frey, *The Technology Trap: Capital, Labor and Power in the Age of Automation* (2019).

[47] R. M. Kanter, *The Change Masters: Innovation and Entrepreneurship in the American Corporation* (1985).

shopping," or "regulatory arbitrage."[48] They also cause them to try to network in an increasingly dense fashion with their peers in other states and simultaneously instill them and their transnational private/public links in state elites too. Among the major losers are trade unions and other groups with few transnational linkages and less clout in an intangible economy where labor has become more "flexible" and, indeed, "commodified," although they are sometimes still in a position to obtain compensatory side payments from national governments.

Operating in such a changing world is leading to new problems of management and control, what Lake has called "the privatization of governance"[49] and others have identified as the emergence of "private authority" in international affairs. Private actors decide the rules of their conduct and act to ensure order in the markets, facilitate trade, and protect private property.[50] Institutions and formal processes of global governance do not have the direct sanctioning power that has been at the core of state development in the modern era – especially in the form of Weber's "monopoly of legitimate violence." In the meantime, the sovereignty of states is only partially and unevenly pooled through the development of intergovernmental institutions and processes – what authors often refer to as the concept of "soft law."[51]

Significant issue areas, including accountancy, auditing, and corporate governance, have witnessed ongoing negotiation processes among firms; private sector organizations representing particular industrial, financial, and commercial sectors; as well as governments and international regimes, in order to reconcile conflicting standards and move toward a more level playing field. Also, decision-making processes related to many significant issues moved from elective arenas to places presented as politically neutral with the consequence of a loss of political character of such issues and the annihilation of divergences and conflicts within the field of political actions.[52] Consequently, it is becoming more and more difficult to organize

48 A. Kellow, Multi-level and Multi-arena Governance: The Limits of Integration and the Possibilities of Forum Shopping (2002) 12 *International Environmental Agreements* 327; H. Murphy and A. Kellow, Forum Shopping in Global Governance: Understanding States, Business and NGOs in Multiple Arenas' (2013), 4:2 *Global Policy* 139.

49 D. A. Lake, Global Governance: A Relational Contracting Approach, in *Globalization and Governance* (A. Prakash and J. A. Hart eds., 1999), 31–53; M. Kahler and D. A. Lake (eds.), *Governance in a Global Economy: Political Authority in Transition* (2003).

50 A. Cutler et al. (eds.), *Private Authority and International Affairs* (1999); K. Ronit and V. Schneider (eds.), *Private Organisations in Global Politics* (2000); R. B. Hall and T. J. Biersteker (eds.), *The Emergence of Private Authority in Global Governance* (2003); E. P. Stringham, *Private Governance: Creating Order in Economic and Social Life Oxford* (2015).

51 A. L. Newman and E. Posner, *Voluntary Disruptions: International Soft Law, Finance, and Power* (2018).

52 M. Flinders and M. Wood, Depoliticisation, Governance and the State (2014) 42:2 *Policy and Politics* 135; R. Belmonte and M. Damiani, The Depoliticization of Immigration: Youngsters and Immigrants in Perugia, in *Changing Democracies in an Unequal Word* (F. Saccà ed., 2021), 88–105.

politically effective resistance to globalization as such, especially in the more developed capitalist states, although recent examples of the growth of populism on both right and left has been at the forefront of recent politics.

Furthermore, in an era where states compete to attract foreign direct investment, transnational corporations can make strategic actions independently of the interests of the countries in which they operate. Also, they have an increasing role in law-making processes that they exercise through lobbying activities. Often, they turn to practices of self-regulation, private governance, risk management, and alternative dispute resolution.[53] Their resources come from private sources – even if governments very often support transnational corporations (TNCs) through public investments and favorable tax conditions[54] – and are used to earn profits for a restricted circle of actors that in most cases are involved in private decision-making processes. At the same time, transnational financial agencies operate in several economic-financial fields, including the insurance, accountancy, and risk management sector, affecting the allocation of resources between social groups, national economies, and commercial enterprises.[55] Indeed, they assume an institutional role consisting in ensuring trust among participants in economic-financial transactions[56].

2.1.2 *Sectoral Differentiation*

In this context, different sectors at different levels and organizational structures play differentially powerful roles in this process. Analysts including Gordon,[57] Piketty,[58] and Stiglitz[59] have argued that the third and fourth industrial revolutions have reduced the profitability of the real economy, leaving capitalists fewer alternatives to financial manipulation to gain income and wealth compared to the second industrial revolution era,[60] leading to growing inequality and economic instability.[61] This process, combined with the increased capacity of transnationally linked financial special interests and pressure groups to lobby and capture state and international policymaking agencies and processes, leads to an uneven heterarchy of the kind we

53 Stringham, *supra* note 48.

54 Mazzucato, *supra* note 25; Cerny, *supra* note 35.

55 S. Strange, *The Retreat of the State: The Diffusion of Power in the World Economy* (1996); A. Pizzorno, Natura della disuguaglianza, potere politico e potere privato nella società in via di globalizzazione (2001) 62 *Stato e mercato* 201; Stringham, *supra* note 48.

56 Pizzorno, *supra* note 52.

57 R. J. Gordon, *The Rise and Fall of American Growth: The U.S. Standard of Living since the Civil War* (2016).

58 T. Piketty, *Capital in the Twenty-First Century* (2014).

59 J. E. Stiglitz, *People, Power, and Profits: Progressive Capitalism in an Age of Discontent* (2019).

60 A. Gemzik-Salwach and K. Opolski (eds.), *Financialization and the Economy* (2017); T. Bayoumi, *Unfinished Business: The Unexplored Causes of the Financial Crisis and the Lessons Yet to Be Learned* (2017).

61 A. Faiola, How Debt is Making Global Inequality Worse, *The Washington Post*, Today's Worldview, November 19, 2021.

have elsewhere labeled "transnational neopluralism."[62] Also, this process includes reorganizing political institutions, realigning political forces and coalitions, reforming policy processes, and restructuring ideological space, thus reinventing the social dimension of politics through new policy and coalition "spaces" populated by a wide range of new and old political actors in both the developed and developing worlds.

These new political processes are therefore differentiated more by sector and issue area than by physical, geographical, or territorial space. They involve a combination of vertical, horizontal, and diagonal restructuring of institutions and policy domains. In purely economic terms, this means that firms with extensive specific assets are more efficiently organized through quasi-monopolistic, hierarchical governance structures.[63] The key dimension here concerns the configuration of interests, characteristic of the industry, or activity concerned. There are essentially two aspects of this dimension: the mobility of physical capital and cross-border price sensitivity.

In firms and sectors that are highly integrated or linked into such structures and processes, especially where there is a "world market price" for a good or asset that determines local prices, lobbying pressure from firms in that sector and from industry organizations is likely to be organized through flexible "pentangles" (coalitions that include transnational actors from outside the national "container" and which operate at the transnational level to influence global governance processes) rather than simpler iron triangles.[64] The politics of key issue areas like financial regulation can play a catalytic role in reshaping global economics and politics as a whole, imposing their particular market and policy structures on other sectors and issue areas too.

2.1.3 *Finance and Politics in the Twenty-First Century*

Finance plays a unique role in the processes outlined above, and financialization is a key independent variable in the structuration of business-politics relations over the past half century. Unlike the "real economy", finance is the ultimate intangible sector, because it links and shapes all the others. On the one hand, economic and social progress have required the development of finance and money to grow. In this sense, finance and politics can be seen to be mutually interdependent, with effective policymaking requiring support for the development and institutionalization of finance in order to pursue wider social and political goals and to develop systemically relevant structures and processes, both macroeconomic and microeconomic. Without finance, whether private or public, there would be no economic development. On the other hand, however, the creation of financial instruments and the

62 Cerny, *supra* note 38.

63 Williamson, *supra* note 4 (both).

64 P. G. Cerny, From "Iron Triangles" to "Golden Pentangles"? Globalizing the Policy Process (2001) 7:4 *Global Governance* 397.

evolution of financial markets in a range of circumstances can permit finance to become autonomous from the real economy and to develop a dynamic of its own.

However, the contemporary evolution of finance and money since the middle to late twentieth century is unique in history. We will examine three distinct but inextricably intertwined trends and variables that are shaping the relationship of politics and finance today. Together they are making finance more independent, opaque, and disconnected from the real economy than ever.

The first of these structural trends is the restructuring of the world political economy around the transnationalization of special financial interests. The second is the structuration of the financial sector itself through the development of a range of complex financial instruments, especially securitization and derivatives, which disconnect finance from the real economy and therefore from political and social objectives. The third trend involves the wider political context and impact of government and transnational regulation of finance.

This leads to various attempts by the "reactive state" and overlapping and competing transnational "regime complexes" to manage the workings of the financial system in ways that support that system and its market mechanisms. These attempts not only led to the Global Financial Crisis (GFC) of 2007–2008 but also have continued in its aftermath.[65] In this context, we will consider a range of crucial social and political consequences of what has been called "financialization."[66] The evolution of the world political economy is widely seen as increasingly problematic and dysfunctional as a result.[67] The role of finance in the world economy has been evolving in the general direction of financialization since the 1950s.[68] There have been several factors driving this process:

- growing trade and pressures on the international system to reallocate capital across borders as a result, with the postwar financial system becoming more flexible and extensive;
- domestic budgetary and other pressures on the postwar welfare state, leading to policies of budgetary belt-tightening and to neoliberal economic policies across various levels and sectors;
- leveraging – of the role of debt – in both the domestic and the international financial systems, including the ideology of "financial inclusion";

[65] B. S. Bernanke et al., *Firefighting: The Financial Crisis and Its Lessons* (2019).

[66] Gemzik-Solwach and Opolski, *supra* note 58.

[67] For an authoritative analysis, see M. Sawyer, Financialisation and the Dysfunctional Nature of the Financial System, in *Progressive Post-Keynesian Economics: Dealing with Reality* (J. Jespersen and F. Olesen eds., 2019), 69–85.

[68] This section draws on a wide range of sources, but in particular: B. Christophers, *Banking across Boundaries: Placing Finance in Capitalism* (2013); R. Faroohar, *Makers and Takers: The Rise of Finance and the Fall of American Business* (2016); A. Nesvetailova, *Fragile Finance: Debt, Speculation and Crisis in the Age of Global Credit* (2007); R. Guttman, *Finance-Led Capitalism: Shadow Banking, Re-regulation and the Future of Global Markets* (2016).

- and the predominance of new financial instruments and institutions like securitization and "shadow banking," which will be examined more closely in Section 2.1.4.

In the post–World War II period, the internationalization of banks and the increasing flow of financial assets across borders led to pressures for significant structural changes in the international financial system. Most writers focus on the emergence of the Eurodollar market in the 1950s and 1960s, in which a combination of international pressures and the role of domestic institutions – originally involving the Midland Bank in the United Kingdom – led to increasing regulatory tolerance for American financial assets, especially those obtained outside the United States, to be deposited in the United Kingdom, outside the scope of US regulations. This process encouraged and reinforced increasing cross-border financial flows in general, augmented politically as well as financially by the tradition of sterling as an international currency and the historical role of the City of London as an international financial center. In this context, financial firms and institutions developed strategies consistent with the wider process of globalization. Indeed, transnational finance has often been identified as the key independent variable driving globalization.[69]

Furthermore, one of the approaches that several important authors have taken is to apply the theories of Hyman Minsky.[70] He argued that financial crises are endemic in capitalism because periods of economic prosperity encouraged borrowers and lenders to be progressively reckless. This excess optimism creates financial bubbles and the later busts. Therefore, capitalism is prone to move from periods of financial stability to instability. This is a type of market failure and needs government regulation. It is the flexibility, complexity, and opacity of finance that gives it its strength and significance in controlling and coping with political and bureaucratic processes such as regulation and, in particular, crisis management, especially in the context of the "Great Recession" of the mid and late 2000s.

2.1.4 *The Development of Financial Instruments and Institutions*

As financial flows expanded in the postwar period and virtually exploded in the 1980s and 1990s and since, financial firms and actors sought to devise new ways of trading on increasingly complex financial markets, moving away from traditional trading

69 Strange, *supra* note 53; S. Strange, *States and Markets* (1988); P. G. Cerny, Globalization and the Changing Logic of Collective Action (1995) 49:4 *International Organization* 595; P. G. Cerny, *Finance and World Politics: Markets, Regimes and States in the Post-Hegemonic Era* (1993).

70 A. Minsky and P. Hyman, *Can "It" Happen Again?: Essays on Instability and Finance* (1982); A. Minsky and P. Hyman, *Stabilizing and Unstable Economy* (1986).

processes and structures including established stock and securities markets. This trend required several developments in the nature of the tradable instruments. The first was flexibility – the ability to trade an increasing range of instruments in a growing array institutional and noninstitutional public and private markets and informal quasi-market networks. The second involved the "tradability" of those instruments, namely their widespread acceptance and use in an interconnected range of settings from the local to the global. The third involved widening the range of financial market actors, from financial firms themselves to households and individuals, which has been called "financial inclusion" or "the financialization of daily life."[71] The fourth has been the restructuring of the overarching financial industry itself into fewer and fewer "SIFIs" – systemically important financial institutions, both controlling the overall process and strengthening special relationships with regulators.[72] The fifth required the extremely rapid expansion of leverage to finance these developments, rather than redistributing profits or assets from the real economy.[73] The sixth has been the doctrine of "shareholder value" capitalism, in which the first priority of all firms is the making of profits that are transferred to shareholders rather than reinvested in a real economy firm's production and exchange processes that include labor and other "stakeholders."[74] The final development, probably the most controversial, has been said to be the consolidation of a new form of rentier capitalism, in which profits are skimmed off by financial elites, impeding rather than enabling growth in the wider economy and leading to increasing inequality.[75] This final trend is also sometimes said to enable and entrench illegal activities and the rigging of economic and financial outcomes, what Veblen called "sabotage."[76] As the result of this set of developments, Sawyer argues that the twenty-first-century financial system is "dysfunctional."[77]

The financial instruments at the core of the process are not technically new but have been dramatically expanded in the context described above. They mainly involve "securitization" and "derivatives." Traditional banks, both commercial and investment, operated on the basis of what has been called "originate-to-hold." In both cases, those banks keep the financial instruments they deal with on their books. In contrast, what have been called "non-bank" financial firms and institutions restructure and sell the instruments they originally "own" in a range of formal and

[71] R. Martin, *Financialization of Daily Life* (2002).

[72] A. R. Sorkin and R. Andrew, *Too Big to Fail: The Inside Story of How Wall Street and Washington Fought to Save the Financial System from Crisis – and Themselves* (2009).

[73] D. Graeber, *Debt: The First 5,000 Years* (2011); T. Di Muzio and R. H. Robbins, *Debt as Power* (2016).

[74] L. Stout, *The Shareholder Value Myth: How Putting Shareholders First Harms Investors, Corporations, and the Public* (2012).

[75] E. Fullbrook and J. Morgan (eds.), *The Inequality Crisis* (2020).

[76] A. Nesvetailova and R. Palan, *Sabotage: The Business of Finance* (2020).

[77] M. Sawyer, *Financialization and Economic and Social Performance*, in Gemzik-Salwach and Opolski, *supra* note 58, 9–25; Sawyer, *supra* note 64.

informal financial markets. They transform them into new kinds of securities in a process known as "securitization" and the value of those securities comes from the prices they attract as well as their salability in various formal and informal markets.[78] Derivatives, in turn, are securities the value of which does not derive from the original securities themselves but from their being based on the market value of these securities themselves when bought and sold. They are, in effect, insurance policies on the prices and market value of the securities from which they are "derived."[79]

Securitization is a complex process in which the original securities themselves are "sliced and diced" into "tranches," namely segments created from a pool of securities that are divvied up by risk, time to maturity, or other characteristics in order to be marketable to different investors. Each tranche of a securitized or structured product is one of several related securities offered at the same time but with varying risks, rewards, and maturities to appeal to a diverse range of investors. Different tranches will have different credit ratings, appealing to different buyers with senior tranches for the highest and safest credit ratings, junior tranches for the riskiest ratings, and mezzanine tranches for a generally small intermediate category. Typical investors of senior tranches tend to be conduits, insurance companies, pension funds, and other risk-averse investors. Junior tranches are more risky investments because they are not secured by specific assets. The natural buyers of these securities tend to be hedge funds and other investors seeking higher risk/return profiles.

Tranches allow for the "ability to create one or more classes of securities whose rating is higher than the average rating of the underlying collateral asset pool or to generate rated securities from a pool of unrated assets."[80] This is accomplished through the use of credit support specified within the transaction structure to create securities with different risk-return profiles. The equity/first-loss or junior tranche absorbs initial losses, followed by the mezzanine tranches, which absorb some additional losses, again followed by more senior tranches. Thus, due to the credit support resulting from tranching, "the most senior claims are expected to be insulated – except in particularly adverse circumstances – from default risk of the underlying asset pool through the absorption of losses by the more junior claims."[81] Some tranches are sold and traded separately and some as parts of single, combined securities.

[78] This process is widely covered in the literature, but this section draws, in particular, on M. Zandi, *Financial Shock: A 360° Look at the Subprime Mortgage Implosion, and How to Avoid the Next Financial Crisis* (2009); cf. Helleiner, Pagliari, and Spagna, *supra* note 37.

[79] See Helleiner, Pagliari, and Spagna, *supra* note 37.

[80] I. Fender and J. Mitchell, Structured Finance: Complexity, Risk and the Use of Ratings (2005) 3:1 *Financial Stability Review* 127.

[81] Committee on the Global Financial System, January 2005.

Virtually the whole political economy literature on securitization and derivatives discusses their complexity, opacity, and disconnectedness from the real economy. However, in the context of the free market, neoliberal and deregulatory ideology of national governments, and transnational regime complexes[82], such financial instruments and processes are still treated lightly and warily by both policymakers and regulators. A crucial part of these developments is the transformation of the financial institutional infrastructure itself. Increasingly important over time is the restructuring in recent years of banking and other financial institutions and markets and the macrofinancial and microfinancial structural shifts involved, adapting ways of doing things from the "shadow" sector in order to compete.

The highly institutionalized commercial and investment banks described above have historically been the core of traditional financial systems and until recently have been highly regulated and insured by governments in order to underpin the stability of the system as a whole. This was particularly true of the US Emergency Banking Act of 1933, which divided up commercial and investment banking and administered them separately. In particular, the act set up the Federal Deposit Insurance Corporation to underpin the commercial banking sector, insuring deposits originally of $2,500, increased over the years to six deposits in different accounts of $250,000, for a total of $1,500,000 in 2011. While these banks are still propped up by the US Government, they have increasingly had to compete with what PIMCO (Pacific Investment Management Company) executive director Paul McCulley at a FED (Federal Reserve System) annual meeting in 2007 called "shadow banks."

Nesvetailova provides a useful definition of the difference:

> While, for instance, traditional banks are assumed to be taking in short-term deposits and converting them into long-term loans, shadow banks do the opposite: they take in long-term savings (e.g. pension fund liabilities) and transform them into short-term savings. If traditional banks take in liquid deposits (e.g. cash and similar instruments) and transform them into less liquid securities, shadow banks do the opposite: through a combination of financial and legal operations they transform illiquid assets (such as mortgages or car loans) into apparently liquid financial securities.[83]

In other words, shadow banks have not only used securitization and derivatives to make greater profits than is available in traditional banking but indeed have triggered a system-wide change in the nature of finance. The authors cited in this chapter and many others have noted that the way shadow banks have done business over recent decades has forced the reconstruction of traditional banks too. In order to compete, other institutions have to jump on the bandwagon because

[82] N. Barofsky, *Bailout: An Inside Account of How Washington Abandoned Main Street While Rescuing Wall Street* (2012).

[83] A. Nesvetailova (eds.), *Shadow Banking: Scope, Origins and Theories* (2018).

that's where the money increasingly goes, creating "long and opaque chains of credit intermediation."[84]

This is particularly true of what are called "universal banks," which originate consumer and corporate loans, package loans into asset-backed securities (one of the major dimensions of the securitization process) and what are called "collateralized debt obligations" (CDOs), create over-the-counter (OTC) derivatives whose value are derived from loans, and distribute the resulting securities and other financial instruments to investors. Furthermore, complex financial institutions have used the OTC strategy to maximize their fee income to reduce their capital charges and to transfer the risks associated with securitized loans to investors. Other structural shifts include the setting up of Special Purpose Vehicles (SPVs), Structured Investment Vehicles (SIVS), and other nonregulated, quasi-independent institutions in which to park, especially less profitable or endangered securities the markets for which have slowed or shut down. Regulated banks in effect become shadow banks because they had to restructure and become opaquer and complex in order to compete.[85]

A major consequence of rise and dominance of shadow banking therefore concerns the shift of investing from cash and investment in the real economy to the circulation of the purely financial instruments described above. For example, pension funds have grown dramatically as the result of the shift from defined benefit to defined contribution pensions (the result of the declining power of labor unions in the real economy), along with money market mutual funds (MMMFs), hedge funds, etc.[86] Thus, there are two tendencies: the accelerating pace of financial innovation and the capture of monopoly-like rents through "'shrouding,' or embracing complexity."[87] In other words, growing demand for profitable investment increasingly creates more and more supply because of and facilitated by the abstract nature of finance itself.[88]

The future of governance of the financial system has not been resolved and some argue the concerns may be growing and intensifying as regulatory stopgaps unravel. All national governments and regional organizations such as the European Union have considered and even attempted to implement a range of regulatory changes in the financial sector, and all of these have been critically scrutinized and found wanting. Furthermore, the Dodd-Frank Act of 2010 in the United States has been seen as in some ways counterproductive because of (a) maintaining competing regulatory bodies (in the United States) that have different approaches, (b) leaving

84 Nesvetailova, *supra* note 79.

85 Ibid.

86 P. Coggan, *Guide to Hedge Funds: What They Are, What They Do, Their Risks, Their Advantages* (2010); S. Lack, *The Hedge Fund Miracle: The Illusion of Big Money and Why It's Too Good to Be True* (2012).

87 Nesvetailova, *supra* note 79.

88 D. Gabor, Shadow Connections: The Hierarchies of Collateral in Shadow Banking, in Nesvetailova, *supra* note 79, 143–162.

actual regulation-making to these bodies in the future, resulting in partiality and whipsawing, (c) insufficient transnational convergence,[89] and (d) limitations on the capacity of the Financial Stability Oversight Council (FSOC) to create policy consistency. Indeed, The Trump Administration engineered a partial rollback of Dodd-Frank in 2018, the Economic Growth, Regulatory Relief, and Consumer Protection Act. Finance is the hegemonic sector in the structural transformation of the simultaneously globalizing and fragmenting intangible economy.

2.2 CONCLUSIONS

A central debate in the business and politics issue area is whether the growing significance of intangibles in the real economy, along with nonproductive financialization and regulatory arbitrage are (a) crowding out investment in the real economy; (b) whether the "intangible" economy is itself creating new forms of monopolization that do not require the kinds of financial investment characteristic of the nation-state–supported second industrial revolution; (c) leading to greater inequality and political backlashes such as populism;[90] (d) creating a growing level of over-indebtedness and leverage, from real economy firms to financial firms that will lead to chronic Minskyian crises; and (e) whether nation-state governments are limited to "firefighting" and "bailouts" to salvage national financial systems – that is, the "reactive state" rather than the "proactive state."

The future of business and politics as the twenty-first century unfolds is thus potentially unstable and increasingly procyclical, with various levels of uneven heterarchical quasi-governance lacking the institutional capacity to shape the system as a public good. While the contributors to this volume show that private actors can exert a positive influence, they also give us reasons to be skeptical about private actors' ability to deliver public goods. In the context of banking and finance, various authors have diverse partial policy prescriptions. For example, D'Arista[91] argues that financial institutions need stress tests to be based on cash reserves rather than capital requirements; Guttmann[92] argues for revising the International Monetary Fund's Special Drawing Rights and giving them a greater international role; and Roos[93] argues for the greater use of debt default to tackle overleveraging, especially of sovereign debt. Nesvetailova and Palan[94] argue that "sabotage" will ultimately be necessary to tame Minskyian tendencies. However, as the proverb goes (variously

[89] Helleiner, Pagliari, and Spagna, *supra* note 37; Gemzik-Solwach and Opolski, *supra* note 58.

[90] M. Sawyer, Financialisation, Financial Crisis and Inequality, in *Inequality: Trends, Causes, Consequences, Relevant Policies* (P. Arestis and M. Sawyer eds., 2018), 43–88.

[91] J. D'Arista, *All Fall Down* (2019).

[92] R. Guttman, *Finance-Led Capitalism: Shadow Banking, Re-regulation and the Future of Global Markets* (2016).

[93] J. Roos, *Why Not Default? The Political Economy of Sovereign Debt* (2019).

[94] Nesvetailova and Palan, *supra* note 73.

attributed to at least two dozen people, from Niels Bohr and Yogi Berra to Woody Allen and Confucius): "Prediction is difficult, especially about the future." The unevenness and complexity of the rapidly evolving system of heterarchy in world political economy is laying the groundwork for future crises at multiple overlapping and interacting levels as the reactive state becomes more and more ineffective at regulating finance – and other sectors – in a "postinternationalist" world.

3

Corporations and the Making of Public Standards in International Law

The Case of China in the International Telecommunication Union

Jan Wouters

3.1 INTRODUCTION

The present contribution has been inspired by a recent regulatory battle in a specialized agency of the United Nations (UN),[1] the International Telecommunications Union (ITU). The theme is particularly rich to illustrate some fundamental questions underlying the relationship between private and public actors and standards in international law, in particular, issues of corporate capture, democratic legitimacy and accountability, and human rights. It is also, from another point of view, a fascinating tale about the rise of China within the UN system; about how Chinese technology corporations are actively proposing new international standards on a number of issues, including a new internet protocol and rules on facial recognition, through international regulatory agencies like the ITU; and how Western governments, including the European Union (EU) and its Member States, have rallied to counter the Chinese offensive.[2] While their actions are officially inspired by concerns for the protection of personal data and the privacy of individuals – in other words, by human rights – there are other matters at stake, including the question of corporate influence in public standard-setting bodies, the coherence

[1] UN specialized agencies are autonomous international organizations established by intergovernmental agreement and having wide international responsibilities, as defined in their basic instruments, in economic, social, cultural, educational, health, and related fields that are brought into relationship with the UN through agreements concluded with the latter's Economic and Social Council (ECOSOC) and approved by the UN General Assembly: see, together with a list of such agencies, J. Wouters, C. Ryngaert, T. Ruys and G. De Baere, *International Law: A European Perspective* (2018), at 290–291.

[2] On the role of the EU in the ITU until ten years ago, see J. Shahin, The European Union's Performance in the International Telecommunication Union (2011) 33:6 *Journal of European Integration* 683.

with existing standards, and, last but not least – and not within the purview of this contribution – the preservation of Western normative dominance.[3]

We start with situating the recent regulatory battles in the ITU (Section 3.2) and delve subsequently in the other issues: corporate influence in public standard-setting bodies (Section 3.3), democratic legitimacy and accountability (Section 3.4), and human rights (Section 3.5).

3.2 THE BATTLE FOR FACIAL RECOGNITION STANDARDS AND A NEW INTERNET PROTOCOL AT THE ITU

3.2.1 *China's Choice for the ITU*

The ITU is one of the oldest global regulatory agencies.[4] Originally founded as the International Telegraph Union in 1865 to promote cooperation among international telegraphy networks, the ITU has contributed for more than 150 years to the connectivity, interoperability, and standardization of telecommunications, from the use of the Morse code to satellite communications. As a UN specialized agency since 1947, it has evolved into a unique platform for global public–private partnerships and has firmly embraced the corporate sector and other stakeholders, proudly announcing on its website that its "global membership includes 193 Member States as well as some 900 corporations, universities, and international and regional organizations."[5] More accurately, there are two types of members: 193 Member States and the 900 "Sector Members." Since 1994, Sector Members are allowed to formally participate in the decision-making processes of the ITU and since 1998 they are recognized as having formal rights of participation under the ITU Constitution.[6] The ITU has three sectors: Radiocommunication (ITU-R), Telecommunication Standardization (ITU-T), and Telecommunication Development (ITU-D). Corporations or organizations may become a member of one or more sectors and may join as a Sector Member or Associate.[7] Importantly, much of the regulatory

[3] In that sense, much of what is studied in this contribution resembles a game of "great powers." For the thesis that great powers remain the primary actors writing the rules that regulate the global economy, see D. W. Drezner, *All Politics Is Global: Explaining International Regulatory Regimes* (2007), at 5. The same author, in his conclusion, predicted that "China has a clear incentive to develop new technology standards" but that "the United States and European Union will be anticipating future attempts at standards creation," at 219.

[4] The ITU is sometimes referred to as "the world's oldest international organization," although that is debatable. See, nevertheless, in that sense D. Westphal, International Telecommunication Union (ITU) (2014) *Max Planck Encyclopedia of International Law* para 1; G. A. Codding Jr., The International Telecommunications Union: 130 Years of Telecommunications Regulation (1995) 23 *Denver Journal of International Law and Policy* 501.

[5] www.itu.int/en/about/Pages/default.aspx.

[6] See I. Walden, International Regulatory Law, in *Telecommunications Law and Regulation* (Ian Walden ed., 2018) 791, at 807–808.

[7] www.itu.int/en/myitu/Membership.

dynamics in the ITU starts in "Study Groups," which are renewed every four years. Each of these Study Groups, in which "thousands of experts representing government, industry and academia" participate, is responsible for progressing ITU work in a specific field of the ITU's mandate; they develop the technical basis for ITU agreements, standards, and reports. The mandates and leadership teams of each Sector's Study Groups are decided by the Sector's respective governing bodies, that is, the Radiocommunication Assembly (RA), the World Telecommunication Standardization Assembly (WTSA), and the World Telecommunication Development Conference (WTDC).[8] It has been observed by members of delegations to the ITU that ITU standards – which typically take around two years to be developed – "are increasingly written by companies, rather than governments".[9]

It is in this context that China has displayed a remarkable drive to shape international standards, reflecting "long-standing concerns that Chinese representatives were not at the table to help set the rules of the game for the global Internet."[10] The country is known for sending the largest delegation to the ITU's Study Groups, including Huawei and other state-owned enterprises. Huawei itself is said to have introduced some 2,000 new standard proposals to ITU Study Groups on topics such as 5G, cybersecurity, and artificial intelligence.[11] More in particular, since the autumn of 2019, through quite a number of its technology corporations, China has been pushing two initiatives in the ITU: (i) a new standard for facial recognition and (ii) a new Internet Protocol ("New IP"). It was the *Financial Times* that disclosed on December 1, 2019, that a battle was looming within the ITU regarding the shaping of facial recognition standards.[12] The newspaper reported that

> Chinese technology companies are shaping new facial recognition standards at the UN ... as they try to open up new markets in the developing world for their cutting-edge technologies. Companies such as ZTE, Dahua and China Telecom are among those proposing new international standards – specifications aimed at creating universally consistent technology – in the UN's International Telecommunications Union (ITU) for facial recognition, video monitoring, city and vehicle surveillance.

[8] www.itu.int/en/mediacentre/backgrounders/Pages/itu-study-groups.aspx.

[9] C. Burt, Standards for Biometric Surveillance Being Drafted for ITU by Chinese Businesses, December 2, 2019, www.biometricupdate.com/201912/standards-for-biometric-surveillance-being-drafted-for-itu-by-chinese-businesses.

[10] J. Ding, P. Triolo and S. Sacks, Chinese Interests Take a Big Seat at the AI Governance Table, June 20, 2018, www.newamerica.org/cybersecurity-initiative/digichina/blog/chinese-interests-take-big-seat-ai-governance-table/.

[11] K. Cordell, The International Telecommunication Union: The Most Important UN Agency You Have Never Heard Of, Center for Strategic & International Studies (CSIS), December 14, 2020.

[12] A. Gross, M. Murgia, and Y. Yang, Chinese Tech Groups Shaping UN Facial Recognition Standards, *Financial Times*, December 1, 2019, www.ft.com/content/c3555a3c-0d3e-11ea-b2d6-9bf4d1957a67.

Another *Financial Times* article, of March 2020, discusses China's attempts since September 2019 to convince ITU delegates of the need to construct an alternative form of the Internet. It explains why the ITU has been chosen for these two initiatives. As a global organization of 193 Member States and one of the oldest specialized agencies of the UN, it is seen as the de facto standards body for telecoms networks:

> Standards produced there legitimise new technologies and systems in the eyes of certain governments – particularly those in the developing world who don't participate in other internet bodies. Ultimately, they give a commercial edge to the companies who have built the tech they are based upon.[13]

It is said that African states in particular tend to follow ITU standards as they do not have the resources to develop standards themselves.[14] Moreover, such standards "are commonly adopted as policy by developing nations in Africa, the Middle East and Asia, where the Chinese government has agreed to supply infrastructure and surveillance tech under its 'Belt and Road Initiative'" (BRI).[15] Chinese corporations – particularly Huawei, Hikvision, Dahua, and ZTE – supply AI surveillance technology in sixty-three countries, thirty-six of which have signed up to the BRI.[16] It is also known that Chinese corporations are supplying surveillance infrastructure to countries in Africa, including Angola, South Africa, Uganda, and Zimbabwe.[17] It has been observed that

> while European and North American businesses participate heavily in the standards bodies such as the Internet Engineering Task Force (IETF), the Institute of Electrical and Electronics Engineers (IEEE), and the 3rd Generation Partnership Project (3GPP), the ITU gives China a chance to leverage its influence in Africa, the Middle East and Asia, where ITU standards are often adopted as policy.[18]

[13] M. Murgia and A. Gross, Inside China's Controversial Mission to Reinvent the Internet, *Financial Times*, March 27, 2020, www.ft.com/content/ba94c2bc-6e27-11ea-9bca-bf503995cd6f.

[14] R. Wingfield, as quoted in T. Parker, Leaked Documents Show State-Owned Chinese Companies Are Shaping Global UN Facial Recognition Standards, December 1, 2019, https://reclaimthenet.org/china-un-facial-recognition/

[15] Gross, Murgia, and Yang, *supra* note 12.

[16] S. Feldstein, The Global Expansion of AI Surveillance, Carnegie Endowment for International Peace Working Paper, September 2019, at 8 https://carnegieendowment.org/files/WP-Feldstein-AISurveillance_final1.pdf.

[17] Avisian, Chinese Facial Recognition Technology Makes Play for Global Acceptance, March 31, 2020, www.secureidnews.com/news-item/chinese-facial-recognition-technology-makes-play-for-global-acceptance/ It has been observed that biometric data are being used by Chinese technology corporations to train their algorithms for improved results: Chris White, 'Chinese Companies Use Zimbabweans As Guinea Pigs To Identify Black Faces', The National Interest, 3 December 2019, https://nationalinterest.org/blog/buzz/chinese-companies-use-zimbabweans-guinea-pigs-identify-black-faces-report-101447.

[18] Burt, *supra* note 9.

While it is often thought that standard-setting organizations like the ITU, the International Organization for Standardization (ISO), or the Electrotechnical Commission (IEC) operate on a mere technical basis with a view to reaching worldwide interoperability, it has been highlighted that their decision-making processes are more political than expected.[19] It is clear that the Chinese government – notably through the upcoming China Standards 2035 strategy[20] – is pursuing a strategy of increasing influence in international organizations, particularly throughout the UN system,[21] and that it is linking this to the offensive interests of its business enterprises, especially in technologically advanced sectors involving 5G, facial recognition, blockchain,[22] and AI. China has recently spread its influence rapidly in the most important organizations for technical standards: Zhao Houlin was secretary-general of the ITU from 2015 to 2022;[23] Shu Yinbiao is president of IEC since 2020; and Zhang Xiaogang was president of ISO from 2015 to 2018.[24]

19 On the politicization of UN specialized agencies, see already in the early 1980s, V.-Y. Ghebaly, The Politicisation of UN Specialised Agencies: A Preliminary Analysis (1985) 14:3 *Millenium: Journal of International Studies* 317.

20 For a relativizing analysis, see N. Wilson, *China Standards 2035 and the Plan for World Domination: Don't Believe China's Hype*, June 3, 2020, www.cfr.org/blog/china-standards-2035-and-plan-world-domination-dont-believe-chinas-hype.

21 At the time of writing, three UN specialized agencies were led by a Chinese national: the ITU, the UN Food and Agriculture Organization (FAO), and the UN Industrial Development Organization (UNIDO): see T. Cheng-Chia and A. H. Yang, How China Is Remaking the UN In Its Own Image, *The Diplomat*, April 9, 2020, https://thediplomat.com/2020/04/how-china-is-remaking-the-un-in-its-own-image/. The International Civil Aviation Organization (ICAO) was led by a Chinese national from 2015 until 2021, when the Colombian Juan Carlos Salazar Gómez took over on August 1, 2021. In 2020, China lost the contest for the election of a new director-general at the World Intellectual Property Organization (WIPO): see B. Glosserman, China Loses a Skirmish in Fight for Global Influence, *Japan Times*, March 9, 2020, www.japantimes.co.jp/opinion/2020/03/09/commentary/world-commentary/china-loses-skirmish-fight-global-influence/.

22 In September 2020, the ITU approved new basic standards on financial applications for blockchain, developed by the People's Bank of China, the China Academy of Information and Communications Technology, and Huawei, the first Chinese-developed international standard on blockchain for finance approved globally: E. Gkritsi, China Sets Global Blockchain Standards, Canaan Is Alive: Blockheads, September 8, 2020, https://technode.com/2020/09/08/blockheads-china-sets-global-blockchain-standards-and-canaan-is-alive/?utm_source=TechNode+English&utm_campaign=947b98a299-EMAIL_CAMPAIGN_2020_06_03_04_13_COPY_01&utm_medium=email&utm_term=0_c785f26769–947b98a299–111988938&mc_cid=947b98a299&mc_eid=978e88078f.

23 For a recent interview with Xinhua, see Interview: China Active Contributor to UN, Says ITU Chief, October 18, 2021, www.news.cn/english/2021-10/18/c_1310253049.htm. From 1 January 2023, the secretary-general of ITU is Doreen Bogdan-Martin, who had been supported by the United States, an American citizen: M. L. Viña, N. Picarsic, and E. de La Bruyère, Biden Takes First Step in Countering China through UN Elections, Foundation for Defense of Democracies (FDD), Policy Brief, 7 April 2021.

24 For the rapid institutional rise of China in the ISO since 2007, see J. Kynge and N. Liu, From AI to Facial Recognition: How China Is Setting the Rules in New Tech, *Financial Times*, October 7, 2020, www.ft.com/content/188d86df-6e82-47eb-a134-2e1e45c777b6. While not delivering the president currently, China seems to keep its influence in the ISO: see C.

3.2.2 *China's New IP proposal*

In September 2019, Huawei Technologies Co. Ltd. (China), China Mobile Communications Corporation, China Unicom, and the Chinese Ministry of Industry and Information Technology proposed to the Telecommunication Standardization Advisory Group (TSAG) of the ITU to study the radical idea of a New IP, that would replace the current TCP/IP (Transmission Control Protocol and Internet Protocol).[25] In its proposal, Huawei asserted that the current IP is unsuited for the development of new digital applications, for which the development of a new protocol is needed. It therefore suggested the Study Groups of ITU-T to start a further long-term research in the then ongoing (2017–2020) and the next (2021–2025) study period.

In the meetings of the TSAG from February 10 to 14, 2020, this proposal (which has been given the new title "New Vertical Communication Networks") encountered critical reactions from Dutch and United Kingdom internet registries. They argued that internet protocols have been developed in a "bottom up" manner and that relevant work is taking place in the Internet Research Task Force (IRTF) and in the IETF.

In the course of 2020, discussions took place in various ITU-T Study Groups, as they are the ones preparing proposals for new study questions to be decided at the WTSA meeting that was scheduled to take place in Hyderabad, India, from March 1 to 9, 2022.[26] The Chinese New IP proposal was discussed in Study Group (SG) 11 ("protocols and test specifications") and SG 13 ("future networks"). The United Kingdom, the EU, and its Member States objected to the proposal for a variety of reasons. They saw no evidence that the current standardization setting had failed in developing new internet functionalities nor that foreseeable requirements, such as those linked to the development of AI, Augmented and Virtual Reality, or Internet of Things (IoT), risked being insufficiently addressed. They also expressed their preference that new protocols and standards be discussed in the relevant Standards Development Organizations (SDOs)[27], in particular in the IETF, where the decision-making process is transparent, bottom-up, and open to all stakeholders (including industry, civil society, and academia), rather than in the ITU, where

Paris, Latest ISO President Has Ties to China, Too, June 4, 2020, www.oxebridge.com/emma/latest-iso-president-has-ties-to-china-too/.

[25] See New IP, Shaping Future Network: Propose to Initiate the Discussion of Strategy Transformation for ITU-T, TSAG C-83, Geneva, September 23–27, 2019. See also the White Paper: Towards a New Internet for the Year 2030 and Beyond, www.itu.int/en/ITU-T/studygroups/2017-2020/13/Documents/Internet_2030%20.pdf.

[26] The meeting was initially scheduled for November 2020 but has been delayed because of the COVID-19 pandemic.

[27] Such SDOs include the IETF, the European Telecommunications Standards Institute (ETSI), the World Wide Web Consortium (W3C), and the 3GPP. In addition, there is the aforementioned IRTF, which focuses on long-term research issues.

decision-making is top-down, intergovernmental, and does not involve all stakeholders. Duplicating work at the ITU could lead to higher costs and undermine interoperability. They also expressed the concern that implementing the Chinese proposal for a top-down, incumbent-controlled internet would bring a high risk of fragmentation of the global internet into locally controlled intranets, of decreased network resilience, and could seriously harm the openness of the global internet. This would not be in line with the European vision for the Internet, which is one of a single, open, neutral, free, and un-fragmented network, supporting permissionless innovation, privacy, and user empowerment.[28]

At an ad hoc meeting of SG 13 on December 11, 2020, around 100 Chinese participants participated, strengthened by Burundi, which on behalf of ten African countries expressed support for the Chinese proposals. They encountered fierce resistance by all EU Member States, the United States, the United Kingdom, Canada, and Japan. At the next plenary meeting of SG 13, it was found that there was no consensus for the project, and the discussion was ended.

3.2.3 *China Telecom's Proposal for Standards on Facial Recognition*

China Telecom introduced a proposal for a new "framework standard" through a document entitled "Requirements for face recognition application in visual surveillance" in ITU SG 16 ("multimedia"). Already in the spring of 2020, the European Commission raised a number of important concerns. The draft recommendation foresees the use of face recognition for a wide variety of use cases, for both public and private bodies, for example, to confirm the identity of a suspect, for police checks of identity cards, for criminal fugitives, transport, entertainment, employee attendance, trajectory tracking, etc. However, it does not contain any safeguards for the protection of personal data and privacy of individuals. From a European perspective, such a lack of safeguards is very problematic regarding its compabitility with the EU's General Data Protection Regulation (GDPR).[29] As the draft recommendation cannot be implemented within the EU (and more broadly the European Economic Area, EEA) and could have a negative impact on transfers of personal data of European to third countries that implement this standard, the Commission

[28] The EU and its Member States support the multi-stakeholder model for internet governance, including for the development of internet standards and protocols: see Council Conclusions on Internet Governance of November 27, 2014 (16200/14, limité): "The Council of the European Union … invites Member States and the Commission to … foster the multi-stakeholder model of Internet governance including for the core Internet discussions, decisions and bodies through: … cooperation alongside other stakeholders with entities in charge of Internet protocol and other information technology specifications whose decisions may have significant public policy implications."

[29] Regulation (EU) 2016/679 of the European Parliament and of the Council of April 27, 2016, on the protection of natural persons with regard to the processing of personal data and on the free movement of such data and repealing Directive 95/46/EC, O.J. 2016 L119/1.

strongly submitted that it should be considered under the ITU's Traditional Approval Process (TAP), which applies to all recommendations with policy or regulatory implications, rather than through the Alternative Approval Process (AAP) proposed by China.

The Commission's concerns, expressed at a virtual meeting of SG 16 in April 2020, were shared by the United States, Canada, and Australia, which also highlighted the very political implications of the draft recommendation and questioned the mandate of the ITU to adopt norms in this field. In a later contribution, Romania added to the concerns by pointing to the specific risks for fundamental rights of facial recognition techniques, arguing that ethical boundaries and principles needed to be defined, setting clear criteria and limits, before standardization could take place. It also referred to serious concerns expressed by other UN entities, such as the Office of the UN High Commissioner for Human Rights,[30] pointing to the fact that the ITU is part of the UN family and its values. We will come back to this latter point (Section 3.5).

At the meeting of SG16 of December 14–16, 2000, China Telecom pushed again for the Study Group to consider the proposal and accept the new standard. Twenty EU Member States, the Commission, the United Kingdom, Canada, the United States, Australia, and Japan mobilized and expressed their disagreement. Interestingly, the meeting was chaired by a staff member of China Telecom, who seems to have had difficulties accepting the lack of consensus.

3.2.4 *Interim Evaluation*

As is clear from the above, the two Chinese proposals concerned have, for the time being, been blocked in the ITU context by a mobilization of Western countries. The latter have become alarmed by China's tactics, consisting of having Chinese corporations launching at first sight technical proposals in ITU Study Groups that, seemingly, are aimed at pushing through China's vision on new technologies and the Internet. It can be expected that China will learn from the recent experience and will seek to fine-tune its strategy and approach. The massive investment of resources, including human resources – compare the presence of 100 Chinese participants at SG 13 in December 2020 – the involvement of lobbyists and chairs of Study Groups, and concerted outreach to developing countries, especially in Africa, have made a deep impression on China's Western counterparts. However, in spite of concerted opposition of Western countries, it can be expected that China and the Chinese corporations and experts concerned will reiterate their

[30] United Nations High Commissioner for Human Rights, Impact of New Technologies on the Promotion and Protection of Human Rights in the Context of Assemblies, including Peaceful Protests, June 24, 2020, A/HRC/44/24, www.ohchr.org/EN/HRBodies/HRC/RegularSessions/Session44/Documents/A_HRC_44_24_AEV.docx.

proposals – possibly with some minor modifications – at future ITU meetings, capitalizing on their strong presence and influence over other delegations.

3.3 CORPORATE INFLUENCE IN PUBLIC STANDARD-SETTING BODIES

The developments detailed in Section 3.2 may raise eyebrows from the viewpoint of the integrity of the standard-setting process in international organizations.[31] How can it be that corporate actors, such as powerful Chinese tech giants, have such an impact in the standardization work of the ITU? To be fair, there has always been a huge corporate role – directly or indirectly, openly or discretely – in the elaboration of technical standards by international organizations. Büthe and Mattli have observed that the key to successfully setting standards in such organizations is that governments and business corporations from their countries (often through domestic standard-setting bodies) "speak with a single voice."[32] For a long time, these organizations have been used by Western countries to exert and perpetuate their normative influence.[33] While the close intertwinement between the Chinese government and Chinese businesses may work particularly in China's advantage, Western countries have also been teaming up with their businesses. In essence, China presents a case of what Büthe and Mattli call high "institutional complementarity":

> firms operating in a hierarchical and coordinated domestic system are likely to win because their system fits more naturally with the global structure, where a single regulator is the clear focal point. Such a domestic system enables a country's stakeholders to speak with a single voice and in a timely fashion on the global stage .... High institutional complementarity implies that the interaction between domestic and global institutions is smooth and easy, yielding decisive strategic benefits to the firm in terms of effective interest representation in global rule-making and timely information.[34]

Nevertheless, the question arises whether decision-making processes in public international organizations should not provide for a number of safeguards in this respect. The UN and other multilateral organizations and processes have been accused of "corporate capture" in a number of instances. The latter concept includes not just policy and legislative interference by corporations but also "revolving door" practices where corporate employees act as (or are part of a team of)

[31] See J. Baron and O. Kanevskaia, "Global Rivalry Over Leadership in ICT Standardization: SDO Governance Amid Changing Patterns of Participation" in this volume (Chapter 14).

[32] See T. Büthe and W. Mattli, *The New Global Rulers. The Privatization of Regulation in the World Economy* (2011), 12–13.

[33] See FreedomLab, *The New Power of Technical Standards*, September 25, 2020, https://freedomlab.org/the-new-power-of-technical-standards/.

[34] Büthe and Mattli, *supra* note 32, at 13.

government representatives in multilateral processes and forms of economic diplomacy where States prioritize corporate interests.[35] Cynically, such corporate capture has apparently also been nurtured by the

> growing dependence of multilateral institutions on private funding, product of governments' failure to pay their ordinary contributions to multilateral institutions, their earmarking of funds for issues that advance their (and their corporations') interests and falling tax revenues/public funding during the era of neoliberalism.[36]

The problem is definitely more widespread than the ITU, and it is not within the purview of the present contribution to come up with overarching suggestions to tackle it. It is nevertheless interesting to point to recent work of the OECD in this respect, which has engaged in a thorough exercise to map best practices in the standard-setting work of international organizations (IOs), including regarding stakeholder engagement.[37] The 2021 OECD report "Compendium of International Organisations' Practices: Working towards More Effective International Instruments" acknowledges that such engagement constitutes a valuable tool to make international instruments more trusted, implemented and complied with, and to strengthen their ownership. However, it adds to this:

> many IOs continue to face significant challenges in engaging with relevant stakeholders in a meaningful and inclusive manner, and reconciling transparency and effectiveness of discussions in the development of international instruments. Stakeholder engagement can be resource intensive, and IO staff may encounter difficulties in investing the necessary time and human capital .... Like in domestic rulemaking, there is a risk of capture of the engagement process by those who have sufficient resources to exert influence.[38]

While the OECD report contains valuable examples of the practice of various international organizations regarding their engagement with stakeholders, both of a non-decisional and decisional nature, it concludes that, "despite the undeniable efforts of a large majority of IOs to engage more systematically with stakeholders, their practices in terms of mechanisms, openness and frequency of consultation vary widely from one organisation to another" and that "few IOs have developed a whole of organisation policy or strategy for stakeholder engagement to date, mapping their stakeholders and defining objectives and key steps to engage them and manage

[35] ESCR-Net Corporate Accountability Working Group, *Corporate Capture at the United Nations*, February 11, 2021, at 2. For interesting considerations on corporate capture in the work of the Codex Alimentarius Commission, see J. Braithwaite and P. Drahos, *Global Business Regulation* (2000), at 408, 417, and 516.

[36] ESCR-Net Corporate Accountability Working Group, *supra* note 35.

[37] OECD, Compendium of International Organisations' Practices: Working Towards More Effective International Instruments, Paris, 2021.

[38] OECD, Compendium of International Organisations' Practices, 80.

risks."[39] It looks like the ITU is in urgent need of such a "whole of organization strategy." This can not only help avoiding cases of capture but also strengthening the legitimacy of new standards, as Buhmann has righthly argued:

> the inclusion of non-state actors that are the potential holders of new duties, whether (soft law) responsibilities or (hard law) obligations, offers a risk of capture if the process is not carefully designed and managed, but also a possibility for support and output legitimacy, if it is well designed and managed. Participation in a process is important for participants to perceive their needs and concerns addressed, but participation must be equalized in regard to access and power in order to avoid the risk of capture and illegitimacy due to or actual or perceived imbalance.[40]

3.4 DEMOCRATIC LEGITIMACY AND ACCOUNTABILITY

It has almost become an evergreen to raise the question of the democratic legitimacy of international standard-setting processes, both within intergovernmental organizations and within private rulemaking bodies.[41] But the examples above of recent regulatory battles in the ITU, in which Chinese technology corporations with the support of China have aggressively tried to have new international standards accepted on internet protocol and facial recognition must touch a raw nerve with democracy watchdogs, from parliamentarians to journalists.

In the more general debate on the legitimacy of international standards, a traditional distinction has been made between "input legitimacy" and "output legitimacy."[42] This contribution will not enter into that discussion but submits that nowadays legitimacy should be preferably understood as "democratic legitimacy"

[39] Ibid., at 91 and 93, respectively.

[40] K. Buhmann, Collaborative Regulation: Preventing Regulatory Capture in Multi-Stakeholder Processes for Developing Norms for Sustainability Conduct in *Sustainability and Law* (V. Mauerhofer et al. eds., 2020), 295 at 305.

[41] See *inter alia* A. Marx, E. Bécault, and J. Wouters, Private Standards in Forestry: Assessing the Legitimacy and Effectiveness of the Forest Stewardship Council, in *Private Standards and Global Governance. Economic, Legal and Political Perspectives* (A. Marx, J. Swinnen, M. Maertens, and J. Wouters eds., 2012), 60; N. Hachez and J. Wouters, A Glimpse at the Democratic Legitimacy of Private Standards: Assessing the Public Accountability of GlobalG.A.P. (2011) 14 *Journal of International Economic Law* 677. This section builds in particular on the latter article.

[42] "Input legitimacy" rests on the fact that the norm reflects the preferences of the people, while "output legitimacy" is based on the contents and effects of the norm as promoting the general interest. It has been argued that a lack of input legitimacy, resulting from a democratic deficit, may be compensated for by a high degree of output legitimacy: see F. Scharpf, *Governing in Europe – Effective and Democratic?* (1999), 6ff. While the present author does not fully agree with this, the discussion exceeds the limits of this contribution. See also the considerations on "cognitive legitimacy" and "moral legitimacy" for the assessment of voluntary sustainability standards in P. Haack and A. Rasche, The Legitimacy of Sustainability Standards: A Paradox Perspective (2021) 2 *Organization Theory* 1, at 5.

and that the democratic character of a norm makes it legitimate.[43] Democracy is indeed considered a most important framework of analysis for assessing the legitimacy of a norm – whether global or local, public or private.[44]

As argued in an earlier publication,[45] democracy may be successfully conceived at the global level by promoting a link between regulation and public deliberations rather than relying on fixed social, institutional, or procedural preconditions.[46] This democratic link can be fruitfully thought of in terms of public accountability. Where regulatory authority is exercised by a governing entity and not by the people directly – as is the case when international organizations or private bodies issue global standards – democracy is ultimately concerned with the connection of such governing entity with the group of people that it intends to govern.[47] This democratic connection can be achieved through mechanisms of public accountability. The democratic character of a governing entity and of the rules it produces is a function of its accountability to the "public."[48]

This raises the following questions in relation to ITU standards: (i) what is the "public" and what is its role? and (ii) what does "accountability" concretely mean?

As to the public, it is submitted that, in a global context, it should not so much be considered as a "global demos" but rather in a deliberative-democratic sense, which

43 See, for example, R. Keohane, Global Governance and Democratic Accountability, in *Taming Globalization: Frontiers of Governance* (David Held and M. Koenig-Archibugi ed., 2003), 130: "We live in a democratic era, and I share the widespread belief that rules are only legitimate if they conform to broadly democratic principles, appropriately adapted for the context.' David Held also argued that there is a 'growing recognition of democracy as the fundamental standard of political legitimacy which finds entrenchment in the Universal Declaration of Human Rights and regional treaties": Cosmopolitanism: Ideas, Realities and Deficits, in *Governing Globalization: Power, Authority and Global Governance* (D. Held and A. McGrew eds., 2002), 315.

44 See *inter alia* S. Bernstein, Legitimacy in Global Environmental Governance 1 (2005) *Journal of International Law & International Relations* 139; S. Bernstein and B. Cashore, Can Non-state Global Governance Be Legitimate? An analytical framework 1 (2007) *Regulation & Governance* 347, at 353ff.; G. De Búrca, Developing Democracy beyond the State (2008) 46 *Columbia Journal of Transnational Law* 221; K. Dingwerth, *The New Transnationalism: Private Transnational Governance and Its Democratic Legitimacy* (2007).

45 Hachez and Wouters, *supra* note 41.

46 See also S. Wheatley, Democratic Governance beyond the State: The Legitimacy of Non-state Actors as Standard Setters, in *Non-State Actors as Standard Setters* (A. Peters, L. Koechlin, T. Förster, and G. F. Zinkernagel eds., 2009), 226–227.

47 See P. Nanz and J. Steffek, Global Governance, Participation and the Public Sphere 39 (2004) *Government and Opposition* 314: "The idea of democratic legitimacy is that the citizens decide for themselves the content of the laws that organize and regulate their political association. Separating the process of rule-making from politically accountable institutions, global governance is argued to suffer a massive 'democratic deficit.'"

48 See, e.g., T. Risse, Transnational Governance and Legitimacy, in *Governance and Democracy: Comparing National, European and International Experiences* (A. Benz and Y. Papadopoulos eds., 2006), 183, at 184: "In democratic systems, a social order is legitimate because the rulers are accountable to their citizens, who can participate in rule-making through representatives and can punish them by voting them out of office."

must not necessarily be territorially defined or linked with particular nation-states but may be approached from a more functional point of view. The relevant public associated with a governing entity and its norms may be identified in relation to a particular issue, on the basis of an "affected" criterion.[49] A public in relation to a particular issue would encompass the circle of persons affected by that issue and by its being regulated, which are often called "stakeholders." In an area such as internet protocol and facial recognition, such public will be extremely wide: it includes internet users of all kinds, both individual citizens, businesses and other private actors, as well as governmental actors, consumers, producers, and so on. The enormous size of the so-defined public leads to important problems of identification, representativeness, or feasibility in designing democratic governance processes.[50] Whereas those problems are real, they are not insoluble (especially in regard of the progress of information technologies), and in any case, they should not be used as excuses to disregard the public's entitlement to democratic accountability in global governance.[51]

Turning to "accountability," it has often been exclusively considered in a retrospective dimension, where it designates a relationship in which an actor – in our case the general public – may require that another – for example, a governing entity – render account of its activities and impose a cost on them as the case may be. In the democratic discourse, such views of accountability emphasize the control exercised by the public on governing entities.[52] In democratic societies, the people must be able to control those who govern them,[53] and this may be achieved in many ways, following different channels.[54] This view of accountability is retrospective because it logically presupposes that the governing entity has already acted, or

[49] See J.-A. Scholte, Reconstructing Contemporary Democracy (2008) 15 *Indiana Journal of Global Legal Studies* 305, at 309; De Búrca, *supra* note 44, at 248ff.

[50] See Risse, *supra* note 48, at 185 and 193, who does not exclude a priori that the concrete accountability mechanisms available to the internal and external stakeholders be differentiated (notably for reasons of practicability) as long as they stay effective.

[51] In this regard, see Wheatley, *supra* note 46, at 232–233.

[52] See examples of such conceptions in R. Grant and R. Keohane, Accountability and Abuses of Power in World Politics (2005) 99:1 *American Political Science Review* 29: "*Accountability*, as we use the term, implies that some actors have the right to hold other actors to a set of standards, to judge whether they have fulfilled their responsibilities in light of these standards, and to impose sanctions if they determine that these responsibilities have not been met." (emphasis in original). See also M. Bovens, Analysing and Assessing Public Accountability: A Conceptual Framework 13 (2005) *European Law Journal* 447, at 450, according to whom accountability is "a relationship between an actor and a forum, in which the actor has an obligation to explain and to justify his or her conduct, the forum can pose questions and pass judgement, and the actor may face consequences."

[53] See M. Kahler, Defining Accountability Up: the Global Economic Multilaterals (2004) 39 *Government and Opposition* 133.

[54] In this regard, Grant and Kehoane (*supra* note 52, at 36) identify seven "accountability mechanisms" in world politics: hierarchical, supervisory, fiscal, legal, market, peer, and public-reputational.

issued, and/or implemented norms before control may be exercised, and it tends to be sanctions- and redress-oriented.[55] However, for the purposes of this contribution, a more extensive view of accountability is advanced, by adding a prospective dimension to the retrospective one. While the retrospective conception focuses on the governing entity "rendering account" of its activities to the public, the prospective dimension insists on the necessity for the governing entity to "take into account" the preferences, interests, and concerns of the public in making government decisions and issuing public norms, through appropriate means. This side of accountability emphasizes the responsiveness that a governing entity must show to the public's concerns.[56] It is most effectively achieved by means of mechanisms of inclusive participation,[57] which can take many forms, such as voting procedures to adopt particular rules (directly or through representatives) or public notice and comment procedures prior to making a decision.

In light of the foregoing, public accountability in democratic governance can be defined as the relationship of a governing entity to its public according to which the former must allow inclusive participation of the latter in its governing activities, in order to take account of the public's preferences in making government decisions, as well as the relationship according to which the public is entitled to control and sanction a posteriori the governing entity for the way it has conducted its government functions (rule-making, rule-implementation, rule-enforcement, rule-interpretation). If such an accountability relationship is effective between the governing entity and the public, the norms issued by the governing entity for the purpose of regulating issues of concern to the public should approximate what is called "democratic" and hence have good chances of being viewed as legitimate.

Again, trying to operationalize responsiveness and control in very technical global governance regimes such as ITU standards on internet protocol and facial recognition may lead to practical problems given the sheer size and diversity of the public. In this respect, much attention is presently given to the incremental formation of a

55 Control may, however, take a more continued form, for example, as a constant monitoring is established to oversee in real time the activities of an agent, notably to pre-empt dysfunctions and create learning curves. See J. Wouters, N. Hachez, and P. Schmitt, Managerial Accountability: What Impact on International Organisations' Autonomy?, in *International Organisations and the Idea of Autonomy* (R. Collins and N. White eds., 2011), 230.

56 R. Mulgan, "Accountability": An Ever-Expanding Concept? (2000) 78 *Public Administration* 555, at 566ff.

57 See Nanz and Steffek, *supra* note 47, at 315: the deliberative theory of politics "claims that democratic legitimation can be generated by means of deliberation between a variety of social actors (e.g. government officials from different national communities, scientific experts, NGOs, etc). Political decisions are reached through a deliberative process where participants scrutinize heterogeneous interests and justify their positions in view of the common good of a given constituency. In [those authors' view], any bestowal of democratic legitimacy on global governance must ultimately depend on the creation of an appropriate public sphere, i.e., an institutionalized arena for (deliberative) political participation beyond the limits of national boundaries."

vibrant and variegated "global civil society," for the explicit purpose of participating in the governing of the global public space.[58] In various domains, global civil society organizations, most importantly nongovernmental organizations (NGOs), have been quite successful in generating debate and in participating in the establishment of truly global sets of norms, either of a public or private nature.[59] The question is, however, the extent to which, and the ways to find out whether, such civil society organizations, through their participation in, and oversight of, global public deliberations, effectively represent the public at large.

Accountability, to function effectively, also needs other supporting principles to be put in place. Transparency is one of them and can be defined as the level of access enjoyed by the relevant public to information about, from, or concerning the governing entity and its activities. Without access of the public to such information, participation will be meaningless, and control will be curtailed.[60] This is why transparency is a major stake in struggles for increased accountability in global governance, even though it should not be understood as a component of the notion of accountability itself, as is sometimes done, but rather as an enabler of accountability.[61] Another principle that is crucial for deliberation in global governance, as well as for retrospective control thereof, is that of stating the reasons for making a government decision.[62] Stating reasons allows shedding light on the deliberative dynamics, and on the arguments at play, and makes the control of the norm and of the governing entity more objective.[63]

The considerations developed above may be considered rather abstract. It is submitted, though, that they are essential in order to ensure the democratic legitimacy of global standard-setting practices, whether of an intergovernmental or private

[58] For an analysis of prospects for increasing the participation of a global public in transnational law-making through the use of ICT platforms, see K. Buhmann and S. Azizi, Towards the Participation of a Global Public in Transnational Law-Making? Everyday ICT Platforms as Legitimacy Opportunities for Bottom-Up Governance, in *Transnationalisation and Legal Actors. Legitimacy in Question* (B. L. Kristiansen, K. Mitkidis, L. Munkholm, L. Neumann, and C. Pelaudeix eds., 2019), 112.

[59] See how civil society and more particularly international NGOs play a role in global norm-formation: M. Finnemore and K. Sikkink, International Norm Dynamics and Political Change (1998) 52 *International Organization* 887, at 896ff. For an account of NGO participation in UN proceedings, see N. Hachez, The Relations between the United Nations and Civil Society (2008) 5 *International Organizations Law Review* 49.

[60] For a study of the interplay between transparency and accountability, see T. Hale, Transparency, Accountability and Global Governance (2008) 18 *Global Governance* 73.

[61] On transparency as an enabler of accountability, see T. Hale and A.-M. Slaughter, Transparency: Possibilities and Limitations (2006) 30 *The Fletcher Forum of World Affairs* 153.

[62] This is already considered a general principle of administrative law in traditional domestic or international administrative settings. See, e.g., in EU law, D.-U. Galetta, H. C. H. Hofmann, O. M. Puigpelat, and J. Ziller, The General Principles of EU Administrative Procedural Law, European Parliament, 2015, at 20.

[63] See Risse, *supra* note 48, at 214, who articulates the procedural requirements that have to be met by private governing entities to ensure democratic legitimacy: transparency, deliberative quality, responsiveness and reliability, responsibility and accountability, and congruence.

nature. It will require further in-depth research to apply them to, and effectuate them practically in, the ITU and other SDOs. As the recent developments in the ITU detailed in Section 3.2 narrate, there is a great practical need to do this.

3.5 HUMAN RIGHTS

While traditionally, the ITU's work stood far off from human rights,[64] it has been rightly observed that in recent years, as the organization has become increasingly involved in internet governance and online communications, the link between its decisions and the human rights of end users have become much more obvious.[65] However, an important concern about ITU standard-setting processes is that they do not involve a human rights screening:

> There are virtually no human rights, consumer protection, or data protection experts present in ITU standards meetings so many of the technologies that threaten privacy and freedom of expression remain unchallenged in these spaces .... When it comes to facial recognition [these standards are] extremely dangerous from a human rights perspective.[66]

For that reason, it has been asserted that

> the ITU, as a technical standards setting body, is not an appropriate forum for discussing privacy, which is ultimately a human rights issue. Other bodies have far greater expertise on privacy, and a much clearer mandate to discuss it: the UN Human Rights Council, Human Rights Committee and Special Rapporteurs, to name but three. If the ITU were to start determining what national laws, policies and regulations related to privacy looked like, this would be a real cause for concern, particularly given the restrictions on the rights to privacy that exist in many of the states which make up the ITU.[67]

As Romania indicated in the discussions regarding China Telecom's proposal for a new standard on facial recognition (Section 3.2.3), as part of the UN family, the ITU should uphold the fundamental values of the UN, including the respect and promotion of human rights. There is a strong legal argument to support this thesis.

64 Interestingly, the ITU describes its core mission very much in a fundamental rights way: it is stated that "it is committed to connecting all the world's people – wherever they live and whatever their means. Through our work, we protect and support everyone's fundamental right to communicate," see www.un.org/en/about-us/un-system and www.itu.int/en/about/Pages/overview.aspx.

65 R. Wingfield, Spotlight on the ITU #1: Why Human Rights Defenders Should Care About the ITU, *Global Partners Digital*, March 15, 2017, www.gp-digital.org/spotlight-on-the-itu-1-why-human-rights-defenders-should-care-about-the-itu/.

66 Mehwish Ansari, as quoted in Parker, *supra* note 14.

67 R. Wingfield, Spotlight on the ITU #3: WTDC 2017 – And Why the ITU Needs to Change, *Global Partners Digital*, November 13, 2017, www.gp-digital.org/spotlight-on-the-itu-3-why-the-itu-needs-to-change/.

In 1947, the UN and the ITU concluded a cooperation agreement, which made the latter a specialized agency of the former. Article IV of this agreement explicitly obliges the ITU to allow for the submission of formal recommendations from the UN "having regard to the obligation of the United Nations to promote the objectives set forth in Article 55 of the Charter" and to enter into consultation with the UN on such recommendations.[68] In Article 55(c) of the UN Charter, the UN is tasked to promote "universal respect for, and observance of, human rights and fundamental freedoms for all." One may submit that the ITU, as a member of the UN family, is bound to respect and promote human rights but also that there may be a case for the UN's ECOSOC to develop recommendations about the need for integrating human rights concerns in all regulatory processes in UN specialized agencies, including the ITU, with possibly an important consultative role for the UN High Commissioner for Human Rights.

3.6 CONCLUDING REMARKS

If it had not been for the *Financial Times*' repeated coverage (Section 3.2), the larger public and academia would probably not have heard about the recent regulatory battles regarding standards for facial recognition and internet protocol that have been going on in the ITU. This finding by itself is rather worrying: global normative power plays are taking place in UN agencies on issues that deeply affect the daily lives of peoples around the world, and most of us are not even aware of it. In this chapter, we situated these recent regulatory battles in the ITU and developed a number of reflections regarding the need to scrutinize the risk of corporate capture, the need to better safeguard democratic legitimacy and accountability, and the need for a stronger scrutiny of such regulatory processes from a human rights point of view.

It is said that the EU and its Member States have recently decided to upgrade their capacity and representation in ITU meetings, having been alarmed by the initiatives of China and Chinese corporations. It is one of the lesser known fallouts of Brexit, as in the past the EU relied strongly on the United Kingdom's participation in ITU bodies. All of this constitutes a wake-up call. Apart from a deeper and more proactive engagement by Western governments in the work of the ITU, there is clearly a need for a much wider reflection on how to enhance the democratic legitimacy and accountability of its regulatory processes and on a more critical engagement with the role that powerful corporations play within those processes, whether or not in sync with their national governments.

[68] Article IV(1) and (2) of the Agreement between the United Nations and the International Telecommunications Union.

PART II

Evolution and Resilience in Banking and Finance

4

Standard-Setting and Organizational Resilience

The Case of the Institute of International Finance

M. Konrad Borowicz[*]

4.1 INTRODUCTION

The fundamental challenges faced by the management of financial trade associations are retaining existing members and attracting new ones. The management's ability to do that defines the long-term success and resilience of such organizations. Not all associations are successful in achieving that goal. In the early 2000s, as many as six trade associations brought together the various creditors of sovereign debt.[1] Only three of them still exist today, and the Institute of International Finance (IIF) is by far the most influential among them; it has over 450 members that fund its activity. How did the IIF manage to hold on to its members and even expand its membership?

The IIF has emerged in the wake of sovereign defaults of the 1980s as an organization entrusted with monitoring sovereign borrowers. Its influence started to wane as sovereign markets appeared to have healed, mainly due to the Brady plan.[2] IIF's membership started to decline as member institutions have begun to

* An earlier version of this chapter has been presented at the conference on the evolution of transnational private rule makers held at Tilburg on December 3–4, 2020. This chapter is part of a project that has received funding from the European Research Council under the European Union's Horizon 2020 research and innovation program (Grant Agreement No 725798).

1 The group, frequently referred to as the "Gang of Six," comprised the following associations: the Emerging Markets Creditors Association (EMCA), the Emerging Market Traders Association (EMTA), the IIF, the International Primary Market Association (IPMA), International Securities Market Association (ISMA), Securities Industry Association (SIA), the Bond Market Association (BMA). In 2005, IPMA merged with the ISMA to form the International Capital Market Association (ICMA).

2 The Brady plan, named after then US Treasury Secretary Nicholas Brady, allowed countries to exchange their commercial bank loans for bonds guaranteed by multilateral lenders, in particular the IMF and the World Bank. J. Sachs, Making the Brady Plan Work (1989) 68 *Foreign Affairs* 87.

question the return on the investment associated with maintaining their membership in the IIF. By all accounts, the IIF was experiencing an existential crisis. Its continued viability as the voice representing private creditors of sovereign debt was uncertain.

IIF's management successfully steered the organization through those uncertain times. Recent literature, particularly the work of two political economists, Abraham Newman and Elliot Posner, has suggested that the IIF's continued success can be attributed to a combination of exogenous and endogenous factors.[3] In the IIF's case, the emergence of a new paradigm for banking regulation brought about by the Basel Accords created a new role for the organization in terms of regulatory advocacy. On the endogenous side, management capable of identifying opportunities for the expansion of the organization's influence was vital to leverage the considerable experience of the IIF with the collection of information, to help it established itself as a credible contributor to the policy work at the Basel Committee on Banking Supervision.

Newman's and Posner's analysis suggests three strategies of organizational resilience that help explain the IIF's success story. First, timely identification of new constituencies that can help support the work of the organization. Second, a reorientation toward new activities, specifically transnational policy advocacy in the realm of banking regulation. Third, the adaption of an internal governance mechanism to accommodate new members and facilitate new activities. Together, Newman and Posner argue, these strategies were critical for the continued relevance of the IIF.

In this chapter, I argue that standard-setting is another strategy adopted by the IIF to maintain relevance. The IIF adopted the strategy of standard-setting in the wake of new regulatory initiatives promoted in the sovereign debt space in the early 2000s. Despite the optimism that the Brady plan injected into sovereign debt markets, problems have not disappeared from those markets. Those problems have been the catalyst for a set of proposals aimed at establishing an official sector bankruptcy-like mechanism to facilitate sovereign debt restructurings known as the Sovereign Debt Restructuring Mechanism (SDRM). For fear of the impact this could have on public sector participation, the IIF, together with the other associations, opposed establishing the SDRM.[4]

The alternative to the SDRM proposal discussed consisted of contractual standards, which the IIF helped to define and endorsed. The standards set, among other things, thresholds of creditor participation aimed at ensuring that a small group of creditors does not undermine the efforts of the rest to restructure or write-off a

[3] A. Newman and E. Posner, Structuring Transnational Interests: The Second-Order Effects of Soft Law in the Politics of Global Finance (October 18, 2016) *Review of International Political Economy* 768.

[4] EMCA, EMTA, IIF, IPMA, ISMA, SIA, BMA, Sovereign Debt Restructuring (Discussion Draft, December 6, 2002).

portion of a piece of distressed sovereign debt. The IIF also played an essential role in developing the Principles for Stable Capital Flows and Fair Debt Restructuring, a code of conduct for the various actors in the sovereign debt market. Two informal groups comprising members from both the public and the private sector to which the IIF serves as a secretariat were entrusted with monitoring the implementation of the Principles.

My main argument in this chapter is that, by endorsing and in part also creating that framework, the IIF created the structural conditions for its continued relevance in the sovereign debt space. The IIF's continued relevance is evidenced by its role in shaping the private sector's response to the looming sovereign debt crisis induced by the COVID-19 pandemic, which I also describe in this chapter. Recognizing that the crisis undermined the ability of many emerging countries to service their external debt, the IIF called on its members to refrain from enforcing the contracts and join the Debt Service Suspension Initiative (DSSI) – an ad hoc regulatory instrument promoted by the G20 Finance Ministers and Central Bank Governors. Still, the IIF insisted that private creditor participation should be voluntary. What was the result? At the time of writing (March 2021), over forty-six countries have taken advantage of the debt relief under the DSSI. However, most of that relief came from public creditors; private creditor participation in the DSSI has been minimal.

By creating the structural conditions for its relevance by endorsing or developing standards, the IIF's management has shown an entrepreneurial attitude that has remained largely neglected in the extant theoretical literature. The analytical framework developed by Newman and Posner and developed further here can help us understand the dynamics of resilience of trade associations. However, it also prompts questions about normative standards through which to view that resilience. When are the activities of such associations beneficial, and when do they create social costs? To the extent they create costs, what degree of control do public policymakers have over the activities of such associations? What are the channels through which public policymakers can exercise such control?

4.2 A BRIEF HISTORY OF THE IIF'S ECONOMIC ACTIVISM

4.2.1 *IIF in the 1980s: Addressing the Information Gap in the Sovereign Debt Market*

The IIF was established in 1983 in response to the perceived deficiencies in the structure of the sovereign debt market increasingly populated by private creditors.[5]

[5] For an early account of the origins of the IIF, see W. S. Surrey and P. N. Nash, Bankers Look beyond the Debt Crisis: The Institute of International Finance, Inc. Perspectives (1985) 23:1

Around that time, several sovereign borrowers, most notably Mexico, Brazil, Argentina, and Poland, experienced problems servicing their external debt. Their perilous situation prompted concerns about the nature of private creditor participation in any future restructuring of the debt of those countries and private creditors' role in the market more generally.

The IIF was formed as a result of a meeting organized by a group of policymakers affiliated with the Committee on Changing International Relations, a committee of the National Planning Association (NPA), a US think tank established in the 1930s. The group brought together representatives of commercial banks involved in sovereign lending to discuss the situation. As recounted by Walter Sterling Surrey, the IIF's first general counsel, and Peri N. Nash, the group identified four major deficiencies: (1) the information made available by the borrowing countries to public lenders, such as the International Monetary Fund (IMF), was typically made available on a confidential sovereign-to-sovereign basis and therefore not readily available to commercial banks, (2) the information was often outdated, (3) the leading commercial banks developed their analyses but did not like to share it with other institutions, and (4) there were no uniform reporting standards.

Discussions about the structure of a new institution were held in New York in the summer of 1982 and brought together some thirty-one major banks from the United States, Japan, the United Kingdom, France, Canada, the Netherlands, the Federal Republic of Germany, and Switzerland as well as representative from the World Bank, the IMF, the Bank for International Settlements, the Bank of England, and the NPA. It was at that meeting that the IIF's Articles of Incorporation had been drawn. Pursuant to the document, the purpose of the IIF was

> to form an organization of commercial banks to promote a better understanding of international lending transactions generally; to collect, analyze and disseminate information regarding the economic and financial position of particular countries which are substantial borrowers in the international markets to provide the Members with a better factual basis on which each member independently may analyze extensions of credit to borrowers in such countries; and to engage in other appropriate activities to facilitate, and preserve the integrity of, international lending transactions.[6]

Columbia Journal of Transnational Law 111. The information about the origins of the IIF in Section 4.2.1 is derived mainly from that article.

6 Articles of Incorporation of the Institute of International Finance, Inc., art. third (January 11, 1983).

The Articles also provided that the IIF would be a nonprofit corporation located in Washington, DC. Its membership would comprise commercial banks active in the market for sovereign debt. The members' voting powers in matters pertaining to the organization's activities would be proportionate to the magnitude of the member's exposure to sovereign debt. A small staff would manage the day-to-day operations of the IIF. The IIF would also seek to facilitate the exchange of views among members through the organization of working groups.

IIF's work in the areas identified above would prove valuable during times of sovereign crises, such as those of the early 1980s. Still, it was not as clear what the benefit of retaining membership would be outside of the context of a challenging macroeconomic environment that typically acts as a catalyst for the emergence of such crises. The future validated those concerns. As noted in an empirical study by Newman and Posner, the Brady Plan of 1989 had resolved much of the debt crisis, and many small commercial banks had left the organization or merged with bigger banks. At the same time, the IMF and Bank of International Settlements (BIS) gradually opened up information to private actors, undercutting the value of IIF surveillance activities. US bank representation fell from 40 banks in 1987 to 18 by 1993. Overall membership declined from 167 full members in 1987 to 135 members in 1991. "By its own account, the organization faced a crisis in the late 1980s as its primary mission had evaporated."[7]

4.2.2 *IIF in the 1990s: Shaping the New Paradigm of Banking Regulation*

The evolving political economy of banking regulation in the wake of revisions to the first Basel Accord of 1988 created a unique opportunity for the organizational revival of the IIF. The first Basel Accord broke ground in that it represented the first-ever international effort at coordinating banking regulation. Still, that Accord is commonly viewed as having been the product of mainly national actors, particularly central banks.[8] Commercial banks, the principal target of the first Accord, may have sought to influence the final shape of the first Accord. However, they did that through national channels rather than directly by seeking to influence the Basel Committee for Banking Supervision (BCBS) – the body established and entrusted with the task of developing the Accord. Only when the proposal for the second Accord was floated did banks seek to exert a greater degree of influence

7 Newman and Posner, *supra* note 3, at 782.

8 C. Goodheart, *The Basel Committee on Banking Supervision: A History of the Early Years 1974–1997* (2011) (quoted in Newman and Posner, *supra* note 3, at 780).

over its shape by lobbying the BCBS directly.[9] This was partly because Basel II was directed at activities of investment banks, many of which operated on a global basis. The IIF identified the opportunity to represent them and sought to capitalize on it.

Targeting large investment and money center banks as potential new members was the first strategy of the IIF identified by Newman and Posner aimed at the organizational revival of the IIF. The second strategy consisted of the comprehensive reorienting toward transnational regulatory policy efforts. As Newman and Posner note, the second strategy followed directly from the first.

> Having identified investment and money center banks as their primary new member targets, IIF's leaders sought to enhance the organization's relevance to these banks' new concerns about the Basel Committee's expanding regulatory agenda. The strategy meant that the IIF would have to engage the new transnational rulemaking arena directly and would have to add a regulatory advocacy dimension to its traditional functions.[10]

In 1990, under the leadership of Managing Director Schulmann, the IIF formally altered its mission statement to broaden its goals, thereby hoping to appeal to a broader set of firms than those it sought to represent in the early days of its existence on matters pertaining to the sovereign debt market. That shift was also reflected in the appointment of a different group of people to its management. As Newman and Posner note, the appointment of Charles Dallara, a long-time US Treasury Department official, was an excellent example of that.[11] Crucially, as they note, the management of the IIF itself initiated that shift. In other words, it was not in another substantial way the result of pressure from the industry. The management also anticipated reluctance from the public sector to engage with the organization

[9] M. K. Borowicz, The Internal Ratings-Based and Advanced Measurement Approaches for Regulatory Capital Under the Basel Regime, in *The Governance and Regulation of International Finance* (G. P. Miller and F. Cafaggi eds., 2013).

[10] Newman and Posnner, *supra* note 3, at 784.

[11] In their discussion, Newman and Posner include the following except from an official IIF document commemorating its first twenty-five years of existence:

> The Board recognized at this time that such a bold regulatory thrust may have a particular appeal to some of the very large banks that had still not joined the Institute .... A broader agenda of the IIF activities and events was seen as part of the strategy to attract these banks .... The challenge to the new Managing Director was to find more effective ways to keep the IIF relevant, to expand its influence and to revitalize its membership. Dallara's response came quickly. In the fall of 1993, following intensive discussions with the IIF's Board of Directors, he forged a new agenda for the Institute that would involve increased advocacy ...." Institute of International Finance, *IIF History Book: The First 25 Years* (2007) (quoted in Newman and Posnner, *supra* note 3, at 784.

on the advocacy front. This is why the shift was implemented carefully and gradually.

The third strategy of adaptation identified by Newman and Posner consists of governance changes. The new focus on advocacy informed the design of internal operations of the IIF. In 1991, the IIF created a working group on capital adequacy.

> Contrary to arguments attributing organizational priorities to the material interest of industry, the IIF's agenda shift was a reaction to Basel I rather than in anticipation of it. The aim of the IIF's leaders in revamping the internal organizational structure was to make the IIF a better interlocutor with Basel and a source of expertise, rendering it more effective as an industry advocate and, ultimately, more attractive to new members.[12]

The strategies of adaptation proved to be successful. The IIF became the BCBS' most influential adviser in large part due to its proven track record to collect information on a confidential basis. Around that time, the industry was increasingly embracing quantitative approaches to finance and relying on risk modeling. The BCBS was keen to build on that expertise, but its access to information about how banks used those models was limited. As Newman and Posner note, the IIF positioned itself as a supplier of that information, which proved instrumental for incorporating the internal risk models into the Basel II framework.

4.2.3 *IIF in the 2000s: Strengthening the Contractual Framework for Sovereign Debt Restructuring*

A series of sovereign crises, in particular the Mexican financial crisis and the Asian financial crisis of the late 1990s, created the opportunity for the IIF to reestablish itself as the preeminent organization in the sovereign debt space. As noted earlier, private creditors started playing an increasingly prominent role in sovereign debt markets, which, in some ways, has made sovereign debt defaults more interesting. Private actors tend to be more determined to recover their investment, as exemplified by the pursuit of Argentinian assets by the so-called vulture funds through much of the 2000s. While this may be a profitable strategy for some investors, overall, it is not a very effective method of policing sovereigns because it will reduce recoveries for creditors as a group.

Creditors as a group would be better off if they engaged in talks aimed at a restructuring of the debt. In the corporate debt context, bankruptcy law helps reduce the transaction costs associated with such talks by providing a set of rules to be followed that aim to maximize the recovery for the creditor group. Unfortunately, there is no bankruptcy law or court for sovereigns. In the early 2000s, senior officials from the IMF proposed the SDRM as an effort to "create some of the features of a

[12] Newman and Posnner, *supra* note 3, at 786.

bankruptcy regime without creating a bankruptcy court,"[13] but the concept never came into fruition.

One of the main reasons for the project's failure was that the IIF, together with several other associations, came out strongly against it in a 2002 paper.[14] The paper identified several theoretical objections to the SDRM. Among other things, it challenged the assumption that there is an inherent collective action problem among private-sector creditors in a sovereign debt restructuring that precludes agreement. It also sought to undermine the analogy between domestic bankruptcy legislation and the SDRM by arguing that the SDRM would lack the necessary procedural checks and balances that render a domestic bankruptcy process fair and effective. However, the principal objection seemed to have stemmed from the private sector's concern that the SDRM will decrease the participation of public creditors in sovereign debt restructurings, erode the rights of private creditors, and increase the frequency of sovereign debt restructurings.[15]

While the proposal enjoyed considerable support from the official sector, it ultimately failed to establish the SDRM. Sean Hagan, the IMF's general counsel at the time, provides an account of the failure.[16] The most important reason for the failure is that the implementation of the SDRM would require an amendment to the IMF's Articles of Agreement. Under the Articles, a majority of three-fifths of the IMF's members holding 85 percent of the voting power was needed. Since the United States held 17.14 percent of the IMF's voting power, its participation was required. The United States ultimately declined to do so largely, as Hagan notes, due to steadfast opposition to the SDRM proposal by the major financial industry associations.

> Not only did such opposition make it much more difficult for the SDRM proposal to be approved in Congress, but there was clearly a reluctance within the U.S. government to forge ahead with such an important reform of the international financial system when a key stakeholder in that system – the private sector – was so resistant.[17]

[13] A. Krueger, first deputy managing director of the IMF, first articulated the proposal in a 2001 speech.

[14] EMCA, EMTA, IIF, IPMA, ISMA, SIA, BMA, *supra* note 4.

[15] The following passage from the letter speaks to that: "In some official quarters, the SDRM is also seen as key to limit the size of official financing packages in the future as well as an instrument to force burden sharing. However, it remains unclear how the presence of an SDRM would constrain political decisions in favor of or against official funding in any given case."

[16] S. Hagan, Designing a Legal Framework to Restructure Sovereign Debt (2005) 36 *Georgetown Journal of International Law* 299.

[17] As he further notes, opposition to the SDRM proposal by financial industry associations was, of course, also an important reason why a number of emerging market countries opposed the SDRM proposal. "The private sector consistently warned that the SDRM, if adopted, would adversely affect the volume and price of capital to these countries." Hagan, *supra* note 16, at 392.

Interestingly, Hagan notes that European and Asian financial institutions were less openly hostile to the SDRM proposal than their US counterparts.[18] Moreover, industry associations made up of investors that actually purchased and held sovereign debt (the "buy-side") were more willing to engage in discussions regarding the design of the SDRM proposal than those responsible for actually placing new bond issuances for emerging market sovereigns (the "sell-side").[19]

The private sector's opposition to the SDRM was also premised on the ongoing work on standard aimed at facilitating sovereign debt restructurings through voluntary means. Those standards took two primary forms: collective action clauses (CAC) in sovereign debt documentation and a code of conduct known as the Principles for Stable Capital Flows and Fair Debt Restructuring.

CACs were a response to a design feature of sovereign debt contracts, which historically required all creditors to agree to a restructuring giving rise to the problem of holdouts or investors unwilling to agree to the terms of the restructuring. Since the mid-1990s, the official sector has encouraged CACs in international sovereign bonds, but that has not changed the market practice much.[20] Data quoted in a 2002 IMF report indicated that the vast majority of international sovereign bonds outstanding in that year did not contain CACs.[21] The two main reasons identified in the report for the resistance in adoption are short-run costs associated with introducing any change in documentation (inertia) and concerns that issuers might face a permanent increase in borrowing costs if they were to introduce such provisions. The report notes that there is no evidence that the use of CACs would systematically raise borrowing costs. Concerning the first issue, short-run costs, and inertia, it notes that these problems could largely be overcome through the broad adoption of CACs. While it was apparent the IMF could play an important role in promoting such adoption, for example, by using clauses as a condition for access to Fund resources and/or special facilities, there was the issue of which clauses to promote exactly?

[18] Ibid.

[19] Ibid.

[20] IMF, The Design and Effectiveness of Collective Action Clauses (June 6, 2002).

[21] Crucially, the report noted, even if new issues of bonds include CACs, it will take a significant amount of time for the majority of international sovereign bonds to contain such provisions because the speed with which non-collective action clauses bonds will be replaced is a function of their maturity profile and assumptions about the growth in net new issuance of bonds. "Assuming that all bond issuance from now on will include collective action clauses and that net new bond issuance grows at a rate of roughly 3 percent per annum, approximately 80 percent of the bond stock would contain collective action clauses by 2010 and approximately 90 percent by 2019." As more recent data from the IMF shows, from end of September 2017 to the end of October 2018, only 8 percent of issuances did not include enhanced CACs. IMF, Fourth Progress Report on Inclusion of Enhanced Contractual Provisions in International Bond Contracts (March 2019).

For a long time, the IMF has monitored the use of CACs in the market. In one of the first documents surveying their use, it classified them into two types: "majority restructuring" provisions, which enable a qualified majority of bondholders of an issuance to bind all holders of that issuance to the financial terms of a restructuring, either before or after default, and "majority enforcement" provisions, which enable a qualified majority of bondholders to limit the ability of a minority of creditors to enforce their rights following a default, thereby giving the debtors and the qualified majority of creditors the opportunity to agree upon a restructuring.[22] There was a large variation of provision within these two types, particularly concerning voting thresholds.

The lack of uniformity in the drafting of CACs presented a unique opportunity for the IIF to engage in standard-setting – an activity it has previously shied away from. Other trade associations benefited from the first-mover advantage in this space. In the late 1990s, the EMCA proposed a model majority restructuring provision that would allow for a restructuring of key terms based on an affirmative vote of 95 percent of the bondholders. Still, that was viewed by the IMF as too high of a threshold, effectively defeating the purpose of the majority restructuring provision. The skeptical reception of the 95 percent threshold led another trade association, the ICMA, specifically its predecessor, the IPMA, which later, together with the ISMA, merged into ICMA to develop the 2003 Model Collective Action Clauses for Sovereign Bonds (under New York Law). The IIF, together with several other associations, endorse the model developed by ICMA, which provided for an 85 percent threshold.

In August 2014, ICMA published the latest sovereign debt contract reforms package, including new and updated CACs, a revised pari passu clause, and a model creditor engagement clause. The updated CACs – which include a menu of voting procedures including two different options for aggregation of votes across series to secure creditor agreement for modification of payment terms – was widely welcomed as a "means of facilitating collective action and avoiding disruption to sovereign debt restructurings that can arise from holdout litigation." In 2015, the IIF – also a collaborator in the drafting process – endorsed the full package of the ICMA contract reforms.

The second prong of the standard-setting activity that the IIF was involved in concerned developing a code of conduct for actors participating in sovereign debt restructurings – what has later become known as the Principles for Stable Capital Flows and Fair Debt Restructuring. The publication of the Principles in 2004 followed from an early 2000s initiative of Jean-Claude Trichet (at the time, the governor of the Banque de France), who launched proposals for a Code of Good Conduct governing creditors and debtor states' behavior. The G20 relegated the development of the Code to a working group led by the Banque de France and the

[22] IMF, *supra* note 20.

IIF. The prominent role played by the IIF in the process can be linked to its increasing advocacy activities described earlier. By the early 2000s, the IIF had already established itself as the principal interlocutor for regulators and policymakers and managed to persuade several prominent figures from the financial industry to become members of its various committees. This included Jacques de Larosière, also a former governor of the Banque de France and in the early 2000, co-chairman of the IIF's Special Committee and advisor to the chairman of BNP Paribas Group. The Principles were endorsed by the G20 in 2004.[23]

The Principles focused on four areas: transparency and timely flow of information, close debtor-creditor dialogue and cooperation to avoid restructuring, good faith actions, and fair treatment. Before 2010, the Principles applied only to sovereign issuers in emerging markets. However, their applicability has since been broadened to encompass all sovereign issuers (voluntarily) and cases of debt restructurings by non-sovereign entities in which the state plays a major role in influencing the legal and other critical parameters of debt restructurings.

As the IIF notes,

> the Principles promote early crisis containment through information disclosure, debtor-creditor consultations, and course correction before problems become unmanageable. They also support creditor actions that can help to minimize market contagion. In cases where the debtor can no longer fulfill its payment obligations, the Principles outline a process for market-based restructuring based on negotiations between the borrowing country and its creditors that involve shared information, are conducted in good faith and seek to achieve a fair outcome for all parties. Such a process maximizes the likelihood that market access will be restored as soon as possible under sustainable macroeconomic conditions.[24]

Adherence to the Principles is voluntary – accordingly, their effective implementation requires acceptance and adherence by both debtors and creditors. The Group of Trustees of the Principles, with the support of the Principles Consultative Group, encourages and monitors the implementation of the Principles. While these groups have no statutory authority, they have earned de facto acceptance by sovereign debtors, their creditors, and the international policy community due mainly to the reputation and stature of their members, who collectively have decades of experience in international policy and capital markets. The IIF serves as secretariat to both groups. What that means in practice is that the IIF, building on its surveillance practice, collects information about individual debtors, asks for input members of the Principles Consultative Group, and produces an (annual) report on the progress in the implementation of the Principles.[25]

23 TBC.

24 IIF, Principles For Stable Capital Flows and Fair Debt Restructuring and 2012 Addendum, at 2.

25 Interview, member of the Principles Consultative Group, April 2021.

The development and continued relevance of the Principles, given the cyclical nature of sovereign debt crises, allowed the IIF to expand its influence through the strategy of standard-setting. The Principles are now viewed as an indispensable feature of the sovereign debt market. The IIF, through its role as a secretariat to the Group of Trustees and the Principles Consultative Group and beyond it, is an organization indispensable to their functioning. More recently, the IIF has taken further initiatives aimed at enhancing its role even further. For example, in 2019, the IIF developed the Voluntary Principles for Debt Transparency. These new Principles build on the key guidelines of the Principles for Stable Capital Flows and Fair Debt Restructuring, and their implementation is also monitored by the Principles Consultative Group as well as the IIF itself.

4.3 THE CONTRACTUAL FRAMEWORK FOR SOVEREIGN DEBT RESTRUCTURING IN THE COVID-19 PANDEMIC

In early 2020, many countries in the world imposed strict lockdowns to control the outbreak of the pandemic, thereby effectively freezing economic activity for months. While the economic hardship these measures would entail was apparent, those measures were believed to be necessary to control the pandemic. Economic policymakers were immediately confronted with the question of how to manage the economic fallout. Domestic policymakers needed to identify resources that would enable them to stimulate aggregate demand through fiscal policies. It was clear that such stimulus requirements would make it more difficult for those countries to service their international debt obligations and necessitate the incurrence of new debt. In other words, it was clear that countries would require cooperation from their creditors.

What was the reaction of the creditor community to the apparent need faced by countries? On March 25, 2020, the president of the World Bank Group and the managing director of the IMF released a Joint Statement calling on official bilateral creditors to suspend debt payments from the member countries of the International Development Association to allow those countries to devote their liquidity to tackle challenges posed by the coronavirus outbreak.[26] Private creditors (and other international creditors, including sovereign wealth funds) should commit, upon specific request by the sovereign debtor, to forbear payment default for the poorest and most vulnerable countries significantly affected by COVID-19 and related economic turbulence for a specified time (e.g., for six months or to the end of 2020), without waiving the payment obligation.

In response to the COVID-19 "call to action" from the World Bank and the IMF, the G20 finance ministers and Central Bank governors announced the DSSI on

[26] Joint Statement World Bank Group and IMF Call to Action on Debt of IDA Countries (March 25, 2020).

April 15, 2020, supporting a net present value-neutral, time-bound suspension of principal and interest payments for eligible countries that make a formal request for debt relief from their official bilateral creditors and encouraging private creditors to participate on comparable terms.[27] The communique called for private creditors to work through the IIF.[28]

The IIF initially agreed with the approach. In a letter addressed to the IMF, World Bank, OECD, and Paris Club, it noted that private creditors (and other international creditors including sovereign wealth funds) should commit, upon specific request by the sovereign debtor, to forbear payment default for the poorest and most vulnerable countries significantly affected by COVID-19 and related economic turbulence for a specified time (e.g., for six months or to the end of 2020), without waiving the payment obligation.[29]

However, in a subsequent letter, dated May 4, 2020, the IIF provided an updated and stressed that participation should be wholly voluntary.[30] In effect, the private creditors declined to participate in the DSSI, other than on a voluntary, case-by-case basis.

The IIF's outreach in the case of the DSSI has been primarily via two IIF policy working groups.[31] The IIF has, among other things, surveyed its members about the status of requests made by DSSI-eligible countries to private creditors concerning debt suspension. As reported by the Principles Consultative Group, a June 2020 survey revealed no such requests had been made.[32] By September, four private creditors have been approached by countries eligible for the DSSI requesting forbearance on comparable terms to official creditors.[33]

While the limited requests from debtors arguably explain the limited involvement of creditors, we should bear in mind that outcome is at least partly the result of the private creditors' refusal to participate in the DSSI other than on a voluntary, case-by-case basis. It was that decision that created the structural conditions for private creditor free-riding. As of August 2020, forty-three countries out of seventy-three

27 G20 Finance Ministers and Central Bank Governors Meeting, Communiqué (April 15, 2020).

28 "We call on private creditors, working through the Institute of International Finance, to participate in the initiative on comparable terms." G20, *supra* note 27, at 1.

29 Institute for International Finance, IIF Letter Debt LICs (April 9, 2020).

30 Institute for International Finance, Letter to IMF, World Bank and Paris Club on a Potential Approach to Voluntary Private Sector Participation in the DSSI (May 4, 2020).

31 "Most of these firms are IIF members; many other private creditors and lenders have also contacted us in recent weeks to learn more about the DSSI. Based on these conversations, we believe there is a deep appreciation for the challenges facing these most vulnerable countries and strong interest in finding ways to support them and the proposed debt service suspension." Ibid.

32 Principles Consultative Group, Principles for Stable Capital Flows and Fair Debt Restructuring: Report on Implementation (October 2020), at 24.

33 Ibid.

eligible have made use of the DSSI; these countries, mainly from sub-Saharan Africa, will benefit from postponed debt payments of an estimated US$5 billion.[34]

Nevertheless, there is the concern that the primary purpose of the debt relief offered by public creditors, whether by way of the DSSI or by other means, will be to pay private creditors. David Malpass, the president of the World Bank, had expressed that concern in a recent interview when he said that "there is a risk of free-riding, where private investors get paid in full, in part from the savings countries are getting from their official creditors."[35] As Bolton et al. note,

> if left entirely to their preferences, commercial lenders will behave in a commercially predictable manner even if this means, as it probably will with the DSSI, being tagged with the mildly opprobrious title of free-rider. Some of the emergency financial assistance being provided to the poorest countries by multilateral financial institutions, and some of the debt relief resulting from debt payment suspensions granted by bilateral creditors, will end up being used by the debtor countries to service their commercial obligations. To this extent, the private sector will free ride on the public sector.[36]

What is the scale of private creditor free-riding? As reported by the European Network for Debt and Development, a nonprofit organization, between May and December 2020, the original duration of the DSSI suspension, the sixty-eight eligible countries for which data is available are paying around $10.22 billion to private creditors.[37] The forty-six countries that are receiving debt service suspension are paying $6.94 billion to private creditors. This is $1.64 billion more than what they are receiving from bilateral lenders as debt suspension.

4.4 STANDARD-SETTING AND ORGANIZATIONAL RESILIENCE

The IIF was not the only and certainly was not the first trade association to contribute to the standard-setting process in the realm of sovereign debt. The process has been initiated by a group of trade associations, sometimes referred to as the "Gang of Six," with ICMA taking the helm of that process. ICMA had considerable experience in drafting model clauses and contracts for capital market transactions. The IIF never sought to compete on that front – to the contrary. It engaged in cooperation with ICMA. Still, it made efforts to reorient its activities and governance toward that process by putting forward the proposal that its Global Policy Initiative Department will act as a secretariat to the Group of Trustees and the Principles Consultative

[34] International Monetary Fund, The World Bank, Implementation and Extension of the Debt Service Suspension Initiative (September 28, 2020).

[35] D. Malpass, World Bank: Covid-19 Pushes Poorer Nations: From Recession to Depression, *The Guardian*, August 19, 2020.

[36] P. Bolton et al., Sovereign Debt Standstills: An Update, VoxEU.org (blog), May 28, 2020.

[37] European Network on Debt and Development, The G20 Debt Service Suspension Initiative: Draining out the Titanic with a bucket? (October 2020).

Group. In 2001, it established the Committee on Sovereign Risk Management, which has played an important role in the establishment of the Principles for Stable Capital Flows and Fair Debt Restructuring and the ongoing development of the voluntary contractual approach to sovereign debt restructuring.

The emerging framework provided an opportunity to strengthen the position of the IIF in the sovereign debt space. The IIF's management skillfully capitalized on this opportunity. The IIF's management did not only reorient the organization toward transnational policy initiatives, such as the Basel Accords, but also created and actively fostered the development of standards, such as the Principles for Stable Capital Flows and Fair Debt Restructuring. Standard-setting can thus be viewed as a strategy of organizational resilience – one that builds on and complements the strategies identified by Newman and Posner. In other words, standards are valuable not only to their users but also to the organizations that develop and promote them. It may be simplistic to only view the economic function of standards from the standpoint of its use cases. We should also recognize and examine how the setting of standards contributes to the empowerment of private standard-setting organizations and their advocacy agenda.

4.5 CONCLUSIONS

Trade associations need to retain existing members and acquire new ones to continue to exist. On that count, the IIF has done a remarkable job, which ensured its continued existence and relevance. The goal of this chapter was to cast light on the strategies adopted by the IIF to achieve that goal. Beyond the maintenance of its original function of monitoring sovereign borrowers, the existing literature has identified three strategies of organizational resilience adopted by the IIF during a period of its relative decline in the early 1990s: first, identifying new constituencies; second, reorienting toward transnational policy advocacy; third, adapting its governance accordingly.

In this chapter, I have argued that in the wake of new regulatory developments in the sovereign debt space, the IIF has successfully adopted a fourth strategy of organizational resilience: standard-setting. Specifically, the IIF has reoriented itself toward the endorsement of a contractual approach to sovereign debt restructurings. Furthermore, it has adapted its governance to reflect this new goal. Finally, it led standard-setting activities that helped entrench it as the leading actor in this space. The IIF's role in shaping the private sector's response to the looming sovereign debt crisis induced by the COVID-19 pandemic is an excellent example of that.

What can we make out of the preceding analysis? The key takeaway is that financial trade associations create structural conditions for their relevance through their standard-setting activities. The process through which they create the conditions and maintain their relevance is a vital source of leverage that public policymakers should seek to exploit. US financial institutions may not have the same interests as European or Asian institutions; the buy-side does not have the same interest as the sell-side. Policymakers should seek to exploit these heterogeneous preferences to promote their goals. The IMF's attempt to create the SDRM was a good attempt to at doing just that. Despite its failure, that attempt could serve as an inspiration for how personality and skilled diplomacy can seek to orient private collective action toward the provision of global public goods rather than club goods.

5

Resilience and Change in Private Standard-Setting The Case of LIBOR

Pierre-Hugues Verdier

5.1 INTRODUCTION

The LIBOR scandal stands out as the most striking failure of private financial standard-setting in the post-crisis era. LIBOR, the London Interbank Offered Rate, is a well-known and widely used benchmark interest rate. For decades, it has been used to set rates for financial transactions around the world, ranging from home mortgages to syndicated loans, debt securities, and derivatives. In aggregate, these transactions amount to hundreds of trillions of dollars.[1] In June 2012, a settlement by Barclays Bank with the US Department of Justice (DOJ), Commodity Futures Trading Commission (CFTC), and UK Financial Conduct Authority (FCA) revealed that this key rate had been manipulated for years.[2] The culprits included brokers at smaller firms on the margins of the global financial system but also dozens of traders affiliated with the world's largest banks – the very same banks that sat on LIBOR's governing committee and provided the daily estimates on which it was based.

These revelations caused scandal and generated intense political pressure to reform LIBOR and other financial benchmarks. The LIBOR scandal and its consequences thus provide a crucial case study for the theory articulated in this project's framing chapter.[3] The chapter's central claim is that "crisis events or other

[1] See P.-H. Verdier, *Global Banks on Trial: U.S. Prosecutions and the Remaking of International Finance* (2020), at 15. This chapter draws on the research conducted on the LIBOR case for chapter 2 of *Global Banks on Trial* but omits much of the narrative detail and concentrates on analyzing the case in light of this volume's theoretical approach to the resilience of private authority. The information on the LIBOR transition process was current as of April 2021.

[2] Barclays Bank PLC Admits Misconduct Related to Submissions for the London Interbank Offered Rate and the Euro Interbank Offered Rate and Agrees to Pay $160 Million Penalty (June 27, 2012), www.justice.gov/opa/pr/barclays-bank-plc-admits-misconduct-related-submissions-london-interbank-offered-rate-and.

[3] See P. Delimatsis, "The Resilience of Private Authority in Times of Crisis" in this volume (Chapter 1).

unfortunate regulatory disasters" tend to further empower, rather than weaken, private authority.[4] Private authority's resilience arises from several factors: its transnational nature,[5] regulatory capture,[6] the value of the system to its actors and their preferences,[7] and the focus of public actors on short-term crisis-fighting rather than reform.[8] Because of these factors, "the State and its public agents will rarely exercise coercion vis-à-vis private regulatory bodies and even less reclaim authority to protect the public interest."[9] The ultimate consequences are twofold: perpetuation of "free riding of private ordering"[10] and reinforcement of "the neoliberal orthodoxy premised on the concepts of market competition and an increasingly limited role for the State."[11]

As this chapter will show, the LIBOR scandal constitutes a hard case for the theory. Indeed, it appears to contradict nearly all its central predictions. Public authorities engaged in resolute enforcement against the actors involved in LIBOR manipulation, including corporate criminal cases against several of the world's largest banks that led to penalties of tens of billions of dollars. Prosecutors also brought individual charges against several brokers and bankers, some of which resulted in substantial prison sentences. As a direct consequence of the scandal, regulators replaced LIBOR's private administrator, the British Bankers Association (BBA), which was widely seen as having failed to respond effectively to indications of possible manipulation. Since then, the public sector has played a central role in creating and administering new, more robust benchmark interest rates and encouraging their adoption. As part of this vast effort, public actors are orchestrating multiple public and private organizations, deploying regulatory tools to steer private actors to adopt the new rates, and addressing many complex legal and logistical issues raised by the massive stock of legacy LIBOR contracts.

Overall, the LIBOR scandal and its aftermath amount to what the theory suggests we should not observe: a substantial reassertion of public authority over a crucial element of the global financial infrastructure in response to a crisis. Neither the transnational nature of the benchmark itself, its users, and the manipulation scheme, nor the fact that the scandal coincided in time with the global financial crisis and the European debt crisis prevented this outcome. Moreover, private governance in this area appears to have shown little resilience once the scandal broke. Although one should be careful in drawing conclusions from a single case

4 Ibid., at 22.
5 Ibid., at 27.
6 Ibid., at 27, 42–43.
7 Ibid., at 37.
8 Ibid., at 43.
9 Ibid., at 44.
10 Ibid., at 22, 39.
11 Ibid., at 21.

study, the LIBOR scandal casts doubt on the idea that the expansion of private authority in economic governance is a one-way trend that even major crises fail to reverse. Instead, this case suggests that the equilibrium between public and private authority can and does shift in response to crises, at least in certain circumstances.

Yet, in other respects, the LIBOR case illustrates the phenomena described in Chapter 1. In the period that preceded the first settlement by a major global bank of US criminal charges in June 2012, the relationship among the public and private bodies involved in LIBOR oversight was characterized by a collaborative approach and a clear preference on the part of public authorities for private design, management, and oversight of financial benchmarks. This remained true even after the first indications of possible manipulation became public in mid-2008. At the time, public bodies, their attention consumed by crisis-fighting, showed limited interest in the problem and underwrote the BBA's tepid and ultimately ineffective reforms. In stark contrast, the Barclays criminal settlement precipitated much broader public intervention in the form of a wide-ranging enforcement campaign and fundamental LIBOR reforms.

This chapter argues that the intervention of a different set of public actors – namely prosecutors and the enforcement arm of the CFTC, a derivatives market regulator – is the key factor that explains this stark difference in outcomes before and after 2012. These public actors' priorities and incentives differ substantially from those of those public actors – namely prudential banking regulators and central banks – traditionally involved in overseeing private standard-setting in the banking industry. Their generalist nature and lack of close cooperative relationship with the industry make them less vulnerable to capture.[12] Because their responsibilities do not include crisis-fighting, they can concentrate on investigating and prosecuting misconduct. And at least for US agencies, the transnational nature of the relevant market poses little obstacle to effective enforcement. Thus, many of the factors described in the framing chapter that perpetuate the resilience of private standard-setting cease to apply when these public actors take center stage.

These considerations suggest that the phenomena described in the framing chapter are characteristic of a particular version of private-public sector relationships, one that reflects preference for private ordering and finds its proponents in agencies whose mission centers on prudential oversight and financial stability. To the extent that this approach creates blind spots, the intervention of other public actors is key to restoring the balance between private standard-setting and effective public oversight. At the same time, one should not expect complete replacement of private standard-setting by public management, even in response to a major crisis, in areas like benchmarks where widespread adoption by private actors is essential to

[12] See M. A. Livermore and R. L Revesz, Can Executive Review Help Prevent Capture?, in *Preventing Regulatory Capture: Special Interest Influence and How to Limit it* (D. Carpenter and D. A. Moss eds., 2013), 434–437.

achieve the benefits of the standard. Thus, the transition to the new benchmarks that will replace LIBOR involves collaboration among central banks, regulators, market participants, and industry bodies. It takes place, however, under a conspicuous shadow of public authority.

Section 5.2 briefly describes the evolution of LIBOR and its functioning prior to the global financial crisis. Section 5.3 examines how the relevant private and public actors, most centrally the BBA and UK authorities, reacted to the first public reports of potential LIBOR manipulation in mid-2008. Section 5.4 examines the June 2012 Barclays settlement and the broader enforcement campaign against LIBOR manipulation, focusing on the role of US prosecutors and market regulators. Section 5.5 describes the regulatory aftermath of the scandal, including immediate steps to reform the LIBOR-setting process and impose new regulation on benchmarks and longer-term reforms that will replace LIBOR with publicly managed, transaction-based benchmark rates. Section 5.6 concludes.

5.2 ORIGINS AND EVOLUTION OF LIBOR

LIBOR grew out of private initiative in the offshore US dollar market. As US dollar holdings overseas grew in the 1950s and 1960s, a vibrant interbank lending market emerged, centered in London. Foreign holders of US dollars deposited them in London banks, including branches of major banks from around the world, which lent dollars to each other through overnight and term deposits. Increasingly, they also lent dollars to end users, funding these loans through interbank deposits. The growth of this market generated demand for standardization of contract terms. One such crucial term was the interest rate, as banks sought a uniform way to link the floating rate paid by borrowers to their own funding costs. Initially, individual loan contracts created mechanisms to aggregate the interbank borrowing rates reported by major London banks. In the 1980s, the BBA consolidated the process and began publishing a single set of rates.

To generate LIBOR for each reported currency and maturity, the BBA received daily submissions from a panel of large banks active in the London interbank market. Each bank submitted an estimate of "the rate at which an individual contributor panel bank could borrow funds, were it to do so by asking for and then accepting interbank offers in reasonable market size just prior to 11:00 London time."[13] The BBA generated LIBOR by eliminating submissions in the top and bottom quartile and averaging the remaining submissions. The rules were designed and the process overseen by a BBA committee composed of representatives of the contributing banks. Thus, the initial creation and management of LIBOR required

[13] British Bankers' Association, Understanding the Construction and Operation of BBA LIBOR: Strengthening for the Future (2008), para. 12.2.

little official assistance or public imprimatur: an industry group simply aggregated and published market information for the benefit of its members.

In doing so, these private actors provided a public good: LIBOR was published in leading financial newspapers and could be used by anyone. Because it was set independently, it circumvented disputes that might arise between parties to a contract as to whether the party responsible for setting the rate did so accurately. It also reduced search and transaction costs for market participants by facilitating rate comparisons and avoiding the need to design a rate-setting mechanism for each contract.[14] Network effects also meant that using the benchmark became more attractive as more market participants did so. Unsurprisingly, LIBOR came to dominate lending markets worldwide, including many transactions and products with no direct link to the London interbank US dollar market.[15]

For decades, the private sector managed LIBOR without much public intervention or oversight. There seemed to be little concern among regulators, the BBA, or market participants that glitches could emerge. However, potentially significant problems were lurking below the surface. Because the contributing banks traded numerous assets whose value was linked to LIBOR, they had significant financial stakes in the daily LIBOR fixings. This was even more so for individual traders or desks within the bank, whose positions would likely be more concentrated. The fact that representatives of these same banks made and oversaw the process generated potential conflicts of interest. The risk of inaccurate or biased submissions was exacerbated by the fact that they were not based on actual transactions but on estimates by traders of the bank's borrowing costs for the relevant currency and maturity. Because many currencies and maturities were illiquid, data from actual transactions provided limited discipline on submitters' discretion.

Bankers often asserted that LIBOR's design ensured that it could not be manipulated.[16] Because outliers were excluded, it was said, a single bank could not meaningfully affect the rate by skewing its submissions. Although this belief was demonstrably false,[17] it appeared to be widely shared among market participants and regulators. This attitude reflected faith in the self-correcting nature of markets: the BBA and reporting banks had incentives to preserve LIBOR's franchise value and therefore to provide effective oversight. UK officials also saw LIBOR as a success story, cementing the centrality of London in worldwide credit markets.

[14] D. Duffie and J. C. Stein, Reforming LIBOR and Other Financial Market Benchmarks (2015) 29 *Journal of Economic Perspectives* 191, at 193–196.

[15] Verdier, *supra* note 1, at 45; Duffie and Stein, *supra* note 14, at 198.

[16] See L. Vaughan and G. Finch, *The Fix: How Bankers Lied, Cheated and Colluded to Rig the World's Most Important Number* (2017), at 17.

[17] P. Gandhi et al., Financial Market Misconduct and Public Enforcement: The Case of Libor Manipulation (2019) 65 *Management Science* 5268.

5.3 THE FINANCIAL CRISIS AND THE BBA'S REFORMS

The first signs of trouble with LIBOR emerged during the financial crisis. In April 2008, after the collapse of US investment bank Bear Stearns, news reports emerged suggesting that major banks might be misreporting their borrowing costs to avoid appearing to be under stress. In fact, studies showed, LIBOR submissions were very close to each other, which experts saw as evidence that they were inaccurate.[18]

These news reports prompted a first round of LIBOR reform. Under pressure from regulators and market participants, the BBA announced that it would review its rules on LIBOR reporting and increase its efforts to detect and sanction inaccurate submissions. It soon became clear, however, that the BBA was unwilling to undertake any major reforms to the LIBOR-setting process or its governance structure. Senior BBA officials declared that any problems were minor and transitory, accused critics of misunderstanding the process, and reiterated that the LIBOR methodology ensured that the rate was accurate. After several weeks, the organization announced that there would be no immediate changes and made vague promises to strengthen LIBOR oversight, with details to be announced later.

The BBA's inaction did not go unnoticed by regulators. Upon learning of it, Mervyn King, the Bank of England's governor, responded to a Bank official: "This seems entirely inadequate. What should we do?"[19] Timothy Geithner, the head of the Federal Reserve Bank of New York, who had also become concerned about LIBOR's integrity, sent King a list of proposed reforms. The proposed changes, while modest, would have addressed some of the most salient vulnerabilities.[20] UK. authorities, however, proved unwilling to press the BBA to undertake such substantive reforms, let alone to increase public oversight. They agreed with the BBA's plan to conduct a months-long consultation. During that process, virtually all the FRBNY's proposals were quietly dropped. In November 2008, as the financial crisis raged, the BBA announced minimal reforms, effectively promising that its existing committee would oversee submissions more closely under the existing rules.[21] Although several commentators criticized the reforms as insufficient, UK and US regulators appeared to accept them.

[18] C. Whitehouse and M. Mollenkamp, Study Casts Doubt on Key Rate, *Wall Street Journal* (May 29, 2008) www.wsj.com/articles/SB121200703762027135.

[19] Further Information and Correspondence in Relation to the BBA LIBOR Review in 2008 (July 20, 2012) (transcript of Mervin King, Governor, Bank of England's written comments on an email entitled "Result of BBA review: just 'strengthen the oversight of BBA Libor'" [May 30, 2008]).

[20] They included measures such as auditing bank submissions, reducing the number of reported maturities, adding more banks to the panels, and randomly selecting a subset of banks to generate daily rates.

[21] The reforms contemplated that the committee would exercise more probing review of banks' submissions, issue warnings, and possibly sanction repeat offenders by excluding them from the panel.

To this point, the story of the LIBOR scandal seems in line with the theory proposed by the framing chapter. Shaken by a major crisis that undermined LIBOR's credibility, the BBA adapted to deflect the scandal. After delaying action, it adopted largely cosmetic reforms that preserved private authority over LIBOR. Public actors proved willing to accede to this outcome. As predicted, their intense focus on crisis-fighting facilitated the BBA's approach: UK and US regulators and central bankers were consumed by the growing financial crisis. Beyond this, internal discussions in the UK government reveal officials' strong reluctance to impose public regulation or oversight and a corresponding preference for a private sector solution, supporting the notion that "cognitive capture" may play a role in perpetuating private authority. The benchmark's transnational nature also inhibited public intervention: US and UK regulators, while appearing to cooperate, in fact clashed. The latter, including officials at the Bank of England and the Financial Services Authority (FSA), apparently believed that the FRBNY was trying to exploit the crisis to undermine the "London-centric" nature of LIBOR. They thus dismissed its suggestions and supported the BBA's modest reforms.

5.4 THE BARCLAYS SETTLEMENT AND ITS AFTERMATH

The Bank of England, FRBNY, and FSA were not the only public actors looking into LIBOR manipulation. The CFTC had launched an investigation, later joined by the DOJ, which culminated in April 2012 in a first criminal settlement with Barclays. Under a non-prosecution agreement, the bank agreed to pay $453 million in penalties.[22]

The settlement revealed extensive misconduct relating to LIBOR setting. As journalists and economists had suspected, Barclays and other banks had understated their borrowing costs during the financial crisis to avoid appearing financially distressed, thus skewing LIBOR downward. In addition, multiple traders and brokers had conspired to fix LIBOR to benefit their trading positions, often at their own customers' expense. At Barclays, derivatives traders routinely asked LIBOR submitters to skew the bank's submissions in their favor, taking advantage of the submitter's relatively junior position and lack of effective compliance oversight. This revelation further undermined LIBOR's credibility.

Barclays was far from the only bank involved in LIBOR manipulation. The bank's leadership apparently hoped that, by settling first, they would minimize the scandal's fallout. That strategy proved a failure: the settlement triggered an enormous scandal that soon spun out of control, forcing Barclays' CEO, COO, and chairman to resign in short order. The public bodies that had approved LIBOR reforms in 2008,

[22] Barclays Bank PLC Admits Misconduct Related to Submissions for the London Interbank Offered Rate and the Euro Interbank Offered Rate and Agrees to Pay $160 Million Penalty, *supra* note 3.

especially the Bank of England and the FSA, came under heavy criticism. The LIBOR scandal triggered parliamentary hearings in the United Kingdom, Congressional hearings in the United States, and an internal review by the FSA. Eventually, the FSA was broken up and its market oversight and enforcement functions were transferred to the newly created Financial Conduct Authority (FCA).

Barclays was the opening salvo of a broader enforcement campaign by the DOJ and CFTC. In subsequent years, US authorities brought criminal and regulatory charges against several other global banks, including UBS, RBS, Lloyds, Deutsche Bank, and Citigroup, imposing fines and penalties of more than $4.5 billion. This enforcement campaign was part of a larger trend of US criminal prosecutions targeting major international banks for a range of violations, including benchmark manipulation, tax evasion, and sanctions violations, that resulted in fines and penalties of more than $34 billion.[23] In subsequent years, prosecutors and regulatory agencies in other jurisdictions joined this enforcement campaign. In several cases, home state regulators participated in US-led enforcement actions; but non-US governments also grew more assertive in initiating their own actions. Investigations spread to related markets and benchmarks, most notably foreign exchange.

Several features characterized this campaign and distinguished these actions from previous regulatory enforcement: the use of broad criminal statutes to reach misconduct not explicitly targeted by more specific regulatory regimes; the use of criminal investigation techniques, such as whistleblower rewards and plea bargain offers to witnesses; and much higher penalties. Another notable feature is the prosecutions' explicit orientation toward organizational reform and self-regulation. US criminal enforcement policies adopted in the late 1990s and expanded since explicitly aim at providing incentives for organizations to establish effective compliance, internal investigation, and reporting policies and procedures in order to mitigate punishment.[24] In addition, prosecutors often impose extensive compliance obligations on organizations that settle criminal cases, requiring adoption of new internal policies, hiring of new staff, and external oversight by corporate monitors or regulatory agencies.[25]

These corporate prosecutions can also be accompanied by individual criminal charges. Prosecutors in the United States and the United Kingdom brought such charges against numerous individuals embroiled in the LIBOR scandal. Tom Hayes, the ringleader of a group of traders and brokers who repeatedly manipulated LIBOR,

[23] Verdier, *supra* note 1, at 8.

[24] J. Arlen and R. Kraakman, Controlling Corporate Misconduct: An Analysis of Corporate Liability Regimes (1997) 72 *NYU Law Review* 687.

[25] B. L. Garrett, Structural Reform Prosecution (2007) 93 *Virginia Law Review* 853; B. L. Garrett, *Too Big to Jail* (2014); J. Arlen and M. Kahan, Corporate Governance Regulation through Nonprosecution (2017) 84 *University of Chicago Law Review* 323; P.-H. Verdier, The New Financial Extraterritoriality (2019) 87 *George Washington Law Review* 239.

was found guilty and sentenced to fourteen years in prison in 2015.[26] In total, at least fifty individuals were indicted, of which several pleaded guilty. Others were acquitted, including six brokers accused of conspiring with Hayes. Although prosecutors found it difficult to extradite individuals,obtain convictions, and sustain them on appeal, the LIBOR scandal represented a significant shift from the lack of post-crisis individual prosecutions.

In sum, beginning with the Barclays case in 2012, prosecutors and regulators engaged in robust enforcement campaign against LIBOR manipulation, which went well beyond the public sector's tepid reaction to indications of manipulation in 2008. This campaign constituted a significant assertion of public authority in an area that had erstwhile been left almost completely to private standard-setting and oversight.

The deterrent effect of the enforcement actions by itself amounted to a form of re-regulation. A recent study found no indication of manipulation by major banks after 2010, which the researchers attributed to that deterrent effect.[27] This is consistent with the idea that, in areas where regulation aims to discipline self-serving behavior and internalize costs, private rule-making is unlikely to be stable unless some actor is available to punish deviations and impose a "penalty default rule."[28] While the BBA's own enforcement mechanism clearly did not fulfill that function, public enforcement of the private standards – in this case through criminal prosecutions of firms and traders who manipulated the process in their own interest – may provide such a background penalty default even without further public regulation.

In any event, prosecutors and regulators did not limit themselves to imposing fines and other sanctions. They also used settlements as vehicles to require banks to implement reforms to improve the integrity of their LIBOR submission process, consistent with their compliance-oriented approach to the resolution of other corporate criminal cases. Finally, as will be seen in Section 5.5, the enforcement campaign and the publicity that surrounded it provided the impetus for broader reforms that substantially increased public oversight of benchmarks and aim to eventually eliminate LIBOR altogether.

What explains this shift in the public sector's approach? The answer lies in the identity of the public actors involved. The central actors in the enforcement campaign that began in 2012 were not central banks and specialized regulatory agencies but prosecutors and, to some extent, the enforcement arms of market regulators.

26 An appeal court later reduced Hayes's sentence to eleven years.

27 Gandhi et al., *supra* note 17.

28 T. Büthe, Private Regulation in the Global Economy: A (P)Review (2010) 12 *Business and Politics* 1; T. Büthe, Global Private Politics: A Research Agenda (2010) 12 *Business and Politics* 1.

The factors that tend to inhibit robust public response to crises or governance failures arising from private standard-setting are much less applicable to these actors. Unlike central bankers and banking regulators, prosecutors and market conduct enforcers have little or no role in immediate crisis-fighting; on the contrary, because of their more direct lines of political accountability, crises generate incentives for them to be seen as acting resolutely. As part of generalist law enforcement agencies, prosecutors are much less vulnerable than specialized agencies to capture – cognitive or otherwise – by a particular regulated industry. They also have little or no stake in fostering private governance for its own sake.

Finally, the transnational nature of private authority matters less to these actors: unlike central bankers and specialized agencies, which must maintain continuing collaborative relationships with regulated entities, industry organizations, and their own foreign counterparts, prosecutors and enforcement agencies are accustomed to acting unilaterally where needed. In the case of US authorities, the broad extraterritorial reach of the relevant US laws and the country's leverage over private actors – through its control of access to US dollar payments and other critical infrastructure – often allows them to bring successful enforcement actions even without meaningful foreign cooperation.

These factors suggest that the resilience of private authority, at least in international finance, is driven in significant part by the nature of the incentives of the specialized agencies that traditionally oversee financial institutions. In LIBOR and other cases, the shift in initiative within the public sector from these agencies to prosecutors and market regulators undermined the resilience strategies of private actors like the BBA and the banks themselves. That shift may be part of a broader trend, apparent since the financial crisis, by which areas such as international finance that were traditionally seen as effectively beyond the purview of ordinary law enforcement are losing the benefit of this exceptionalism.

5.5 REFORMING BENCHMARKS, REPLACING LIBOR

The Barclays settlement and subsequent prosecutions, by exposing widespread LIBOR manipulation, made it clear that the BBA's 2008 reforms had been ineffective and that public oversight was lacking. Ultimately, it convinced policymakers that continued private management of this vital benchmark was untenable and that it must be replaced altogether. Thus, LIBOR reform proceeded in two stages, the second of which remains ongoing.

The first stage followed immediately upon the Barclays settlement. The UK government appointed Martin Wheatley, an experienced regulator, to conduct an independent review of LIBOR. The report, released later in 2012, recommended a series of reforms amounting to substantially stronger public oversight. They included introducing new legislation to regulate LIBOR-setting, including specific criminal penalties for benchmark manipulation; transferring LIBOR to a new administrator selected by public tender; and discontinuing LIBOR for insufficiently liquid currencies and maturities.[29]

Most of Wheatley's recommendations were incorporated in the Financial Services Act 2012.[30] LIBOR management was transferred from the BBA to a new operator, an affiliate of the Intercontinental Exchange (ICE), by public tender.[31] European authorities also reacted: the Market Abuse Directive was amended to cover benchmark manipulation and the European Commission introduced a proposal that led to the adoption in 2016 of a regulation imposing extensive oversight of financial benchmarks.[32] IOSCO, for its part, adopted global principles for benchmark administrators.[33] The LIBOR scandal thus led directly to a substantial assertion of public authority, not only over LIBOR itself but over financial benchmarks generally.

Reforms, however, could not stop at this increased oversight. The scandal had exposed deeper weaknesses in LIBOR: manipulation was not just the result of poor governance but of the fact that the underlying market for interbank dollar lending had shrunk. As that trend continued, even the historically more active currencies and maturities would increasingly be based on estimates rather than actual transactions, threatening the accuracy of the benchmark and making it more vulnerable to manipulation. A 2014 report by the Financial Stability Board recommended reforms to financial benchmarks to base them on actual transactions rather than discretionary estimates; it further recommended the creation of entirely new, transaction-based risk-free reference rates to replace flawed benchmarks like LIBOR.[34]

In response to these recommendations, a series of national and regional coordinating committees were created to develop accurate and useful risk-free benchmark rates that could be used in a variety of financial instruments, and to foster their adoption. The US Alternative Reference Rates Committee, convened in 2014, selected the Secured Overnight Financial Rate (SOFR) as the main US dollar risk-free rate. Unlike LIBOR, SOFR is managed by a public sector entity, the FRBNY, and based on actual transactions in overnight repos on US treasuries, the world's largest funding market. Among the risk-free rates adopted by committees in

[29] The Wheatley Review of LIBOR: Final Report (HM Treasury 2012).

[30] Financial Services Act 2012, c. 21 (UK).

[31] While the ICE is also a private operator, unlike the BBA it is not managed by the banks who provide the submissions and stand to benefit from manipulation.

[32] Directive 2014/57/EU of the European Parliament and of the Council of 16 April 2014 on criminal sanctions for market abuse (market abuse directive) [2014] OJ L173/179; Regulation (EU) 2016/1011 of the European Parliament and of the Council of 8 June 2016 on indices used as benchmarks in financial instruments and financial contracts or to measure the performance of investment funds and amending Directives 2008/48/EC and 2014/17/EU and Regulation (EU) No 596/2014 [2016] OJ L171/1.

[33] Principles for Financial Benchmarks: Final Report (July 2013), www.iosco.org/library/pubdocs/pdf/IOSCOPD415.pdf.

[34] Reforming Major Interest Rate Benchmarks (July 22, 2014) www.fsb.org/wp-content/uploads/r_140722.pdf.

other jurisdictions, several will also be publicly managed, such as SONIA (Bank of England), STR (European Central Bank), and TONAR (Bank of Japan).[35]

The initial expectation was that these rates would coexist with the reformed LIBOR and similar IBORs for other currencies and locations. In July 2017, that expectation changed radically. In a widely reported speech, Andrew Bailey, the FCA's chief executive, explained that despite improvements to LIBOR, it was becoming increasingly unsustainable and would need to be phased out. Panel banks, he said, "feel understandable discomfort about providing submissions based on judgements with so little actual borrowing activity against which to validate those judgements."[36] While the FCA could use its regulatory powers to compel panel banks to continue to provide LIBOR submissions, "it is not only potentially unsustainable, but also undesirable, for market participants to rely indefinitely on reference rates that do not have active underlying markets to support them."[37] Accordingly, the FCA did not intend to compel submissions after the end of 2021, meaning that most or all LIBOR rates would end on that date. Bailey's remarks were widely perceived as sounding LIBOR's death knell. The predicted end of LIBOR in 2021 raised serious concerns as trillions of dollars of contracts worldwide still referenced the benchmark, few of which had workable fallback provisions.

These events triggered a second, much more ambitious stage of reform: the enormous task of shifting market practices – including trillions of dollars in legacy contracts – to new benchmarks and ensuring that these new rates would be robust and useful to market participants. The FCA's announcements proved insufficient by themselves to shift market practices. Many participants apparently assumed that LIBOR would in fact continue after 2021 or that substitute synthetic LIBOR rates would be published that could be used seamlessly for existing contracts. The estimated volume of financial contracts based on USD LIBOR actually increased between the announcement and early 2021, reaching $223 trillion.

Regulators responded by acting to compel market participants to accelerate the transition away from LIBOR. The FCA issued further statements making it increasingly clear that market participants should not expect LIBOR to continue, culminating in March 2021 when it announced that most LIBOR settings would cease at the end of 2021 and that even the most widely used US dollar rates would cease in June 2023.[38] That statement added that even if synthetic LIBOR rates were published after these dates, they would not be considered representative, thus prohibiting their use in new contracts. US financial regulators issued a joint supervisory

[35] A. Schrimpf and V. Sushko, Beyond LIBOR: A Primer on the New Benchmark Rates [2019] *BIS Quarterly Review* 29.

[36] A. Bailey, The Future of LIBOR (July 26, 2017), www.fca.org.uk/news/speeches/the-future-of-libor.

[37] Ibid.

[38] Announcements on the End of LIBOR (March 4, 2021) www.fca.org.uk/news/press-releases/announcements-end-libor.

letter in November 2020 warning that issuing new LIBOR-based contracts after the end of 2021 "would create safety and soundness risks" and could lead to regulatory action.[39] In addition to stopping the issuance of new LIBOR-based contracts, regulators also required that market participants develop plans to include fallback language in existing contracts that may be affected by LIBOR's cessation.[40]

Regulators, the ARRC, and the private sector cooperated in designing and implementing contractual fallback language for existing contracts. The International Swaps and Derivatives Association (ISDA), an industry association heavily involved in developing model contracts for swaps and other financial derivatives, issued an IBOR Fallbacks Protocol under which participating firms agree to amend their existing LIBOR-based derivatives to add fallback provisions.[41] The ARRC and its multiple working groups issued model fallback clauses for numerous categories of LIBOR-based contracts, including mortgages, business loans, debt securities, and securitizations.[42] For legacy contracts that parties are unable to amend, the ARRC lobbied the New York State legislature to adopt legislation to automatically switch to a prescribed fallback rate upon termination of the benchmark.

Perhaps the most challenging aspect of the LIBOR transition has been to make available a full set of term rates that can substitute for LIBOR. SOFR, for example, is an overnight rate: it measures the interest rate charged on overnight lending transactions secured by US Treasury securities. Because it is based on a large volume of actual transactions, it is very robust. But it does not directly substitute for the principal use of LIBOR, which is to prospectively set the interest rate for a given period, for example, three months, under a contract. To generate term rates based on SOFR that are also robust and transaction-based, the administrator must have access to a pool of relevant transactions. The market for such transactions – in this case, SOFR-based swaps – is still in its infancy. The ARRC and regulators have also tried to foster its development, and as of the fall of 2020 the latest signs were encouraging, but it remains much smaller than the market for LIBOR-based swaps.

For that reason, the contractual fallback clauses mentioned above typically do not prescribe a specific alternative term rate to be used upon LIBOR termination. Instead, they incorporate into the relevant contracts language such as "the forward-looking term rate … that has been selected or recommended by the

39 SR 20-27, Interagency Statement on LIBOR transition (November 30, 2020), see also SR 21-7, Assessing Supervised Institutions' Plans to Transition Away from the Use of LIBOR (March 9, 2021); see also FCA, Letter to CEOs re: Firms' Preparations for Transition from LIBOR to Risk-Free Rates (September 19, 2018).

40 SR 21-7, Assessing Supervised Institutions' Plans to Transition Away from the Use of LIBOR (March 9, 2021)

41 ISDA 2020 IBOR Fallbacks Protocol (October 23, 2020), www.isda.org/protocol/isda-2020-ibor-fallbacks-protocol.

42 Fallback Contract Language, www.newyorkfed.org/arrc/fallbacks-contract-language.

Relevant Governmental Body."[43] While this language reflects continuing uncertainty about the availability and exact nature of SOFR-based term rates, it also represents a remarkable conferral of authority to the public sector to effectively rewrite the terms of hundreds of trillions of dollars of financial contracts at the stroke of a pen.

5.6 CONCLUSION

The LIBOR scandal and its aftermath appear to be a clear case in which a major failure of private regulation led directly to a substantial reassertion of public authority over a vital aspect of the international financial infrastructure. As such, it calls for qualification of the conjecture in the framing chapter that the shift from public to private authority constitutes a one-way ratchet that even severe crises cannot reverse and even tend to accelerate.

At the same time, the LIBOR case also demonstrates several tendencies described by the framing chapter: the difficulty of coordinating public regulation of transnational markets, governmental focus on immediate crisis-fighting measures rather than long-term reform, and ideological preference for market-based regulation. These tendencies, however, dominate only as long as the main public actors involved are those – principally bank regulatory agencies and central banks – traditionally charged with prudential oversight of the banking industry. The intervention of public actors with different objectives and incentives – namely prosecutors and market regulation agencies – marks a major shift in the nature and scope of public regulation and oversight.

These observations suggest that the balance between public and private authority in regulating markets can indeed adjust in response to crises and failures. A key factor may be the existence and active involvement of public actors outside the traditional regulatory paradigm and less bound by the tendencies outlined above. In other words, the case argues for private authority to be overseen not by one but by multiple pairs of eyes in the public sector.

To be sure, one must be wary of drawing general conclusions from a single case. The future of LIBOR remains uncertain, and new opportunities for manipulation or other unintended consequences of the reforms may arise. Even if the transition proves entirely successful, specific features of the LIBOR case may not recur in other areas. For instance, the long-term decline of the underlying lending market on which LIBOR submissions were based and the limited benefits and increased risks

[43] ARRC Recommendations Regarding More Robust Fallback Language for New Issuances of LIBOR Floating Rate Notes (April 25, 2019), www.newyorkfed.org/medialibrary/Microsites/arrc/files/2019/FRN_Fallback_Language.pdf. The term "Relevant Governmental Body" is defined as "the Federal Reserve Board and/or the Federal Reserve Bank of New York, or a committee officially endorsed or convened by the Federal Reserve Board and/or the Federal Reserve Bank of New York or any successor thereto."

of participation for the contributing banks created demand for public involvement in coordinating the transition. Market participants may not have been as eager to participate in public-led reforms of a vibrant benchmark.

In addition, while prosecutors and enforcement-focused agencies can provide a strong impetus for reform, they can only respond to a limited class of crises, namely those that involve misconduct that can credibly be characterized as criminal. Where private authority generates other kinds of problems or externalities, these actors may lack the ability to intervene. Finally, other public actors may lack the resources or influence of US prosecutors and regulators, raising the risk that negative impacts of private authority on the public outside powerful countries may go unchecked. The circumstances in which crises may favor expansion or retrenchment of private authority thus constitute a rich area for further research.

6

The Basel Committee on Banking Supervision in the Post-crisis International Governance of Banking Regulation

Continuity Despite Weakness

Matteo Ortino

6.1 INTRODUCTION

The regulatory regime applicable to the banking sector consists of multiple sets of principles, rules, and standards: international, regional, and national law; hard law and soft law; public law, private law, and private rules; political and technical decisions. Although to varying degrees, each component of that regime plays a part in the setting of goals to be pursued and standards of conduct to be followed. As the components or/and their combination change so does the regime as a whole and thus its functioning. The regulatory regime applicable to the banking sector can therefore be thought of as an ecosystem characterized by diversity and interdependence.

But is the ecosystem of banking regulation also characterized by resilience – another essential characteristic of ecosystems? What drives the evolution of that regime and what explains its resilience, particularly in the face of a crisis, such as the financial crisis of 2007–2008?

The remainder of this chapter is organized as follows: first, we introduce the Basel Committee on Banking Supervision and the standards its members develop. Second, we survey the failures of the Basel regime leading to the global financial crisis of 2007–2008 and some possible explanations thereof. Then, we discuss the reasons why the fundamental features of the regime are still in place even after its evident inadequacies and why the reforms adopted in the wake of the crisis are a way to safeguard the resilience of such features.

6.2 THE BASEL COMMITTEE OF BANKING SUPERVISION (BCBS) AND THE REGULATORY REGIME FOR BANKING

The cross-border trade of goods and services, foreign investment, and finance as well as other activities central to the functioning of the global economy are each governed by distinct legal and regulatory regimes. All those regimes carry out the same three basic regulatory functions, that is, rule or standard-setting, monitoring, and enforcement. However, the way in which these functions are discharged differs a great deal. While the regimes in trade and in foreign investment mainly rely on binding international law, the most important components of the regulatory regime in banking are international soft law and national law.[1] The structure of the international financial architecture is characterized by what has been called "Transnational Regulatory Networks,"[2] or "loose network of soft-law standard setters,"[3] or "International regulatory forums."[4] The ecosystem that has the Basel Committee of Banking Supervision (BCBS or Basel Committee) at its epicenter is emblematic of the regulatory regime in banking.

The BCBS is the most important international standard-setting body in the field of financial regulation. Its remit concerns banking regulation and particularly prudential requirements of internationally active banks.

Established in 1974 by the central bank governors of the G10 group of countries, it currently has forty-five members from twenty-eight jurisdictions, consisting of central banks and authorities with formal responsibility for the supervision of banking business. Therefore, it is composed not of governmental representatives but of officials from domestic technocratic authorities; however, representatives from political institutions such as the European Commission sit as observers, a status that in practice is equivalent to proper membership. The internal organizational structure of the Basel Committee comprises the Committee (the ultimate decision-making body), Groups, Working Groups, and Task Forces, the chairman and the secretariat. The Committee can be analyzed against the three regulatory functions of standard-setting, monitoring, and enforcement.

The Basel Committee's main objective is financial stability. Its Charter states that its "mandate is to strengthen the regulation, supervision and practices of banks worldwide with the purpose of enhancing financial stability" (Section 1).[5] A minimum harmonization of national or regional banking laws and regulation protects fair competition and particularly prevents banks that are subject to adequate prudential requirements from being at a competitive disadvantage relative to banks coming instead from more permissive jurisdictions. In this way, a related objective is being pursued by the BCBS, that is, to prevent a dangerous and unfair inter-jurisdictional competition in laxity in the field of banking.

1 R. Lastra, Do We Need A World Financial Organization? (2014) 17 *Journal of International Economic Law* 787; C. Brummer, Why Soft Law Dominates International Finance – and Not Trade (2010) 13 *Journal of International Economic Law*, 623.

2 E. Avgouleas, *Governance of Global Financial Markets: The Law, the Economics, the Politics* (2012) 2; A.-M. Slaughter, *A New World Order* (2004).

3 Lastra, *supra* note 1, at 795.

4 See, for example, N. Moloney, Institutional Design: The International Architecture, in *The Oxford Handbook of Financial regulation* (N. Moloney et al. eds., 2015), 129, at 145.

5 Basel Committee Charter, www.bis.org/bcbs/charter.htm.

The BCBS has become a synonym for powerful international sources of informal law. The principles and standards that are adopted by the Committee are widely implemented at the domestic level, not only in its members' legal systems but also in third-country jurisdictions. Informality is a feature characterizing the very nature of such an entity, as well as its decision-making processes and the legal nature of the standards it adopts. Its Charter is not an international treaty. The BCBS is not an international organization, nor does it possess any legal personality; agreements reached internally by its members do not formally constitute a source of law. As explicitly stated in its Charter, "The BCBS does not possess any formal supranational authority. Its decisions do not have legal force. Rather, the BCBS relies on its members' commitments, as described in Section 5, to achieve its mandate." The BCBS represents an international forum for the "negotiation" and development of principles and standards aimed at protecting a sound international financial system.

The BCBS is part of a wider system, composed of international and national principles/rules/standards and actors (BCBS-system). The BCBS' standards, as essential as they are, constitute only a segment of a composite legal regime, in which further important and complementary roles are played inter alia by the Group of 20 (G20)[6], the Financial Stability Board (FSB),[7] and national authorities. The G20, the FSB, and the BCBS are all sources of decisions meant to be implemented by domestic regulators in their own legal system.[8] In line with the organizing principle of specialization and division of labor, each plays a different role in the regulation of banking markets.[9] Collectively, they provide some of the legislative, executive, and technical components of financial regulation that find their way into domestic jurisdictions and applied to financial institutions by domestic regulators. The G20 "specializes" in taking meta political decisions, while the FSB focuses on proposing

6 The G20 is a forum for discussion of financial and economic issues between a mix of the world's largest advanced and emerging economies, representing about two-thirds of the world's population, 85 percent of global gross domestic product, and over 75 percent of global trade. The G20 started in 1999 as a meeting of finance ministers and central bank governors in the aftermath of the Asian financial crisis. Since 2008, the G20 Leaders' Summit is held annually, comprising prime minister/heads of state, finance ministers, and central bankers. Such summits have played a key role in responding to the global financial crisis.

7 The FSB was established in 2009 when the G20 London Summit took the decision to transform the Financial Stability Forum into a body with an enhanced institutional role with regard to safeguarding the stability of the international financial system. The statutory objective of FSB is to coordinate multi-sectorial regulatory activities of domestic regulators directly and through international networks of regulators (e.g., IOSCO and BCBS). Compared with the G20, the FSB has more of an executive role. As requested by the G20, the FSB also develops general principles and standards on specific topics.

8 D. Zaring, The Emerging Post-crisis Paradigm for International Financial Regulation, in *Comparative Law and Regulation. Understanding the Global Regulatory Process* (D. Zaring and F. Bignami eds., 2016), 497, at 502.

9 M. Ortino, The Governance of Global Banking in the Face of Complexity 2019 *Journal of International Economic Law* 1.

and implementing these decisions by coordinating technical decision markers, and, finally, the BCBS works to articulate prudential banking regulatory and supervisory standards. In 1988, the Committee adopted the Capital Accord, also known as "Basel I," which underwent a radical revision in 2004, known as "Basel II." Finally, in response to the 2007–2008 global financial crisis, the Basel Committee members approved a comprehensive package of reforms collectively known as "Basel III." These reforms have sought to address problems in the banking system exposed by the global financial crisis, including unsustainable levels of leverage, insufficient high-quality loss-absorbing capital, excessive variability of banks' modeled risk-weighted assets, a mispricing of liquidity risk, and the buildup of system-wide risks.

Since its creation, there has been a progressive expansion of the BCBS' mandate, of its membership as well as of its capacity to influence the content of domestic banking regulation and supervision. This trend has continued even after the global financial crisis, which as it is well known was triggered in the banking sector. Interestingly, in the wake of the crisis, there has been a further increase in the BCBS' powers and scope of influence, notwithstanding the fact that its standards not only were not able to prevent the crisis but in fact contributed to its outbreak and spread. The Basel Committee was in fact part of the problem, not part of the solution. According to Rodrik, the BCBS

> has produced largely inadequate agreements. The first set of recommendations (Basel I) encouraged risky short-term borrowing and may have played a role in precipitating the Asian financial crisis. The second (Basel II) relied on credit rating agencies and banks' own models to generate risk weights for capital requirements, and is now widely viewed as inappropriate in light of the recent financial crisis. By neglecting the fact that the risks created by an individual bank's actions depend on the liquidity of the system as a whole, the Basel Committee's standards have, if anything, magnified systemic risks.[10]

6.3 THE WEAKNESSES OF THE BCBS

The failings of the BCBS system can be found in all of its basic regulatory functions: standard-setting, monitoring, and enforcement. They are interconnected weaknesses that feed into one another.

With respect to standards setting, there is a partial conflict between the goal formally attributed to them by the BCBS, that is, international financial stability, and the goals that individual members in the Committee may ascribe to them, that is, the protection and competitiveness of their own national banking sector. The compromises that often follow from this conflict detract from the realization of the statutory purpose of the Committee.

[10] D. Rodrik, *The Globalization Paradox: Why Global Markets, States, and Democracy Can't Coexist* (2011), at 224.

Further, the substantive content of the standards adopted by the Committee has been found wanting, in at least three respects. First, the conduct prescribed for the banks by the standards tends to be insufficiently rigorous for the stability of the financial system. The inadequate technical quality of the Basel standards is exemplified by the excessively low capital requirements and the reliance on self-regulation in the form of banks' own risk assessment determinations. In this respect, Basel II mirrored the inadequacies of national banking regulation and supervisory practices, particularly in the United States, in the years leading to the crisis.

The inadequacy of Basel standards in their specific prescriptions and level of harmonization have various causes, including insufficient understanding of financial markets, regulatory capture, and national interests. The financial crisis revealed gaps in the policymakers' understanding of the functioning and effects of financial markets and of financial and technological innovation, especially in terms of risks to the general well-being.[11] This gap – which private interests have taken advantage of – has given rise to flawed economic theories and misconceptions, which in turn have produced ineffective banking regulation, both at the international and at the national level. Lastra points out that before the crisis widespread was "the belief . . . that financial markets are best left to their own devices."[12] The substantive regulatory flaws in the Basel standards stemmed, in large part, from the failure of the Anglo-American legal and theoretical framework in the field of financial regulation, which constituted until 2007 the reference model for the definition of the international standards regime.

Furthermore – stressing the "capture" explanation for the failings of Basel – Rodrik states that "if the regulations were written by economists and finance experts, they would be far more stringent."[13] The "over-reliance on private sector input"[14] evident in the Basel standards – and deemed as one of the reasons of their failure – is probably the product of both gaps in the policymaker's understanding of the functioning and effects of financial markets and of financial and technological innovation and regulatory capture. Furthermore, the wide range of national preferences and interests that confront each other at the Basel negotiation table tends to

[11] Avgouleas, *supra* note 2, at 3–4, who describes the financial revolution as a knowledge revolution. The complexity of banking and of banking institutions has reached such a level that a proper level of understanding is not only missing in banking supervisory authorities but even within the private side of the sector. According to R. P. Buckley, The Changing Nature of Banking and Why It Matters, *Reconceptualising Global Finance and Its Regulation* (R. P. Buckley et al. eds., 2016) 11, at 25: "It is apparent from multiple discussions with bankers that while each may well understand their own role well, very few bankers, and only those at the very highest levels of the bank, actually understand the bank's entire business."

[12] Lastra, *supra* note 1, at 797.

[13] D. Rodrik, *Straight Talk on Trade: Ideas for a Sane World Economy* (2018), at 129. On regulatory capture in international banking regulation, see K. Alexander, *Principles of Banking Regulation* (2019), at 73–77.

[14] Avgouleas, *supra* note 2, at 2.

result in poor regulatory compromises, consisting in weak and ineffective standards.[15]

Second, because of ongoing conflicting national interests, the level of harmonization reached in the Basel agreements is usually not high enough to prevent the negative effects of a regulatory competition or the "race-to-the-bottom" problem. Particularly when the standards affect politically sensitive domains, they tend to be weaker.

Third, when a substantial degree of harmonization is achieved, the standards are often not adequate to the needs of many countries, particularly the less developed ones. This is because they are conceived to suit, in the first place, the more advanced economic and banking systems of the real rule-making members in the BCBS.

Some of these failings have a common institutional underlying factor: the Basel Committee's decision-making structure and process. The BCBS' governance structure failed to produce effective regulations and supervisory standards; first, because it lacked transparency, accountability, and legitimacy, thus enabling, among other things, special interest group pressure from major banks and international finance associations to have disproportionate influence on the regulators that were members of the Committee, stirring the process in their favor and to the detriment of an adequate regulatory outcome.[16] And second, because the countries and the banking industry that developed the standards did not consult countries that were not members of the Committee (mainly developing and emerging market economies).

The Basel system has proven to be inadequate also with respect to enforcement. In fact, many commentators, be they academics or regulators, seem to hold the belief that the single biggest institutional failing of the BCBS is not its standard-making structure and process but on the enforcement side. According to this view, Basel standards were not effective in preventing the 2007–2008 financial crisis because they were poorly implemented at the domestic level, in the sense that implementation, and as a result enforcement, was lacking or varied across jurisdictions. Agreed standards were not (fully) adopted in some jurisdictions or were not uniformly implemented or enforced across national legal systems, to the detriment of international financial stability and the level playing field. Therefore, what attracts a great part of the commentary on the Basel institutional system is its failure to properly carry out the enforcement function. For example, according to Lastra, the global banking system requires legal and institutional changes especially at the surveillance and enforcement stages, rather than in the law-making function.

[15] D. Howarth and L. Quaglia, The Comparative Political Economy of Basel III in Europe (2016) 35 *Policy and Society* 205, at 212, examining how the preferences of European regulators on Basel III explain "the disagreements that emerged in Basel and ultimately the weakness of the reforms eventually agreed by the BCBS, despite the severity of the international financial crisis."

[16] Alexander, *supra* note 13, at 73–74.

While formal international standard-setters like the Basel Committee are "adept" at the regulatory function and thus "can continue with their rule-making role," what is really missing is an effective enforcement of these standards.[17]

The reasons for inadequate implementation and enforcement are various and to a certain extent link back to the function of standard-setting. First, the non-binding nature of Basel standards means that any deviation from them is, from a strictly legal point of view, formally costless for national jurisdictions. This makes it easier for domestic interests – be they public and/or private, general or special – when it is time to implement or enforce these standards, to prevail over conflicting international commitments and the goal of international financial stability. Second, as already mentioned, Basel standards, to the extent that their regulatory content is determined by the most influential members of the Committee, may not be adequate for the other jurisdictions and their specific economic and financial system. This is particularly the case of nonmember countries from less economically advanced part of the world, which are not even represented in the Basel negotiations. These other countries are likely to proceed at best with a lukewarm implementation, also because a full implementation can be disproportionately costly.[18]

6.4 THE RESILIENCE OF THE BCBS

6.4.1 *Exogenous Factors Accounting for Resilience*

The most characteristic component of the BCBS regime, that is, the soft-law nature of its standards and the related informality of the standard-setting body, is unlikely to be replaced anytime soon. According to Arner, "outside of the EU, there continues to be very limited interest in moving from soft law to hard law approach to international financial regulation."[19] What explains the continued resilience of the BCBS and its standards?

At least four exogenous factors can explain this resilience. First, a certain degree of institutional inertia or path dependency certainly contribute to the continued relevance of the BCBS and its standards.[20] A radical transformation of the regulatory approach, like the switch from an informal network of national regulators to a proper hard-law organization or agreement would be, conceptually and practically, more difficult to put in place than incremental revisions of the status quo. This is particularly true in a regulatory space as complex as international banking, which

[17] Lastra, *supra* note 1, at 800–801.

[18] C. Monticelli, *Reforming Global Economic Governance: An Unsettled Order* (2019), at 163.

[19] D. Arner, The Politics of International Financial Law, in *The Changing Landscape of Global Financial Governance and the Role of Soft Law* (F. Weiss and A. J. Kammel eds., 2015), 81, at 89.

[20] P.-H. Verdier, The Political Economy of International Financial Regulation (2013) 88 *Indiana Law Journal* 1405.

does not simply or mostly provide for liberalization measures (like the trade and the foreign investment regimes) but instead entails the harmonization of national regulation of financial institutions and activities. The latter task becomes even more difficult to carry out if the political conditions at the international level are missing, as when international multilateralism is receding and replaced by a stronger unilateral or bilateral approach to international relations.

Second, soft law provides a series of practical and legal advantages that make it a very useful – and thus resilient –instrument of setting standards in the field of banking, domestically and internationally. Generally, soft law represents a sort of regulatory compromise between conflicting needs. It is still law but without the obligation to comply with many substantive and procedural legal requirements that are attached to hard law. It carries out the same principal regulatory function as hard law, namely, standard-setting, but generally with more flexibility, speed, and technical expertise and much less formality. This is why soft law is extensively relied upon, especially by specialized agencies, in the field of financial services. The latter is characterized by technical complexities and by the speed of financial and technological innovation and market developments. For its flexibility and malleability, soft law is particularly suitable to cope with the infinite variations of regulated financial activities and institutions.

The same underlying reasons explain the use by the BCBS of soft law as opposed to binding international legal acts. Soft law standards represent the useful compromise to solve the tension between, on one side, the BCBS members' lack of legal authority and legitimacy to impose international hard law prescriptions and, on the other side, the need for cross-border regulatory and supervisory consistency. Similarly, BCBS' soft law standards and principles are meant to solve the tension between an international regulation sufficiently ambitious and universal in its applicability and appropriately transparent to be assessable by market participants and national authorities,[21] with the need for some degree of flexibility in their implementation and enforcement so as to be compatible with different legal and economic systems.[22]

The third factor behind the resilience of soft law in international banking regulation is the protection of certain interests by and in major countries, which makes the latter ambivalent about stepping up international cooperation. Such interests want to gain from international coordination by promoting some degree of inter-state commitment, while avoiding the costs associated with proper hard law agreements. In its standard-setting function, the Basel regime is shaped in a way as to simultaneously increase the advantages and reduce the disadvantages of international coordination in the banking field as much as possible. On the one hand, by providing some degree of conduct harmonization across global financial markets

[21] Monticelli, *supra* note 18, at 148.

[22] C. Brummer, *Soft Law in the Global Financial System: Rule-Making in the 21st Century* (2015).

through common standards and the relative behavior-changing mechanisms, the regime narrows down the margin for regulatory race to the bottom and reduces the sources of international financial instability. On the other hand, the absence of formal binding obligations and dispute resolution systems simplifies the efforts to adjust – if, when, and to the extent necessary – the national implementation and enforcement of international standards according to conflicting (public or private) domestic interests. Verdier[23] has highlighted three domestic actors that are keen on leveraging the characteristics of the Basel regime to further their own interests, even if it is to the detriment of internationally agreed policy goals: developed jurisdictions (such as the United States, the United Kingdom, and the EU), their financial industries, and their specialized financial regulators. According to this account, the pursuit of their own interests by these three forces has greatly contributed to the decades-long resilience of an international regulatory approach based on non-binding standards and on delegated and somewhat discretionary implementation and enforcement. Thus, soft law will remain the dominant legal form in international banking regulation until for those actors its benefits exceed the costs or until other actors and interests prevail.

Finally, the fourth exogenous factor, strengthening the resilience of the Basel regime, has to do with political international credibility. National implementation of what is agreed in the BCBS has also an important international political dimension. Since 1974, the BCBS standards, once adopted by its members by consensus, have been endorsed by the Group of Central Bank Governors and Heads of Supervision (originally of the G10). However, since 2008, the G20 has started holding summits at the level of heads of state or government; and in that composition in November 2010 (G20 Seoul Summit), it endorsed the Basel III agreement.

Therefore, through its highest-profile political composition, the G20 has brought to the international economic governance of financial markets a higher level of political and institutional commitment. The latter in turn can bring a higher degree of legitimacy and authority to international legal standards. More specifically, while remaining soft law, the BCBS standards can become a little "harder" because of the official commitment by the highest-level political institutions to their implementation at the domestic level. The mechanism increasing the standards' compliance pull is not strictly legal but political: it is a question of international credibility. If and to the extent that international political commitments are not followed through by a country's domestic institutions, damaging consequences can follow in terms of reduced international credibility, and thus of future negotiation strengths, of that country and of its internationally active representatives and organs (starting from the very central bank and supervisory authorities that sit in the BCBS).

[23] Verdier, *supra* note 20.

6.4.2 *Endogenous Factors Accounting for Resilience*

After having highlighted the most important exogenous drivers of the resilience of the Basel regime, it is important to turn to the endogenous factors.

The fact that international financial regulation is still based on soft law standards does not mean that the reforms that have been introduced within the Committee after the start of the crisis have left such component unchanged. Rather, the reforms can be viewed as an attempt to reconcile the almost inevitability – at least for now – of having to rely on soft law standards with the need to reduce the weaknesses of this very type of regulatory approach. In other words, the changes brought to some parts of the international regime of banking are meant to make up at least partially for the continued reliance on an informal standard-setting body and nonbinding legal standards, so as to have the advantages of soft law while reducing its drawbacks as much as possible. At least to some extent, these changes contribute to the resilience of the regime, in an attempt to avoid more radical reforms.

In this regard, two important endogenous factors in the resilience of the Basel regime will be highlighted below:[24] the membership enlargement of the BCBS and the BCBS internal mechanism of peer assessment (of the two, the latter will be examined in more detail). These reforms can be seen as means to improve especially the implementation and enforcement of BCBS standards, notwithstanding their continued soft-law nature. In some way, the objective of such reforms is to make the BCBS standards less soft, not in a formal sense but de facto, that is, to facilitate, or apply pressure for, a higher degree of compliance, even in the absence of a legally binding obligation.

6.4.2.1 Extended Membership

The first reform, which could improve the implementation of BCBS standards, is the broadening of the Basel Committee's membership. The expansion was decided

[24] To be sure, these are not the only relevant reforms enacted at the international level. As regards the functions of standard-setting, for instance, as already mentioned, in 2009 there was the establishment of the Financial Stability Board (replacing the Financial Stability Forum), which, as a mix of political and technocratic support of the G20, has been given the task of agenda setting and coordinating the work of international standard-setting bodies (including the BCBS). Instead, as regards the function of monitoring, the surveillance of compliance has been strengthened: the IMF and the FSB have made Financial Sector Assessment Program (FSAP) a regular part of their members' obligation as well as imposing publication of their results (International Monetary Fund, Press Release, IMF Expanding Surveillance to Require Mandatory Financial Stability Assessments of Countries with Systemically Important Financial Sectors [September 27, 2010], www.imf.org/en/News/Articles/2015/09/14/01/49/pr10357). Additionally, in 2009, the FSB set up a series of peer review mechanisms to monitor the progress made by its members in implementing FSAP regulatory and supervisory recommendations (for a description and a list of relevant documents: www.fsb.org/work-of-the-fsb/implementation-monitoring/peer_reviews/).

and took place in 2009, carrying forward the call from G20 leaders for major standard-setting bodies, including the FSB and the BCBS, to review their membership.[25] By involving additional countries and making them part of the standard-setting process, two beneficial effects can arise, at least in principle. Due to the involvement and representation of additional jurisdictions, the standard-making process – and the resulting standards – might be seen as more legitimate. Furthermore, in this way, also less influential countries' financial and economic needs and specificities are more likely to be taken into account and incorporated in the final agreements. Consequently, the final BCBS standards can be more easily accepted, and thus more consistently implemented, by a wider network of countries. However, whether and to what extent these effects are effectively going to materialize is another matter.

6.4.2.2 The BCBS' Peer Assessment Program

The second reform that can increase the compliance pull of BCBS standards is the Regulatory Consistency Assessment Program (RCAP) established within the Basel Committee in 2012 for monitoring and evaluating the adoption and implementation by its members of its agreed standards. The program can work in synergy not only with the political credibility-based implementation mechanism mentioned above but also with other functionally equivalent mechanisms normally associated with nonbinding international financial law. As explained below, these mechanisms are based on market discipline and on the possible regulatory reaction and retaliation by foreign financial banking regulatory and supervisory authorities to deviations from Basel agreements.

The RCAP consists of two distinct but interlinked parts: the monitoring of timeliness and the assessment of consistency. The first part monitors the timely adoption of Basel standards. It takes place every semester and is based on the data provided by each member. The second part assesses the consistency and completeness of domestic implementing measures, highlighting possible deviations from agreed standards.

The second part results in a "report card" given to each individual member regarding compliance with the commitments undertaken within the Committee. The report card contains two evaluations. Each assessed jurisdiction receives a grade concerning the key components of a specific legal framework (e.g., risk-based capital framework) and a grade on the framework as a whole. The best grade that members can obtain is "compliant," where all the minimum requirements have been observed; the second highest rating is "largely compliant," where only the main

[25] See www.bis.org/press/p090313.htm. Nout Wellink, chairman of the Basel Committee, stated that "this expansion in membership will enhance the Committee's ability to carry out its core mission, which is to strengthen regulatory practices and standards worldwide."

standards have been met; negative judgments of ""materially non-compliant" follow, when fundamental provisions are not met or differences have been found between international standards and domestic legislation capable of seriously affecting financial stability or conditions of equal competition at international level; and of "non-compliant," when the applicable Basel requirements have not been adopted or differences have been found that could seriously affect financial stability or international competitive parity.

The assessment part of the RCAP has two strands: jurisdictional peer reviews and thematic assessments of regulatory outcomes. While the first concerns the assessment of domestic legal regimes, the other concerns banks, in the sense that in addition to evaluating the correspondence between the standards and the legal regimes adopted by the individual jurisdictions, the application of the same standards by individual banks (sampled) is also assessed to determine whether, how much, and how this application diverges across banks and countries.

The part of the RCAP that most interests the present analysis is jurisdictional assessment, due to its relevance as a monitoring mechanism that is aimed at promoting consistent domestic adoption and implementation of the Basel standards. The objectives, the object, the parameters, and the evaluation procedures are illustrated in a guide prepared by the Committee: the Handbook for Jurisdictional Assessments.[26] The guide explains the complete assessment program and describes the RCAP questionnaires, which member jurisdictions complete ahead of the assessment and update regularly.

The evaluation of individual legal regimes aims to promote the full and correct implementation of the Basel standards by the members of the Committee. To this end, the RCAP identifies domestic rules and requirements applied to international banks that are not in line with the letter or spirit of the relevant Basel standards. The assessment relates to domestic regulations aimed at regulating the aspects covered by Basel standards, while a broader analysis on the functioning of the regulatory framework and the effectiveness of supervision is not carried out.

The evaluation process is divided into several phases and involves various institutional actors. After a preparatory and preliminary phase, there is the evaluation phase focused on the work of the Evaluation Group (the Assessment Team) set up ad hoc for the preparation of a draft report; then there is the revision phase in which a different Group – the Review Team – reexamines the draft report and then transmits it together with its observations to other bodies (the Peer Review Board [PRB] and the Supervision and Implementation Group [SIG]) "hierarchically" superordinate, for approval and possible sending to the Committee for discussion and final approval.

[26] BCBS, Regulatory Consistency Assessment Programme (RCAP). Handbook for jurisdictional assessments, March 2018, www.bis.org/bcbs/publ/d434.htm.

The pressure to comply with Basel standards exerted on members through the RCAP stems from the cumulative negative consequences that the publication of negative assessments can produce. Despite the euphemistic tones used in explaining the objectives of the RCAP – according to which its assessments "help member jurisdictions to undertake the reforms needed to make them more aligned with Basel standards"[27] – the implicit purpose is to increase the costs for those jurisdictions that decide to deviate from Basel standards. The main costs are of three types. First, there are reputational and credibility costs at the political level (G20 and FSB) and at the technocratic level (among the participants to the Basel Committee), which can negatively impact the strength of a member's future negotiation position. Second, there are market costs stemming from market discipline, if and to the extent to which national deviations from internationally agreed standards are perceived by market participants as a sign of weakness of the corresponding domestic banking system. And third, there are regulatory costs which derive from the additional legal requirements imposed across jurisdictions on internationally active banks whose country of origin deviate from Basel standards. Foreign regulators and banking supervisory authorities can deem those banks as a greater source of financial instability and/or can retaliate seeing such deviations as undermining the sought-after level playing field in the global banking market.

These deterrent effects are potentially the stronger the more authoritative the evaluation process and its final assessment – in addition to the substantive content of standards – is perceived. To this end, although these are in any case peer reviews, and therefore not carried out by an impartial third party, the RCAP is based on a procedure with various elements aimed at reasonably ensuring a "fair" evaluation.

The RCAP procedure does not end with the assessment but essentially provides for continuous control by the Committee on the subsequent progress made by the competent domestic authorities to correctly implement the Basel standards. Among other things, at least one year after the non-positive evaluation, the assessed jurisdictions must draw up a report indicating the legislative and regulatory amendments adopted or proposed to correct the nonfulfillment and gaps highlighted by the evaluation approved by the Committee. In addition, subsequent RCAP assessments may also include in the examination those elements of the domestic regime that in the previous assessment had been reported as being corrected. So, in essence, the RCAP monitoring mechanism exerts ongoing pressure on members. This pressure is further strengthened by the involvement of the more strictly political actors of international cooperation in economic and financial matters: for accountability, the BCBS periodically reports to the G20 and the FSB, in addition to other external stakeholders, on progress achieved in the implementation of the agreements concluded within the Basel Committee.

[27] Ibid., at 3.

Only time will tell if, even in the absence of any enforcement authority, this new monitoring mechanism will actually work in fostering "more consistent implementation through peer pressure and public identification of noncompliant jurisdictions."[28]

6.5 CONCLUSION

The fundamental question addressed by this chapter was what explains the resilience of the Basel Committee and its standards, particularly in the aftermath of the crisis. The Committee has been criticized much in the same way as private standard-setters and the delegation of rule-making powers to private bodies have.[29] In the European Union (EU), for example, the reliance on private standard-setters to achieve legal harmonization across Member States has been questioned for lack of legitimacy and accountability. Concerns have been expressed that their decision-making is not sufficiently transparent, prompting the risk of capture by the industry to be regulated and thus to the exclusion of other stakeholders' voice and interests.[30]

However, still in relation to EU law, these legitimacy concerns have not determined any real change of course on the part of EU policymakers, the reason probably being that the standard-setting process is deemed to be actually working.[31] In other words, the acceptance of such "non-democratic" bodies, processes, and networks may be based on their effectiveness on the ground and thus on output legitimacy. This sets these private standard-setters apart from the Basel Committee, whose standards have instead failed to concretely achieve their objectives, depriving such international regulatory approach of much of its output legitimacy.

This chapter has highlighted some of the reasons behind paradigm continuity in the post-crisis international governance of financial regulation, still dominated by an approach based on informal networks of national regulators. The decision, taken at the political (G20) and at technocratic (Committee) level, has been to favor incremental changes of the existing institutional structure and workings rather than a system overhaul. The chosen strategy is therefore to keep on relying on the Basel Committee and on nonbinding international standards, while introducing some institutional reforms to the way the BCBS system works in order to address at least some of its most problematic issues. In particular, important changes have been adopted with a view to making standard-setting more legitimate and receptive to a

[28] N. Véron, *The G20 Financial Reform Agenda after Five Years* (2014), 1, at 6.

[29] Alexander, supra note 13; M. Borowicz, The Internal Ratings-Based and Advanced Measurement Approaches for Regulatory Capital under the "Basel regime," in *The Governance and Regulation of International Finance* (G. Miller and F. Cafaggi eds., 2013), 167–208.

[30] Ibid.

[31] C. Barnard, *The Substantive Law of the EU* (2019), 597.

wider range of national interests and specificities, and standards implementation more widespread and fuller across jurisdictions.

However, fundamental problems with the BCBS system have not been addressed (limited legitimacy, regulatory capture, disproportionate influence of some jurisdictions on the standard making process, lack of involvement of an adequately wide range of stakeholders also beyond the financial sector, lack of international dispute-settlement mechanisms, diversity of financial and economic systems across jurisdictions, etc.). The fact that not even a crisis as disruptive as the 2007–2008 global financial crisis was able to trigger enough political will and technical ingenuity to overcome the actual governance model – toward a more formal international law approach or, in the opposite direction, an increased nationalization/diversification of the prudential regulation of international banking[32] – is testament to the resilience of the factors – including path dependence, practicality, and the diversity of national regulatory preferences reflecting public and private interests – behind such model.

[32] Rodrik, *supra* note 13.

PART III

Evolution and Resilience in Sustainability and Food Safety Regimes

7

Human Rights Due Diligence and Evolution of Voluntary Sustainability Standards

Enrico Partiti

7.1 INTRODUCTION

Private regulators of social and environmental sustainability such as voluntary sustainability standards (VSS) have proliferated. Private schemes such as the Forest Stewardship Council (FSC), FairTrade, and the Marine Stewardship Council (MSC) define sustainability-related product features and production processes by means of voluntary standards. VSS discipline aspects of production including human rights, labor rights, and environmental impacts ranging from pollution prevention to impact on forests and biodiversity. Like other private governance structures,[1] VSS are characterized by contingency and context-dependency that makes them receptive to critical events[2] including regulatory developments, even prospective ones. Legislative developments at the national level such as the convergence around criteria of timber legality in EU, US, Australian, and South Korean legislation contributed to align VSS requirements. In addition, the goals of VSS were partially refined toward assessing compliance with national provisions and demonstrating due diligence of legality of timber origin as required by those instruments.[3]

Not only events and rules at the national level are capable to affect this form of private authority. Transnational private regulation is a vehicle to "harden" voluntary obligations and make them applicable to individuals.[4] Transnational private

[1] E. J. Balleisen and E. K. Brake, Historical Perspective and Better Regulatory Governance: An Agenda for Institutional Reform (2013) 8:2 *Regulation & Governance* 222.

[2] See Section 1.2.1 in this volume.

[3] T. Bartley, Transnational Governance and the Re-centred State: Sustainability or Legality (2014) 8:1 *Regulation & Governance* 93; C. Overdevest and J. Zeitlin, Assembling an Experimentalist Regime: Transnational Governance Interactions in the Forest Sector (2014) 8:1 *Regulation & Governance* 22

[4] F. Cafaggi, New Foundations of Transnational Private Regulation (2011) 38:1 *Journal of Law and Society* 20.

regulators are therefore also affected by relevant international soft law instruments in their field of operation.[5] For standards such as VSS, the emergence of human rights responsibilities of corporations represents a major, albeit understudied, development. The 2011 adoption of the United Nations Guiding Principles on Business and Human Rights (UNGP) affirmed a corporate responsibility to respect human rights throughout business activities, parallel to a State duty to protect human rights and a right for victims to obtain remedies.[6] As an integral part of the responsibility to respect, firms must perform human rights due diligence (HRDD) to identify, assess, avoid, mitigate, remedy, and report about human rights impacts in their value chains, which include both social and environmental aspects.[7] Some counties passed legislation making HRDD mandatory. EU rules currently require HRDD in the supply chains of minerals associated with armed conflict in Central Africa, and a proposal for a general HRDD Directive is expected soon.

VSS, like other transnational private regulators, are characterized by considerable flexibility and organizational resourcefulness,[8] insofar as they are capable to rapidly adapting governance structures, procedures, and content of their standards to better fit their contextual environment. Organizational resourcefulness confers resilience to private regulators, as they can reorganize in the face of change affecting the pursuit of their objectives and withstand discontinuity while adapting to new environments.[9] Given VSS' receptivity to soft law and, especially, to (perspective) national legislation, an alignment of standards in line with the responsibilities, processes, and constructs of HRDD is expected to be visible. With respect to norms of responsible business conduct, voluntary standards defining responsible production and sourcing must be aligned with HRDD and its requirements if they are to support certified firms at different levels in the value chain toward compliance with their HRDD responsibilities and emerging legal obligations. However HRDD also directly affects VSS, as they are private organizations with their own responsibility to conduct HRDD. Responsibility, or even legal liability under future legislation, could result from VSS association to human rights impacts caused by certified entities or members or to that which they contributed. VSS must also implement grievance mechanisms in line with the UNGP and perform their own HRDD toward firms with which they have a business relation such as certified and noncertified members.

5 L. H. Gulbrandsen, Dynamic governance interactions: Evolutionary effects of state responses to non-state certification programs (2014) 8:1 *Regulation & Governance* 82.

6 Human Rights Council, Guiding Principles on Business and Human Rights: Implementing the United Nations "Protect, Respect and Remedy" Framework, A/HRC/17/31 (March 21, 2011).

7 UNGP's Principle 17.

8 See Section 1.2.4.2 in this volume.

9 C. S. Holling, Resilience and Stability of Ecological Systems (1973) 4:1 *Annual Review of Ecology and Systematics* 1.

Studying the evolution of VSS in light of HRDD allows us to better understand the influence of requirements established by public authority on private standards. Is public authority capable to influence transnational private regulation or is it bound to fail? To what extent does the resilience stemming from the capacity of VSS to adapt to change (in regulatory frameworks) allow them to retain their regulatory prerogatives or bring private regulators to (partially) reorient their goals?[10] This chapter focuses on private standards connected to deforestation, conversion of ecosystems, and human rights concerns that certify forest products and agricultural commodities. While it does not focus on one case study, it adopts a comparative perspective to analyze the effects of HRDD on some of the most relevant multi-stakeholder and industry-driven initiatives in this domain. The analysis takes place on the basis of requirements contained in production standards, codes of conduct for members, other documents and policies, and NGO reports. These sources are complemented by fifteen semi-structured interviews centered on the impact of HRDD on standards held with NGO representatives and certification managers from ISEAL and from six schemes active in the domain of timber, palm oil, soy, sugarcane, cocoa, and coffee certification.

This chapter is structured as follows. Section 7.2 situates emergence and evolution of VSS in connection to regulatory crises and a recently changed climate toward certification that also contributed to the demand for mandatory legislation. Section 7.3 explains how HRDD can be seen as an organizational crisis, which could be both an opportunity for VSS to consolidate their regulatory prerogatives and a potential threat in light of the establishment of other risk management tools and initiatives. Section 7.4 illustrates relevant aspects of HRDD for VSS. Section 7.5 discusses how VSS are aligning their requirements and policies to the value chain dimension of HRDD and its engagement dimension. Section 7.6 concludes by reflecting on the refinement of VSS relation of complementary with public rules generated by HRDD and the capacity of public authority to align transitional private regulators to public rules. It also reflects on the resilience of VSS and their capacity to expand their activities to novel domains intersecting with HRDD.

7.2 REGULATORY FAILURES AND TRANSNATIONAL PRIVATE REGULATION

Regulatory crises are a critical moment for private regulators.[11] These crises are events of varying scale and scope resulting from the unintended or unforeseen consequences of the design or operation of a regulatory system and its interactions with other systems.[12] A regulatory crisis may pressure the industry to self-regulate to

[10] See Section 1.3.2 in this volume.

[11] See Section 1.2.4 in this volume.

[12] J. Black, Learning from regulatory disasters (2014) 10:3 *Policy Quarterly* 3.

protect reputation and avoid liability but also to preempt more demanding regimes. In the domain of sustainability, private regimes appeared as a response to a regulatory crisis exposing shortcomings in the regulation of global production. Certifications for forestry products, coffee, and other agricultural commodities were established after the collapse of commodity prices and the worsening of deforestation caused by agricultural production.[13] Labor schemes, such as Social Accountability International and the Fair Labour Association, emerged in the aftermath of extensive campaigns in the mid-nineties exposing sweatshop conditions and incidents in the garment industry.[14] The first wave of biofuel certification (before EU regulatory intervention) was linked to the 2007/2008 food crisis to avoid biofuel production displacing food crops.[15] Many of these VSS appeared in an environment characterized by a lack of binding international frameworks that resulted in the emergence of heterogeneous standards.

Where a crisis is connected to a regulatory failure, it may reverberate on public authority as well, which may expressly support private regimes as a solution. Remarkably, voluntary private regulation in the area of sustainability was often suggested as a possible solution also by the very NGOs that brought up attention to the crisis in question.[16] However, in recent years, the wide acceptance of HRDD and the demands for making it mandatory were accompanied by a growing dissatisfaction from certain civil society organizations about the effectiveness and impact of corporate social responsibility[17] and voluntary initiatives including private standards and certifications. NGOs campaigned for the introduction of mandatory legislation aimed at value chain transparency and mandatory HRDD noting how voluntary private standards failed and that they should only play a very limited function in future instruments.[18] NGOs are also experiencing "certification fatigue" in participating in VSS and offering monitoring functions to ensure that firms comply with the standards – a role that they consider as very resource-intensive and better performed by public authority.[19] In recent years, prominent civil society organizations left the VSS that they contributed to establish. Among several instances, the most visible is arguably that of Greenpeace International leaving the FSC, of which

[13] E. Meidinger, The Administrative Law of Global Private-Public Regulation: The Case of Forestry (2006) 17:1 *European Journal of International Law* 47.

[14] MSI Integrity, Not Fit-for-Purpose: The Grand Experiment of Multi-stakeholder Initiatives in Corporate Accountability, Human Rights and Global Governance (2020), at 37.

[15] P. McMicheal, A Food Regime Analysis of the "World Food Crisis" (2009) 26:4 *Agriculture and Human Values* 281.

[16] MSI Integrity, *supra*, at 14.

[17] A. Ramasastry, Corporate Social Responsibility versus Business and Human Rights: Bridging the Gap between Responsibility and Accountability (2015) 14:2 *Journal of Human Rights* 237.

[18] D. Brack and S. Ozinga, Enforcing Due Diligence Legislation "Plus," Fern, October 2020, www.fern.org/fileadmin/uploads/fern/Documents/2020/Enforcing_due_diligence_legislation_plus_16102020.pdf.

[19] Interview with NGO representative.

it was a founding member, in 2018 due to the controversies around the "FSC Mix" certificate.[20]

Some environmental NGOs are also growing frustrated at what they consider as an obstructive attitude of business toward attempts of reform in VSS about transparency, auditing, and stringency of the requirements.[21] NGOs filed complaints against Bonsucro and RSPO for breaches of international standards for responsible business conduct.[22] A recently published report by the Institute for Multi-Stakeholder Initiatives Integrity went as far as concluding that VSS "have peaked" and that they will be replaced by alternative, rights-centered, models of private governance similar to the Bangladesh Accord.[23] While quantifying effectiveness and impact of VSS remains complex and debated,[24] certification managers respond to this alleged lack of impact of VSS by noting how certification was never intended to be a "silver bullet" capable to tackle deeply rooted structural problems that can only be solved with the involvement of all public and private actors and mandatory rules. Part of the disappointment among certain civil society organizations would stem from having put too high expectations on certification,[25] which should be seen as a complement rather than a replacement of public governance.[26] This is also the position of VSS in public consultations and lobbying activities.[27]

Regulatory crises not only brought private actors together in the establishment of voluntary sustainability regimes but also mobilized civil society and governmental support for private solutions instead of more profound public intervention. This establishes competitive dynamics under which private regimes hinder or delay the emergence of more profound and mandatory public rules.[28] Competition arises where private and public regimes fight for legitimacy, uptake, support, the authority to set rules and key terms thereof, or the acceptance of a regulatory regime over the

[20] www.greenpeace.org/static/planet4-international-stateless/2018/03/6b3d1c70-greenpeace-statement-on-forest-certification-and-guidance-for-companies-and-consumers_final.pdf.

[21] Interview with NGO representative.

[22] Swiss NCP: *TuK Indonesia* v. *Roundtable on Sustainable Palm Oil (RSPO)*; before the UK NCP: *IDI, EC, and LICADHO* v. *Bonsucro*.

[23] MSI Integrity, *supra* 14, at 46. See also J. Reinecke and J.Donaghey, "The Politics of Collaborative Governance in Global Supply Chains: Power and Pushback in the Bangladesh Accord" in this volume (Chapter 8).

[24] UNFSS Voluntary Sustainability Standards, Trade and Sustainable Development, 3rd Flagship Report of the United Nations Forum on Sustainability Standards (2018).

[25] Interview with certification manager.

[26] Ibid.

[27] See the FSC submission to the fitness check for the EUTR: https://ec.europa.eu/info/law/better-regulation/have-your-say/initiatives/11630-Illegal-logging-evaluation-of-EU-rules-fitness-check-/F506597.

[28] N. Malhotra, B. Monin, and M. Tomz, Does Private Regulation Preempt Public Regulation? (2019) 113:1 *American Political Science Review* 19.

other.[29] Competition could result in substitution where public rules are challenged by, or replaced with, private regimes that are less stringent than public regimes or limit their effectiveness, pursue business interests to a larger extent than public goals, or that are ineffective and "symbolic." The fact that public authorities, at least in the EU, are committed to introduce or have already introduced mandatory legislation on the social and environmental impact of global production therefore stands in contrast to initiatives hitherto enacted on both sides of the Atlantic and grounded on voluntarism and multi-stakeholderism. It arguably testifies to a possible co-optation outcome, where public regulation takes over private regimes, either by turning elements of private regulation into a (mandatory) public regime or by narrowing down the regulatory space for private governance.[30]

7.3 HRDD AS THREAT AND OPPORTUNITY FOR VSS

From the internal perspective of transnational private regulators, the perception of critical factors or a change in (regulatory) context as threats to the status quo is linked to the notion of organizational crises. An organizational crisis represents a threat for an organization that prevents it from attaining its goals or reduces its ability to do so. Organizations seek to resolve such crises also because they are an opportunity to achieve their goals even further – and beyond the issue in question.[31] Organizational crises catalyze opportunities to cooperate in new or existing institutions and experiment with alternatives that would not otherwise be considered, resulting in rethinking, reorganization, and new institutional settings.[32] The introduction of HRDD, especially in mandatory legislation, from the perspective of VSS can be seen as an organizational crisis.

The goals of VSS do not just include the regulation of sustainability. VSS also pursue institutional goals such as increasing market uptake and gaining legitimacy from their association to legislation.[33] HRDD and mandatory HRDD constitutes an opportunity for schemes to extend their uptake among firms and consolidate their regulatory prerogatives, possibly even in new regulatory domains and through new regulatory tools. As VSS contribute to social and environmental risk management, HRDD could incentivize their use as part of companies' responsibilities and

[29] B. Eberlein, K. W. Abbott, J. Black, E. Meidinger, and S. Wood, Transnational Business Governance Interactions: Conceptualisation and Framework for Analysis (2014) 8:1 *Regulation & Governance* 11.

[30] B. Cashore, J. S. Knudsen, J. Moon, H. van der Ven, Private Authority and Public Policy in Global Context: Governance Spheres for Problem Solving (2021) 15:4 *Regulation & Governance* 1166.

[31] T. W. Milburn, R. S. Schuler, and K. H. Watman, Organisational Crisis: Definition and Conceptualisation (1983) 36:12 *Human Relations* 1144.

[32] P. L. Berger and T. Luckmann, *The Social Construction of Reality* (1967), at 107–108.

[33] J. Black, Constructing and contesting legitimacy and accountability in polycentric regulatory regimes (2008) 2:1 *Regulation & Governance* 157.

obligations. The UNGP raised awareness and demand for supply chain transparency that VSS are well placed to provide, by giving firms a tool showing that they "do not harm" and to monitor progress and improvements.[34] HRDD also requires firms to engage with their value chains, as further illustrated in Section 5.2, thereby generating a demand for guidance and new institutional forms to that purpose.

In parallel, however, HRDD could push firms to design their own internal due diligence systems for sourcing and tackling social and environmental risks, which could be less stringent and less transparent than private certification, nor based on a multi-stakeholder approach and without third-party assurance mechanisms.[35] Private business programs in the context of sustainability supply chain management[36] proliferated in sectors covered by VSS. There is evidence that they displaced certification especially in the cocoa space.[37] These initiatives cover a company's entire sourcing and could create fragmentation and ultimately additional burdens for compliance by upstream producers. Scheme managers are concerned with this increased competition by firms' proprietary systems:

> We need to be very clear what is the difference with other [firm-level] schemes. Legal deforestation is not the same as zero deforestation. Third-party certification with accreditation is not the same as one simple, single audit firm certifying every scheme.

In connection to deforestation, alternative forms of private governance have indeed emerged that are not necessarily alternatives to VSS but that could reduce their role in regulating sustainability in value chains. Multiparty pledges such as the Soy Moratorium reduce the relevance of voluntary certification initiatives at least for deforestation-related concerns as they include public enforcement and strong enforcement mechanisms to avoid that noncompliant products are traded. Auditing is also supplanted as a monitoring mechanism by the possibility to use remote sensing and publicly available satellite imageries,[38] which are, however, also integrated in VSS under the awareness of the limits of audit systems.[39] A respondent from a nongovernmental organization summarized the implications of HRDD as follows:

[34] Interview with certification manager.

[35] Ibid.

[36] T. Thorlakson, J. F. de Zegher, and E. F. Lambin, Companies' Contribution to Sustainability through Global Supply Chains (2018) 115:9 *Proceedings of the National Academy of Sciences* 2072; E. Meidinger, Governance Interactions in Sustainable Supply Chain Management, in *Transnational Business Governance Interactions: Advancing Marginalised Actors and Enhancing Regulatory Quality* (S. Wood, R. Schmidt, E. Meidinger, B. Eberlein, and K. W. Abbott eds., 2019), 52.

[37] S. Subramanian, Is Fair Trade Finished?, *The Guardian*, July 23, 2019.

[38] Interview with NGO representative.

[39] Interview with scheme manager.

> If [VSS] look at the mandatory human rights due diligence requirements that are increasing particularly in Europe, and realize that they have to lift their game and this is what they're going to need to do to essentially provide that service for companies so that they can make their human rights due diligence requirements, then that's an opportunity. If they do it, that's an opportunity but on the other hand, if they don't rise to that challenge then companies will decide they're not an effective tool for human rights due diligence and find other ways to do it .... it will only be a legitimate process for human rights due diligence if the [VSS] and its own process of certification, etcetera, is robust.

As organizations, VSS themselves also bear the responsibility in the UNGP not just to respect human rights but also to avoid associations to human rights violations to which they are directly linked through their commercial relations. Recent dispute resolution before the national contact points (NCP) for the OECD Guidelines confirmed that this can be the case, thereby opening the door to other complaints. In two cases against RPSO and Bonsucro in Switzerland and the United Kingdom, both NCPs confirmed previous practice to expand what they considered as a "multinational corporation" under the OECD Guidelines for Multinational Corporations[40] – an instrument that expressly operationalizes the UNGP. This notion was interpreted to include other transnational private actors such as NGOs and sport bodies such as FIFA. The Swiss NCP's involvement in the RSPO case was rather narrow in light of jurisdictional limitations.[41] In the Bonsucro case, however, the UK NCP held that it could be possible for a multi-stakeholder initiative to breach provisions of the OECD Guidelines such as the presence of a human rights policy and the continuous performance of HRDD including the exercise of leverage and mitigation of adverse human rights impact.[42] Membership was explicitly considered as a business relation directly linking human rights harms committed by a (prospective) member to a VSS.[43] The factual assessment of these claims is currently pending after failure of the parties to reach a mutually agreed solution.

This process was described as:

> an important wake-up call [for VSS] in the sense that, "Look, we have to be more reactive to this type of thing and we need to have a system where really what we're asking of our members is broader than just our standard and that certification part of it. It's that broader alignment with human rights over to the UNGP."[44]

[40] D. Carolei, Survival International v World Wide Fund for Nature: Using the OECD Guidelines for Multinational Enterprises as a Means of Ensuring NGO Accountability (2018) 18:2 *Human Rights Law Review* 371.

[41] Before the Swiss NCP: *TuK Indonesia* v. *Roundtable on Sustainable Palm Oil (RSPO)*.

[42] UK National Contact Point (NCP) for the OECD Guidelines for Multinational Enterprises, Decision: Initial assessment by the UK National Contact Point for the OECD Guidelines for Multinational Enterprises: complaint from IDI, EC and LICADHO against Bonsucro Ltd, para. 13.

[43] UK NCP, para. 14 and 24.

[44] Interview with scheme manager.

7.4 RELEVANT ASPECTS OF HRDD FOR VSS

The type of due diligence legislation currently discussed in the EU,[45] with specific rules for agricultural commodities and ecosystem conversion,[46] will likely require companies to undertake due diligence for all human rights and environmental impacts in the entire value chain. This would reflect the UNGP and sector-specific OECD Guidance documents asking firms to account for the entire adverse social and environmental impact they caused, to which they contributed, or are directly linked through their business relations.[47] Within mandatory HRDD and with respect to the business responsibility to exercise HRDD the function of VSS must be explained. Firms demand supply chain risk-management tools, to manage risks, ensure conformity, and enhance productivity, reputation, and profitability[48] and also to ensure respect of legal requisites. The requirements of a scheme must therefore be aligned to HRDD as provided in the UNGP, OECD Guidelines, and the specifications of future regulatory instruments for a VSS to be of assistance in firms' responsibilities. Where issues and risks covered by a scheme align with those faced by a firm, standards are suitable for integration in that firm's HRDD processes as a non-dispositive evidence of low risk,[49] as also done under the EU Timber Regulation.[50] As a consequence of a possible narrower scope of VSS, compliance with a scheme would not grant a presumption of conformity with legislation but would serve as a rebuttable presumption of "low risk." This approach has been problematic for VSS in the timber legality space, as certified firms were disappointed that the cost of certification did not lead to opening up market access and ensuring legal compliance in the EU.[51]

The limitations of VSS must be clear. Firstly, HRDD responsibilities include all possible human rights affected by business operations,[52] but VSS may have a narrower human rights scope. For example, FSC does not generally refer to all

45 European Parliament resolution of March 10, 2021 with recommendations to the Commission on corporate due diligence and corporate accountability (2020/2129 INL).

46 European Parliament resolution of October 22, 2020 with recommendations to the Commission on an EU legal framework to halt and reverse EU-driven global deforestation (2020/2006 INL).

47 For discussion over these categories of involvement and their interpretation: E. Partiti, Polycentricity and Polyphony in International Law: Interpreting the Corporate Responsibility to Respect Human Rights (2021) 70:1 *International and Comparative Law Quarterly* 133.

48 S. Ponte and P. Gibbon, Quality Standards, Conventions, and the Governance of Global Value Shains (2005) 34:1 *Economy & Society* 1.

49 E. Partiti, The Place of Voluntary Standards in Managing Social and Environmental Risks in Global Value Chains (2022) 13:1 *European Journal of Risk Regulation* 114.

50 Regulation (EU) No. 995/2010 of the European Parliament and the Council of May 11, 2009, laying down the obligations of operators who place timber and timber products on the market. OJ L 295/13 (EUTR).

51 Interview with certification manager.

52 UN Office of the High Commissioner for Human Rights, The Corporate Responsibility to Respect Human Rights. An interpretative guide (2012), at 13.

human rights in its Principles and Criteria but, as its focus lies on forest operations, it covers human rights affected by forest management operations such as workers', customary, community, and Indigenous Peoples' rights.[53] The effectiveness of VSS as risk mitigation tools depends also on the extent to which a given social and environmental concern or harm can be detected. This links to the vexed question of whether certification is an effective mechanism to verify and ensure that the scheme's criteria are implemented properly.

Secondly, HRDD responsibilities apply throughout the entire value chain. From the perspective of a downstream firm marketing in a jurisdiction with (future) HRDD legislation, HRDD must identify, mitigate, and remedy possible risks and harms all the way upstream. Furthermore, a downstream firm could be implicated in adverse impact through a producer from which it sources both certified and noncertified material and in which human rights violations occur in the context of noncertified volumes. Different would be a scenario where harm occurs in a production unit whose products are not traded or marketed by downstream firms. While some NGOs are keen to expand the possible responsibilities of downstream firms,[54] there would not be a "direct link" with adverse impact through business relations. A similar situation would arise where harm is generated by a subsidiary or associated entity of a firm with which the downstream firm does business but with which there is no direct relation. However, from the perspective of the human rights responsibility of that upstream entity, there would be association to human right harm. This situation is particularly challenging for VSS' own HRDD, as they would be certifying entities causing or contributing to human rights violations and also breaching their standards in noncertified operations.

However, most requirements of schemes apply to the level of harvest, plantation, and unit of production. Even where the entire value chain must be certified under forms of chain of custody certification, intermediary entities such as mills, plants, and processing facilities are rarely requested to comply with requirements concerning environmental impacts and human rights. A 2019 comparative study of FSC and PEFC's principles and criteria and chain of custody requirements[55] concluded that the forest management standards are aligned to the ILO Fundamental Conventions, the UNGP, and the OECD Guidelines, and these are assessed by auditors. However, the chain of custody requirements include only compliance with ILO Conventions and are limited to an indirect reference to FSC Policy for Association and a self-declaration of compliance by firms.[56] Scheme holders consider that the purpose of chain of custody standards is to assure credibility of claims, and therefore

[53] FSC, FSC Support to Respect for Human Rights (2019), at 3.

[54] Interview with NGO representative.

[55] R. Kusumaningtyas, *Labour Rights and Human Rights in Forest Certification Standards: An Analysis of FSC and PEFC Adherence to the UN Guiding Principles, ILO Fundamental Conventions and OECD Guidelines* (2019).

[56] FSC Chain of Custody Certification FSC-STD-40-004 V3–0, Art 1.3.

human rights issues are not necessary, also because they consider risk to lie at the farm level.[57] Furthermore, requirements for nonproducing members have traditionally been lower than those for producers in order to attract downstream firms to participate.[58] However, as Section 7.5 illustrates, these features of VSS are changing.

7.5 IMPACT OF HRDD ON VSS

Some VSS are attempting to build in respect for human rights, including an obligation to perform HRDD, within membership requirements applicable also to downstream actors and retailers, that is, the noncertified members. The emergence of HRDD responsibilities for upstream entities is also visible in the expanded criteria for certification to noncertified volumes and entities. Some schemes are introducing the principle that producers whose only part of their operations is certified cannot breach key requirements in the noncertified areas or production units. For intermediary supply chain actors such as mills, this approach results in extending criteria to all sourced volumes, thereby transmitting upstream a request for certification-compliant production. Additional human rights criteria are also appearing in chain of custody certification. This expands the substantive obligations so that the scheme covers broader supply chain segments for the downstream firms and therefore better aligns with HRDD requirements. Section 7.5.1 discusses these developments concerning VSS regulatory activities. Section 7.5.2 focuses instead on the recent expansion of novel forms of nonregulatory activities centred on value chain collaboration and engagement.

7.5.1 *Expanding Requirements*

FSC established in 2011 a Policy for Association that attempts to extend FSC standards beyond certified operations. Certificate holders, certification bodies, partners, or members associated with FSC can be disassociated if responsible – as a company or because of activities of subsidiary companies or subcontractor – for violations of key criteria including illegal logging or trade, destruction of high conservation value forests, significant conversion of forests to planation, GMO use, violations of traditional rights, human rights, and breaches of ILO Core Conventions.[59] The Policy of Association is enforced by FSC and is part of the due diligence performed by the organization. FSC is attempting to move beyond a self-declaration for prospective members toward actively performing due diligence

[57] Interview with scheme manager.
[58] Ibid.
[59] FSC Policy for Association. FSC-POL-01-004 V2–0 EN.

about whether firms are involved in unacceptable activities under the Policy for Association.[60]

Between 2015 and 2017, FSC attempted to reform the Policy for Association by formalizing how it performed due diligence. The proposed policy provided that prospective members will be subject to additional screening in high-risk cases. Data is collected via a self-assessment complemented by stakeholder input.[61] If there is evidence of violations, the matter would be dealt with under the procedure to process complaints against breaches of the Policy for Association, with a Complaint Panel that will make recommendations about association. Disassociation should take place only in the presence of repeated violations, as the organization prefers to address violations through cooperation given that dissociation would not produce positive outcomes for forests.[62] Revision and expansion of the Policy for Association has been complex, and an attempt to strengthen its enforcement by FSC, as well as clarifying when a member may breach the key criteria,[63] produced no result and had to be put on hold.[64] Another attempt for revision started in 2020. Through its Shared Responsibility policy, RPSO included the requirement that all members such as NGOs, banks and investors, retailers, manufacturers, processors, and traders must respect human rights, especially free prior and informed consent, in their entire operations and have grievance mechanisms in place.[65] In this way, RSPO supports respect for human rights and the performance of HRDD within its membership requirements for downstream firms.

Similarly, Bonsucro scaled-up its membership requirements through a Code of Conduct. In March 2020, Bonsucro aligned it to the UNGP and the OECD/FAO Guidance for Responsible Agriculture Value Chains by recognizing human rights responsibilities of members in relation to their suppliers. The Code therefore requires certified and noncertified members (i.e., respectively, mills and all other supply chain actors) to commit to continuous improvement, respect human rights and protect natural ecosystems, embed this commitment in operations, and communicate progress.[66] By incorporating the UNGP's concept of "direct link" to human rights harm that determines the boundaries of companies' responsibility to respect, the Code applies also to products and services linked to sugarcane

60 FSC, Due diligence evaluation for the association with FSC. FSC-PRO-10-004 V2–0 EN Draft 2 (2016).

61 Ibid., Art. 2.1 and 2.2.

62 FSC, Processing Policy for Association Complaints in the FSC certification scheme. FSC-PRO-01-009 (V3–0) EN, Art. 5.21.

63 FSC, Second Consultation Report on FSC-POL-01-004 V3–0.

64 https://fsc.org/en/current-processes/policy-for-the-association-of-organizations-with-fsc-fsc-pol-01-004

65 RSPO Shared Responsibility Task Force, Shared Responsibility Requirements and Implementation, at 26.

66 Bonsucro Code of Conduct, 1.2.

production, processing, and sourcing.[67] The self-assessment performed by members requires them to improve compliance of their production, processing, and sourcing. As under the UNGP,[68] the expected commitment of members varies according to the risks at hand and the nature and size of operations.[69] Members are also expected to provide remedies to adverse impact, including via operational-level grievance mechanisms and remediation in line with UNGP Principle 31.[70]

Bonsucro ensures compliance with its Code of Conduct not by including its requirements in audits but via reporting appraised by the organization. Action plans may be requested in case of noncompliance, with the possibility to refer to Bonsucro's Grievance Mechanism.[71] Bonsucro also acknowledges their own responsibility toward members through risk assessment.[72] An enhanced due diligence of members was introduced, assessing their social and environmental risk. The process entails online searches, consultation of court records in the country of operation and with other organizations that may possess information about relevant social and environmental impacts of the perspective member, and comments by interested parties on the basis of which the level of risk and expected actions are determined.[73] The process may lead to additional requirements imposed on the (candidate) member. In a recent case, Bonsucro engaged in discussion with local stakeholders and used its leverage to require a prospective member to establish corrective plans including disengagement with suppliers breaching human rights.[74] Where allegations were raised about the involvement of another candidate member's with forced evictions of indigenous communities, Bonsucro engaged with different stakeholders and ascertained that, while the candidate was not directly involved, some of its suppliers might have been responsible. Bonsucro thus requested in the action plan the implementation of risk management systems, a requirement of continuous dialogue, and a disengagement strategy.[75] This is in line with the UNGP requirement that leverage should be exercised as much as possible, and disengagement should only take place where leverage failed to achieve results.

Concerning the expansion of certification requirements to noncertified volumes and organizations to account for the human rights responsibility of the firms at hand, some VSS are expanding the human rights requirements applicable in their chain of custody certification. Some schemes "don't want to create a Chain of Custody Standard that is covering human rights issues. The purpose of that standard is to

[67] Ibid., 2.1.
[68] UNGPs Commentary to Principle 12.
[69] Interview with certification manager.
[70] Bonsucro Code of Conduct – Implementation Guidelines, Point H-J.
[71] Bonsucro Code of Conduct – Reporting Guidelines.
[72] Interview with scheme manager.
[73] Ibid.; see also Bonsucro – Membership Application Procedure, point 4.
[74] Interview with scheme manager.
[75] Ibid.

assure credibility of claims."[76] Other VSS are instead broadening the applicable requirements under chain of custody standards. FSC recently incorporated core labor standards into auditing requirements in chain of custody.[77] As they become part of the audit criteria, this update strengthened enforcement of human rights provisions that would otherwise only be covered under FSC Policy for Association and its self-assessment. In addition, the expansion of human rights in chain of custody allows downstream entities sourcing FSC-certified products to receive assurance of low risk of at least certain human rights violations in the entire supply chain. In a similar manner, various additional social and environmental requirements have been introduced in Rainforest Alliance's 2020 version of its supply chain standard.[78]

Bonsucro is introducing additional rules for certification of mills and processors concerning noncertified volumes. In the current standard, the supply area included in the unit of certification comprises the farms supplying cane in conformity with Bonsucro requirements. Where this is less than 100 percent of the supply, a respective percentage of production is considered as certified.[79] In fact, mills on average select an area to certify that represents only 23 percent of the mill supply, and the production standard applies only to that area. Bonsucro is revising its standards to introduce a system where human rights requirements apply to the entire mill supply, including areas neither controlled by the mill nor certified but that are managed by smallholders whose certification is complex and where environmental and social risks lie.[80] These requirements include enacting "sustainability policies" to respect human rights, mapping vulnerable stakeholders, and assessing risks.[81] While auditing is limited to assess whether sustainability policies and other requirements are int place, these new criteria – if implemented successfully by mills – are capable to expand the reach of human rights standards under the HRDD responsibility of the mill. The standard would therefore acknowledge that mills' responsibility extends beyond certified volumes and includes all entities to which they are directly linked via their sourcing activities.

Also RSPO similarly introduced in the 2018 revision of its Principles and Criteria requirements that mandate the entire unit of certification, in all its business operations and transaction, to have a policy to respect human rights at all value chain levels.[82] Other standards focusing on GMO such as ProTerra require mills and processors employing inputs from noncertified farms to design and implement

76 Ibid.

77 Ibid.; https://fsc.org/en/current-processes/incorporating-the-fsc-core-labour-requirements-into-the-coc-standard.

78 Rainforest Alliance, Sustainable Agriculture Standard: Supply Chain Requirements (2020).

79 Bonsucro/Bonsucro EU RED Production Standard V4.2 2016, at 12.

80 Interview with certification manager.

81 Bonsucro Draft Production Standard Version 5, Criteria 1.1, www.bonsucro.com/wp-content/uploads/2020/05/Bonsucro-Production-Standard-V5.1.pdf.

82 RSPO 2018 P&C, Criteria 1.2 and 4.1.

supply chain control systems to ensure that core GMO and social and environmental indicators are met.[83] While these requirements avoid commingling of GMO and non-GMO materials, where human rights requirements are monitored, the standard also covers the entire human rights responsibility of the mills concerning the farms to which it is directly linked. Verification of supply at the farm level is undertaken over a five-year period through third-party audit.[84]

In light of HRDD responsibilities, VSS are spurred to reflect over their own due diligence structures.[85] "Some of these elements were already considered good practices, but now from this lens of mandatory due diligence, these issues are going to become probably more important."[86] In addition to a more thorough screening of prospective members discussed above, where schemes are not detecting noncompliance with certain criteria in spite of the presence of a high risk, they may be expected to carefully assess whether audits are working properly and whether they should not employ additional venues to have access to information, or establish complaints and grievance tools to accede to it.[87] In the 2020 standards revision, UTZ-RA strengthened mechanisms to collect geospatial data complemented by remote sensing and baseline mapping to supplement auditing in determining whether land conversion occurred. In this way, the scheme already knows which farms present a high risk of past deforestation and will inform auditors about possible concerns.[88]

Generally, VSS also have to tackle the unintended adverse impact stemming from compliance with their standards. While certification may make visible existing conflicts,[89] in other cases, the standard may generate adverse impact or may have to balance between different types of harm. To lessen the negative environmental impact of burning sugar cane by farmers, standards may contemplate requiring increased mechanization. This may however impact on human rights of the workforce. Bonsucro includes this type of risk into its risk management systems. As a form of impact mitigation, the scheme and the certified entities offer retraining programs, and information is shared with other certified firms that aim to increase mechanization and could generate similar harms.[90]

In the context of deforestation-related criteria and their possible human rights implications, a scheme is in the process of implementing enhanced definitions of forests and covered ecosystems for the entire production of farmers and mills located

83 See, for example, ProTerra Standard for Social Responsibility and Environmental Sustainability Version 4.1 September 25, 2019, point 1.2.

84 Interview with scheme manager.

85 ISEAL, Assuring Compliance with Social and Environmental Standards. Code of Good Practice (2018).

86 Interview with scheme manager.

87 Ibid.

88 Ibid.

89 Ibid.

90 Ibid.

in the Brazilian Cerrado independently from whether certain areas will be certified or destined to certified processors and mills. Both definitions and elements of verification system will build on those provided by the Accountability Framework initiative (AFi),[91] a global benchmark for deforestation claims across value chains established by NGOs and aligned to the UNGP. Benchmarking criteria therefore affect VSS substantive requirements. The effects of AFi on other definitional elements that scale-up standards' formal requirements are also visible. The 2020 revision of Rainforest Alliance's production standards has explicitly incorporated AFi's approach centered on non-conversion of forests and natural ecosystems and has embedded relevant concepts and definitions.[92] Other standard-setters are in the process of including aspects of AFi relevant to their schemes in their requirements, and others – such as the Responsible Leather Roundtable – already use AFi definitions.[93]

7.5.2 *Collaboration in Risk Mitigation and Remediations*

Human rights abuses and social conflicts within value chains are likely to endure without collaboration and engagement among all stakeholders involved.[94] HRDD requires collaboration between downstream firms and upstream entities.[95] Collaboration is also essential with non-business stakeholders and human rights holders to ensure mitigation of impacts and remediation. Collaboration may require investment in value chain mapping and transparency and even supporting upstream producers. Firms should avoid risk-adverse behavior such as disengaging from noncompliant suppliers (which may in fact aggravate the situation for human rights) or stop sourcing from high-risk areas.[96] Finally, HRDD also requires that human rights violations, where they occur, are remedied and the status quo is restored, a requirement that is more easily fulfilled through collaboration.

Engagement can take various forms, such as committing to higher wages or purchase volumes, longer-term contractual relations, as well as investment by downstream firms to improve working, social, and environmental conditions upstream.[97] The provisions of economic incentives and tools to improve

91 Ibid.

92 Interview with certification program manager.

93 Ibid.

94 J. Rotter, P.-E. Airike, and C. Mark-Herbert, Exploring Political Corporate Social Responsibility in Global Supply Chains (2014) 125:4 *Journal of Business Ethics* 581.

95 Shift Project, Using Leverage in Business Relationships to Reduce Human Rights Risks (November 2013), www.shiftproject.org/resources/publications/leverage-business-relationships-reduce-human-rights-risk/.

96 UN Office of the High Commissioner for Human Rights, The Corporate Responsibility to Respect Human Rights. An interpretative guide. HR/PUB/12/02 (2012), at 50–51.

97 Shift Project, Bringing a Human Rights Lens to Stakeholder Engagement, Shift Workshop Report No. 3, August 2013, https://shiftproject.org/wp-content/uploads/2013/08/Shift_stakeholderengagement2013.pdf.

productivity intend to remove some of the economic drivers of social and environmental harm. At the same time, engagement ensures change on the ground and avoids that certification creates segregated markets where compliant products are sold in Western markets and noncompliant produce is sold elsewhere. However, this principle is complex to operationalize as companies lack the knowledge and incentives to actively engage. Engagement may be burdensome, requiring cost-sharing and direct financing. The allocation of costs and responsibilities remains unclear and contestable unless fairness considerations are incorporated to offset frequent downstream firms' exploitation of their suppliers.[98]

While offering risk mitigation and remediation through collaboration is the responsibility of firms, requiring engagement has proven difficult for standards, but this is an area where VSS are increasing their focus:

> That's where you need organizations to take companies by the hand, bring them together, and say, "Look, this is where your investment is going to go." The great thing about a mandatory law would be that then they actually have to put in that investment, they can't just walk away, but you're still going to need that glue between companies to actually do something in a more collective sense. I think standard system to a certain degree, they can be that glue although, again, they are still maybe not active enough in that space to think about what this really comprehensive mitigation or remediation look like. Some of them have developed mechanisms and to a certain degree, just the noncompliances in the standard, you can build investments around it .... Anyway, the interesting role or where I definitely hope that standard systems will play a greater role is exactly in that wider remediation and mitigation space where it's not just that they provide some information about which producers are compliant or noncompliant, but they can actually provide an entry point for companies that have to invest in mitigation and remediation because their inspections are linked to those problems.[99]

Beside their traditional multi-stakeholder structures, VSS are introducing or strengthening collaborative features traceable to the UNGP requirement of engagement between upstream and downstream in mitigating and remedying impacts. This pathway confirms the intuition of those suggesting a reframing of VSS functions, one less concerned with authoritative rule-making and more centered on assistance in broader practices concerning sustainable supply chain management.[100] One area where collaboration was enhanced concerns the amount of certified products that entities downstream commit to purchase. Purchase commitments ensure a steady demand for certified products that guarantees price premiums for

98 M. C. Schleper, C. Blome, and D. A. Wuttke, The Dark Side of Buyer Power: Supplier Exploitation and the Role of Ethical Climates (2017) 140 *Journal of Business Ethics* 97.

99 Interview with scheme manager.

100 L. Fransen, Beyond Regulatory Governance? On the Evolutionary Trajectory of Transnational Private Sustainability Governance (2018) 146 *Ecological Economics* 772.

producers to undertake the necessary investments.[101] Certification managers raised concerns about the "magnificent claims" made by downstream companies joining an initiative while only sourcing a limited amount of certified products and receiving a positive image return.[102] While some schemes tackle this issue by strengthening their rules concerning claims about certified sourcing,[103] some organizations took structural steps to actively engage chain actors and require downstream entities to provide support to farmers in facilitating compliance with the standards. This allocates responsibilities for the costs of sustainability, mitigates the risk of social and environmental harm, and possibly scales up impact to areas and products also not sold in Western markets.

RSPO introduced in 2019 a "Shared Responsibility" policy applicable to all members but is particularly relevant for noncertified members. Similar to the FSC and Bonsucro cases discussed above, RSPO members comply with a Code of Conduct requiring them to implement requirements for their own entire organization that must align with the RSPO standards.[104] This broad requirement was expanded though the notion of Shared Responsibility defining the commitments for collective action, collaboration, and accountability needed to transform palm oil markets toward more responsible outcomes.[105] Members must comply with common principles and policies, support small farmers, raise awareness, and offer training as well as technical and personnel support to RSPO. The most salient aspect concerns the identification of volume targets for buyers. Manufactures and retailers commit to purchase an extra 15 percent of certified palm oil in the first year of implementation, while traders and processors have a 2 percent target. This commitment from downstream firms matches the commitment from farmers to comply with more stringent standards.[106] Members must report on their purchase commitments, which are independently verified and included in the audit under the Chain of Custody Standards. Systems for sanctions and incentives are currently being discussed, as well as the provision of financial contributions to support smallholders.[107]

A similar approach was introduced by RA-UTZ in the 2020 standards revision to ensure that risks, costs, and benefits of sustainability transformations are evenly distributed between producers and buyers. The new standard introduced a "sustainability differential," i.e. a price premium to certified producers to recognize farmers'

[101] C. Gallemore, A. Guisinger, M. Kruuse, D. Ruysschaert, and K. Jespersen, Escaping the "Teenage" Years: The Politics of Rigor and the Evolution of Private Environmental Standards (2018) 152 *Ecological Economics* 83.

[102] Interview with scheme manager.

[103] RTRS, Use of the Logo & Claims Policy. Version 2.0 (2011).

[104] RSPO, Code of Conduct for Members, Art. 3.2 (2015).

[105] RSPO, Shared Responsibility Task Force. Shared Responsibility Requirements and Implementation (2019), at 7.

[106] https://rspo.org/news-and-events/news/what-are-the-new-shared-responsibility-rules.

[107] RSPO, *supra* note 105, at 16.

efforts and to support sustainable production. While a price premium is already present in schemes such as FairTrade, buyers of certified products under RA-UTZ certification are also required to make (and report about "sustainability investments" necessary to enable farmers in their value chains to comply with production requirements or the cost of audit and on the basis of investment plans designed by certificate holders themselves.[108] Both sustainability differential and sustainability investment are paid by the first buyer, included in the sale contract, and recorded in RA's traceability system.[109] Bonsucro's Implementation Guidelines of the 2020 Code of Conduct also require continuous commitments and improvements that can be demonstrated by sourcing increasing percentage of certified material or supporting suppliers toward certification.[110]

Remediation for social and environmental harms has also been introduced in recent iterations of RA and RSPO standards. Since 2014–2015, RSPO requires certified members that engaged in noncompliant land clearance for plantation or other facilities after the 2005 cutoff date to use remediation and compensations mechanisms. Members will have to designate protected areas to offset previous conversion.[111] If land-use change impacts on the human rights of affected communities, social remediation and compensation plans must be negotiated with right holders.[112] In the 2020 revision of RA standards, in line with HRDD, a separate protocol was introduced requiring remediation and offering guidance on how to effectively remediate human rights violations.[113] A strong remediation guidance is also included in AFi,[114] which was developed building on the UNGP requirements.[115]

Also VSS' growing involvement with integrated jurisdiction and landscape management shows an extension beyond individual producers as a unit of analysis, in combination with strong elements of engagement with and among public and private actors. As the eradication of adverse social and environmental impacts requires addressing structural issues with the involvement of all relevant public and private actors,[116] VSS are supporting efforts in specific jurisdictions to identify smallholder lands and establish district-level multi-stakeholder governance structures to monitor, report, and verify land-use change. These approaches are part of

[108] RA, Sustainable Agriculture Standards (2020), at 8.

[109] RA, Annex 6 – Traceability and Shared Responsibility (2020), at 16–17.

[110] Bonsucro (2020) Code of Conduct – Implementation Guidelines, Point B.

[111] Interview with certification manager.

[112] RSPO Remediation and Compensation Procedure (RaCP) Related to Land Clearance without Prior High Conservation Value (HCV) Assessment RSPO-PRO-T02–001 V2.0, at 15.

[113] RA, Annex 4 – Rainforest Alliance Remediation Protocol v. 1 (2020).

[114] AFi, Operational Guidance on Remediation and Access to Remedy (2020).

[115] Interview with certification manager.

[116] P. Pacheco, G. Schoneveld, A. Dermawan, H. Komarudin, and M. Djama, Governing sustainable palm oil supply: Disconnects, complementarities, and antagonisms between state regulations and private standards (2020) 14:3 *Regulation & Governance* 568.

a trend linking private initiatives with REDD+.[117] However, the focus of landscape and jurisdictional initiatives moves beyond certified producers and aims at structurally involving other supply chains actors including the financial industry.

While VSS have already been cooperating within landscape and jurisdictional initiatives for a few years,[118] some are beginning to offer jurisdiction-based certifications. RSPO has finalized a second consultation on a "Jurisdictional Approach to Certification" that aims to establish, in partnership with public authorities, a stepwise process toward granting certification against RSPO standards to an entire jurisdictional organization.[119] ISEAL recently released a code of good practices applying not to standard systems but to both landscape and jurisdictional initiatives that wish to make credible claims about their activities and to other initiatives developing frameworks for landscape and jurisdictional projects.[120] While recognizing the potential of these initiatives, ISEAL stresses that they remain complementary to current supply chain tools like standards systems, which are capable to verify and incentivize specific sustainability improvements at the farm level.[121] Also here, the perceived risk for schemes is that firms may decide to source from certain landscapes or jurisdictions, giving up certifications.[122]

7.6 CONCLUSION

As public authority intervenes in the regulation of sustainability and human rights across value chains, both through soft law and via mandatory rules, isomorphic pressures among private certifications generate convergence among VSS requirements and approaches, with VSS increasing also their nonregulatory activities. A visible trend among private schemes is the expanded application of key requirements to noncertified volumes and firms to account for the human rights responsibilities of entities at different levels of the value chain. As a form of transnational private governance applicable to the firms and producers that wish to comply with their standards, VSS are complementary to international and national provisions in the social and environmental domains.[123] This happens by design, so that VSS can be used by firms to demonstrate compliance and manage social and environmental

[117] C. Meyer and D. Miller, Zero Deforestation Zones: The Case for Linking Deforestation-Free Supply Chain Initiatives and Jurisdictional REDD (2015) 34 *Journal of Sustainable Forestry* 559.

[118] ISEAL, How Sustainability Standards Can Contribute to Landscape Approaches and Zero Deforestation Commitments (2016).

[119] RSPO, RSPO Jurisdictional Approach to Certification. Second Draft (2020).

[120] ISAL, Making Credible Jurisdictional Claims. ISEAL Good Practice Guide Version 1.0 (October 2020).

[121] Ibid., at 2

[122] Interview with scheme manager.

[123] E. Partiti, Orchestration as a Form of Public Action: The EU Engagement with Voluntary Sustainability Standards (2019) 25:1 *European Law Journal* 115.

risks. If VSS want to retain their complementarity, they must adapt to emerging public requirements. This allows schemes to better fit in firms' HRDD systems as they cover risks for a broader number of value chain entities. VSS themselves are enacting enhanced due diligence and risk management procedures to account for their own HRDD responsibilities vis-à-vis possible human rights impacts by members and certified firms.

With emerging obligations of HRDD, schemes are no longer competing with public rules in a transnational space or deterring their emergence. As public regulators step up the regulation of responsible business conduct, it will be public requirements that determine what represents sustainable or responsible conduct across value chains. This process can be seen as a co-optation of VSS where VSS do not anymore independently define sustainable practices but operationalize detailed requirements of what constitutes HRDD that are emanations of public authority both at the international and at the national/regional level. In this context, the implementing functions of VSS in transposing legal obligations in the social and environmental domains are diminished in autonomy. Therefore, public intervention is capable to effectively align transitional private regulators to public rules. This could be seen as an instance where public authority has been capable, if partially, to get a handle on economic private activism.[124] However, HRDD spurs VSS to account for impacts of various entities associated to them, thus further expanding the application of their standards to more firms across value chains. The extension of this form of indirect public control is therefore counterbalanced by an increased relevance of VSS in the supply chain they govern.

The impact of HRDD on VSS is linked to its double nature of opportunity and threat for VSS, in line with the notion of organizational crisis discussed in Section 7.3. HRDD gave VSS the possibility to leverage their organizational resourcefulness to engage in new activities and establish new institutional features. By strengthening their efforts in the area of engagement and collaboration between firms at different levels in the value chain, VSS function is also expanding and partially realigning. By providing standards and associated services, VSS also increasingly engage in non-regulatory activities such as offering fora for engagement for risk mitigation, remediation, and sharing costs of social and environmental compliance required by HRDD. This does not fully shelter VSS from the possible threat stemming from other alternative tools for HRDD. However, it creates a novel goal to which VSS are arguably well placed to contribute. The capacity of VSS to expand their activities to new nonregulatory domains despite the influence of public authority on their regulatory function also testifies to their resilience.

[124] See P. Delimatsis, "The Resilience of Private Authority in Times of Crisis" in this volume (Chapter 1).

8

The Politics of Collaborative Governance in Global Supply Chains

Power and Pushback in the Bangladesh Accord

Juliane Reinecke and Jimmy Donaghey

8.1 INTRODUCTION: COLLABORATIVE ACTION AND TRANSNATIONAL GOVERNANCE

On April 23, 2013, the Rana Plaza building complex collapsed claiming the lives of over 1,100, mainly women, ready-made garment workers and injuring many more. This was just the latest in a series of fatal factory fires and collapses that killed hundreds of garment workers in Bangladesh, many despite factories being audited against international private accountability standards, including some of those in the Rana Plaza complex. The collapse also demonstrates the failure of prevailing business practice to deal with labor issues in the global supply chain based on individual social auditing by international brands of factory compliance against accountability standards and codes of conducts. To date, the main approaches to transnational labor governance have been either the development of business-driven codes of conduct[1] or agreements between individual multinationals and international trade unions in the form of global framework agreements.[2] However, as discussed elsewhere, neither solves the chimera that is transnational labor governance. In this chapter, we focus on a novel transnational governance initiative that was developed after the Rana Plaza crisis: the Bangladesh Accord for Building and Fire Safety.

[1] R. M. Locke, *The Promise and Limits of Private Power: Promoting Labor Standards in a Global Economy* (2013).

[2] N. Hammer, International Framework Agreements: Global Industrial Relations between Rights and Bargaining (2005) 11:4 *Transfer: European Review of Labour and Research* 511. M. Helfen, E. Schüßler, and S. Botzem, Legitimation Strategies of Corporate Elites in the Field of Labor Regulation: Changing Responses to Global Framework Agreements (2015) 43 *Research in the Sociology of Organizations* 243; S. Ashwin, C. Oka, E. Schüßler, R. Alexander, and N. Lohmeyer, Spillover Effects across Transnational Industrial Relations Agreements: The Potential and Limits of Collective Action in Global Supply Chains (2020) 73:4 *Industrial and Labor Relations Review* 995.

In common with a central theme of this volume, a central feature of this chapter is the role that crises played in determining the dynamics of transnational private governance. Drawing on the work of Louis Althusser, we view the idea of crisis as "a critical moment" for institutions where "we're uncertain and don't really know whether the crisis [or "situation" to avoid being tautological] will culminate in death or rebirth."[3] While not seeing crises as necessarily leading to such stark binary outcomes, we share the idea that the defining feature of a crisis is a period of extreme uncertainty and this uncertainty may force actors to make decisions that mark a departure from previous practice in order to emerge from the uncertainty. In this context, the chapter focuses on two primary crises that were central to the dynamics of the Accord. First, the role that the very crisis nature of the Rana Plaza disaster played in developing the collective approach that drove the Accord. Second, once established, the Accord itself faced a crisis in the form of a conflict between the transnational level governance of the Accord and the national regulatory system of Bangladesh. While the Accord had many novel features,[4] in this chapter, we focus on one particularly novel aspect of the Accord – the nature of the collective action created through the Accord – and highlight both the institutional design features that were at its foundations but also how the collective action was highly political in nature and why ultimately this contestability of its actions became a weakness in the end.

The supply chain model, where both buyer and supplier firms are involved in multiple contracts and implementing multiple private governance standards, has led to fragmentation of labor governance.[5] Thus, as globalization has deepened and multinational corporations seek to reduce labor costs, private transnational labor governance has emerged as a key area of focus where MNCs seek regimes with low labor standards while simultaneously wanting to avoid association with the most egregious labor abuses.[6] This private governance often emerges in response to pressures exerted by civil society actors, such as unions and NGOs, particularly when crises emerge.[7] In this context, neither public governance nor individual

[3] L. Althusser, The Crisis of Marxism, *in Power and Opposition in Post-revolutionary Societies* (1979), 225.

[4] J. Donaghey and J. Reinecke, When Industrial Democracy Meets Corporate Social Responsibility: A Comparison of the Bangladesh Accord and Alliance as Responses to the Rana Plaza Disaster (2018) 56:1 *British Journal of Industrial Relations* 14. J. Reinecke and J. Donaghey, After Rana Plaza: Building Coalitional Power for Labour Rights between Unions and (Consumption-Based) Social Movement Organisations (2015) 22:5 *Organization* 720.

[5] J. Donaghey, J. Reinecke, C. Niforou, and B. Lawson, From Employment Relations to Consumption Relations: Balancing Labor Governance in Global Supply Chains (2014) 53:2 *Human Resource Management* 229. J. Morris, J. Jenkins, and J. Donaghey. Uneven Development, Uneven Response: The Relentless Search for Meaningful Regulation of GVCs (2021) 59: 1 *British Journal of Industrial Relations* 3.

[6] A. Hassel, The Evolution of a Global Labor Governance Regime (2008) 21:2 *Governance* 231.

[7] E. Schuessler, S. J. Frenkel, and C. F. Wright, Governance of Labor Standards in Australian and German Garment Supply Chains: The Impact of Rana Plaza (2019) 72: 3 *Industrial &*

actors have the capacity to provide meaningful governance. In this chapter, we examine an example of how collaborative governance, in the immediate aftermath of a crisis, helped to overcome governance gaps inherent in prevailing practice that emphasizes individual actions but also how the collective action literature needs to be more cognisant of the politics within collectives and those outside the collective.

A collective action dilemma describes a situation where the action of individuals leads to a lack of investment or resources being overexploited unless an external authority, typically the government, intervenes to regulate access.[8] However, due to structural changes in the global economy, where states often compete against each other for investment based on how liberally regulated their economies are (or not), the possibility of government regulation is slim. Elinor Ostrom suggested an alternative to either regulation, polycentric systems of governance, in which formally independent centers of authority interact to make allocation, regulatory, and sanctioning decisions.[9] In such a system, private actors may seek to avoid the "tragedy of the commons" if governance systems are designed to tie in actors to a collective approach. In this chapter, we take the Bangladesh Accord as an example of collaborative governance and explore the key features that prompted its efficacy as a governance mechanism. However, while certainly the collective action features of the Accord had a positive effect on workplace safety in the Bangladesh garment sector, our findings highlight that the political consequences of collective action by private actors require greater attention from transnational governance scholars.

The argument developed here is that by understanding worker safety as a collective action problem, a more robust approach to global labor governance may be achieved, depending on the prevailing circumstances. However, while such an approach may be effective in terms of improving some governance areas, we highlight that the private power generated by collaborative governance to overcome the collective action problem made it a highly politically contested approach. This calls for greater attention to the dynamics of contestation and how these can affect the operation of collective approaches. We illustrate our arguments by examining our empirical research on a key response to the Rana Plaza tragedy, the Bangladesh Accord for Building and Fire Safety (Accord),[10] from which wider lessons for labor rights in global supply chains may be drawn. The research is based on a six-year longitudinal project (2013–2019) with a total of 140 interviews conducted in

Labor Relations Review 552. See also E. Partiti, "Human Rights Due Diligence and Evolution of Voluntary Sustainability Standards" in this volume (Chapter 7).

8 E. Ostrom et al. (eds.), *The Drama of the Commons* (2002).

9 E. Ostrom, Beyond Markets and States: Polycentric Governance of Complex Economic Systems (2010) 100 *American Economic Review* 641.

10 See also J. Donaghey and J. Reinecke, When Industrial Democracy meets Corporate Social Responsibility – A Comparison of the Bangladesh Accord and Alliance as responses to the Rana Plaza disaster (2018) 56:1 *British Journal of Industrial Relations* 14.

Bangladesh and buyer countries with supplier companies, buyer companies, trade unionists, NGOs, and other related parties.

8.2 WORKER SAFETY AS A COLLECTIVE ACTION PROBLEM IN APPAREL SUPPLY CHAINS

The apparel sector has become the epitome of how globalization is driving down labor standards. Single brands have neither the willingness, incentive, nor leverage to make individual mechanisms work, as the failure of social auditing demonstrates. Wary of exposure to negative publicity by mainly Western NGOs, labor activists, and unions, brands have heavily invested in social auditing of factory compliance to corporate codes of conduct, which accounts for up to 80 percent of their ethical sourcing budget.[11] Yet, while social auditing has helped companies manage their supply chains, safeguard individual reputations, and claim social responsibility, it has largely failed to improve working conditions.[12] Shortcomings have been tragically demonstrated by the failure to prevent a series of fatal industrial accidents: Rana Plaza famously housed two factories, Phantom Apparels and New Wave Style, which were audited against the Business Social Compliance Initiative's (BSCI) standard.[13]

Critics have long argued that social auditing is primarily designed to limit buyers' legal liability and to manage reputational risk, rather than improving working conditions[14]. In theory, the threat of sanctions – withdrawal of orders – is meant to encourage suppliers to address noncompliances. In practice, social auditing creates a collective action dilemma of its own. Even in cases of major noncompliances, there is little follow-up by buyers and contracts are rarely terminated, not least because this would create disruption to the supply chain and/or increase production costs for buyer firms.[15] This renders the threat of an individual buyer withdrawing orders ineffective. In turn, the knowledge that individual action is likely to make little difference reinforces a buyer's incentives to keep "eyes wide shut," even if suppliers are found noncompliant with a company's code of conduct. Companies

[11] ETI , Auditing Working Conditions | Ethical Trading Initiative (2013), www.ethicaltrade.org/in-action/issues/auditing-working-conditions.

[12] G. LeBaron and J. Lister, Benchmarking Global Supply Chains: The Power of the "Ethical Audit" Regime (2015) 41: 5 *Review of International Studies* 905. G. LeBaron, J. Lister, and P. Dauvergne, Governing Global Supply Chain Sustainability through the Ethical Audit Regime (2017) 14:6 *Globalizations* 958.

[13] J. Reinecke and J. Donaghey. The "Accord for Fire and Building Safety in Bangladesh" in Response to the Rana Plaza Disaster, in *Global Governance of Labour Rights* (A. Marx, J. Wouters, G. Rayp, and L. Beke eds., 2015).

[14] V. Mele and D. H. Schepers, E Pluribus Unum? Legitimacy Issues and Multi-stakeholder Codes of Conduct (2013) 118:3 *Journal of Business Ethics* 561; S. B. Banerjee, Corporate Social Responsibility: The Good, the Bad and the Ugly (2008) 34:1 *Critical Sociology* 51.

[15] G. LeBaron, J. Lister, and P. Dauvergne, Governing Global Supply Chain Sustainability through the Ethical Audit Regime (2017) 14:6 *Globalizations* 958.

and their suppliers then both have an interest in hiding labor violations rather than reporting them. The result is corporate complicity in a system where multiple buyers re-monitor the noncompliances of their supplying factories, leading to duplication of audits and "audit fatigue," yet without significant remediation taking place.

This failure has implications for the interests of all actors and at all levels in the supply chain in the apparel sector:

- At the brand level, even though safe and sustainable factories carry collective benefit for the entire industry, buyers face individual disadvantage when pursuing costly sustainable actions, as such costs may not be borne by competitors. Brands are competing against each other on a low-cost model and competitors may have an incentive to free-ride based on safety upgrades that another firm has made. Without assurances that all buyers invest in safe and sustainable factories, it is difficult to convince individual buyers to take action due to this risk of free-riding.
- At the supplier level, competition between factories both from within the country and from other countries is cutthroat due to low entry barriers. Suppliers compete with each other on a cost-basis and push downwards pressure on workers in terms of wages, safety, and many other labor issues regimes.
- At the worker level, as long as an unlimited supply of labor is ready to take up work in garment sector, workers lack market power to demand safer workplaces. Efforts at developing a collective voice in the form of trade unions face strong resistance from employers and often government officials alike. As a result, out of over 4,500 officially registered garment factories in Bangladesh, only about 10 percent have registered unions. But according to local estimates, many fewer are functioning properly due to the immature system of industrial relations, fragmentation of unions and lack of organizing capacities.
- At the supply chain level, highly complex global webs of purchasing relationships involve multiple buyers sourcing from multiple suppliers with parties spreading their relationships across geographical spaces to minimize risk. The combined effect has been increasing fragmentation, multiple tiers involving subcontracting, and an overall lack of transparency. Fragmentation has produced a situation where, in the absence of state oversight, brands have not taken responsibility for labor standards within the factories that produce the goods which they sell.
- At the host government level, competition among sourcing destinations for low cost production drives down standards and wages. Bangladesh for many years has been the world's second-largest exporter of ready-made garments, though has now slipped to third, and it faces increasing competition from neighboring Myanmar, Cambodia, Laos, and

> increasingly East Africa. The Bangladeshi government has generally resisted effective regulation out of fear that compliance will increase production costs and decrease the competitiveness of this sector that makes up 80 percent of exports in a highly competitive and mobile global market.

These contrasting interests made the issue of worker safety much more complex and certainly makes the question of what is the problem to be solved far from straightforward. In the Accord, for international brands and the trade unions, the shared problem they were seeking to solve through a collective approach was how they could establish and enforce a governance system to make Bangladeshi factory owners improve the safety in their factories. In this way, what they were seeking to establish was a new system that required the greatest change from an actor other than those actually involved in the design of the governance system. Thus, the collective action was one of trying to force other actors who each had their independent agency to change their behavior and invest resources, rather than the Accord actors themselves shifting their approach. Therefore, and unsurprisingly, the collective action became one of intense internal and external politics in terms of the creation and implementation of the Accord. While the internal politics played a role in both making the Accord more encompassing and probably more effective,[16] as will be developed below, the external politics, particularly in terms of those who were the subjects of the collective action, ultimately led to the ending of the Accord.

8.3 LABOR GOVERNANCE IN THE BANGLADESH RMG SECTOR

Since the 1980s, Bangladesh grew to become the second largest exporter of garments after China, growing from growing from $12,000 in exports in 1978 to annual exports exceeding $21.5 billion and 13 percent of GDP at the time Rana Plaza occurred. Despite Rana Plaza, the sector still grew to $34 billion by 2018[17] and has been credited with creating employment for around 4.1 million people directly, about 65 percent of whom are women, and 5 million workers indirectly.[18] At the time Rana Plaza occurred, workers only earned a minimum wage of $38, which increased to US$68/month in 2013 and US$95 in 2019. Despite these low wages, employment has contributed to the country's rapid economic development and poverty reduction,

[16] J. Donaghey and J. Reinecke, When Industrial Democracy Meets Corporate Social Responsibility: A Comparison of the Bangladesh Accord and Alliance as Responses to the Rana Plaza Disaster (2018) 56:1 *British Journal of Industrial Relations* 14. J. Reinecke and J. Donaghey. Towards Worker-Driven Supply Chain Governance: Developing Decent Work through Democratic Worker Participation (2021) 57:2 *Journal of Supply Chain Management* 14.

[17] BGMEA Sustainability report, http://download.bgmea.com.bd/BGMEA%20Sustainability%20Report%202020.pdf.

[18] Ibid.

halving halved the percentage of people living under the $1.90 poverty line since 1991.

The Bangladesh RMG sector epitomizes the global supply chain model, both in terms of the economic development and job opportunities it brought to the country, as well as in terms of the lack of regulation and exploitation of labor. It is a prime example of how the hypercompetitive market dynamic of globalized, industrial capitalism has overwhelmed the traditional bulwarks against capitalist exploitation – protective labor market institutions of the state and trade unions – and shifted the human cost of cheap fashion to the most vulnerable element of the chain – the garment worker in developing countries. Bangladesh is also an example of the "competition state,"[19] where states compete for inward investment through cheap labor and lack of public regulation to keep prices low. As a result, public regulation has largely failed to protect workers' rights in the Bangladeshi ready-made garment industry as the Bangladesh Labour Law and Building Code have remained largely unenforced. At the time Rana Plaza occurred, the government's labor inspectorate had fewer than 100 inspectors for more than 24,000 factories across all industrial sectors, 3 million shops and 2 major ports, including the over 4,300 export-oriented garment factories.

In terms of labor relations, Mark Anner[20] describes Bangladesh as "despotic market labor control" where workers lack market power alongside ineffective state protection. Since Rana Plaza, the government has publicly criticized efforts to increase unionization in the ready-made garment sector. A hostile context for trade unionism, low density, lack of unity with thirty-four union federations in the garment sector alone, an immature system of industrial relations, and political corruption point to the limitations of traditional labor regulation in the sector. Following a change in the labor law post–Rana Plaza, the International Labour Organization[21] reported a rise in factory-level union registrations to 437 by March 2015 out of at least 4,500 officially registered garment factories. Yet, according to the AFL-CIO Solidarity Center in 2019, only 200 were still active with many fewer functioning properly due to both employer resistance and lack of union organizing capacities and, with international pressure subsiding, the government rejected 73 percent of applications for new union registrations in 2015.

Weak labor power and hypercompetitiveness have not only depressed wages but investment in factory safety. With uncontrolled growth of the RMG sector, residential and commercial buildings in densely populated urban areas were repurposed for industrial use, often by adding additional stories without permission as in the case of

[19] P. G. Cerny, Paradoxes of the Competition State: The Dynamics of Political Globalization (1997) *Government and opposition* 251.

[20] M. Anner, Labor Control Regimes and Worker Resistance in Global Supply Chains (2015) 56:3 *Labor History* 292.

[21] Internatuional Labour Organization Bangladesh Newsletter (2015) www.ilo.org/wcmsp5/groups/public/—asia/—ro-bangkok/—ilo-dhaka/documents/publication/wcms_381573.pdf.

Rana Plaza. As the industry grew, so did the number of industrial disasters: before Rana Plaza, more than 600 Bangladeshi garment workers had died due to unsafe buildings since 2006, often despite factories having been certified by reference to CSR auditing standards. Sixty-four were killed in the Spectrum Sweater factory disaster in 2005, 21 killed in the Garib & Garib sweater fire in 2010, 117 killed by the Tazreen factory fire in 2012, and eventually over 1,100 died and a further 2,000 got severely injured in the Rana Plaza collapse in 2013.

8.4 THE BANGLADESH ACCORD FOR BUILDING AND FIRE SAFETY

The Accord was signed in the immediate aftermath of the Rana Plaza building collapse in 2013 to develop a more robust approach to worker safety in the Bangladesh ready-made garment industry. The Accord grew out of an earlier attempt to create a "Memorandum of Understanding" following the Tazreen fire that killed 112 workers but never came into force as only two brands, PvH and Tchibo, had signed up.[22] The idea behind the Memorandum of Understanding was that brands would take a collective approach to developing greater worker safety in an initiative jointly managed with labor actors in the form of NGOs and unions. It was only, however, after the crisis of Rana Plaza that a number of labor actors including the Global Union Federations, IndustriALL Global Union, and UNI Global Union, as well as the labor rights NGOs Clean Clothes Campaign and Workers Rights Consortium were able to pressurize a critical mass of brands into signing up to this five-year, legally binding agreement between brands and unions that was unprecedented in global supply chain governance.

The Accord, at its peak in 2017, had been signed by 215 signatory companies, global and local unions, with labor rights NGOs as witness signatories. Its main governing body is the Accord Steering Committee, which is composed of three brand representatives and three union representatives with the ILO acting as its independent chair. Signatory companies include global brands such as H&M, Inditex, C&A, Primark, and Hugo Boss; large Western retailers such as Aldi, Carrefour, or Tesco; as well as a number of smaller apparel brands. The Accord was never intended on being a permanent approach to the governance of worker safety: it grew as a crisis response to Rana Plaza but was always viewed as a mechanism that could be leveraged to develop nationally based institutions. The original Accord had a five-year duration and expired in July 2018, to be replaced by the "Transitional Accord" to carry on the work with a proposed term of two to three years, depending on the progress made in terms of establishing a Bangladeshi-based alternative in which brands and unions had confidence. This, however, as will be

[22] J. Reinecke and J. Donaghey, After Rana Plaza: Building Coalitional Power for Labour Rights Between Unions and (Consumption-Based) Social Movement Organisations (2015) 22 *Organization* 720.

outlined below was effectively brought to a premature end by court action in Bangladesh.

The Accord set out as its goal "to enable a working environment in which no worker needs to fear fires, building collapses, or other accidents." Program activities included:

- Rigorous program of fire, electrical, and structural safety inspections carried out by trained Accord engineers
- Monitoring remediation progress and facilitating brand support for remediation
- Online publication of all Corrective Action Plans (CAPs)
- Mobilizing collective brand leverage through escalation and termination of business relationships with nonparticipating supplier factories
- Training program for joint labor-management safety committees
- Accord Safety and Health Complaints Mechanism to resolve safety complaints

By signing the Accord, company signatories made legally binding commitments that were enforceable in the national courts in the country within which they were registered. Thus, while the initiative was essentially a private governance mechanism, national regulatory mechanisms were to be the ultimate enforcer of the agreement. The legal commitments included financial responsibility for funding the Accord's activities above. In terms of the operations of the Accord, the Accord employed its own engineers and other members of its secretariat who acted to implement a unified approach to safety across all factories who supplied its members. This was specifically designed to reduce the multiplicity of different codes of conduct where minor differences between multiple codes and multiple inspections by each brand meant that suppliers lacked a clear approach in terms of their buyers requirements.

The success of the Accord is most clearly demonstrated by improvements to safety, reducing workplace accidents. The average remediation rate had reached over 84 percent by the time the first Accord expired in April 2018, rising to 93 percent by December 2020 (see Figure 8.1).

The Accord found more than 80,000 safety issues in its first round of inspections of 1,100 factories. Critical issues were found in almost each factory often despite having previously passed multiple social audits. As of 2017, 74 percent of identified safety issues have been reported or verified as fixed,[23] such as fire proofing the electrical wiring, installation of fire doors and fire systems, as well as redistributing weight loads and strengthening the factory building's columns.

The Accord illustrated how a collaborative approach by brands and unions had, in the context of a crisis, the potential to generate leverage to change the system

[23] Ibid.

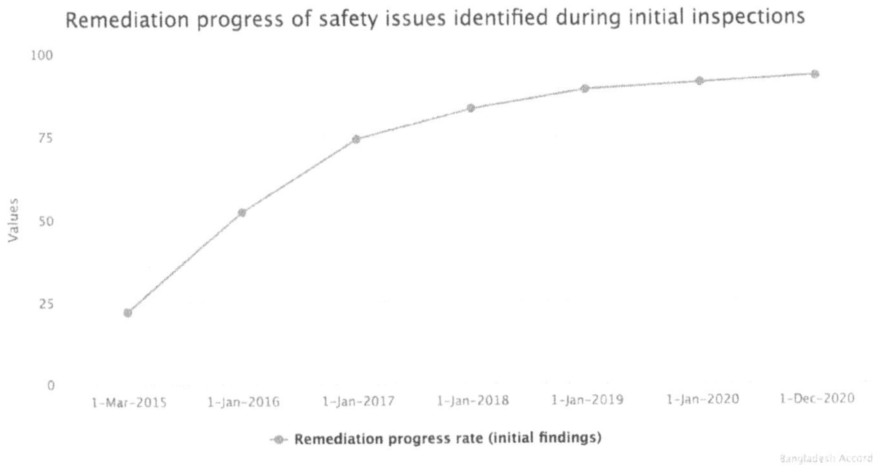

FIGURE 8.1. Remediation progress
Source: Accord, 2020[24]

through collective action. What features made this approach effective? Eight dimensions helped to establish the institutional conditions that made the Accord a successful example of collaborative labour governance. These will be divided into institutional design for collective action and operating principles for collective action.

While the term "institutional design" is often used in a loose way, in the Accord, there was a very deliberate "design" adopted as a mechanism of developing the Accord as a governance approach. These four design features of the Accord both enabled the development of a collective approach and gave other actors assurance that their interests would be represented through the governance structures. The four design features as follows:

Transnational Co-determination

A central feature of the Accord was that it was a jointly governed initiative by representatives of business and labor: worker representatives, and not just representatives of capital, were included in the design and oversight of the transnational labor governance regimes. Rather than other initiatives where business organizations coopted NGOs and the like onto their bodies in advisory-type capacities, in the Accord, equal status of business and worker interests within the institution underscored its purpose. Two Global Union Federations and six local Bangladeshi unions are full signatories with 50 percent voting rights on the Accord Steering Committee. In addition, four NGOs (Clean Clothes Campaign, Workers Rights Consortium, International Labor Rights Forum, Maquila Solidarity Network) are "witness

[24] http://bangladeshaccord.org/progress.

signatories" who enjoy observer status only. The International Labour Organization (ILO) acts as neutral chair.

Rather than promoting common business interests in protecting reputation[25], inclusion of recognized labor representatives meant representation of interests of the agreement's intended beneficiaries: garment workers. Through such a collective approach, different parties were able to cooperate and build a consensus through which problems were solved, even if their individual interests were in competition or the definition of the problem differed. In this way, the Accord was built around the idea that while interests may be mutual, they are not necessarily shared. Mutuality is built upon the recognition that, at times, the interests of the parties involved, typically workers and managers/owners, may not be shared but that a common solution can create mutual benefit despite divergent interests.[26] An obvious actor missing from the Accord as an employment relations agreement are the Bangladeshi employers. For this reason, the Bangladesh Garment Manufacturers and Exporters Association (BGMEA) and Government of Bangladesh fiercely contested the quasi-regulatory authority of the Accord, leading to a High Court case which will be discussed later in the chapter.

Industry-wide, Pre-competitive Collaboration

Tragedies such as Rana Plaza have demonstrated that an industry's reputation is a shared resource, subject to reputational spillovers.[27] In collaborative approaches, encompassing interest groups thus need to collaborate to achieve collective action and sanction free-riding. In this aspect, under the Accord, brands effectively were accepting the need for pre-competitive collaboration as a way of removing from competition issues of collective concern, such as labor rights. Collective action then spreads the cost of economic adjustment, increases sanctioning capability, and reduces the incentives for free-riding.

Legally Enforceable Commitment

By signing the Accord, company signatories make legally binding commitments that were enforceable in the national courts in the country within which they are

[25] In contrast, the Alliance for Bangladesh Worker Safety, a competing, corporate-driven self-regulatory initiative insists that "the Corporation is a voluntary association of business organizations the primary purpose of which … is to further their common business interests by strengthening worker safety conditions."

[26] T. A. Kochan and S. A. Rubinstein, Toward a Stakeholder Theory of the Firm: The Saturn Partnership (2000) 11:4 *Organization Science* 367.

[27] M. L. Barnett and A. A. King, Good Fences Make Good Neighbors: A Longitudinal Analysis of an Industry Self-Regulatory Institution (2008) 51 *Academy of Management Journal* 1150.

registered. Due to its legally binding nature, the Accord departs from voluntary CSR standards. The Accord created an enforceable contractual relationship in the home country of the buyer brands. The point about the establishment of a legally enforceable contract was a very significant new departure in global supply chain labor governance. Through the Accord, brands transferred oversight of their supply chain to a body that had a right to initiate legal action against the brands where they did not meet their commitments. While heavily resisted in the past, a legally binding agreement was achieved due to the pressure placed on brands by the harnessing of the complementary capacities of labor rights NGOs and trade unions. This legally binding nature was tested when two cases were filed in October 2016 at the Permanent Court of Arbitration in The Hague by IndustriALL Global Union and UNI Global Union to hold two unnamed signatory companies to account for failing to meet Accord terms [28] – in particular, to require their suppliers to complete their remediations and to agree on commercial terms that are financially feasible for their suppliers to cover the remediation costs. The first case settled in December 2018. The second case settled in January 2018, involving agreed payments of $2.3 million to cover remediation in more than 150 garment factories in Bangladesh ($2 million) and pay into IndustriALL and UNI's joint Supply Chain Worker Support Fund ($0.3 million).[29]

Developing Worker Voice

Central to the Accord, and pushed by the labor caucus, was the idea that having a transnational apparatus was not enough: the governance of factory-level safety needed to have worker participation at all levels. Worker voice was thus seen as central to the Accord as it recognizes the potentially competing interests of management and workers over core organizational issues[30]. As such, the Accord oversaw the development of a more comprehensive structure of worker voice in the area of workplace safety, including joint worker-management safety committees in all factories and a robust complaints mechanism. By December 2020, the Accord Safety and Health Complaints Mechanism had resolved over 693 complaints raised by workers and ensured the creation and training of over 1,260 Joint labor-management Safety Committees. The training foresees a central role for workers and worker representatives, including direct trade union participation in factory training and factory inspections.

[28] https://pca-cpa.org/en/cases/152.

[29] www.industriall-union.org/global-unions-reach-us23-million-bangladesh-accord-settlement-with-multinational-brand.

[30] J. Donaghey, Trojan Horse or Tactic? The Case for Partnership, in *Developing Positive Employment Relations* (S. Johnstone and A. Wilkinson eds., 2016).

Alongside these design features of the Accord, four operating principles became essential to the establishment of the collective approach.

Leverage through Collective Action

The Accord creates collective leverage through the combined power of its corporate signatories. Unlike codes of conduct or International Framework Agreements, which are generally agreed between one MNC and a GUF, the Accord covers multiple brands (in excess of 200 in the first Accord). Collective action by a large proportion of buyers provided far greater leverage for effective sanctioning than any buyer would have individually. As expressed by a buying brand: "If you don't remediate you lose your orders from 215 brands. That's leverage, that's how you get things done in Bangladesh." Under Accord rules, signatory firms agreed to terminate contracts with factories that failed to make safety improvements. Facing the loss of orders from not just one but a large group of buyers committed the factory to invest in remediation. Effective sanctioning led to the most unsafe factories being temporarily or permanently shut, with remediation efforts monitored in almost all other factories, potentially saving the lives of thousands. In 17 factories safety concerns were so severe that the Accord recommended immediate evacuation, and immediate remedial actions were necessary in another 110 factories. While not all factories were covered by the Accord, approximately half of all workers in the sector and most of those in directly exporting firms are covered by the Accord. The collective brand approach of the Accord also brought benefits to supplier firms in Bangladesh by having a unified set of standards, rather than suppliers attempting to satisfy a multiplicity of codes of conduct for different buyers.

Accountability through Collective Oversight

Collective oversight over inspections meant it was possible to overcome some of the limitations of previous auditing approaches, such as lack of transparency. By including unions, the ILO, and NGOs in oversight, as well as placing factory reports and Steering Committee minutes in the public domain, buyers were incentivized to act on noncompliance. Parties without profit rationales, such as unions and NGOs, can expose firms who seek to circumvent the collective approach. Transparency also reenforced collective leverage, because even brands not covered under the Accord were less likely to source from factories that have found to be unsafe.

Pooling of Resources

The Accord brought brands together to pool resources and share costs, information, responsibility, and risk. Pooling of resources increased marginal per capita return, which incentivizes participants because they know that their individual contribution made a bigger difference.[31] With industry-wide contributions, a collective safety mechanism funded higher-quality inspections with engineering teams specializing in fire, electrical, and structural safety. Companies assume responsibility for funding the activities of the steering committee, safety inspectors, and training coordinators based on their annual volumes of garment purchases from Bangladesh on a sliding, pro-rata scale up to $500,000 per annum. With industry-wide contributions, a collective safety mechanism was argued to fund a program of high-quality inspections and remediation monitoring with engineering teams specializing in fire, electrical, and structural safety. To illustrate the scale of the task, by the time the first Accord expired in April 2018, Accord engineers had carried out a total of 25,656 follow-up inspections in a total of 2,055 factories. This yielded 134,489 findings, with safety hazards present in each and every factory, such as lack of fire escapes. Respondents repeatedly stated that another large-scale disaster would have been imminent without immediate intervention. Pooling of resources was argued to overcome the deficiencies of single-brand approaches such as lack of expertise, under-funding of specialized inspections, and protocols for follow-up action and remediation. Cost sharing was also viewed as making governance more accessible especially for smaller buyers with limited resources and further reduces incentives for free-riding.

Highly Focused Approach

One of the criticisms of the Accord was also one of its strengths. The Accord had a narrow focus on building, electrical, and fire safety. In order to build an agreed approach encompassing so many brands, as well as union and NGO actors, meant such a narrow focus was necessary as maintaining agreement is easier. This also meant that a highly specialized approach was enabled to be taken by the engineers employed by the Accord in terms of implementing an agreed common standard across all factories who wished to supply for any Accord brands. While preventing fatalities within the industry, one criticism though was that it has done little to increase poverty wages or extend worker rights beyond safety. In contrast, wide-ranging approaches such as the UN Global Compact on the other end of the spectrum have been criticized for achieving few of their many wide-ranging objectives. Similarly, global framework agreement negotiation by GFU with MNCs cover a wider variety of industrial relations issues but are often less able to deliver in terms of the expertise required and monitoring involved. Focusing on a clear and tangible problem enabled the Accord to concentrate actions and resources on delivering more effective problem solving.

[31] A. Poteete, M. Janssen, and E. Ostrom, *Working Together: Collective Action, the Commons, and Multiple Methods in Practice* (2010).

8.5 CONTESTING THE REGULATORY POWER OF COLLABORATIVE GOVERNANCE: THE BANGLADESH HIGH COURT CASE

A theme of the chapter to this point has been the central role that crisis played in initiating collective action and in developing the Accord. Without doubt, the Accord's focus on creating structures and processes for collective action was a key feature that explains its relative success compared to other private governance initiatives. While the work on collective action by the likes of Ostrom is attractive in explaining the emergence of collaborative governance initiatives, two particular problems are worth highlighting in relation to our case. First, the literature on collective action is underpinned by a rational-economic mindset. In contrast, we highlight that a more political approach to developing collective action is necessary. Take, for example, Ostrom,[32] where she argues that "collective-action problems occur when it takes the inputs and efforts of multiple individuals in order to achieve joint outcomes – and it is difficult to exclude beneficiaries of these actions from benefiting even if they do not contribute." Here Ostrom is working from the perspective that the problem is actually relatively easy to identify but that the difficulty arises over who pays the price for such action. While problems such as free-riding have long been acknowledged as potential problems in collective approaches,[33] such an approach ignores the political nature of organizational life where, not just the solution or cost of that solution are contested but the very nature of the problem to be solved is one that is contested.

Secondly, by definition, collective action is about bringing parties together and including them in a decision-making process. However, who is included or excluded is often a cause of political tensions within any cooperative arrangement.[34] A central feature of this literature is that collective action is viewed as parties coming together in order to solve shared or mutual problems. However, such a picture paints an idealized picture where all parties are equally invested in solving the problem. As we will develop, while there was significant unity to form a collective initiative, one of the reasons for forming the collective initiative was to take action against parties who were perceived as being the root cause of the problem for which a solution was to be developed: Bangladeshi employers, factory owners and government cast as "negligent" in providing workplace safety. The Accord thus also created a separate but related crisis for the industry and government in Bangladesh. The latter

[32] E. Ostrom, Polycentric Systems as One Approach for Solving Collective-Action Problems, Indiana University, Bloomington: School of Public & Environmental Affairs Research Paper 2008-11 (2008), at 2.

[33] M. Olson Jr., The Logic of Collective Action: Public Goods and the Theory of Groups (1965) 124 *Harvard Economic Studies*, www.hup.harvard.edu/catalog.php?isbn=9780674537514.

[34] J. P. Galvis, Remaking Equality: Community Governance and the Politics of Exclusion in Bogota's Public Spaces (2014) 38:4 *International Journal of Urban and Regional Research* 1458; M. Webber, *Inclusion, Exclusion and the Governance of European Security* (2013).

perceived the Accord to be a threat to their competitive advantage – cost leadership – in the international garments sector. This was a substantially different crisis due to the nature of the interests involved. Our argument is that the role of interests and how they relate to "problems" that require solving is central to understanding the dynamics of collective action in transnational labor governance. In the context of the Accord, we will highlight that in terms of its creation, implementation, and de facto termination, the nature of collective action in the Accord was highly politicized in nature.

Within the literature on collaborative governance, there is an underlying assumption that parties cooperate to solve a shared problem and generate "win-win" solutions. While the "solutions" to such problems may be contested, the idea is that those participating do so with a clear understanding of what the actual problem is. However, this approach implies that there is one objective and identifiable factor that can be identified as the problem that requires fixing. As outlined above, for both the MNCs and the labor actors in the form of unions and NGOs, the problem was the state of repair of the Bangladeshi factories and the main obstacle identified as causing that problem were Bangladeshi factory owners. This, however, is an oversimplification and this came to be highlighted through the Accord. In our interviews with factory owners and managers in Bangladesh, a consistent picture emerged that they felt extreme pressure from the MNC buyers to drive down their prices. As we have argued in our research elsewhere,[35] problems that multinational corporations seek factory owners to remedy often arise out of the pressures associated with the sourcing model that the multinationals impose on their suppliers. Thus, factory owners in Bangladesh did not share the same understanding of the problem.

Initially, the opposition of factory owners and the government did not prevent the Accord from operating. With both the MNCs and unions viewing the Bangladeshi employers as the problem, the employers were excluded from the governance arrangements of the Accord. As such, they were clearly placed in the role of subjects of the initiative. This proved to be very controversial for both the employers and the government of Bangladesh. In our research, the metaphor of "being a guest in someone's house, and then telling the host to change your house" was frequently raised by employers and managers in Bangladesh. Thus, since the start of the Accord, there was much opposition from industry and government actors in Bangladesh about not cooperating with the Accord. However, having the collective buying power of up to 220 brands from Europe, North America, and Southeast Asia meant that the vast majority of factory owners allowed the Accord to inspect their premises. Without doubt, though, there was a feeling among Accord actors that

[35] J. Reinecke and J. Donaghey, Political CSR at the Coalface: The Roles and Contradictions of Multinational Corporations in Developing Workplace Dialogue (2021) 58:2 *Journal of Management Studies* 457; J. Reinecke, J. Donaghey, N. Bocken, and L. Lauriano, Business Models and Labour Standards: Making the Connection, Ethical Trading Initiative, London (2019).

some factory owners in Bangladesh were "dragging their heels" in terms of implementing the remediation to "ride out" the period until 2018 when the initial Accord was due to expire.

A second feature of the Accord was that the fire, electrical, and particularly structural aspects of complying with the Accord meant that a significant cost had to be paid to raise the standards of factories in Bangladesh: under the approach of the Accord, while brands had a duty to help suppliers through loans or advance payment for orders, ultimately it was the suppliers who were expected to pay the cost. While the brands did face a cost in terms of being Accord members, which was to pay for the operational costs of the Accord, this was capped at an annual maximum of US$500,000. In contrast, costs associated with remediation were to be covered by factory owners that could run substantially higher. The IFC in 2016[36] estimated that total remediation costs for factories covered by the Accord would amount to ~US$403 million, or between US$120,000 and US$320,000 for the majority of factories (80 percent). As Accord signatories, brands were obliged to "ensure" that it was financially feasible for their supplier factories to cover these costs. But brands insisted that "ensuring" by no means meant covering the costs. Thus, the collective action in this case was not simply a positive sum game but rather was a zero-sum game with the actor responsible for paying the cost being the subject of governance rather than being a participant in it.

This exclusion and cost model caused considerable resentment within Bangladesh. The government, the industry bodies in the form of the BGMEA and Bangladesh Knitwear Manufacturers and Exporters Association, and individual employers engaged in a series of pushbacks against the Accord. From the outset, the government opposed the Accord and portrayed it, and the Rana Plaza disaster itself, as part of a conspiracy to undermine the lucrative RMG sector in Bangladesh. Both the prime minister and the minister for commerce were vocal in their opposition, but more significantly, stating that the Accord would not continue to operate past its initial five-year term ending in 2018. While there was much rhetoric from the political class in Bangladesh opposing the Accord, state actors did not take direct action to stop it from operating, presumably due to the dependence on the sector for exports.

However, ultimately it was the actions of the state, through the Bangladeshi court system that effectively ended the role of the Accord in Bangladesh. In this case, a factory owner was deemed to be noncompliant with the Alliance, an alternative system to the Accord but one that crucially shared findings and had a system of mutual recognition of noncompliant factories with the Accord. Thus, the factory owner was excluded from supplying either Accord or Alliance brands. After

[36] IFC, Remediation Financing in Bangladesh's Ready Made Garment Sector (2016), www.ifc.org/wps/wcm/connect/Topics_Ext_Content/IFC_External_Corporate_Site/Sustainability-At-IFC/Publications/p_report_remediation_financing.

undertaking some remediation works, the factory owner applied to the Accord to be deemed compliant but the Accord deemed that the factory still had not met the required standards. In response, the factory owner applied to the national body for non-exporting factories to be deemed compliant. This was forthcoming and the factory owner went to court claiming that as his factories were compliant with the national body, his factories should be deemed compliant with the requirements of the Accord. In response to the case, the Supreme Court of Bangladesh took the unusual step of opening up a *suo moto* case on the entire legality of the operation of the Accord in Bangladesh.

In this case, the Supreme Court of Bangladesh, when ruling on the operation of the Accord, argued that in 2013, when Bangladesh was facing an emergency situation, the Accord taking on some of the responsibility of the Bangladeshi state was acceptable. But by 2019, when the Transitional Accord came into effect, this emergency state was no longer in existence. The Supreme Court's decision ruled that the authority of the Accord to end contracts was based on the Accord being focused on implementing the National Action Plan and placed the Accord on the same footing as the less stringent National Tripartite Plan. In addition, the Court ruled that where a factor was regarded as being safe by the National Tripartite Plan, under Bangladeshi law, the Accord could not deem it as being unsafe. The Court then went further and argued that given the national emergency of 2013 had now passed, the Accord was given 281 days to end its operations within Bangladesh.[37] This judgment prompted a series of negotiations opening up between the Accord, its constituents, the BGMEA, and the government of Bangladesh. This ultimately brought an end to the operations of the Accord in Bangladesh in April 2020 and established a new governance body, ostensibly run in its operations by the BGMEA but with BGMEA, brand, and union representatives making up its governing body.

Much of the literature on collective action and also the literature on joint problem solving is one where parties seek to take joint action on a commonly held problem. What happens though where the collective action is effectively to get another party or parties to make changes that they see as contrary to their interests? This became the key political question in the case of the Accord. A key feature of the design of the Accord was that it was essentially designed to force Bangladeshi employers to take the substantive action to improve labor conditions in their factories. A second source of pushback came from the Bangladeshi state for whom the Accord raised issues on two levels. First, the Bangladeshi government viewed the Accord as impinging on is right as a sovereign government to govern within its jurisdiction. Secondly, the Bangladeshi government, as being heavily reliant on the garments sector for exports, had a key interest in maintaining the competitiveness of the industry in Bangladesh. Ultimately, the exclusion of these groups and how they

[37] Accord can stay for 281 days from May 8: SC, www.thedailystar.net/country/bangladesh-supreme-court-okays-accord-stay-281-days-may-8-1745779.

framed the problems and responsibilities for remedying safety issues in the Bangladesh RMG sector initiated considerable resistance from those outside but subjected to and affected by the operation of the collective action of the Accord.

8.6 CONCLUSION

The Accord was an unprecedented example of how collaborative governance can generate collective action in global supply chains and solve a collective action problem – despite a lack of reinforcing institutional support, even resistance, from the host government. Without doubt, the crisis following the Rana Plaza disaster enabled the development of a collective approach that has halted the deadly incidents in the factories. The nature of the crisis played a central role in its success by bringing together a plurality of interests and having inbuilt mechanisms for ensuring accountability through participation of unions and NGOs. Viewing governance as a collective action problem helps improve our understanding of the complex institutional arrangements that can contribute to collaborative governance within complex global supply chains. A number of key lessons can be drawn. First, the collaborative approach enables a system that provides collective leverage between participants but also against those who may seek to free-ride. Secondly, collective oversight from an independent body provides a mechanism through which diverse actors can be guided down a common path. Third, the inclusion of multiple interests enables the identification of mutual solutions to interests affecting particular parties. A final and more general lesson to be drawn is that, in the current neo-liberal environment, individual action and intense competition is often elevated above the benefits of cooperative and collaborative behavior. Taking individual action as illustrated by the social auditing model adopted by many supply chains creates an inferior regime in terms of health and safety governance. The Accord demonstrates that collective responses have a central role to play in developing meaningful and sustainable governance mechanisms that can deliver common solutions despite competing interests.

However, two more cautionary tales emerge in terms of collective action and the nature of private governance. The first is that private governance, regardless of the parties who participate, operates in the shadow of public governance. This relationship between the public and private sphere is one that has attracted increased attention in recent years[38] but ultimately private initiatives can be overridden by public institutions. In the case of the Accord, the Bangladeshi state, through its High Court, took a decision to reassert national sovereignty over a transnational

[38] T. Bartley, *Rules without Rights: Land, Labor, and Private Authority in the Global Economy* (2018); J. S. Knudsen, Government Regulation of International Corporate Social Responsibility in the US and the UK: How Domestic Institutions Shape Mandatory and Supportive Initiatives (2018) 56:1 *British Journal of Industrial Relations* 164.

governance initiative: the Bangladeshi state certainly faced a legitimacy crisis in terms of its ability to defend its main export industry. Obviously, all those brands could have chosen to exit and withdraw their sourcing from Bangladesh in protest against the ruling, thus threatening nearly the entire export base of the country. But ultimately brands' commercial interests triumphed. However, this does not mean that the Bangladeshi state was able to claw back on economic private activism entirely. A plethora of private social auditing regimes are still in place, requiring buyers to comply with the codes of conduct of their suppliers. In this sense, the very feature that endowed the Accord with its regulatory power – stringent enforcement through the collective leverage of signatory brands – was also the one that rendered it vulnerable to state backlash.

Secondly, collective action in this case was inherently political in nature and steeped in the extreme power asymmetries of the global supply chain. While a problem was identified that few could have argued was not a problem (the deaths of workers in Bangladeshi garment factories), the root cause of it was highly contested (negligent employers and factory owners or a "broken" supply chain where brands' squeezing of suppliers creates downward pressure). As such, the "solution" of devising a private governance system that excluded the Bangladeshi employers while placing on them the main burden of paying the cost of the Accord and associated remediation, created an oppositional force. Employers had an inherent interest to bring the initiative to an end. Thus the creation of collective inclusion also implicitly meant the creation of exclusion and thus "problem solving" actually became a highly contested territory.

Finally, the case of the Bangladesh Accord contains important insights about the episodic nature of crises in transnational governance. While the crisis of the immediate aftermath of the Rana Plaza disaster for brands sourcing from Bangladesh played a key role in shaping the collective action by brands, unions, and NGOs, by creating a hitherto unmatched level of inspection and enforcement, a crisis was created for the Bangladeshi government and the factory owners. In response, they took action through public institutions that pushed back against the private governance. At time of writing, the dynamics are still playing out with efforts being made to recast the Accord with a more international focus, demonstrating the ebbs and flows of the interface of national regulation and transnational governance, as well as the dynamic effects which the episodic nature of crisis responses may have.

9

The Evolution of the Global Food Safety Initiative

The Dynamics of the Legitimacy of a Transnational Private Rule-Maker

Tetty Havinga and Paul Verbruggen

9.1 INTRODUCTION

The Global Food Safety Initiative (GFSI) is an industry-driven meta-regulator that has proven to be influential in shaping both industry practices and public policy making in the field of food safety across the globe. GFSI makes a particularly promising case for investigating how a transnational private regulator has changed over time and shown resilience in overcoming deep-rooted legitimacy challenges (or "crises") to its private authority. In 2000, a group of leading international supermarket chains founded the Global Taskforce on Food Safety, Quality and Security "to set voluntary standards for food products sourced by retailers around the world."[1] Twenty years later, GFSI has become a leading global business organization in the food industry, promoting "continuous improvement in food safety management systems around the world".[2] That goal is principally pursued by the assessment or, as GFSI calls it, "benchmarking" of private food safety certification schemes that regulate food production and processing to a common, global industry standard. In 2021, over 150,000 certificates from 12 GFSI-recognized food safety certification programs had been issued in 162 countries and numerous food safety experts participated in its committees and events.[3]

In our analysis of the evolution of GFSI, we will discuss its governance structure, its activities, and its framing. The lens through which we assess that evolution is the concept of legitimacy understood in terms of institutionalization theory. To survive, any organization needs social acceptability and credibility.[4] In other words, they

[1] D. Orgel, CIES planning Global Food Safety Initiative, *Supermarket News*, May 22, 2000, www.supermarketnews.com/archive/cies-planning-global-food-safety-initiative.

[2] GFSI, What Is GFSI, www.mygfsi.com/about-us/about-gfsi/what-is-gfsi.html.

[3] GFSI, GFSI Governance Model and Rules of Procedure, Version 042021 (2021), at 81; GFSI, Recognised Certification Programmes, www.mygfsi.com/certification/recognised-certification-programmes.html.

[4] W. R. Scott, *Institutions and Organizations: Ideas, Interests and Identities*, 4th ed. (2014), at 71

require legitimacy from those actors that have an interest in their activities. For private, non-state regulatory organizations such as GFSI, building and maintaining legitimacy is of vital importance.[5] In the spirit of this book, one can say that this labor is an essential means to harness endogenous and exogenous forces that undermine the organization's regulatory effectiveness and thus lead to its crisis, in order to adapt and demonstrate resilience.[6] Whereas traditional state authority is often taken for granted, non-state regulators "must obtain legitimate rule-making authority . . . from salient constituencies in their organizational field."[7] Legitimacy provides justifications and a shared understanding of what is acceptable or appropriate. GFSI needs the cooperation of other parties in order to achieve its regulatory goals. More specifically, GFSI depends on the participation of retailers, certification program owners, food manufacturers, food producers, and others in the food supply chains, as well as on the support of authoritative organizations and persons, whether public or private. These actors constitute different legitimacy communities with their own values, priorities, and interests.[8] Changes in these traits challenge the legitimacy of GFSI, put it at risk of organizational crisis, and thus require from it a response of resilience to find a new equilibrium allowing for the continuation of its activities.

We will argue that GFSI has evolved as a transnational private rule-maker through continued processes of pluralization of its constituents, increased transparency, ratchetting up of food standards' quality, and globalization of its benchmarking activities. In these dynamics, we suggest, GFSI has sought to respond to criticisms and changing demands of its legitimacy communities. GFSI has evolved from a relatively limited retailer-led initiative into a leading actor in the field of global food safety. The GFSI benchmarking requirements are regarded as top of the bill and both national and international governmental organizations have accepted GFSI as a reliable industry partner in policy debates on food safety. In short, GFSI has expanded on many fronts as a transnational regulator, thus widening and deepening its legitimacy basis. Despite its growth and diversification in terms of (board) membership, GFSI has not changed its initial objectives: it still is an industry-led organization, of which the constituents are food safety experts of large

5 S. Bernstein and B. Cashore, Can Non-state Global Governance Be Legitimate? An Analytical Framework (2007) *Regulation and Governance* 1; J. Black, Constructing and Contesting Legitimacy and Accountability in Polycentric Regulatory Regimes (2008) 2 *Regulation and Governance*, 137, at 148–149; D. Casey, Interactions, Iteration and Early Institutionalization: Competing Lessons of GLOBALGAP's Legitimation, in *Transnational Business Governance Interactions: Empowering Marginalized Actors and Enhancing Regulatory Quality* (S. Wood, R. Schmidt, K. Abbott, B. Eberlein, and E. Meidinger eds., 2019), 183; D. Fuchs, A. Kalfagianni, and T. Havinga, Actors in Private Food Governance: The Legitimacy of Retail Standards and Multistakeholder Initiatives with Civil Society Participation (2011) 28:2 *Agriculture and Human Values* 353.

6 Cf. Sections 1.2.1, 1.2.5, and 7.3 in this volume.

7 L. H. Gulbrandsen, Accountability Arrangements in Non-state Standards Organizations: Instrumental Design and Imitation (2008) 15 *Organization* 563, at 568.

8 Black, *supra* note 5; Casey, *supra* note 5.

food corporations. We will show that many of the changes the organization has gone through can be interpreted as a response to the opposition voiced by internal and external actors in the light of developments in the field of food safety and its certification.

Our account of the evolution of GFSI is mainly based on the content analysis of publicly available documents and on the research we carried out on GFSI before. We studied GFSI publications, newsletters, and press releases. More in particular, we analyzed how the governance structure of GFSI and the benchmarking requirements changed between 2000 and 2020. We also verified what activities GFSI has undertaken over the years and how it frames its mission. In addition, we use information from interviews with two member of the GFSI Global Regulatory Affairs Working Group and other interviews that we conducted in earlier research in the field of food safety governance.[9]

We start this chapter by discussing the concept of legitimacy as developed in the work of Richard Scott and of Julia Black.[10] Subsequently, we will introduce GFSI as a transnational private rule-maker. This introduction lays the ground for the analysis of GFSI's evolution, in which we focus on the processes of pluralization, transparency, globalization, and ratchetting up of standards' quality. We will show how these processes have contributed to the gaining and maintaining of legitimacy, and we will analyze how GFSI has sought to manage the conflicting interests involved and be resilient to these dynamics.

9.2 DYNAMICS OF LEGITIMACY IN TRANSNATIONAL PRIVATE RULE-MAKING

Legitimacy, it has been recognized in academic literature on regulation and governance, constitutes a necessary attribute of any actor in the successful pursuit of regulatory goals.[11] Most scholars of regulatory governance would agree that legitimacy essentially turns on "the acceptability and credibility of the organization to those it seeks to govern."[12] For lawyers, that may imply that a legal mandate is bestowed upon the regulator by a recognized state authority, such as a Parliament or a court,

9 T. Havinga and P. Verbruggen, The Global Food Safety Initiative and State Actors: Paving the Way for Hybrid Food Safety Governance, in *Hybridization of Food Governance: Trends, Types and Tesults* (P. Verbruggen and T. Havinga eds., 2017), 183; P. Verbruggen and T. Havinga, Food Safety Meta-controls in the Netherlands (2015b) 6:4 *European Journal of Risk Regulation* 512; T. Havinga, Private Regulation of Food Safety by Supermarkets (2006) 28:4 *Law & Policy* 515.

10 Scott, *supra* note 4; Black, *supra* note 5.

11 R. Baldwin, M. Cave, and M. Lodge, Introduction: Regulation: The Field and the Developing Agenda, in *The Oxford Handbook of Regulation* (R. Baldwin, M. Cave, and M. Lodge eds., 2010), 25.

12 Black, *supra* note 5, at 144.

and that the actor operates within the bounds of that mandate.[13] Political scientists may stress the democratic representativeness of beliefs, expectations, and interests of those affected by the regulatory activities or the effects and costs of these activities on the attainment of the regulatory goals.[14]

Private rule-making at the transnational level presents a challenging case for the construction of legitimacy. In that domain, traditional state-based mechanisms of democratic legitimacy are generally absent. Legitimacy is not self-evident and must be socially developed by the regulatory organization in relation with those that are sought to be governed.[15] In the absence of such legitimacy, the risk of regulatory failure is apparent and can lead the regulator into organizational crisis. In the same vein, Bernstein and Cashore stress the "political legitimacy," that is, the general support for a regime or governance institution, which transnational private governance systems require to be effective.[16] In their view, it "requires institutionalized authority (whether concentrated or diffuse) with power resources to exercise rule as well as shared norms among the community."[17] In this sociological conception, legitimacy is an empirical observation that results from the acceptance of the organizations' conduct by others. Legitimacy, then, is dynamic and may come and go with the change of legitimacy demands from those in and outside the regulatory regime, such as regulated entities, regulatory intermediaries, and beneficiaries.[18]

Richard Scott has provided a powerful and widely accepted theoretical framework to capture the dynamics of institutionalization and legitimation. In his framework, institutions are built on three pillars: regulative, normative, and cultural-cognitive systems.[19] Related to these three pillars, he discusses three general mechanisms that may lead to institutionalization: (i) increasing returns stressing the role of incentives and interests as motivating force, (ii) increasing commitments stressing the role of identity and mutual social relations, and (iii) increasing objectification of shared beliefs embedded in routines and forms stressing the role of ideas (Table 9.1).[20]

[13] E.g., C. M. Donnelly, *Delegation of Governmental Power to Private Parties: A Comparative Perspective* (2007); M. Eliantonio and C. Cauffman, *The Legitimacy of Standardisation as a Regulatory Technique in the EU – a Cross-disciplinary and Multi-level Analysis: An Introduction*' (2020), at 23–26. See also Section 1.3.2 in this volume stating that "private power accumulation is a continuous process that starts with the delegation (explicit or tacit) of power and thus the transfer of legitimacy to a private body."

[14] E.g., F. W. Scharpf, *Governing in Europe: Effective and Democratic?* (1999), at 7–21.

[15] Black, *supra* note 5, at 144; C. Scott, Standard-Setting in Regulatory Regimes, in *The Oxford Handbook of Regulation* (R. Baldwin, M. Cave, and M. Lodge eds., 2010), 113.

[16] Bernstein and Cashore, *supra* note 5.

[17] Bernstein and Cashore, *supra* note 5, at 351.

[18] K. W. Abbott, D. Levi-Faur, and D. Snidal, Theorizing Regulatory Intermediaries: The RIT Model (2017) 670 *The Annals of the American Academy of Political and Social Science* 14. To be sure, many political scientists view legitimacy as a dynamic property of institutions. See also Scharpf, *supra* note 14, at 26, who astutely notes that "Legitimacy cannot be considered an all or-nothing proposition."

[19] Scott, *supra* note 4, at 59.

[20] Scott, *supra* note 4, at 144–151.

TABLE 9.1. *Three pillars or reasons for institutionalized legitimacy*

Pragmatic	Moral	Cognitive
In line with economic interests	Goals perceived as morally appropriate	Accepted as inevitable
Increasing returns	Increasing commitments and norm generation	Increasing objectivation of shared beliefs embedded in routines
Strategic / cost-benefit calculations	'Thick' institutionalization in procedures, routines, rituals, and symbols	Objectivation of shared believes in a community
Low resilience	Intermediate resilience	High resilience

In line with this triptych, Black distinguishes between three sets of reasons for organizational legitimacy.[21] "Legitimacy may be pragmatically based: the person or social group perceives that the organization will pursue their interests directly or indirectly. It can be morally based: the person or social group perceives the goals and/or procedures of the organization to be morally appropriate. Finally, legitimacy can be cognitively based: the organization is accepted as necessary or inevitable." Black argues that the degree of resilience of organizational legitimacy of a transnational private regulator differs for the three types of legitimacy: pragmatic legitimacy is least resilient, cognitive legitimacy is most resilient, normative legitimacy is in between.[22]

As Scott stresses, "robust institutionalization is often the product of multiple mechanisms that interact with and reinforce each other."[23] The three distinctive mechanisms or sets of reasons may be perceived as phases in an institutionalization process: first, cost benefit calculations are dominant. Subsequently, "thick" institutionalization may take place creating social entanglements by hardening rules and procedures and creating rituals and symbols. In a final stage of institutionalization, shared beliefs are objectified resulting in the assumption that things could not be otherwise. In line with this thinking, Bernstein and Cashore have shown for non-state market driven (NSMD) governance systems that political legitimacy is constructed in a three-phase process with different relationships between the actors and participation of different actors.[24] They distinguish between three phases in the process of gaining political legitimacy:

- the initiation phase, early support of a small number of firms based on strategic calculations;

[21] Black, *supra* note 5, at 144.
[22] Black, *supra* note 5, at 145.
[23] Scott, *supra* note 4, at 151.
[24] Bernstein and Cashore, *supra* note 5.

- the phase of widespread support, gaining support from firms whose practices are further away from the NSDM requirements, norm generation begins; and
- the phase of political legitimacy, participation in shared community, strategic calculations occur within, not about, NSMD systems. The systems that were included in the study of Bernstein and Cashore had not reached this phase yet.

These three phases echo the triad of institutionalization mechanisms flagged by Scott and the reasons for organizational legitimacy discussed by Black. The early stage of NSMD governance systems is characterized by a logic of consequences and calculations based on self-interest; later on, a logic of appropriateness and normative motivations become more important. Bernstein and Cashore elaborate in detail the building of political legitimacy for what they call NSMD.[25] Key elements are the conflicting interests between firms and NGOs and that NSMD governance systems deal with global problems that firms have little incentive to address, such as fair trade or sustainable forestry. As these issues are not key to GFSI (NGOs are not involved in GFSI and food safety is a major concern for most companies in the food industry) this specific elaboration is not relevant for our study. What is relevant, however, is the question of whether we can recognize similar mechanisms of institutionalization of legitimacy in the evolution of GFSI.

Casey recently applied the thinking of private regulators as responding to legitimacy demands in an empirical study of the GlobalGAP, the world's most widely adopted private food safety certification program, which has also been benchmarked by GFSI. Casey contends that for GlobalGAP "early institutionalization of structures, practices and processes have a significant influence on legitimacy by cementing the distribution of power within an organization and crystallizing a dominant organizational logic."[26] We will assess whether and how the distribution of power and the dominant logic within GFSI has changed since its initial phase.

In our comparative analysis of the evolution of GFSI, we focus on changes in its governance structure, its activities, and its framing. We will see how these changes in the distribution of power, in the benchmarking requirements, in the kind of activities undertaken, and in the dominant narrative have contributed (or not) to the construction of legitimacy and to what extent they can be attributed to legitimacy demands.

9.3 THE RISE OF GFSI

GFSI was launched in 2000 against the background of the proliferation of multiple overlapping and competing private food safety standards initiated by retailers and

[25] Ibid.

[26] Casey, *supra* note 5, at 188.

food firms in the aftermath of the BSE crisis and other incidents.[27] In the 1990s, leading supermarket chains such as Tesco and Sainsbury in the United Kingdom and Albert Heijn in the Netherlands, started to develop their own comprehensive quality assurance schemes specifying detailed requirements for their suppliers. These retailers wanted to reduce risks and liability costs and inspire confidence for consumers.[28] Private retail-driven food safety standards have expanded ever since. Food retailers collaborated and created industry standards such as the British Retail Consortium (BRC) Global Standard (1998), EurepGAP (1997),[29] and the International Food Standard (2003).

GFSI was established to promote globally accepted food safety standards. The original taskforce consisted of thirteen European-based supermarket chains predominantly from the United Kingdom and France.[30] Two and a half years later, the taskforce had grown to fifty-two members, mostly from Europe.[31] The retailers wanted one or a limited number of global food safety standards that they could ask their suppliers to meet. This should produce significant cost savings for retailers and suppliers by reducing the number of food safety audits. Rather than developing one single normative standard of its own, GFSI benchmarks rival standards following a set of requirements laid down in the GFSI Guidance Document in order to coordinate, converge, and ratchet up existing standards. The first version of this meta-regulatory standard was published in 2001. The GFSI Benchmarking Requirements are frequently updated, with Version 2020 being the eight edition. In December 2022, twelve certification program owners have earned GFSI recognition, and three government-owned voluntary certification standards were found "technically equivalent."[32] The GFSI Benchmarking program has become a powerful tool in the global food market, because many major supermarket chains and food manufacturers require their suppliers to be certified against a GFSI-recognized

[27] Havinga and Verbruggen, *supra* note 9; M. Webb, Overview of Food Safety Standards, in *Food Safety, Market Organization, Trade and Development* (A. Hammoudi, C. Grazia, Y. Surry, and J.-B. Traversac eds., 2015), 45.

[28] L. Fulponi, Private Voluntary Standards in the Food System: The Perspective of Major Retailers in OECD Countries (2006) 31 *Food Policy* 1; Havinga, *supra* note 9.

[29] The EuropeGAP standard evolved into the GlobalGAP standard. While both GlobalGAP and GFSI were initiated by supermarket chains headquartered in Europe, it is important to point out that the two are very different. GlobalGAP is a standard-owner setting food safety standards for agricultural produce. GFSI is a meta-regulator benchmarking standards (such as GlobalGAP's standard) and organizing events and campaigns to encourage standard development, harmonization, and implementation.

[30] Ahold, Asda/Walmart Europe, Carrefour, Delhaize Le Lion, ICA Sweden, Marks & Spencer, Metro, Migro, Opera, Safeway UK, Sainsbury, Superquinn, Tesco. The plan was to soon add US supermarkets: Kroger, Albertson's, Supervalu, Wegmans Food, Loblaw (Orgel, *supra* note 1).

[31] In January 2013, fifty-two supermarket chains had joined the GFSI taskforce, thirty-seven from Europe, seven from the United States, and eight from other non-European countries.

[32] https://mygfsi.com/how-to-implement/recognition/certification-programme-owners; https://mygfsi.com/how-to-implement/technical-equivalence/.

standard. Accordingly, we have suggested, GFSI should be seen as an industry-driven meta-regulator that has proven to be influential in shaping both industry practices and public policy making.[33]

9.4 GFSI'S ORGANIZATIONAL AND REGULATORY EVOLUTION

The evolution of GFSI from its inception can be studied through four distinctive processes: (1) pluralization of its constituents, (2) increased openness and transparency of its governance and rulemaking activities, (3) expansion and ratchetting up of food standards' quality, and (4) globalization of its benchmarking activities.

9.4.1 *Pluralization of Its Constituents*

GFSI started as a taskforce within CIES – The Food Business Forum, a membership organization of major food retailing companies and their suppliers.[34] The taskforce consisted exclusively of supermarket chains. Its membership expanded from thirteen European retailers in 2000 to fifty-two retailers in 2003. In 2004, a board was formed consisting of eight retail members. In 2005, GFSI transformed its organization structure from a membership organization to a not-for-profit foundation under Belgium law managed by the CIES,[35] which later merged into the Consumer Goods Forum (CGF).[36] It was CIES/CGF who took the final decisions on important governance issues for GFSI, including its structure, strategy, and membership.

The board of the separate legal entity GFSI was dominated by retailers in those first years. Gradually, this power distribution has changed. In October 2008, GFSI announced that it has created a new governance structure for the board. In addition to retailers, from that moment on food manufacturers and food service companies were also awarded membership on the noard. Two vice-chairs of the board are appointed from each of these two categories.[37]

33 P. Verbruggen and T. Havinga, The Rise of Transnational Private Meta-regulators (2016) 21 *Tilburg Law Review* 116.

34 CIES membership is by invitation only and there are an equal number of retailer and of supplier member companies.

35 Orgel, *supra* note 1; Verbruggen and Havinga, *supra* note 33, at 125.

36 CGF is a global, parity-based industry network, driven by its members. It brings together the CEOs and senior management of over 400 retailers, manufacturers, service providers, and other stakeholders across 70 countries and reflects the diversity of the industry in geography, size, product category, and format. Forum member companies have combined annual sales of EUR 3.5 trillion. The CGF is governed by its board of directors, which includes 50 manufacturer and retailer CEOs and chair(wo)men, www.theconsumergoodsforum.com/.

37 GFSI press release October 30, 2008, Retailers, manufacturers and food service join forces globally to ensure safe food for consumers.

In 2020, the board consists of eleven retailers, ten manufacturers, and two food service providers.[38] So, retailers lost their majority. All retailer and manufacturer board members are from CGF member companies,[39] which are prioritized in the board and other GFSI committees.[40] In 2021, the board was replaced with a steering committee to align GFSI with the governance model of the CGF.[41] In the steering committee, manufacturers have the majority.[42] The implications of this "modernization" are unclear at the moment of writing.

In 2020, for the first time, the board elected its own chairs. They chose two co-chairs and two vice-chairs representing retail and manufacture in a parity-based system of governance. Previously, the chair was appointed by CGF. This seems to indicate that GFSI has gained some independence from the CGF. However, in the 2019 version of the governance model, the GFSI office managed by CGF was given more duties and powers.[43] And this is even more so in the 2021 version.[44]

GFSI thus remains an industry-driven organization run by large international food corporations. According to its governance rules: "Steering Committee membership is not assigned to service providers … including associations, certification programme owners, certification or accreditation bodies, food safety related service providers."[45] A balanced representation is one of the criteria for appointment in the steering committee: "Balanced geographical and industry sector representation i.e. manufacturing and retail, including the need to have significant representation from both large and small industry companies to ensure that decisions take into account the divers perspectives within the industry."[46]

Although GFSI was an organization exclusively for retailers, from the start other stakeholders in the global food supply chain were involved in its activities and the pursuance of its regulatory goals. A draft version of the first edition of the guidance document (2001) was circulated for external consultation and "external comments have been incorporated" in the second edition (2002). In 2002, GFSI announced the formation of a "Stakeholder group, open to representatives of all links in the food chain in order to participate in the endorsement [benchmarking] process."[47] The Stakeholder Advisory Forum currently consists of retail, manufacturer, certification

38 https://mygfsi.com/who-we-are/gfsi-board.

39 Thirteen of them are from a company that is also represented in the board of CGF. We checked membership on the CGF website, www.theconsumergoodsforum.com/.

40 GFSI, GFSI Governance Model and Rules of Procedure, February 2015, mygfsi.com; GFSI, GFSI Governance Model and Rules of Procedure, May 2019, mygfsi.com.

41 CGF/GFSI, The Consumer Goods Forum (CGF) Coalition of Action on Food Safety: The Global Food Safety Initiative (GFSI) (2021).

42 Thirteen manufacturers and nine retail and food service steering committee members from thirty-seven CGF coalition members, https://mygfsi.com/who-we-are/governance.

43 GFSI 2015, *supra* note 40; GFSI 2019, *supra* note 40.

44 GFSI 2021, *supra* note 3, art III

45 Ibid., art V B, at 12. Compare GFSI 2015, *supra* note 40; GFSI 2019, *supra* note 40, article IV C.

46 GFSI 2021, *supra* note 3, art C2, at 14

47 Information from www.ciesnet.com/global_food/main.html.

program owner members, audit and certification organizations, and an accreditation organization.[48] In September 2006, the "retailer only" taskforce was replaced by a technical committee including other stakeholders in the food chain as well as the certification industry.[49] This committee provides technical expertise and advice for the GFSI Board. For example, the committee formulates the benchmarking requirements, which are then determined by the Board. Technical working groups are composed of four manufacturers, four retailers, four certification/accreditation bodies, four service providers, and all recognized certification program owners.[50] The benchmarking committees were composed of experts from retailers, suppliers, or food service companies (balanced) and a representative from a national accreditation body.[51] The 2020 benchmarking document states that the assessment of a certification program is performed by the GFSI technical manager and the benchmark leader.[52] So again, more tasks for the GFSI management.

In addition, GFSI has strategically coordinated its regulatory activities with government representatives. One of the four top priorities of the organization in 2002 was "to encourage co-operation between the world-wide food sector and national and pan-national governments and authorities." GFSI staff and participating firm representatives engaged in talks with national and international governments to explain GFSI's mission and the value of third-party certification.[53] GFSI's objective is to establish partnerships with governments. Over time, GFSI has entered into agreements, partnerships, and Memoranda of Understanding (MoUs) with various international and national government organizations, such as the International Accreditation Forum (2003), several Chinese agencies (2015), the United Nations Industrial Development Organization (UNIDO) (2016), and the Mexican National Service for Agroalimentary Public Health, Safety and Quality (2017).[54]

[48] https://mygfsi.com/who-we-are/working-groups/.

[49] CIES, What We do: Food Safety Global Food Safety Initiative, www.ciesnet.com. For example, in March 2008, the Technical Committee had fifty-four members from fifty organizations: fourteen retailers, three retailer associations, ten manufacturers, twelve certification bodies, five standard owners, and one accreditation body.

[50] GFSI 2015, *supra* note 40; GFSI 2019, *supra* note 40. This specification of the composition of technical working groups is not found in the 2021 version of the governance model anymore. The working group composition is determined by the steering committee "ensuring balance where possible between stakeholders from different relevant sectors." GFSI 2021, *supra* note 3, art. VII B, at 29.

[51] GFSI 2015, *supra* note 40; GFSI 2019, *supra* note 40.

[52] GFSI, GFSI Benchmarking requirements, Version 2020 (2020), part I, at 4.

[53] Information from www.ciesnet.com/global_food/main.html. Havinga and Verbruggen, *supra* note 9; and P. Verbruggen and T. Havinga, Transnational Business Governance Interactions in Food Safety Regulation: Exploring the Promises and Risks of Enrolment, in *Transnational Business Governance Interactions: Empowering Marginalized Actors and Enhancing Regulatory Quality* (S. Wood et al. eds., 2019), 28, discuss the interactions between GFSI and governments.

[54] In a presentation on its website the following public private partnerships are listed: Canada (CFIA 2015), China (CNCA 2015), Japan (MAFF 2016), Mexico (Senasica 2016), United States (FDA 2016), Argentina (ministry of agribusiness 2017), Chile (Achipia 2017), Europe (Heads of

From 2016 onwards, GFSI has hosted at its annual Global Food Safety Conference (GFSC) a meeting of governmental food officials and international governmental organizations, followed by a meeting of governments with the GFSI Board.[55] These meetings provide a global platform to discuss ongoing national food safety reforms and the role that third-party audits and certification can play. In these meetings, GFSI representatives explained the GFSI system and governmental representatives pointed out where areas need to be strengthened. National governments essentially voiced two concerns: (i) the quality and reliability of audits and auditors and (ii) the equivalence of the GFSI requirements with national food safety regulations. International governmental organizations such as the Food and Agricultural Organization (FAO) of the United Nations and the World Trade Organization (WTO) were very skeptical about private standards and perceived private food safety standards mainly as a trade barrier in emerging markets.[56] The organization of the government-to-business (G2B) meeting has been formalized with the creation of an organizing committee in September 2020. The committee has eighteen members (eleven representatives of national governmental organizations, six representatives of international public organizations, and one representative of the GFSI Board).[57] Members are expected to "commit to the GFSI outcome of building trust in GFSI" and to "engage their organisation."[58]

In 2014, GFSI introduced the option for government-owned voluntary certification programs to be benchmarked as a technical equivalent. Unlike GFSI recognition, technical equivalence does not include the assessment of the program's governance and operational management. The reason for introducing this possibility seems to be the desire to accept Chinese certification programs that are managed by governmental agencies. Public voluntary certification programs that applied and achieved technical equivalence are China HACCP, Canadian Grain Commission HACCP, and USDA Agricultural Marketing Service. The fact that not only China but also Canada and the United States have had public standards benchmarked by GFSI is an indication of the dominance and the credibility and authority that GFSI has acquired globally.

food safety agencies group 2017), Vietnam (IFC 2018). Partnerships with international governmental organization include: Unido, Oio, WTO/STDF, IFC, Government-to-Business (G2B) Meetings, GFSP and Codex Alimentarius. See: GFSI, Global Food Safety Initiative. Safe Food for Consumers everywhere. General presentation (2020).

[55] Organized by the G2B Organizing group. Its mandate, appointments, and decision making process is regulated in the Governance rules, art X (GFSI 2021, *supra* note 3).

[56] M. Martens and J. Swinnen, Private Standards, Global Food Supply Chains and the Implications for Developing Countries, in *Private Standards and Global Governance: Economic, Legal and Political Perspectives* (A. Marx et al. eds., 2012), 153; G. H. Stanton, Food-Safety Related Private Standards: The WTO Perspective, in *Private Standards and Global Governance: Economic, Legal and Political Perspectives* (A. Marx et al. eds., 2012), 235.

[57] Government-to-Business (G2B) Organising Committee, https://mygfsi.com/who-we-are/working-groups/.

[58] GFSI, Government to Business Charter & Mandate (2020).

GFSI Board members are CEOs from major food corporations – retailers, manufacturers, and food services who purchase many food products and raw materials. SMEs and farmers who produce and supply these products and other stakeholders are not represented in the board and in working groups. On its website, GFSI emphasizes the existence of a GFSI community: "GFSI exists thanks to a global community of passionate people who volunteer their time and expertise because they believe that everyone has a right to safe food. They share a common understanding that collaboration is the key to achieving what no one company or country can achieve alone . . .. Countless individuals from over 150 companies have contributed to over 25 Technical Working Groups, Local Groups, Task Forces, Committees and the Board of Directors."[59]

Finally, it should be noted that none of the recognized certification programs covers the retail of food, even though major corporate retailers initiated GFSI and still are a powerful constituent of GFSI. This illustrates that GFSI is meant to develop the private regulation of supply chains belonging to major food retail and food manufacturing corporations. Apparently, there was no need to regulate the retail sector itself.

9.4.2 *Advances in Openness and Transparency*

In the early years, the governance of GFSI was only loosely organized as a taskforce of retailers within CIES, the food business forum. Over the years, the openness and transparency of the organization has gradually increased. This applies to the governance of GFSI, its benchmarking procedure, and the transparency of the certification programs submitted to the benchmarking procedure.

The benchmarking requirements are publicly available on the GFSI website and outline the benchmarking procedure and requirements. The current GFSI governance model and rules of procedure specifies its objectives and the internal governance of GFSI: mandates, decision-making procedures, the frequency of meetings, eligibility criteria, election and responsibilities of the steering committee and subcommittees, the working groups, and local groups. A code of ethical conduct, obligatory statements of commitment, and a complaints procedure are also included.[60] The internal organization has now been highly formalized through a rulebook of eighty-seven pages.

Appointment of members of the GFSI board and committees was initially "by invitation only." Currently, a call for candidates is distributed and interested parties can apply to be appointed. The eligibility criteria, the appointment process, and – in some cases – the distribution of members over categories are laid down in the GFSI

[59] https://mygfsi.com/who-we-are/alumni/.
[60] GFSI 2021, *supra* note 3.

governance model.[61] The 2015 and 2019 version contained the provision that GFSI holds a register of Benchmarking Committee members on its website.[62] However, this register could not be found on the website. According to the benchmarking document from 2020 a "list of all GFSI-approved Benchmark Leaders is available from GFSI upon request."[63] So it seems that this information is not easily available (anymore). The benchmarking process is regulated in the Benchmarking Requirements document.[64] The benchmark leader and the GFSI technical manager perform the assessment of a certification program and give their recommendation whether to recognize the program. It is the board who approves the benchmark leader and takes the final decision on approval.

GFSI publishes on its website which standards are recognized and which are under review. The latter was not so obvious in 2005. Hugo Byrnes, director of food safety at CIES noted: "There are three other standards under review, which cannot be made public yet. If these are rejected by GFSI, it could cause embarrassment under their respective owners."[65] Elsewhere, we can read which three standards were "under consideration."[66] The current website provides information for each certification program in which of the seven steps of the benchmarking process it is.[67]

On its website, GFSI has a library of free downloadable documents including training material of the Global Market Program, consultation documents and reports and case studies. GFSI is less transparent about financial issues. It is clear that the participation of food safety experts on the board, working groups, and local groups is paid for by the food companies where these experts are employed. There are complaints about the high fees for conferences and the reluctance of the management of GFSI to account for this.

The benchmarking requirements include ever more requirements related to the governance structure of standard owners. Certification programs need to be available for all food firms and all certification bodies should be able to certify against the program. Information that a standard owner should make publicly available include the normative document, the list of certification bodies that are accredited to certify for the standard, rules to prevent conflicts of interest, and a register of valid certificates.

61 GFSI 2015, *supra* note 40; GFSI 2019, *supra* note 40; GFSI 2021, *supra* note 3.

62 GFSI 2015, *supra* note 40; GFSI 2019, *supra* note 40, art VIII c.

63 GFSI, *supra* note 52.

64 Ibid., at 8.

65 L. Joppen, Extension of GFSI Family. Efsis Out, SQF Europegap in, *Food Engeneering & Ingredients*, February 2005, at 9.

66 In *Food Engineering & Ingredients*, April 2005: "The following standards are 'under consideration': Dutch HACCP, the China Retailers Standard and the New Zealand Fresh Produce Programme." Only Dutch HACCP was recognized by GFSI. The other two standards probably failed the test.

67 https://mygfsi.com/how-to-implement/cpos-undergoing-benchmarking.

9.4.3 *Expansion and Ratchetting up of Food Standards' Quality*

From its inception, GFSI aimed at improving the quality and credibility of food safety standards. This includes the substantive norms in the benchmark requirements, transparency and integrity of food scheme owners and certification bodies, and the quality and reliability of audits.

Already, the first GFSI benchmarking requirements were based on international authoritative norms from the Codex Alimentarius Commission and the ISO/IEC Guide 65. Initially, the benchmark requirements only consisted of a list of items that an application should contain, the consequent steps in the procedure, and some time limits.[68] With every new edition, the benchmarking requirements have been tightened and new themes have been added. Usually, when a weakness or issue that needs attention is in the spotlight, GFSI decides to introduce a new technical working group to investigate the matter and to make recommendations as to how to tackle the issue. Such groups were introduced for third-party certification, auditor competences and auditor training, alignment with national authorities, capacity building in global markets, food defense, food safety culture, and managing risks in produce and leafy greens. The activity of these groups often results in new or adapted requirements in the GFSI guidance document. New topics that were introduced in the benchmarking requirements include, for example:

- reducing the risks of food fraud (in response to the horsemeat scandal);
- auditor competences and auditor training;
- stricter requirements for the frequency and scope of audits;
- unannounced audits were added, first optional, later mandatory;
- extended requirements related to scheme owner management and governance; and
- requirements related to food safety culture.

Subsequently, new scopes and sector-specific requirements followed. The first editions only had general requirements for all schemes. The 2020 edition consists of general requirements for all certification programs and specific requirements for twenty scopes covering the whole food supply chain from farming, processing, distribution, and the retail and supply industry, such as feed production, food safety services, and food packaging.

What remains constant, despite all the new themes, is the exclusive focus on food safety. Other themes such as animal welfare and environment or ethical sourcing are explicitly kept out.[69] Moreover, just like the very first edition, the 2020 edition

[68] GFSI, The Global Food Safety Initiative Guidance Document, 2nd ed, February 12, 2002, part III.

[69] GFSI, *supra* note 54.

contains three key elements: HACCP; a food safety management system; and Good Practices for Agriculture, manufacturing, and distribution (GAP).

One of the main concerns over the past twenty years has been the reliability of food safety audits and certificates. This is a crucial issue as the value of the recognized certification programs depends on thorough and reliable food safety audits. Doubts about food safety certificates are voiced over and over again by governments, media, and parts of the food industry. GFSI recognizes these weaknesses and tries to explain the system to everyone and to ratchet up the quality of food safety audits. The first step was the choice for third-party certification, adding an independent observer to the scene. Despite checks and balances in the system of third-party certification[70] concerns remain. In each updated edition, requirements for audits and auditors were tightened. There have been years of discussing and negotiating the introduction of unannounced audits and requirements related to auditor competence and training. Due to conflicting interests and resistance, several of these changes took a long time before a final decision was made and the adaptation could be implemented. Recently, GFSI concluded that benchmarking of food safety certification programs was not sufficient. "There has been an understandable concern about the efficacy of audits and more specifically the competence of some food safety auditors themselves." GFSI introduced its Race to the Top (RTTT) plan. This plan "is intended to address the specific challenges GFSI has been facing in relation to trust and confidence in GFSI certification outcomes …. driving improvements in the food certification system is vital to achieve our mission."[71] In 2021, GFSI introduced its benchmarking and harmonization of professional recognition programs for food safety auditors.[72]

Over time, more detailed requirements were imposed related to the scheme governance and management. For example, the 2020 edition introduces the requirement for CPOs to carry out annual performance reviews of certification bodies. The relation between scheme owner and GFSI is increasingly formalized. Cooperation with the IAF resulted in adaptation of the guidance document. Efsis, a standard that belonged to the first four accepted standards, subsequently declined a new application because the requirements that the program should not be limited to members or own customers and that a scheme owner could not be the organization performing the audits, could not be met.

In addition to benchmarking, the dissemination of knowledge and the exchange of experiences is an important characteristic of GFSI's activities. GFSI provides a global platform for professionalization of food safety experts working at certified food companies, at certification bodies, at certification program owners, at consultancy

70 C. Daugbjerg, Accountability and Integrity in Private Food Safety Regulation: Evidence from the Australian Food Sector (2020) *Australian Journal of Public Administration* 1.

71 GFSI, Stakeholder Engagement Plan. Implementing the GFSI Conceptual Framework The Race to the Top (2020), at 40, 41, 45.

72 GFSI, GFSI Benchmarking Requirements Professional Recognition Bodies, version 2021.

firms, and at regulatory agencies and departments. To pursue this objective, GFSI organizes annual global food safety conferences, focus days in different continents and countries to promote GFSI, and the system of third-party certification.

The modifications and increase in requirements make it ever more difficult and more expensive for certification programs to meet all requirements. For this reason, one of the first recognized schemes has decided not to register anymore. The organization behind this scheme has split into two systems, FSSC 2000 as a GFSI-recognized system and Dutch HACCP as a local system for traditional production.

9.4.4 *Globalization of Benchmarking Activities*

GFSI started in Europe and it was dominated by Europe-based retailers for a long time, although its ambition always was to be a global initiative. Soon after its launch, some US and Canadian supermarkets joined the taskforce. The first four standards that were recognized by GFSI were European.[73] In January 2004, a US retail standard was approved, SQF 2000. The breakthrough to the United States food industry was in 2007, after Walmart made GFSI certification mandatory for its suppliers.

Not only the member companies and the recognized food safety certification programs but also the other activities employed by GFSI were during the first phase located in Europe only. One of five strategic priorities 2011–2015 was to "continue presence in Europe, build momentum in North America and develop a strategy for APAC."[74] Of the twenty annual global food safety conferences (GFSC), fifteen took place in Europe. It was not until 2011 that the first GFSC outside Europe was held, in Orlando, Florida, in the United States. Four years later, in 2015, the first GFSC was held in Asia.

From 2011, GFSI organized focus days in sourcing countries in Latin America, Asia, and Africa. "GFSI Focus Days and Regional Events aim at raising awareness around the benefits of GFSI in regional markets. They were initiated to provide local stakeholders in the food industry with an opportunity to find out more about the Global Food Safety Initiative. They also serve as a unique opportunity for networking and knowledge exchange."[75] In China and Japan, GFSI organized such a meeting every year. Local groups are regional networks of companies that want to promote GFSI and share knowledge to improve food safety. The first local group was located in Japan (2012). Now there are local groups in Mexico (2013), China

[73] The first four standards are BRC Global Standard Food (UK retailers), Dutch HACCP Code (Netherlands), EFSIS (UK private auditing company), and International Food Standard (German retailers) (GFSI, Year Book 2004).

[74] GFSI, GFSI & the Consumer Goods Forum (2010).

[75] The first Focus Day was in 2011 in Brasil, Japan (2011), South Africa (2013). From 2011/2012 every year there has been a Focus Day in China and Japan.

(2013), US-Canada (2013), South Latin America (2015), Europe (2016), and Australia-New Zealand (2019).[76]

GFSI also aimed at cooperation with governments and international organizations all over the world. Responding to critics that private food safety standards are a barrier for SMEs and food businesses on non-Western markets, GFSI launched its global markets program in 2011 (manufacturing) and 2012 (primary production). The GFSI Global Markets Programme is designed to assist companies who have underdeveloped food safety systems to learn and adhere to best food safety practices. It is a systematic continuous improvement process that companies can follow to establish, and achieve recognition for, effective food safety systems. The Programme is "a stepwise pathway towards GFSI-recognised certification for companies that lack or wish to improve their food safety systems."[77]

In 2012, the majority of certifications for most recognized schemes were in Europe, exceptions are SQF (N-America) and FSSC 22000 (more equal distribution).[78] GFSI-recognized certificates have been issued in 162 countries.[79]

9.5 CONSTRUCTING AND MANAGING GFSI'S LEGITIMACY

9.5.1 *Legitimacy Dynamics*

To what extent can the processes that we have highlighted be understood from the perspective of legitimacy? Some of the processes are clearly a response to the criticisms and demands expressed by external or even internal actors. Prominent examples of this are the reliability of food safety certificates, the vulnerability for food fraud, and capacity building in emerging markets. From the very start, the reliability of certification schemes has been the subject of persistent criticism by governments, NGOs, and businesses in the supply chain. GFSI could not simply ignore these critiques, as they go to the core of the organization's regulatory goal, that is, to promote improvement in food safety management systems around the world. To provide these critiques with an answer, bolster its legitimacy, and be resilient, GFSI has sought to make these systems more reliable by promoting third-party certification and by imposing increasingly stringent benchmarking requirements for audits, auditors, and the certification bodies that employ them. The collaboration between GFSI and IAF, and the requirement that certification bodies must be accredited by an accreditation body that is a member of the IAF, are expressly meant to improve credibility. The modernization program, Race to the Top (RTTT), presented in

76 GFSI, *supra* note 2.

77 https://mygfsi.com/how-to-implement/global-markets/.

78 Verbruggen and Havinga, *supra* note 33.

79 GFSI, *supra* note 54, at 22.

2020, is an explicit response to systematic doubts about the functioning of the certification system. The program aims at a fundamental shift from compliance being enough to continuous improvement at all touchpoints.[80] Accordingly, it seeks to address the concern among governments, NGOs, and part of the food industry itself regarding poor auditor performance and a lack of a sufficiently strong food safety culture in the industry.

GFSI stresses in its communication the existence and the importance of a GFSI community: "GFSI has grown into a vast, global multi-stakeholder movement."[81] At GFSI conferences and meetings – as one of the authors has observed as an invited speaker and participant – there certainly is a kind of community of global food safety experts.[82] However, within this community, GFSI has to deal with, at least partly, conflicting interests of stakeholder categories. Governments, transnational corporate retailers, transnational top food manufacturers, farmers, SMEs, certification bodies, certification program owners, and economic development organizations all have a certain interest in securing safe food, but they also have different interests. GFSI is finding the middle ground in all of this. The politics involved in global food safety standards can, for example, explain why it took years before some form of mandatory unannounced audits were included in the GFSI benchmark requirements. Also, how to deal with the issue of auditor training and competences is contentious. Some recognized schemes preferred their own existing training program and examinations. Certification bodies feared that auditors would need to pass various exams, resulting in higher costs while no added value is expected. Since 2019, auditors are required to take and pass the GFSI Knowledge Exam. The examinations are provided by the certification programs and the requirements include mutual recognition of exam results between CPOs to assure that an auditor only needs to pass the exam once.[83]

To sum up, the continuous improvement of the quality of the food safety certification programs is associated with GFSI's desire to build and maintain its legitimacy as a transnational private rule-maker. This organizational concern closely aligns with the original regulatory goal of GFSI, namely to enhance global food safety.

Advances in openness and transparency can also be interpreted as reactions to criticism and changing international norms. Transparent procedures and requirements to ensure integrity, independence, as well as checks and balances in the certification system are in line with international authoritative norms and concerns voiced by governments and IGOs.

[80] GFSI, *supra* note 71, at 45.
[81] https://mygfsi.com/who-we-are/overview/.
[82] GFSC Tokyo March 5–8, 2018.
[83] https://mygfsi.com/news_updates/gfsi-releases-its-new-auditor-knowledge-exam-required-from-july-2019/.

However, the first and foremost driver for the globalization of certification and GFSI's benchmarking activities are the commercial interests of the retailers and manufacturers represented in GFSI. Transnational retailers and manufacturers want to source products and ingredients from all over the world. For that reason, it is important that their suppliers, not only in Europe but also in Asia, Latin America, and Africa, can deliver products from certified firms complying with the GFSI requirements. The Global Markets Programme helps in building and extending this supplier network. At the same time, however, this program also is a response to the concerns that international governmental organizations such as the Codex Alimentarius Commission and the STDF have voiced around the barriers to trade that private food safety standards create for developing countries.[84]

The pluralization of its constituents is more difficult to directly link to GFSI's desire for legitimacy. From the perspective of legitimacy, it would seem wise to include all stakeholders in the decision-making process. However, in GFSI's organizational structure, this is only partly what happened. In the decision-making bodies, the GFSI steering committee/board and the CGF, many categories of stakeholders are not represented. This includes certification program owners, certification bodies, auditors, farmers, SMEs, governments, IGOs, consultants, accreditation bodies, and consumers. Although some of these categories are represented in working groups providing advice to the board/steering committee, they lack formal voting rights. Nevertheless, this degree of pluralization did bolster GFSI's credibility and regulatory clout. GFSI has created a global platform around food safety and succeeded in forming a kind of GFSI community working together to improve food safety and exchanging knowledge and experiences. GFSI also succeeded in establishing partnerships with governmental organizations. Collaboration and partnerships with (international) governmental organizations further add to the legitimacy of GFSI as governments are widely believed to serve the public interest, while industry is believed to put self-interest first.[85]

9.5.2 *Institutionalizing Legitimacy*

To what extent do we observe the three phases in the process of institutionalizing legitimacy as discussed in Section 9.2 in the evolution of GFSI as a transnational private rule-maker? During the first years, it indeed seems that economic reasoning is the most important driver for GFSI's regulatory activities. Other arguments have gradually gained weight. Nevertheless, economic interests remain the most fundamental considerations. The ratchetting up of the benchmarking requirements leads

[84] Stanton, *supra* note 56; Martens and Swinnen, *supra* note 56.
[85] Verbruggen and Havinga, *supra* note 53.

to higher compliance costs, usually for parties up of the supply chain. These involve the companies that want to obtain a certificate and the firms that conduct audits and carry out certification. Too high costs could drive these actors out of the GFSI system. GFSI therefore treads carefully and proceeds step-by-step in laying down more stringent benchmarking requirements for the certification programs. Also, other actors, including the transnational supermarket chains and food manufacturers that are the driving forces behind the private standards, are sometimes tempted to opt for low costs. Nevertheless, so far GFSI has managed to build a fair degree of legitimacy both in the world of the food industry and food safety experts.

The discussed changes are predominantly gradual. Clearly distinguishable phases as suggested by Bernstein and Cashore are hard to uncover. The same is true for a (causal) link between changes in GFSI's regulatory standards and food safety crises. What is clear in the case of GFSI is that, as Casey has argued for GlobalGAP, the first phase of institutionalization lays down the aims, structure, and power distribution within the transnational private rule-making body. Despite its growth and the inclusion of other participants next to retailers, GFSI stays true to its initial mission: "to enhance food safety, ensure consumer protection, strengthen consumer confidence, benchmark requirements of food safety systems and improve cost efficiency throughout the supply chain."[86] Similarly, GFSI remains an industry-led organization relying on the participation of food safety experts of large food corporations, some of which have been represented from the very start. Also, GFSI's main regulatory activity still is the benchmarking of food safety certification schemes. The ambition "once certified, recognised everywhere" still stands.[87]

At least three changes have brought about change in GFSI's initial organizational structure and regulatory activities: the joining of food manufacturers in the board and retailers losing the majority in board and committees, the introduction of the Global Market Programme, and the introduction of the Technical Equivalence Procedure. The latter implies that government-owned food standards are subjected to assessment by an industry organization such as GFSI. For example, the USDA-harmonized GAP audit was augmented to meet GFSI equivalence standards.[88] This collaboration inevitably lends legitimacy to GFSI as a global private rule-maker.

86 GFSI, *supra* note 68, at 3. In 2011 it read: "1. Reduce food safety risks by delivering equivalence and convergence between effective food safety management systems 2. Manage cost in the global food system by eliminating redundancy and improving operational efficiency 3. Develop competencies and capacity building in food safety to create consistent and effective global food systems 4. Provide a unique international stakeholder platform for collaboration, knowledge exchange and networking" (GFSI, An Overview of GFSI and Accredited Certification, March 2011).

87 GFSI, Once Certified, Accepted Everywhere. Standards, Harmonisation and Co-operation in the Global Food Industry, Position paper (2007?): GFSI, *supra* note 52, at 3

88 www.ams.usda.gov/services/usda-harmonized-gap-plus-audit-service-questions-and-answers.

To conclude, GFSI has been deeply concerned in constructing and maintaining its legitimacy as a transnational private rule-maker. It has succeeded in gaining acceptance and credibility among major parts of the global food industry and even in governmental circles by being responsive to needs and criticism of various stakeholders. As such, GFSI has shown strong potential for adaptation, nourishing its resilience and dominance. However, responsiveness cannot explain all organizational changes we have discussed. Economic self-interest of the leading constituents of GFSI has initiated some of these changes yet delayed or prevented others.

PART IV

Evolution and Adaptation in Sector-Specific Regimes

10

Organizational Responses of Transnational Private Regulators after Major Accidents

The Case of the American Petroleum Institute and the Deepwater Horizon Oil Spill

Margarita Nieves-Zárate

10.1 INTRODUCTION

Since 1924, the American Petroleum Institute (API) has developed nearly 700 safety standards and recommended practices covering all segments of the oil and gas industry. Many of API's standards and recommended practices are incorporated into public regulations, to the point that they are considered the most used standards by national regulators in the oil and gas industry.

This chapter analyzes the organizational changes of the API as a response to pressures and demands from public authorities and investigations in the aftermath of the Deepwater Horizon (DWH) oil spill, the major environmental accident in the oil and gas industry in the United States. The DWH oil spill created new incentives and rationales for API to internalize the need for change.

This exogenous event, and the reaction of the API, will contribute to shine light on the mechanics and dynamics of resilience of transnational private regulators and on the relation between public and private authority – in particular on the capacity (or lack thereof) of the former to effectively enroll, steer, and influence the latter. The organizational response of the API to the regulatory crisis created by the DWH accident support the findings of other chapters in this book that argue that that private bodies grow stronger out of episodes and shocks.[1]

Besides API, this chapter focuses on the Bureau for Safety and Environmental Enforcement (BSEE), the federal regulator for offshore oil and gas exploration and production in the United States, in order to investigate how public authorities react to changes undertaken by private regulators in times of crisis. Qualitative research methods such as case studies and the analysis of regulations and investigation reports are used to explain the reorganization of private and public regulators after major accidents in the offshore oil and gas sector.

[1] See P. Delimatsis, "The Resilience of Private Authority in Times of Crisis," Chapter 1.

Section 10.2 explains the emergence of the API as a transnational private regulator and its dynamics such as the resistance to federal safety regulations. Section 10.3 analyzes how the DWH oil spill and the introduction of safety regulations by BSEE became drivers for API's change. Section 10.4 examines the organizational responses introduced by the API in order to adapt itself to the new demands from the public regulator. Section 10.5 discusses the co-regulatory scheme adopted by BSEE legitimizing the response of API. Taking into account the transnational nature of the API and its organizational changes, Section 10.6 identifies the lessons that regulators beyond the United States may learn in order to promote safety in the offshore oil and gas industry, and monitor compliance with safety standards. Section 10.7 provides conclusions.

10.2 THE API'S STRENGTH AND RELATIVE INFLUENCE AS A TRANSNATIONAL PRIVATE REGULATOR

10.2.1 *The Origins of API and Its Growth in Significance*

Transnational private regulators have emerged and multiplied in the oil and gas industry[2] in areas such as safety regulation that are considered as the preserve of public authority. The most ancient and influential transnational private regulator in this sector is the API, whose standards are the most used by national regulators worldwide.[3] In 1919, API was founded in the United States as a nonprofit national trade association to promote the interests of the petroleum industry in all its branches.[4] Soon after its foundation, it was clear that in order to be more effective, API had to develop its own standards for the oil and gas industry.[5] In 1923, API created its Standards Department, and one year after, the API published its first standard on drill pipe threads.[6] Since then, the API has developed nearly 700 standards and recommended practices covering all segments of the oil and gas industry.[7]

2 See A. Wawryk, Adoption of International Environmental Standards by Transnational Oil Companies: Reducing the Impact of Oil Operations in Emerging Economies (2002) 20:4 *Journal of Energy & Natural Resources Law* 406; S. Trevisanunt, Is There Something Wrong with the Increasing Role of Private Actors? The Case of the Offshore Energy Sector, in*What's Wrong with International Law?* (C. Ryngaert, E. Molenaar, and S. Nouwen eds., 2015), at 69.

3 See: API, API Standards: International Usage and Deployment (2020); The International Association of Oil and Gas Producers (OGP), Regulator's Use of Standards. Report No. 426 (OGP, 2010), at 54. In this report, the OGP analyzed fourteen national regulators' use of standards in their regulatory documents and evidenced that API standards were the most used with 225 references.

4 API, Origins, www.api.org/about#tab-origins. In late 1969, API made the decision to move its offices to Washington, DC, where it remains today.

5 API, Timeline, www.api.org/about#tab-timeline.

6 Ibid.

7 API, Overview and Mission, www.api.org/about#tab-overview-and-mission.

Many of those standards and recommended practices are incorporated into public regulations.

The wide use of the API's standards by national regulators beyond the United States consolidates the influence of the API as a transnational private regulator. This transnational role is reflected by the API's twofold mission of not only influencing public policy in support of a strong, viable US oil and natural gas industry but also promoting safety across the oil and gas industry globally.[8] In order to strengthen its global presence, between 2007 and 2010, the API opened three international offices in Beijing, Dubai, and Singapore.[9] The API has around 600 members from international major oil companies to small independent firms in all sectors of the industry, including exploration and production, pipeline operators, marine transportation, refining, marketing, and service and supply firms.[10]

10.2.2 *The API's Influence and Resistance to Governmental Safety Regulations*

The API has sought to expand its influence by promoting the uptake of its standards for the offshore oil and gas industry by BSEE. Historically, the BSEE has formally adopted the standards developed by the API, incorporating them into its own regulations.[11] In parallel, the API has also opposed government initiatives to adopt safety regulations. An example of this opposition is the case of the Safety and Environmental Management Systems (SEMS). From 1991 to 2009, the federal offshore safety regulator unsuccessfully tried to introduce SEMS to manage the risks of offshore oil and gas operations. However, its Minerals Management Service (MMS), the predecessor of BSEE, found strong opposition from the API.

The first attempt was in 1991, when, in response to several investigations, MMS initiated a rule-making procedure to require operators to implement a safety and environmental management program (SEMP).[12] The API was averse to this initiative and asked MMS to postpone the rule-making procedure in order to allow the API itself to elaborate an offshore safety standard. MMS acceded to this proposal and participated in the API's standard-setting process, which was concluded in 1993 when the API published its "Recommended Practice 75" (API RP-75) as a guidance document.[13]

8 Ibid.

9 R. Goodman, API Standards and the Standards Development Process, www.bsee.gov/sites/bsee.gov/files/research-guidance-manuals-or-best-practices/structures/6-api-standards-r-goodman-bsee-workshop1.pdf.

10 API, *supra* note 3.

11 National Commission on the BP Deepwater Horizon Oil Spill and Offshore Drilling, Deep Water, Report to the President (2011), at 225.

12 Ibid., at 71.

13 Ibid.

The second rule-making attempt to introduce SEMS was in 2006 and 2009, when, after a period of advocating for voluntary implementation of the API RP-75, the MMS proposed a rule that required operators to implement SEMS. Once more, the API opposed this regulation, arguing that the implementation of SEMS should remain voluntary. The API presented several arguments for this request: (a) the offshore industry had an admirable safety record, (b) voluntary programs that have enough flexibility to suit the culture of each company are the best way to promote safety in the industry, and (c) having a detailed plan on paper will not ensure an improvement in performance.[14] In the middle of this rule-making procedure, the DWH accident occurred, and the federal government adopted SEMS regulations, taking the API RP-75 as its backbone.

The API's consistent opposition to safety regulations by the federal government has been explained as a reaction to the potential high costs that such regulations could imply for oil and gas operations.[15] Therefore, the API favors regulatory initiatives that foster industry autonomy from government oversight.[16] Such was the API's influence, that only two decades after its first rule-making attempt and a major event such as the DWH accident, the federal government found the momentum to make the SEMS programs mandatory by regulations. The Section 10.3 describes this exogenous event and the criticisms to the role of the API as standard-setter.

10.3 THE DWH ACCIDENT

10.3.1 *The DWH Accident, Criticisms to the Regulatory Regime, and the Adoption of SEMS Regulations*

On April 20, 2010, a sudden explosion and fire occurred on the Deepwater Horizon oil rig in what later became one of the largest marine oil spills in history. The rig was located approximately fifty miles southeast of Louisiana in the Gulf of Mexico and had a 126-member crew onboard. The accident resulted in the deaths of eleven workers and seventeen others were seriously injured. For eighty-six days, oil flowed into the Gulf of Mexico reaching an expanse of shoreline. In total, more than 4.9 million barrels of oil were spilled causing serious environmental damage into the Gulf of Mexico.[17]

[14] API and Offshore Operators Committee (OOC), written comments on the subject proposed rule to add a new Subpart S-Safety and Environmental Management Systems (SEMS) (September 15, 2009), www.bsee.gov/sites/bsee.gov/files/safety-alerts/regulations-and-guidance/oocapicommentletter9-15-09.pdf.

[15] National Commission, *supra* note 10, at 225.

[16] Ibid.

[17] United States Coast Guard, BP Deepwater Horizon Oil Spill Incident Specific Preparedness Review, Final Report (2011), at 109.

The DWH accident originated a regulatory crisis in the United States. We define regulatory crisis as periods of instability or disorder caused by unexpected internal or external events that threaten or affect the normal functioning of an organization or system and bring into question the building blocks of the regulatory framework that govern them. The term "crisis" has been deployed by several scholars to describe "an unexpected event that creates uncertainty and poses a direct or perceived threat to the goals and norms of an organization or society";[18] "a phase of disorder in the seemingly normal development of a system . . . crises are transitional phases, during which the normal ways of operating no longer work,"[19] and "periods of disorder . . . along with widespread questioning or discrediting of established policies, practices and institutions."[20] These definitions have features of the three components that according to Boin et al. a crisis possess: a threat, uncertainty, and urgency.[21] In this sense, our definition of "regulatory crisis" as a specific type of crisis contributes to expand the definition of the term "crisis: provided by the aforementioned scholars as well as in other chapters of this book such as the one by Partiti ("Human Rights Due Diligence and Evolution of Voluntary Sustainability Standards," Chapter 7), in which he analyzes human rights due diligence and evolution of voluntary sustainability standards.

The DWH accident was an external and unexpected event that brought into question the regulatory regime to prevent accidents and marine pollution from offshore oil and gas operations in the United States. After the accident, both public and private regulators in the offshore oil and gas industry introduced reforms that aimed at changing building blocks of the regulatory regime, such as the regulators, the rules to promote safety in the industry, and monitoring mechanisms.

Regarding rule-making and monitoring mechanisms, one of the major findings of the investigations conducted after the DWH accident was the high reliance of the regulatory framework on prescriptive rules and checklist inspections to manage the risks of offshore oil and gas operations in the United States.[22] In order to overcome such weakness, several investigations advised the federal government to complement prescriptive regulations with a risk-based performance approach. This was precisely one of the first measures that BSEE implemented in reaction to the accident. In October 2010, the BSEE issued its Workplace Safety Rule, also known as the SEMS regulation, requiring all oil and gas operators in the US Outer Continental Shelf

[18] C. Coyne, Constitutions and Crisis (2011) 80:2 *Journal of Economic Behavior & Organization* 351.

[19] A. Boin, et al., *The Politics of Crisis Management: Public Leadership under Pressure* (2005).

[20] D. Nohrstedt and C. Weible, The Logic of Policy Change after Crisis: Proximity and Subsystem Interaction (2010) *Journal of Risk, Hazards, & Crisis in Public Policy* 1.

[21] Boin, et al., *supra* note 18.

[22] National Commission, *supra* note 10, at 68.

(OCS) to develop, implement, and audit a SEMS program. The SEMS regulation was amended in 2013 (SEMS regulation II). The SEMS regulation is considered the first environmental and safety performance–based rules adopted by the offshore oil and gas federal regulator in the United States.[23]

The SEMS program is a comprehensive system to reduce human error and organizational failure. It is defined by the SEMS regulation as a program where the operator identifies, addresses, and manages safety, environmental hazards, and impacts throughout the life of their offshore operations, comprising the design, construction, start-up, operation (including, but not limited to, drilling and decommissioning), inspection, and maintenance of all new and existing facilities, including mobile offshore drilling units (MODUs) when attached to the seabed. The SEMS program must address the elements described by BSEE's regulations and meet or exceed the standards of safety and environmental protection of the API RP 75 in its third edition, 2004.[24]

BSEE does not supervise the SEMS program directly. Instead, it has created a third-party audit scheme to conduct such task. The reasons for this approach are not explicated in the background of SEMS regulations. However, there are at least two hypotheses on the motives for this approach. The first is that BSEE lacked personnel, budget, and expertise to audit the SEMS programs.[25] The second is that BSEE did not want the industry to rely on the government to manage the SEMS program.[26] Indeed, in 2006, when the federal government presented an advance notice of proposed rule-making to seek comments on the introduction of SEMS, it asked the industry whether the MMS or an independent third party should verify the SEMS plan. Most commenters were not in favor of the MMS approving the SEMS plans. Instead, they suggested that such review should be conducted by a third party because the MMS might not have the resources and expertise to approve a minimum of one plan for each operator.[27]

Under the third-party audit scheme, operators must maintain and keep up to date with the SEMS program by means of periodic audits.[28] Initially, SEMS regulations

[23] J. Weaver, Managing Offshore Safety in the United States after the Macondo Disaster, in *Managing the Risk of Offshore Oil and Gas Accidents: The International Legal Dimension* (G. Handl and K. Svendsen eds., 2019), at 55.

[24] Office of the Federal Register of the United States, Code of Federal Regulations (CFR) §250.1900, §250.1902.

[25] Weaver, *supra* note 22, at 69.

[26] US Chemical Safety and Hazard Investigation Board, Drilling Rig Explosion and Fire at the Macondo Well Investigation Report, Volume 4 (April 20, 2016), at 77.

[27] Federal Register of the United States, 74 Fed. Reg. 28639, A Proposed Rule by the Minerals Management Service on 06/17/2009, Safety and Environmental Management Systems for Outer Continental Shelf Oil and Gas Operations, www.federalregister.gov/documents/2009/06/17/E9-14211/safety-and-environmental-management-systems-for-outer-continental-shelf-oil-and-gas-operations.

[28] Office of the Federal Register of the United States, *supra* note 23, CFR §250.1909

established that the audits might be conducted either by the operator's personnel or by independent third parties.[29] However, in 2013, a reform to the regulations required operators to audit the SEMS program only by an independent third party. One of the aims of this change was to improve the quality of audits based on the experience of the first cycle of audits.[30] Indeed, after the first audits, BSEE found several flaws in the audit processes including the use of diverse audit methodologies, reporting formats, and scope of activities. Due to these shortcomings, BSEE could not assess the status of implementation and effectiveness of many SEMS in the first cycle of audits.

10.3.2 *Criticisms of the Role of the API as Standard-Setter*

The investigations after the DWH accident not only revealed the shortcomings of the federal government's regulatory approach to managing the risks of offshore oil and gas operations but also raised concerns about the influence of the API as a standard-setting organization. The National Commission on the BP Deepwater Horizon Oil Spill and Offshore Drilling (hereinafter the National Commission) indicated that the API's role as a standard-setter for drilling safety was undermined by its role as the industry's main lobbyist.[31] Furthermore, industry officials asserted that the API's safety standards had failed to reflect "best industry practices" and that the reliance of the MMS on those standards had affected the entire federal regulatory system for offshore oil and gas safety.[32]

As regards the oil and gas industry, the National Commission's final report primarily advised to create a safety self-regulator, similar to the one established in the nuclear sector in the United States.[33] The commission warned that since the API was culturally ill-suited to drive a safety revolution in the industry, it was essential that the new safety regulator operate apart from the API.[34] The report highlighted that the new industry's safety regulator should prompt continuous improvement in standards and practices by incorporating the highest safety standards achieved globally, including but not exclusively those adopted by the API.[35]

In the aftermath of the accident, the API reacted to these new demands with an organizational change: the creation of the Center for Offshore Safety (COS).

[29] Ibid., CFR § 250.1920 (a).

[30] BSEE, SEMS Program Summary – First Audit Cycle (July 23, 2014), www.bsee.gov/sites/bsee.gov/files/memos/safety/sems-program-summary-8132014.pdf.

[31] National Commission, *supra* note 10, at 225.

[32] Ibid.

[33] Ibid., at 241.

[34] Ibid.

[35] Ibid., at 242.

10.4 THE API'S ORGANIZATIONAL RESPONSE TO THE DWH ACCIDENT

10.4.1 *Creation of the Center for Offshore Safety (COS)*

In March 2011, the API created the Center for Offshore Safety (hereinafter COS or the Center) in response to both the Commission's recommendation to the industry of establishing a new safety self-regulator for oil and gas operations and the adoption of the SEMS regulations. The COS is an industry-sponsored group focused on safety of offshore oil and gas operations on the US Outer Continental Shelf (OCS). The mission of the Center is "to promote the highest level of safety for the U.S. offshore oil and natural gas industry through effective leadership, communication, teamwork, utilization of disciplined management systems and independent third-party auditing and certification."[36]

COS works as a unit of the API's Global Industry Services division that is responsible for standards development, certification, training, publications, and safety programs for onshore, offshore, and refinery operations.[37]

Initially, COS membership was limited to deep-water operators, contractors, and service companies. In 2015, COS allowed membership to all companies operating on the US Outer Continental Shelf.[38] Since then, membership for COS is mandatory for the API members who operate offshore but voluntary for non-API members.[39] From the around sixty operators and seventeen drilling contractors that work on the US Outer Continental Shelf, as of March 2021, COS had eighteen members. From these members, eleven are operators, three are rig contractors, and four are service companies.[40] Section 10.4.2 examines the key role of the API and the members of COS in the governance of the Center.

10.4.2 *The Governance of COS*

COS is governed by a charter, governing procedures, and the governing board. The charter establishes COS' objectives, guiding principles, responsibilities, and API oversight and interfacing. In turn, the governing procedures provide information on the policies and procedures for COS' governing board, its activities, and guidelines for its conduct. The Center's governing board consists of a maximum of twenty-four

36 The Center for Offshore Safety, Charter, at 1, https://centerforoffshoresafety.org/~/media/COS/Membership/2018-112_COS_Charter_062518.pdf.

37 Ibid.

38 National Academies of Sciences, Engineering, and Medicine, *Beyond Compliance: Strengthening the Safety Culture of the Offshore Oil and Gas Industry* (2016), at 15.

39 The Center for Offshore Safety, *supra* note 35.

40 The Center for Offshore Safety, Member Organizations, www.centerforoffshoresafety.org/Membership/Member-Organizations.

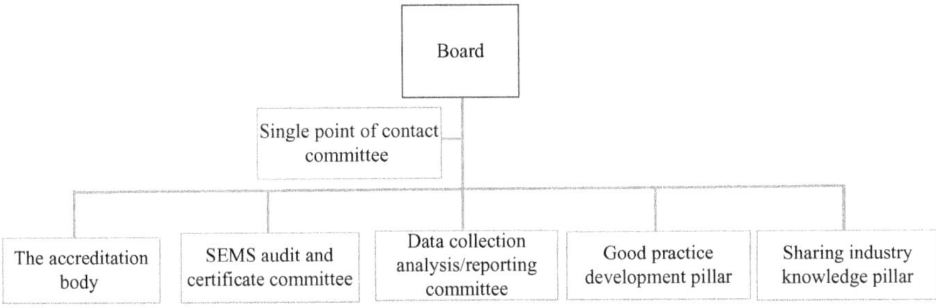

FIGURE 10.1. The structure of COS
Source: The author, adapted from COS, 2020

members that represent oil and gas producers, drilling contractors, service companies, and industry associations. As stated in COS' charter and governing procedures, the API has several mechanisms to control the Center. These mechanisms comprise the approval of COS' board members, charter, and annual plans, reporting obligations, and the revision of all work products developed by COS intended to inform member companies, industry, and the public.[41] The Center is accountable to, and must interact with, several API committees and follow the API's internal policies and procedures.[42] Regarding its structure, COS works through subordinate groups approved by the board, which are designated as committee, subcommittee, or work group.[43] Figure 10.1 presents an overview of the COS's structure.

Besides the governing board, COS has six groups. The first group is a single point of contact committee to manage communication between COS and member companies. The five remaining groups are the accreditation body, the SEMS audit and certificate committee, the data collection analysis/reporting committee, the good practice development pillar, and the sharing industry knowledge pillar. From all the activities developed by the Center, the groups in charge of the accreditation body and the SEMS audit and certificate committee perform functions directly related to the monitoring of the SEMS program.

10.5 CHANGES TO SEMS REGULATIONS: INTRODUCING A CO-REGULATORY SCHEME

10.5.1 *The Role of COS for the Implementation of SEMS Regulations*

The role of COS in the implementation of SEMS regulations has increased over time. Just a few years after its creation, BSEE embraced the Center and provided it

[41] The Center for Offshore Safety, Governance Procedures COS-100-01 (August 2016); The Center for Offshore Safety, *supra* note 35.
[42] The Center for Offshore Safety, *supra* note 35
[43] Ibid.

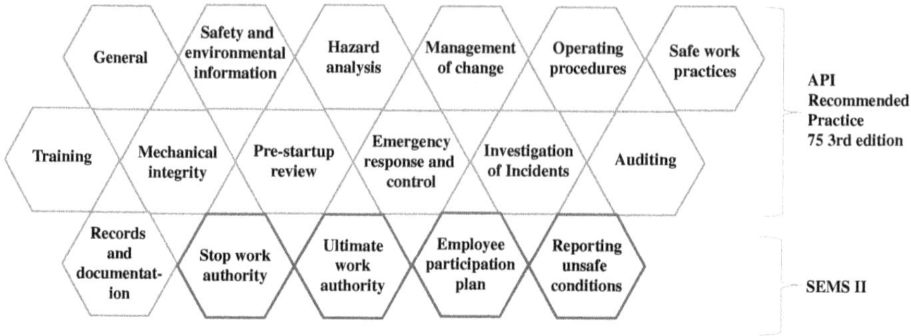

FIGURE 10.2. The seventeen elements of the SEMS program.
Source: The author, based on SEMS II

with a formal role in the implementation of SEMS programs. Such a formal role was the result of acknowledging the leadership that COS displayed to guide operators in their audits. In order to assume leadership in the audits processes, in 2012, COS started an audit service provider (ASP) accreditation program.[44] The goal of the program was to improve the audits through a consistent and unified set of requirements for ASP and their auditors.[45] For this purpose, in 2012, COS adopted a series of standards to guide operators on how to conduct audits (SEMS toolkit) and the competences that ASP's and auditors should fulfill (ASP – accreditation program). The proactive role of COS was acknowledged by BSEE in 2013 when it adopted SEMS regulations II (SEMS II).

SEMS II modified several aspects of the SEMS program both in its content and the auditing process. With respect to the content of the SEMS program, SEMS II included best practices that were not covered by the API RP-75 regarding the involvement of the workforce in the SEMS program. Therefore, besides the thirteen elements established by the API RP 75 third edition, operators must include four new elements in their SEMS program: stop work authority, ultimate work authority, employee participation plan, and reporting unsafe working conditions.[46] Figure 10.2 presents a diagram with the seventeen elements of the SEMS program, highlighting in blue those established by the API RP-75 and in yellow those incorporated by SEMS II.

Regarding the audit process, SEMS regulations II indicate that audits should only be conducted by independent third parties, which were called audit service providers (ASPs). In turn, the ASPs must be accredited by an accreditation body (AB) approved by BSEE as an independent third-party organization that assesses and

44 The Center for Offshore Safety, 2019 Annual Performance Report (2020), at 42.
45 Ibid.
46 Office of the Federal Register of the United States, *supra* note 23, CFR §250.1902 (b); §250.1903 b; §250.1911; §250.1921; §250.1931; §250.1932; §250.1933.

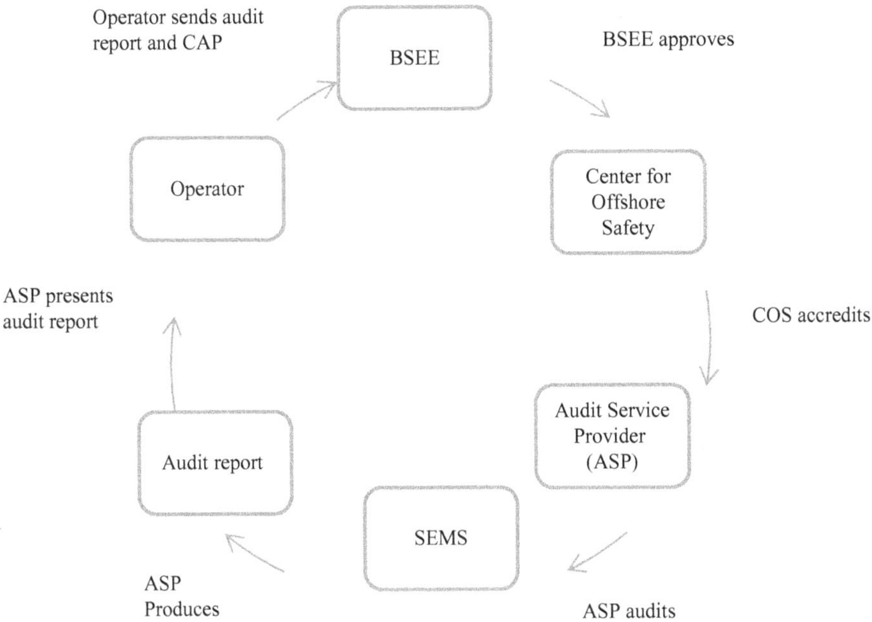

FIGURE 10.3. SEMS II third-party audit scheme.
Source: The author, based on SEMS II

accredits ASPs.[47] In 2015, BSEE approved COS as the first and, so far, only AB to accredit ASPs.[48] Since June 2015, all SEMS programs must be audited by a COS-accredited ASP. As of March 2021, COS had accredited five ASPs.[49] Figure 10.3 illustrates the roles of BSEE, COS, and ASPs in the audit scheme.

Besides these changes, SEMS II required operators to comply with three COS standards related to the third-party audits. With SEMS II, BSEE introduced a model of co-regulation to monitor the implementation of the SEMS program elements of which are analyzed in Section 10.5.2.

10.5.2 *SEMS Regulations through the Lens of Co-regulation*

Co-regulation is a form of regulation that combines elements of private self-regulation and state or public regulation.[50] Under this approach, a government

[47] Ibid., CFR §250.1903 a, b; §250.1922 a.
[48] Ibid., CFR §250.1903 (a).
[49] The Center for Offshore Safety, SEMS Audit Providers, https://centerforoffshoresafety.org/sems-audit-providers/find%20a%20cos%20accredited%20asp.
[50] R. Baldwin, M. Cave, and Martin Lodge (eds.), *Understanding Regulation* (2nd ed., 2011), at 147; N. Gunningham and J. Rees, Industry Self-regulation: An Institutional Pespective (1997) 19:4 *Journal of Law & Policy* 366; C. Coglianese and E. Mendelson, Meta-regulation and Self-regulation, in *The Oxford Handbook on Regulation* (M. Cave, R. Baldwin, M. Lodge, eds., 2010), at 24.

regulator identifies a problem and commands the industry to develop plans aimed at solving it.[51] In response, the industry, as a self-regulator, develops its own internal regulations.[52] By implementing a scheme of co-regulation, the government transfers part of its regulatory tasks – either rule-making, monitoring, or enforcement – to the regulated industry.

In the case of the SEMS regulations, BSEE transferred part of its rule-making and monitoring powers to the oil and gas industry. An example of the delegation of rule-making responsibilities is the adoption of the API RP-75 as the backbone of the SEMS program. By requiring operators to implement a SEMS program on the basis of a standard developed by the API, BSEE yielded part of its rule-making tasks to the industry self-regulator.

The SEMS program gives the opportunity to oil and gas operators of developing risk management systems identifying the mechanisms to address their safety and environmental risks. For example, operators can devise their instruments for risk analysis, monitoring, maintenance, and procedures for managing change.[53] Thus, these mechanisms become the rules that operators must comply with.

However, management systems do not operate alone.[54] Their effectiveness depends not only on the capacity of regulatees to comply with their obligations but on the regulator's capacity to monitor and enforce the management system.[55] Precisely, this is another co-regulatory element in SEMS regulations: the delegation of the government's monitoring task to the oil and gas industry through different mechanisms. The two main mechanisms that BSEE chose to monitor the implementation of SEMS regulations are a form of meta-regulation that involves the offshore oil and gas industry and third-party audits. Meta-regulation is described as the activity of "regulating the regulators, whether they be public agencies, private corporate self-regulators or third party gatekeepers."[56]

Through meta-regulation, a regulator oversees another and sets standards for its activities.[57] Meta-regulation may involve the delegation of regulatory activities by a public authority to private actors aiming at improving voluntary compliance with regulations, reinforcing the ownership of responsibilities among the regulates, and decreasing public enforcement costs.[58]

In the case of the SEMS regulations, BSEE (meta-regulator) approved the COS (industry self-regulator), which, in turn, accredits the third parties that audit SEMS programs. The involvement of the COS is not limited to accrediting the auditors.

[51] Coglianese and Mendelson, *supra* note 49, at 7.
[52] Ibid.
[53] Ibid.
[54] Ibid.
[55] Ibid.
[56] C. Parker, *The Open Corporation: Effective Self-regulation and Democracy* (2002), at 15.
[57] P. Verbruggen and T. Havinga, The Rise of Transnational Private Meta-regulators (2016) 21 *Tilburg Law Review* 116, at 119–122.
[58] Ibid.

The BSEE has also adopted several of COS standards, therefore, influencing the rule-making tasks of the meta-regulator.

Taking into account the role of the API and COS in both the rule-making and monitoring aspects of the co-regulatory scheme introduced by SEMS regulations, one of the main concerns is the role of BSEE as meta-regulator. This concern was highlighted by the US Chemical Safety and Hazard Investigation Board in its last report on the DWH accident, indicating that if BSEE does not independently assess the quality and effectiveness of the third-party audits, the scheme could "devolve into ineffective industry self-regulation."[59]

Taking into account that, by design, the role of BSEE as meta-regulator is to oversee the third-party audit scheme, Section 10.5.3 will describe the tools that BSEE has to perform such functions and its relations with COS.

10.5.3 *The Role of BSEE as Meta-regulator and Its Interactions with the COS*

The interactions between the BSEE and COS as public and private authority are shaped by several mechanisms developed by both authorities in their respective domains. In the case of BSEE, there are at least seven of those mechanisms in SEMS regulations. The first three mechanisms are in relation to COS and the remaining four mechanisms are in relation to the audit scheme. In relation to COS, the first mechanism is the approval of BSEE to COS as the AB.[60] SEMS regulations establish the requirements that COS had to fulfill in order to obtain such approval, as it did in 2015. Those requirements include standards from the International Organization for Standardization[61] and from COS itself.[62] The relation between the BSEE and COS is governed through a memorandum of understanding that authorizes the Center to review auditors and accredit those qualified to conduct the SEMS audits.[63] The second and third mechanisms that BSEE has to steer the work of COS and monitor its performance are the establishment of new regulatory requirements for the AB and audits.[64] The objective of such audits is to verify the compliance of COS with the accreditation requirements. Beyond these

[59] US Chemical Safety and Hazard Investigation Board, *supra* note 25, at 79.

[60] Office of the Federal Register of the United States, *supra* note 23, 30 CFR § 250.1922.

[61] The ISO standard required by SEMS II is ISO/IEC 17011, Conformity Assessment – General Requirements for Accreditation Bodies Accrediting Conformity Assessment Bodies, 1st ed., September 1, 2004; corrected version, February 15, 2005.

[62] Office of the Federal Register of the United States, *supra* note 23, 30 CFR § 250.1922. The AB must have an accreditation process that meets or exceeds the requirements contained in Section 6 of Requirements for Accreditation of Audit Service Providers Performing SEMS Audits and Certification of Deepwater Operations, COS-2-04.

[63] The Center for Offshore Safety, Continual Improvement of SEMS Audits (April 20, 2020), at 6, www.centerforoffshoresafety.org/-/media/COS/COSReboot/2020SEMSAuditingWebinarSlides.pdf?la=en&hash=B928B14370F9B5797D69085503B5ACBFBB2C13D9.

[64] Office of the Federal Register of the United States, *supra* note 23, 30 CFR § 250.1922 (a) (2).

mechanisms, it is important to notice that SEMS regulations do not establish enforcement tools against the AB.

In relation to the audit scheme, the fourth instrument of BSEE to oversee it are all the instances where BSEE receives information from the audits, including the audit plan, the audit report, and the CAP.[65] In the case of the audit plan, operators must send it to BSEE before the audit, and BSEE reserves the right to modify the list of facilities proposed to audit. Regarding the CAP, the BSEE may notify the operator if the proposed schedule to correct the deficiencies identified in the audit is not acceptable or if the CAP does not effectively address the audit findings.[66]

The fifth monitoring tool of BSEE over the co-regulatory scheme is direct evaluations of the SEMS. BSEE retains power to evaluate or visit facilities directly or through its authorized representative.[67] These evaluations or visits may be random and may be based upon the operator's performance or that of its contractors.[68]

The sixth monitoring mechanism of BSEE is directed SEMS audits. If based on the results of BSEE's inspections and evaluations, or as a result of an event, BSEE identifies safety or noncompliance concerns, BSEE may direct the operator to have an ASP audit of his SEMS program.[69] BSEE-directed audit is an additional requirement to the regular audit required by SEMS II. BSEE can also opt for conducting the SEMS audit directly.[70]

Finally, if BSEE considers that the operator is not in compliance with SEMS regulations, it can issue a notice of noncompliance (NNC). By NNCs, BSEE informs the operator in the case of an event of noncompliance and the actions needed to correct it in order to avoid the use of enforcement tools against the operator.[71] According to the severity of the violation, BSEE can use several enforcement tools, including a warning, shut-in, civil penalty, performance improvement plan, referral for criminal penalties, and a disqualification referral.

In turn, COS has developed its own mechanisms to interact with the BSEE and, eventually, influence its behavior. The main mechanism is the issuance of guideline documents or standards on the third-party audits. COS has been successful in developing several documents that BSEE has incorporated by reference in SEMS regulations. The second mechanism is an External Stakeholder Group where BSEE and other governmental organizations celebrate regular meetings with COS to review the progress of the Center.[72]

65 Ibid., 30 CFR § 250.1920.
66 Ibid., 30 CFR § 250.1920 (d) (4).
67 Ibid., 30 CFR §250.1924 (a).
68 Ibid.
69 Ibid.
70 Ibid.
71 Ibid., 30 CFR §250.1451 a, §250.1927 (a).
72 The Center for Offshore Safety, *supra* notes 35 and 40; Weaver, *supra* note 22, at 70–71.

After the introduction of this co-regulatory scheme, the question whether the BSEE provides effective oversight of the operator's implementation of SEMS.[73] This question brings also concerns upon the transparency of the system and how BSEE has used the tools at its disposal to oversee the co-regulatory scheme.

10.5.3.1 The Oversight of BSEE to the Third-Party Audit Scheme

Under the BSEE-COS co-regulatory scheme, BSEE became to a large extent a receiver of information from the operator, mainly the audit plan, the audit report, and the CAP. With those documents, BSEE can assess the implementation of the SEMS programs at both the industry and operator's level, and even more importantly, it can assess the improvement of safety in the industry. Therefore, the role of BSEE assessing the information delivered by the operator and making decisions on the basis of such information is paramount for the success of the co-regulatory scheme. This section analyzes, first, how BSEE has assessed such information and, second, whether it has used its enforcement tools to ensure compliance with SEMS regulations.

The third-party audit scheme introduced in 2015 applied to the second and third cycle of SEMS audits completed by early 2017 and 2019, respectively. However, from 2015 to 2019, BSEE published limited information on the implementation of SEMS programs and the audit results. In addition, since 2017, BSEE has not published annual reports informing the public on the results of its regulatory functions. Only in 2020, BSEE published two documents on the results of the second and third SEMS audits on its website.

The first document is a safety alert issued by BSEE in May 2020 with the analysis of SEMS audits from forty-one operators in the Gulf of Mexico. The safety alert identified several common deficiencies for each SEMS assessed. However, it was not a complete report on the results of SEMS audits but an alert to operators.

The second document is an analysis of the results of the third SEMS audits published on BSEE's website in October 2020. This document does not indicate its author nor date. The fact that it is not signed by BSEE's officials, does not have the logo of BSEE, and based on the wording that it uses, it may be inferred that the document was prepared by a firm hired by BSEE.[74] The document includes as an appendix a memorandum issued by BSEE in October 2017 with a review of the second cycle of SEMS audit reports. This "anonymous" document and its appendix are the main information published on the BSEE's website on the results of the second and third cycle of SEMS audits.

[73] J. Weaver, *supra* note 22, at 76.

[74] SEMS Successes, Challenges and Recommendations Based on Analysis of 3rd Round SEMS Audit Results and SEMS Corrective Actions, www.bsee.gov/sites/bsee.gov/files/analysis-of-sems-audit-reports-october-20-2020.pdf.

In its memorandum issued in October 2017, BSEE presented the results of sixty SEMS audits conducted in the second cycle. BSEE highlighted the success of COS accreditation program in several aspects. COS held the third-party auditors to account for their adherence to quality auditing standards and to standardize reporting formats, which was reflected in more consistent audits. This improvement allowed BSEE to review the audit findings more in depth, as well as the status of implementation of SEMS. In this way, the work of the Center supported BSEE to address the auditing and reporting challenges found during the first audit cycle.[75]

BSEE also found opportunities for improvement in the auditing process. The main concern was that the assessment of the SEMS was general and not centered on the operations conducted by operators such as exploration, drilling, construction, production, well maintenance, and decommissioning. Therefore, BSEE considered to implement a more risk-based approach in future audits, focused on the riskiest operations, with high volume of accidents or with more concerns on the effectiveness of SEMS. In this way, future audits could evidence where SEMS work and not.[76]

Regarding the result of the second cycle of SEMS audits, 47 percent of the findings were considered as deficiencies, 28 percent opportunities for improvement, and 25 percent good practices. Six SEMS elements accounted for the most deficiencies (60 percent): safe work practices, hazards analysis, mechanical integrity, general (policy and leadership), operating procedures, and management of change.[77] Beyond this analysis, the report did not refer to the results of implementing the CAP after the audits.

In turn, the document published on BSEE's website in October 2020 analyzed the audit reports of the third cycle where fifty-two SEMS were evaluated.[78] Though the report did not refer to whether the third cycle of audits addressed the recommendations of the second cycle of focusing the audits on the riskiest operations, the report presented conclusions regarding the adoption of SEMS, the audit process, and the corrective action plan. With respect to the adoption of SEMS, the main findings were that all the operators included in the report had developed their SEMS program, however the main challenge was to implement it. More than 60 percent of the deficiencies were related to the same five SEMS elements found in the second cycle of audits: safe work practices, mechanical integrity, hazard analysis, operating procedures, and management of change. Half of all deficiencies were regarding the implementation of the SEMS policies and procedures.[79]

[75] BSEE, Summary – Learnings from Second SEMS Audit Cycle (October 2, 2017), www.bsee.gov/sites/bsee.gov/files/analysis-of-sems-audit-reports-october-20-2020.pdf.

[76] Ibid.

[77] Ibid.

[78] *Supra* note 73.

[79] Ibid.

Despite these findings, the report found that SEMS were moving toward a level of maturity in comparison to the results of the first and second audits.

With regard to the audit process, the report concluded that the quality of the SEMS audit reports increased significantly compared to the first and second cycles. However, it found opportunities of improvement in the audit process. The report indicates that the approach of the audits was to review the seventeen elements of the SEMS program through a checklist included as a reference by SEMS regulations. In this regard, the report recommended to adopt performance-based audit practices, instead of the checklist approach, and to inform the audit plans with performance indicators based on incident history, leading and lagging indicators, and the a risk-based sampling of operations by the auditors.[80] The latter recommendation, replicated to some extent BSEE's conclusion after the second cycle of SEMS audits.

With respect to the CAP, the report recommended two measures: (a) to adopt COS standards and (b) to implement surveillance audits as part of the corrective plan close out process, in order to verify that the deficiencies found in the auditing process were addressed.

From the two documents published by BSEE on the implementation of the co-regulatory scheme, this chapter draws several conclusions regarding both the audit process and the implementation of SEMS by operators. The first one is that BSEE is satisfied with the role of COS. The Center has supported BSEE to improve the third-party audits, accrediting the auditors and making audits more standardized. However, the audit process needs to move from checklist audits to risk-based audits focused on the riskiest operations in order to assess how effective SEMS programs are in improving safety in the real world and beyond the information documented on paper.

The second conclusion regards the adoption of SEMS. The message from the analysis of SEMS audits is that the implementation of SEMS programs is moving toward a level of maturity. Nevertheless, multiple deficiencies persist and most of them are constantly found in the same core SEMS elements: safe work practices, mechanical integrity, hazard analysis, operating procedures, and management of change.

Other conclusions relate to the oversight of BSEE to the third-party audit scheme. In first instance, the role of BSEE needs to be more transparent. Such transparency is insufficient due to the fact that BSEE has not published annual reports since 2017 and the only two documents related to the analysis of SEMS audits by third-parties were published five years after the implementation of the scheme. A second challenge of the BSEE is related to how it analyzes the information provided by the operators and how implementing SEMS has impacted the levels of safety and environmental protection in offshore oil and gas operations.

80 Ibid.

Since offshore safety depends on identifying relevant indicators, and making them matter,[81] it is important to correlate the findings of SEMS audits with leading and lagging indicators. Some indicators include numbers of loss of containment events, gas releases and fires, explosions, loss of well control, injuries, blowouts, speed or response to well kicks, numbers of cementing failures, numbers of times gas alarms are triggered,[82] and incident investigations.[83]

In the analysis of the second SEMS audit cycle, BSEE already mentioned the importance of performance metrics, indicating that it would track metrics, particularly number and gravity of incidents, and examine if SEMS deficiencies and corrective actions were leading operators to improve their underlying systems.[84] Yet this analysis continues as a pending task for BSEE.

At this point, the question remains regarding what the enforcement approach of the BSEE toward the co-regulatory scheme is. Though there is not complete information on how BSEE has used its enforcement tools and directed audits to enforce SEMS regulations, a few documents published by BSEE evidence that the regulator mainly uses its enforcement tools when operators do not comply with deadlines to submit, for instance, their audit report or CAP. For example, in November 2013, BSEE posted on its website that it had issued INCs against twelve operators for their failure to comply with SEMS regulations. BSEE ordered five operators to halt operations because they did not submit their audit plans and SEMS audits. The remaining seven companies failed to complete the audits before the deadline and were directed to provide BSEE with a copy of their SEMS programs and complete the audits.[85]

Furthermore, in 2019, BSEE published its SEMS Oversight and Enforcement Program (OEP) where it establishes a policy to standardize its approach to the oversight and enforcement of compliance by operators.[86] The main approach is the limited use of INCs. The policy indicates in which specific cases BSEE specialists can issue enforcement tools in the case of violations of SEMS regulations. Most of the cases listed in the policy are related to failures to submit the audit plan, audit report, the CAP, and other documents required by SEMS regulations.

81 A. Hopkins, *Disastrous Decisions: The Human and Organisational Causes of the Gulf of Mexico Blowout* (2012), at 150.

82 Ibid.

83 Text taken from M. Nieves-Zárate, Ten Years After the Deepwater Horizon Accident: Regulatory Reforms and the Implementation of Safety and Environmental Management Systems in the United States (SPE/IADC, 2021), at 10.

84 BSEE, *supra* note 74. On the importance of performance indicators, see also, *supra* note 25.

85 See BSEE, BSEE Cites Offshore Operators for Failure to Complete Safety and Environmental Management System Audits (2013), www.bsee.gov/site-page/bsee-cites-offshore-operators-for-failure-to-complete-safety-and-environmental-management.

86 BSEE, BSEE Safety and Environmental Management Systems (SEMS) Oversight and Enforcement Program (OEP) (2019).

Besides the information on the initial INCs and the OEP, there is not concrete information on how BSEE has used its enforcement tools and directed audits to enforce SEMS regulations. In the analysis of the second SEMS audit cycle, BSEE mentioned that on the basis of performance metrics, it will consider using its "directed audit" to explore unidentified deficiencies that may be contributing to incidents and noncompliance events.[87]

Though BSEE publishes a list of all incidents of noncompliance issued to offshore operators on its website, the list does not indicate the motive of noncompliance. This missing information and the lack of BSEE's annual reports from the years 2017 to 2019 hamper the analysis on how often BSEE has used its enforcement tools due to noncompliance with SEMS regulations, and how SEMS directed audits have been used as an enforcement tool.[88]

In addition to the self-assessment of the BSEE, external organizations to the co-regulatory audit scheme have also examined the implementation of the scheme and highlighted its strengths and weaknesses. Section 10.5.3.2 presents some of the assessments from the US Chemical Safety and Hazard Investigation Board, the National Academies of Sciences, Engineering, and Medicine (NAS), as well as the analysis of the author of this chapter.

10.5.3.2 The Strengths and Weaknesses of the BSEE-COS Co-regulatory Scheme

In its last report, the NAS admitted that COS is making important contributions to offshore safety.[89] The Center plays an important role not only in its capacity as AB but also sharing safety information from its members on a regular basis. Indeed, since its creation, COS has published six annual performance reports from 2014 to 2019. In its annual performance reports, COS presents safety performance indicators and data from the learning from incidents and events shared voluntarily by its members under confidentiality agreements.

Though the information published by COS is limited to the information provided by its members, in the annual report from 2019, it included an analysis of forty-seven SEMS audits submitted between 2017–2019 to BSEE by COS members and non-members.[90] The data was supplied to COS by BSEE, excluding identifying information of operators in order to ensure confidentiality and reduce any bias.[91] Taking into account that BSEE had not published information on the results of the third cycle of SEMS audits, the COS report contributed providing transparency to the co-regulatory scheme regarding the partial results of the third audits.

[87] BSEE, *supra* note 74.

[88] Text taken from Nieves-Zárate, *supra* note 82, at 11.

[89] National Academies of Sciences, Engineering, and Medicine, *supra* note 37, at 16.

[90] The Center for Offshore Safety, *supra* note 39.

[91] Ibid.

Regarding the weaknesses of the co-regulatory scheme, one of the major points of concern is that BSEE misses the opportunity of developing its own expertise in a scheme where it does not audit SEMS programs directly.[92]

The second major point of concern is related to the independence of the co-regulatory scheme. The independence of this scheme has been criticized from at least two angles: independence of COS from the API and independence of the third-party auditors from the operators. As it was discussed in Section 10.2, the National Commission provided a warning regarding the need for creating an industry safety self-regulator separated from the API. However, as it was described in the section on the governance of COS, the Center is not only part of the API, but the latter has many mechanisms to control COS's work. The criticisms on such dependence have persisted in several investigation reports, bringing into question the Center's credibility and objectivity.[93]

The other concern on the independence of the scheme is grounded on the fact that SEMS regulations do not establish any requirement regarding the independence of the ASP from the operators.[94] In the case of the AB, the regulations require that it must establish measures to avoid conflict of interests with the ASPs, however, there are not similar requirements regarding the independence of ASPs and operators.[95]

Another weakness is the low number of COS members. Indeed, the number of COS members has decreased from twenty members in 2016 to eighteen members in 2021. The NAS considers that all companies conducting offshore oil and gas operations should participate in the safety institute advised after the DWH accident. However, several barriers may prevent them to join COS, including the annual cost of membership or the requirement to provide to the Center the resulting data of audits.[96]

Besides these concerns, several aspects of the governance of COS could improve in order to represent different interests of the oil and gas industry beyond oil and gas producers, drilling contractors, service companies, and industry associations. For instance, COS could allow the workforce to have representatives in its governing board. This may be an aspect to improve, considering the key role of workers to advance safety in the offshore oil and gas industry.

So far, this chapter has explained the organizational changes undertaken by the API after the DWH accident in the United States. To conclude this research, this chapter will explore the transnational dimension of the API's organizational changes

92 US Chemical Safety and Hazard Investigation Board, *supra* note 25, at 80.

93 US Chemical Safety and Hazard Investigation Board, *supra* note 25, at 79; other investigations highlighting this point were undertaken by National Academies of Sciences, Engineering, and Medicine, *supra* note 37, at 7–8, 17, 104.

94 US Chemical Safety and Hazard Investigation Board, *supra* note 25, at 80.

95 Office of the Federal Register of the United States, *supra* note 23, CFR § 250.1922 (b).

96 National Academies of Sciences, Engineering, and Medicine, *supra* note 37, at 17.

and what lessons regulators outside the United States that rely on the API RP-75 standard can learn.

10.6 THE TRANSNATIONAL DIMENSION OF THE API'S ORGANIZATIONAL CHANGES AND LESSONS FOR REGULATORS BEYOND THE UNITED STATES

The API has taken several steps to strengthen the transnational dimension of its organizational changes both around COS and the API RP-75. Since 2012, COS has developed a SEMS certificates program to demonstrate that an organization has completed a SEMS audit by an accredited ASP and satisfies the requirements of the API RP 75.[97] Though initially the certificate was only allowed for COS members, in 2020, COS allowed non-COS member companies and operations outside the United States to obtain the SEMS certificate.[98] The certification program is open not only to operators but also to drilling contractors and other offshore service providers. Furthermore, in 2019, the API published a new edition of its RP-75 in order to strengthen its global relevance.

Even before these changes, other regulators around the world had adopted the API RP-75 in their regulations.[99] Safety regulators beyond the United States that endorse the API RP-75 for offshore oil and gas operations may have several lessons to learn from the experience in the United States. One of the lessons is that the sole adoption of the API RP-75 does not guarantee that oil and gas companies are implementing best safety practices in their operations.

Indeed, SEMS regulations II by BSEE and several investigation reports evidenced that API RP-75 does not reflect several good practices in the offshore oil and gas industry, such as the involvement of the workforce in the management system and current process safety principles, including a risk reduction goal, a focus on major hazards, measurements, and metrics.[100] The first deficiency was addressed by SEMS II, however, the other issues were not tackled by the regulation nor by the new version of the API RP-75. Therefore, regulators should consider to complement the API RP-75 with their own regulations in order to incorporate good practices missing in this standard.

Another lesson is on the implementation of the API RP-75. The BSEE has developed a whole third-party scheme to audit the SEMS programs. Other regulators should be aware that it is not sufficient just to adopt the API standards in their

[97] Center for Offshore Safety, *supra* note 43, at 9.

[98] Ibid.

[99] Some examples of countries whose regulators have adopted API RP-75 are India, Nigeria, and Colombia. For India, see OGP, *supra* note 2; for Nigeria, see API, *supra* note 2; for Colombia, see Ministry of Mines and Energy, Resolutions 40687 of 2017 and 40295 of 2020.

[100] For a complete analysis on process safety principles and the defficiencies in API RP-75, see US Chemical Safety and Hazard Investigation Board, *supra* note 25.

regulations, it is important to follow up with mechanisms to ensure that oil and gas companies are actually complying with such standards. Regulators can verify the compliance with standards directly or use third parties. When developing third-party audit schemes, a good practice is to put in place mechanisms to ensure their independence from the regulated industry.

10.7 CONCLUSION

After the major accident in the history of the oil and gas industry in the United States and the criticisms that emerged against the API as private standard-setter, it would have been expected that the regulatory reforms adopted after the accident reduced the reliance of the federal regulatory framework on the API. Looking back, during the decade after the accident, BSEE not only neglected the recommendation of reducing its dependence on the API but increased it in more dimensions than the regimen that preceded the oil spill. Despite the criticisms, the API adapted to the post DWH–era, strengthening the influence of its safety standards in the federal regulatory framework and through organizational responses that allowed it to fill some of the gaps identified by investigation reports. The resilience of the API in the wake of the DWH disaster is the result of its decades of expertise, resources, and leadership in the offshore oil and gas industry that contrast with a public regulator in need of those resources. Over time, BSEE has been receptive to the solutions provided by the API and endorsed them with the introduction of a co-regulatory regime for the implementation of SEMS regulations.

Though this new co-regulatory regime still has to stand the test of time, there are already concerns on its effectiveness. The most significant concern is that the goal of BSEE endorsing the API RP-75 was to implement a performance-based rule to manage the risks of offshore oil and gas operations. Yet the formulation of the API RP-75, its implementation, and the audits are far from a performance-based approach. The model remains prescriptive with the risk of reducing the SEMS program to paperwork disconnected from operations in the real world and far from achieving its goal of improving the safety and environmental performance of oil and gas companies. Precisely, the disconnection between the implementation of SEMS, its effectiveness, and the lack of indicators that show how the environmental and safety performance of operators has evolved since the implementation of SEMS is one of the aspects that undermine the co-regulatory scheme. The scheme could benefit from more transparency by the BSEE as a meta-regulator, analyzing those indicators on an annual basis and evidencing how it has used its oversight powers to ensure compliance with the scheme or introduce the changes needed to make it effective.

Given the transnational nature of the API, its response to the DWH accident has also implications for regulators outside the United States, who have several lessons to learn regarding the strengths and weaknesses of the API RP-75 and the challenges to implement it.

In this way, the analysis on the resilience of the API in times of crisis and the increase of the interdependence between public and private authorities contributes to the empirical evidence on proactive free-riding discussed in this book, particularly in the chapter on the resilience of private authority in times of crisis. The reorganization of the API after the DWH accident provides an example of the perpetuation of private regulatory power not only regarding rule-making but also monitoring the implementation of standards.

11

The Accountability Response of the Global Anti-doping Regime to the Russian Doping Scandal (2015-2020)

Slobodan Tomic and Rebecca Schmidt

11.1 INTRODUCTION

This chapter looks into the response of the global, public–private regime of anti-doping regulation in sports to the Russian doping scandal from late 2014,[1] which revealed a state-sponsored doping scheme that enabled Russian athletes to take prohibited doping substances during their preparation for and participation at several international tournaments. The scandal highlighted the inadequacy of the system's regulatory framework and raised multiple accountability issues relating both to the "field level" and the governing level. The former includes actors involved in the operational aspect of the anti-doping policy, namely athletes, local anti-doping agencies, and testing laboratories, and the latter includes the governing body of the sports governance regime, the International Olympic Committee (IOC) and its anti-doping regulator, the World Anti-Doping Agency (WADA).

The scandal put enormous pressure on the IOC and WADA to demonstrate a strong accountability response. In this chapter, we explore the resilience of the regime by examining whether and to what extent it has been responsive to accountability calls. We look into two key aspects of the regime's response: Its ad hoc accountability measures as well as systemic changes to its accountability framework. This is to address both notions of accountability – "as a virtue" and "as a mechanism."[2] The former refers to the normative dimension of accountability and focuses on whether an actor takes measures that others see as signs of responsible conduct. The latter refers to the prescriptive-legal dimension of accountability and analyzes whether appropriate accountability provisions are set out in the regime's legal framework.

[1] The timeframe for the analysis is until 2020. It is possible that, between 2020 and the time of reading, further developments and changes within the antidoping and Olympic regime occurred, but they go beyond the timeframe of the analysis.

[2] M. Bovens, Two Concepts of Accountability: Accountability as a Virtue and as a Mechanism (2010) 33 *West European Politics* 946.

The anti-doping regime is an interesting case for the study of organizational resilience and adaptability because, at the time of the scandal outbreak, it lacked an accountability mechanism for its governing organizations – the IOC and WADA. Neither of them was subject to the formal scrutiny of stakeholders, their performance indicators were not defined, and they could not bear any consequences for their potential failures or underperformance.

Prior to 2015, the Olympic regime's legal framework and related statutory documents, such as the Olympic Charter and World Anti-Doping Code, defined none of Mashaw's five parameters of accountability: To whom, how, for what, in accordance with what standards, and with what consequences its governing organizations are accountable.[3] Furthermore, the regime has featured a favorable political economy for non-responsiveness to stakeholders, as athletes from around the world and other regime stakeholders, such as sponsors, sports clubs, and sports federations, could not defect to or create a competing international sporting regime. This has rendered the IOC and the wider sports governing regime a "hard case" for the pursuit of accountability.

Given this constellation, the Russian doping scandal has posed a curious empirical puzzle: On the one hand, the regime has found itself under enormous legitimacy pressure. A theoretical expectation is that, in such situations, regimes seek to demonstrate a strong accountability response. The exercise of accountability is crucial for repairing lost legitimacy,[4] and legitimacy represents a critical "ingredient" for regimes' survival. On the other hand, the regime's "foreclosed" political economy has afforded it a position from which it could demonstrate little responsiveness to stakeholders' concerns at almost no cost to the formal position and power of its governing organizations.[5] What, then, has the regime's accountability response been in this constellation featuring two contrasting forces, namely soaring legitimacy pressures versus a "foreclosing" structure?

11.2 THE PRACTICE AND SYSTEMS OF ACCOUNTABILITY IN TRANSNATIONAL REGIMES

11.2.1 *Defining and Conceptualizing Accountability*

The pursuit of accountability is a process in which one actor is justifying its own conduct to another actor, or a group of actors, with the possibility of bearing

[3] J. L. Mashaw, Accountability and Institutional Design: Some Thoughts on the Grammar of Governance, Yale Law School, Public Law Working Paper No. 116, in *Public Accountability: Designs, Dilemmas and Experiences* (M. W. Dowdle ed., 2006), at 115.

[4] J. Black, Constructing and Contesting Legitimacy and Accountability in Polycentric Regulatory Regimes (2008) 2 *Regulation & Governance* 137, at 146.

[5] There are sanctions such as a reprimand and suspension for a specific period that the IOC Session, Executive Board or disciplinary commission can take against individual members of the IOC that have violated "Olympic Charter, the World Anti-Doping Code, the Olympic Movement Code on the Prevention of Manipulation of Competitions or any other decision or applicable regulation issued by the IOC". (see Olympic Charter 2021, s 59).

sanctions for this conduct.[6] The pursuit of accountability can be part of a formalized process, but it can equally be less institutionalized – accountability can be sought and demonstrated without a formal obligation. Alongside a controlling function, accountability has a learning function, too.[7] It can help the regime's authorities to identify and remove failings that have been plaguing regime constituents/users. Addressing such failings will increase the regime's resilience[8] making it fit for purpose. As such, the regime would continue operating without a breakdown or demise.

While some authors have discussed accountability referring to arguably equivalent concepts such as responsibility,[9] others see accountability as a unique concept, often understood as comprising multiple dimensions. One of the most prominent multidimensional frameworks that deconstructs the meaning of accountability is that by Koppell, which points to five conceptions of accountability: transparency, liability, controllability, responsibility, and responsiveness.[10] To map out the accountability response of the global anti-doping regime to the Russian scandal, we have deployed Koppell's framework, questioning to what extent the regime has demonstrated each of its five conceptions (Table 11.1).

TABLE 11.1. *The five dimensions of accountability*[a]

Conception of accountability	Key determination
Transparency	Did the organisation reveal the facts of its performance?
Liability	Did the organisation face consequences for its performance?
Controllability	Did the organisation do what the principal desired?
Responsibility	Did the organisation follow the rules?
Responsiveness	Did the organisation fulfil the substantive expectation (demand/need)?

[a] Koppell, Pathologies of Accountability, at 96.

11.2.2 *Accountability and Legitimacy in Transnational Regulatory Regimes*

Legitimacy is a key factor for motivating regulatees' compliance and stakeholders' support,[11] and it is the pursuit of accountability that enables the building,

[6] M. Bovens, Analysing and Assessing Accountability: A Conceptual Framework (2007) 13 *European Law Journal* 447, at 451.

[7] Ibid, at 464.

[8] P. Delimatsis, The Resilience of Private Authority in Times of Crisis: A Theory of Free-Riding of Private Ordering, in *The Evolution of Transnational Private Rule-makers: Understanding Drivers and Dynamics* (P. Delimatsis ed., 2021).

[9] Bovens, *supra* note 5.

[10] J. G. S. Koppell, Pathologies of Accountability: ICANN and the Challenge of "Multiple Accountabilities Disorder" (2005) 65 *Public Administration Review* 94, at 96.

[11] M. C. Suchman, Managing Legitimacy: Strategic and Institutional Approaches (1995) 20 *Academy of Management Review* 571.

maintaining, and repairing of legitimacy.[12] Regimes enjoying low legitimacy can hardly prevent stakeholders' defection to or creation of competing regimes. It has been argued that the adoption of a robust accountability framework is an important strategy for repairing legitimacy particularly during crisis times.[13]

Outside the context of nation-states, developing accountability systems is far from a standardized and predictable process. In the context of transnational governance, there is no democratic legitimation, and the regime complex can involve multiple actors and interdependencies.[14] Allocating power within and across stakeholder groups can be difficult and deciding who should be accountable, to whom, for what, and under which standards[15] is not straightforward. Further, accountability processes can be hindered by an ongoing power dynamic among the regime actors, particularly where there is one or more predominant "veto-player" actor. That is the case with the International Olympic Committee, which, before the creation of the hybrid (public–private) anti-doping regime and its regulator WADA in 1999, had been building for about a century its supreme authority as the (sole) owner of the private transnational system of Olympic governance.

11.3 THE SETUP OF THE ANTI-DOPING REGIME PRIOR TO THE SCANDAL OUTBREAK

The anti-doping regime is a hybrid, polycentric regime, nested within the global system of sports governance.[16] It is comprised of several actors who come from two main communities, namely the sporting and anti-doping communities (See Figure 11.1).

At the uppermost level is the IOC, which is the supreme authority of the global sports governance system. The IOC is a nongovernmental sports organization based in Switzerland, created in 1894, responsible for promotion of the Olympic movement and organizing of the Summer and Winter Olympic Games.[17] At a lower, medium level of the governing tier of the regime, is WADA, the global anti-doping regulator whose task is to develop and oversee the implementation of the anti-doping policy in international sports. WADA was established in 1999[18] after a group of

[12] Black, *supra* note 3. R. Mulgan, "Accountability": An Ever-Expanding Concept? (2000) 78 *Public Administration* 555.

[13] Black, *supra* note 3, at 146–147.

[14] C. Scott, F. Cafaggi, and L. Senden, The Conceptual and Constitutional Challenge of Transnational Private Regulation (2011) 38 *Journal of Law and Society* 1.

[15] Mashaw, *supra* note 2.

[16] L. Casini, Global Hybrid Public–Private Bodies: The World Anti-doping Agency (WADA) (2009) 6 *International Organizations Law Review* 421.

[17] R. Bartlett, C. Gratton, and G. Christer, *Encyclopedia of International Sports Studies* (2012), at 678.

[18] WADA is registered as "a Swiss private law, not-for-profit Foundation." See WADA, Governance: Overview of WADA's Governance, www.wada-ama.org/en/governance.

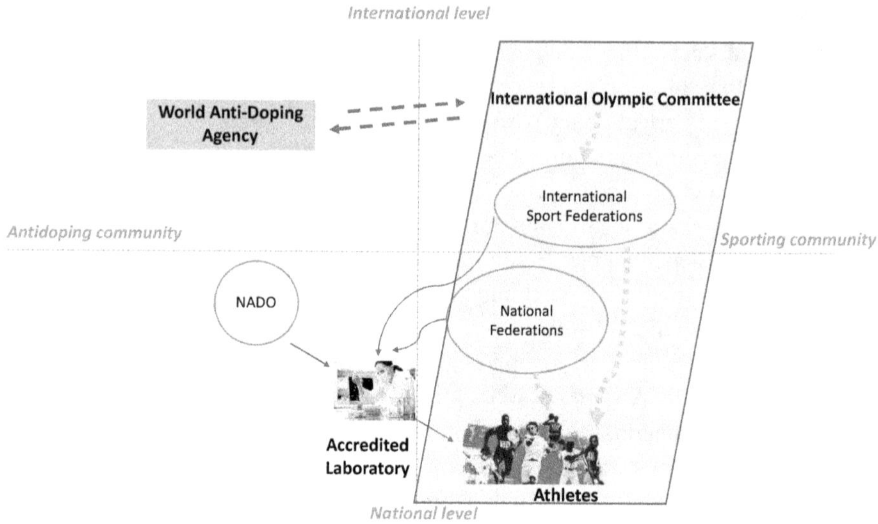

FIGURE 11.1. The structure of the anti-doping regime as a regime nested within the broad international system of sports governance

governments put pressure on the IOC to create a specialized anti-doping regulator as a response to the doping scandal in cycling.[19]

WADA's mission is to direct and monitor the work of specialized anti-doping organizations. Its tasks include research, education, development of anti-doping capacities, and monitoring of how the World Anti-Doping Code (henceforth, Code) is enforced by anti-doping organizations and by members of the Olympic system.[20] WADA's work is governed by the regime's statute and the Code, whose provisions have been incorporated into international legislation through UNESCO provisions and the Council of Europe Convention on Sports.[21] The Code is globally harmonized, having been adopted by a large number of Code signatories, including the IOC, the vast majority of international and national sports federations, national and regional anti-doping organizations, local anti-doping laboratories, and other actors.

Although it is a stand-alone regulator, WADA, by institutional design, enjoys low institutional autonomy[22] from the IOC. Since its creation, WADA has been run (and funded) in equal proportions by IOC representatives and representatives of

[19] D. V. Hanstad, A. Smith, and I. Waddington, The Establishment of the World Anti-doping Agency: A Study of the Management of Organizational Change and Unplanned Outcomes (2008) 43 *International Review for the Sociology of Sport* 227.

[20] World Anti-Doping Code 2021, pt 1.

[21] Hanstad et al., *supra* note 18.

[22] K. Verhoest, B. G. Peters, G. Bouckaert, and B. Verschuere, The Study of Organisational Autonomy: A Conceptual Review (2004) 24 *Public Administration and Development: The International Journal of Management Research and Practice* 101.

national governments, who each nominate eighteen members[23] out of the maximum thirty-eight of the WADA Foundation Board. Similarly, the Executive Board of WADA, a twelve-member body elected by the Foundation Board, comprises an equal number of government and IOC delegates.[24] Despite this parity, in practice, the IOC's influence over WADA is perceived as greater because its members, both on the WADA Executive Committee and on the Foundation Board, make for a more homogenous bloc and mobilize more easily.[25] A WADA director general is not allowed to hold dual roles, although all of WADA's presidents in their prior career had served as IOC members (most of them coming from a prior governing role in an international or national sports federation).

At the lowest operational level of the anti-doping regime are specialized anti-doping bodies and sport governing organisations. These specialized bodies include regional and national anti-doping organizations (RADOs/NADOs) and testing laboratories. Sport governing bodies include international sports federations (IFs, of which there are more than fifty globally, one for each sport in the Olympic realm). While WADA sets the anti-doping policy, develops doping standards, and monitors their implementation, these standards are in practice implemented by the RADOs and NADOs, whose mission is to develop strategies that set out when and which athletes will be tested. RADOs and NADOs direct and execute the testing of athletes, and when they discover that an athlete has violated the Code by taking a prohibited substance, they are supposed to inform the athlete's sports organization, which then determines the sanction (within the statutory prescribed range). The appellate body for doping-related sanctions is the Swiss-based Court for Arbitration in Sports (CAS).[26] The work of RADOs and NADOs is overseen by WADA.[27]

11.3.1 A 'Void Accountability Mechanism' for the Governing Bodies and a Weak Accountability Framework at the Operational Level

When the Russian doping scandal hit, WADA and IOC were widely perceived as the foremost responsible entities for the anti-doping policy. However, at that point, neither was subject to the usual mechanisms of accountability, such as, for instance, dismissal of functionaries, ex-post reporting, and other sorts of performance audit and sanctions. The Code, like the Olympic Charter, did not designate WADA as answerable for the anti-doping policy to external forums, the IOC included. Like the Olympic Charter, the Code did not specify performance benchmarks, sanctions, or

[23] WADA Constitutive Instrument of Foundation 2016, Article 6.
[24] Ibid., Article 11.
[25] B. Houlihan and D. V. Hanstad, The Effectiveness of the World Anti-Doping Agency: Developing a Framework for Analysis (2019) 11 *International Journal of Sport Policy and Politics* 203, at 210.
[26] Olympic Charter 2021, s 61, at 108.
[27] World Anti-doping Code 2021, Article 25.1, at 157.

means through which sanctions shall take place (in cases of policy failure and underachievement).

The effectiveness of RADOs and NADOs is crucial for preventing and suppressing doping among athletes. However, in the period preceding the scandal, WADA had lacked the necessary capacity and authority to adequately monitor them and to make sure their conduct was within the prescribed standards. WADA's lack of ability to exert strong control over the sporting and specialized anti-doping organizations operating at the local level directly impacted the prospects of accountability for the doping athletes. Further, the system's design, prior to the scandal, featured various in-built conflicts of interest. For instance, the sanctions for athletes who were caught doping were decided by national and international sports federations, whose commercial and sport promotion interests could prevail over anti-doping efforts.[28] This could lead them to abstain from imposing (harsh) punishments[29] or to avoid them altogether.[30] Also, domestic authorities could collude with the NADO or national laboratories to produce deliberately ineffective targeting strategies for athlete testing or to tamper with or misreport evidence in potential discoveries of doping.

The result of the weak control framework at the operational level was that the system of anti-doping was ineffective, as indicated by recurring low rates of positive tests. In 2016, out of about 300,000 tests conducted worldwide, only 4,822 were adverse findings,[31] amounting to a catching rate of only 1.6 percent. Based on their anonymous survey of elite athletes, Ulrich and colleagues[32] estimate a 30–31 percent prevalence of doping among athletes at the world championships level. The targeting strategies by NADOs were thus suboptimal, and "dopers" enjoyed an advantage over the authorities in the use of the latest medical technology.

The monitoring framework was sporadically tightened through measures such as the introduction of the "whereabouts rule," which mandated athletes to report their whereabouts for one hour each day and to make themselves available every day for

[28] D. Read, J. Skinner, D. Lock, and B. Houlihan Legitimacy Driven Change at the World Anti-Doping Agency (2019) 11 *International Journal of Sport Policy and Politics* 233, at 241.

[29] R. W. Pound, The Russian Doping Scandal: Some Reflections on Responsibility in Sport Governance (2020) 1 *Journal of Olympic Studies* 3, at 8–9.

[30] A notable example is a Russian athlete who was fined in 2009 by the IAAF after repetitive indications in blood markers of such extreme levels of red blood cells that a heart attack was a possibility. See House of Commons Digital, Culture, Media and Sport Committee, Combatting Doping in Sport: Fourth Report of Session 2017–19 (February 27, 2018), para 18, at 8.

[31] WADA, 2016 Anti-doping Testing Figures (2016), www.wada-ama.org/sites/default/files/resources/files/2016_anti-doping_testing_figures.pdf, at 1.

[32] R. Ulrich, H. G. Pope, L. Cléret, A. Petróczi, T. Nepusz, J. Schaffer, G. Kanayama, R. D. Comstock, and P. Simon, Doping in Two Elite Athletics Competitions Assessed by Randomized-Response Surveys (2018) 48 *Sports Medicine* 211. The estimates were based on surveys conducted at the IAAF World Championships in Athletics in 2011.

a potential no-notice drug test.[33] Another examples was the introduction of so-called Athlete Biological Passports – a WADA database of athletes' testing results that enables cross-time tracing of athletes' markers and identification of suspicious sample patterns even when they are within the prescribed limits. However, despite the progress that these measures allowed for, the system could still be "cheated" on the ground. As the investigation into the Russian doping scandal revealed, state authorities were able to obstruct the control process by pressing the RUSADA (the national Russian NADO) to under-target expected cheaters or misreport the sample analysis[34] during their preparations for international competitions such as the London Summer Olympics 2012,[35] or, in the case of the Russian hosting of the Winter Olympics in Sochi 2014, by coercing on site, at the Olympic village, the lab staff to tamper with the collected samples.

Overall, the regulatory system that was in place prior to the outbreak of the Russian doping scandal suffered from two major accountability deficits. First, at the governing level, its main organizations – IOC and WADA – were not subject to any formal accountability obligations. Second, WADA's capacity to monitor the enforcement of its policies through a network of local anti-doping bodies was weak. This increased the possibilities for athletes to dope with impunity, reducing accountability prospects for this "target" population.

11.3.2 *The Role of the State*

While, back in 1999, the anti-doping regime emerged due to pressure by nation-states, whose representatives have since co-participated in the running of WADA, the state has generally had limited capacity to intervene in the regime's mechanics within the wider context of the IOC's ownership and running of the global Olympic regime. It is one of the rare transnational regimes that originated "organically" as a private actor, through "entrepreneurial development of authority"[36] (the regime was created in the late nineteenth century, by Pierre de Coubertin)[37] rather than through delegation by the state.[38] Over time, it has independently developed its expertise, and reinforced its position as the sole possible owner of a global sports competition. Due to the regime's monopolistic position in running Olympic Games, creating a competing transnational regime has de facto not been viable. Historically, the IOC did not need the state's recognition and support to obtain

33 World Anti-doping Code 2015, Articles 2, 4, and 5.

34 House of Commons Digital, Culture, Media and Sport Committee, *supra* note 29, at 10.

35 Ibid, at 8.

36 S. Eckert, *Corporate Power and Regulation* (2019), at 7.

37 https://olympics.com/ioc/pierre-de-coubertin#:~:text=Pierre%20de%20Coubertin%3A%20Visionary%20and%20Founder%20of%20the%20Modern%20Olympics&text=International%20Olympic%20Committee.

38 J. F. Green, Transnational Delegation in Global Environmental Governance: When Do Non-state Actors Govern? (2018) 12 *Regulation & Governance*, at 263–276.

legitimacy. Today, despite the state's presence in WADA the IOC still has a crucial say over what the anti-doping regime will look like. As such, it has enjoyed better preconditions for resilience than the majority of other transnational private regimes and has been less dependent on the state for survival, including with regards to financial and operational considerations.

So far, the state has mainly acted as a disruptor, that is, an underminer of the current regime, rather than as a facilitator of its resilience and survival. As will be seen in the review of the Russian doping scandal, the state has the possibility to obstruct the anti-doping system of controls on the ground.[39]

11.4 THE OUTBREAK OF THE SCANDAL AND THE REGIME'S ACCOUNTABILITY REACTIONS

News of the Russian doping scandal broke in 2015 after German TV channel ARD released a documentary in which two Russian whistleblowers – a medal-winning runner and her coach – confessed that the Russian authorities had orchestrated a doping scheme in order to maximize the achievement of Russian athletes at international competitions.[40] The scheme had been going on for several years, enabling a number of Russian athletes to compete doped at several major international competitions, including the 2012 Olympic Games in London and the 2014 Winter Olympics in Sochi. About a year later, a Russian doctor, Grigory Rodchenkov, who had defected to the United States from the Moscow Anti-Doping Center (Russia's laboratory), confirmed the scheme in an interview with the *New York Times* in which he revealed further details of Russian public authorities' involvement.[41]

As the scandal gained public traction, WADA decided to investigate it. Thus, within a year (November 2015–December 2016), WADA undertook two investigations that resulted in three reports, all finding considerable evidence of a state-orchestrated doping scheme.

The first investigation, led by the former WADA President Richard Pound, found evidence that, both voluntarily and under pressure, athletes were taking doping substances in order to improve their individual and team performances.[42] The report

[39] Other states, such as those belonging to the "Western bloc," have often acted from an "enlightened self-interest" position when calling for reform of the anti-doping system, as a fair and doping-free competition would arguably them to capitalize on their allegedly superior recruitment and work with sport talent.

[40] H. Suppelt, Top Secret Doping: How Russia Makes Its Winners (December 3, 2014), www.imdb.com/title/tt5922854.

[41] R. R. Ruiz, J. Macur, and I. Austin, Even with Confession of Cheating, World's Doping Watchdog Did Nothing, *The New York Times* (June 15, 2016).

[42] Independent Commission, The Independent Commission Report #1: Final Report, (WADA, November 9, 2015), at 11.

also found that the cheating was facilitated and covered up by doctors, coaches, and laboratory personnel, indicating "a deeply rooted culture of cheating" in the Russian Olympic team.[43] In some sports, such as athletics, cheating was further facilitated through corruption at the international federation level, where intermittent reports of possible doping were ignored or covered up.[44]

The second investigation, led by Richard McLaren, a Canadian attorney and a former president of WADA, focused on the 2014 Winter Olympics. This investigation resulted in two successive reports. The first report, published prior to the Rio Olympics in July 2016, drew on witness testimony, analysis of thousands of documents, forensic analysis of seized hard drives, urine samples, and laboratory results.[45] The report found, beyond reasonable doubt, that there had been an orchestrated doping scheme during the Sochi Olympics, which was perpetuated through a so-called disappearing positive (test) methodology at the testing premises, where state intelligence agents were swapping dirty urine samples with pre-supplied clean samples at the lab, located in the Olympic Village.[46] From a tiny fraction of reexamined samples that were declared clean following the initial laboratory analysis, the investigation found that as many as 643 were, in fact, positive.[47] The full scale of the cheating could not be determined though, since the vast majority of the samples were still being withheld by Russian authorities.[48]

The second McLaren report was published after the Rio Olympics in December 2016. It discovered more than 1,000 new positive samples of Russian athletes[49] relating to prior competitions. Based on this, the report concluded that the scheme had been in place for several years at least, and that, over time, particularly prior to and during the 2012 London Olympics and the Winter Olympics in Sochi, it was further refined.

Overall, the WADA investigations found that the doping scheme involved over 1,000 Russian athletes in more than 30 sports who were assisted or pressured by their medical staff to take doping substances. These findings put pressure on the anti-doping regime to act in two main directions: (a) to sanction the perpetrators of the scheme and those actors whose omissions, or complicity, allowed the scheme to continue until the scandal broke and (b) to improve the governance structure of the anti-doping regime in order to reduce opportunities for athletes to dope with impunity.

43 Ibid., at 10.
44 Ibid., at 11–12.
45 R. H. McLaren, The Independent Person Report: WADA Investigation of Sochi Allegations (July 16, 2016), at 5.
46 Ibid., at 67–72.
47 Ibid., at 36.
48 Ibid., at 39.
49 R. H. McLaren, The Independent Person 2nd Report: WADA Investigation of Sochi Allegations (December 9, 2016), at 57.

11.5 ANALYZING THE REGIME'S RESILIENCE THROUGH ITS ACCOUNTABILITY RESPONSE

This section analyses the anti-doping regime's response in the five years after the scandal, looking across the five dimensions of accountability set out by Koppell.[50]

11.5.1 *Transparency*

Transparency is the component where the regime's accountability response throughout the observed period (2015–2020) was the strongest, although this increase in transparency was mostly based on ad hoc responses rather than the institutionalization of transparency mechanisms. Furthermore, there are still objections from stakeholders that, in some mechanisms, transparency needs to be further strengthened, primarily within the governing tier of the regime, where calls have been made for the adoption of permanent transparency measures.

It is WADA that spearheaded the regime's efforts to respond to the scandal with increased transparency and, subsequently, with building new transparency mechanisms into the regulatory system. The IOC was making pledges during the observed period to enhance its transparency level as well, but in practice it adopted fewer transparency measures than WADA.

WADA's publication of the three investigation reports could in itself be seen as a significant measure of ad hoc transparency, although a previously leaked memo revealed that its president instructed its staff to monitor public reaction before deciding whether to start an investigation, a detail that indicates WADA's opportunism.[51] Nonetheless, the significance of the WADA investigations into the Russian doping scheme was paramount for the regime's later developments in accountability. The resulting investigation reports brought to light a number of key facts and findings in relation to the suspected doping scheme. They not only confirmed that the scheme happened but also highlighted the weak spots in the regulatory system. The findings increased the initially dismissive IOC to take more than a symbolic action in response to the scandal. They also reduced the credibility of early denials of other organizations from the sports movement that the doping scheme claims are fabricated or ill-intentioned. As WADA's investigation reports revealed, new details and evidence of the doping scheme, the IOC could no longer resist taking stronger accountability measures and could hardly oppose the reform initiatives launched by WADA.

[50] Koppell, *supra* note 9.

[51] For instance, on August 4, 2015, Lord Coe, then a vice-president of the International Athletics Federation (IAAF), described the doping scheme stories published by journalists in the United Kingdom, and Germany as "a declaration of war on our sport." See House of Commons Digital, Culture, Media and Sport Committee, *supra* note 29, at 7.

Regarding its internal governance, over the last few years WADA adopted several rules, including the one on publication of all details related to the work of its bodies, from the Foundation Board to various commissions and other units. Note, though, that the Executive Committee has been a partial exception to this positive transparency trend. As critics observed, instead of verbatim minutes, edited minutes – in third person – were published for meetings of the Executive Committee; those minutes were often published late, several months or even more than a year after a meeting.[52] Recently, the US Anti-Doping Agency and Olympic & Paralympic Committee required WADA to make all Executive Committee and Foundation Board decisions publicly available.[53]

WADA also started producing and publishing annual compliance reports,[54] which present detailed information about the activities undertaken in the previous year to advance anti-doping efforts and their effects. It also introduced external audits to strengthen "outside" monitoring of its work. These measures could be seen as including two accountability dimensions, namely transparency and controllability. Still, WADA also adopted a rule to move the promulgation of actors' noncompliance with the Code from the Foundation Board's to the Executive Committee's remit. This was criticized by the athletes as a measure that reduces transparency, given that the work of the Executive Committee was not open to the public and the athletes could not get real-time updates regarding the promulgation of actors' noncompliance with the Code.

At the operational level of the regulatory system, WADA's reform of the monitoring framework has led to the adoption of several instruments that have helped the collection of information on developments in the field. These instruments include the Code Compliance Questionnaire (CCQ), which every NADO/RADO are obliged to fill in on an annual basis. CCQ include reports of all relevant information related to the NADOs'/RADOs' work environment and developments on the ground, starting from their capacities, through challenges that might pertain to their specific environment, to other details that could affect the anti-doping fight. CCQ are followed by physical audit visits of WADA inspectors.

In its response to the scandal, the IOC demonstrated much less ad hoc transparency, contributing little to WADA's early efforts to investigate the doping allegations. In a later development, the IOC visibly intensified its public communication, however, it has not implemented any new major mechanism to make it obligatory

52 A. Brown, Athletes: WADA Continues to Mislead You, The Sports Integrity Initiative (London, September 23, 2020), www.sportsintegrityinitiative.com/athletes-wada-continues-to-mislead-you.

53 USOPC Athletes' Advisory Council and U.S. Anti-doping Agency, Joint Statement from USOPC AAC and USADA on WADA Reform (March 29, 2021), www.usada.org/statement/joint-statement-usopc-aac-usada-wada-reform.

54 WADA, WADA Publishes First Code Compliance Annual Report (March 26, 2020), www.wada-ama.org/en/media/news/2020-03/wada-publishes-first-code-compliance-annual-report.

for its governing bodies to release all important details related to their work and the decision-making process. This was despite the fact that, previously, IOC had set out and has worked on an Olympic 2020 Agenda, which highlighted increased transparency as one of its pledges[55].

11.5.2 *Liability*

Liability, the second aspect of the "accountability bundle," is about consequences of one's own actions, which could be imposed both for a rule violation or for performance failure. In our case study, liability has both reactive and proactive aspects. The reactive aspect concerns the imposition of sanctions for a discovered instance of cheating; the proactive form of liability is being realized when an organization adopts stronger liability measures for its future operation.

Regarding the reactive aspect, we have seen that only limited sanctions have been imposed for the discovered cheating scheme. Instead of imposing immediate and wholesale sanctions against the Russian team, the IOC prioritized "individual responsibility." Under this "route," an individual ban request is directed to the Court of Arbitration for Sport (CAS) for every Russian athlete for whom a review of the prior test samples had indicated the presence of prohibited substances.[56] For the then fast approaching Rio 2016 Olympics, the IOC delegated the process of sanctioning to the IFs rather than making a binding and harmonized decision itself (the latter was a statutory possibility). Some IFs, such as the IF of athletics (then IAAF, now World Athletics), imposed a wholesale ban on the Russian team, but others did not. The result was that one-third of the Russian Olympic team was allowed to compete.[57] This led to growing pressure and criticism of the IOC during and after the 2016 Rio Olympics.[58] Later on, as the criticism of the IOC's handling of sanctions of Russian athletes increased, it decided to impose a wholesale ban on the Russian Olympic team ahead of the 2018 PyeongChang Winter Olympics, in which, according to the ban, Russian athletes could only compete under a neutral flag, that is, as individuals rather than representatives of their country.[59]

[55] IOC, Olympic Agenda 2020: Closing Report (2020), https://stillmedab.olympic.org/media/Document%20Library/OlympicOrg/IOC/What-We-Do/Olympic-agenda/Olympic-Agenda-2020-Closing-report.pdf#_ga=2.160713853.1322075367.1617398607-1394957741.1617230692.

[56] IOC, Decision of the IOC Executive Board concerning the Participation of Russian Athletes in the Olympic Games Rio 2016 (July 24, 2016), www.olympic.org/news/decision-of-the-ioc-executive-board-concerning-the-participation-of-russian-athletes-in-the-olympic-games-rio-2016.

[57] BBC, Rio Olympics 2016: Which Russian Athletes Have Been Cleared to Compete? (August 6, 2016), www.bbc.co.uk/sport/olympics/36881326.

[58] Pound, *supra* note 28, at 12.

[59] R. R. Ruiz and T. Panja, Russia Banned from Winter Olympics by I.O.C., *The New York Times* (December 5, 2021), www.nytimes.com/2017/12/05/sports/olympics/ioc-russia-winter-olympics.html.

The sanctioning situation was further complicated from 2018 onwards, after a series of doping-related suspensions of Russian athletes were overturned by CAS.[60]

The IOC and WADA also suspended the Moscow laboratory; however, a later decision by the IOC to open talks about the laboratory's relaunch and WADA's work on readmission of the Russian Anti-Doping Agency (RUSADA) were criticized by a group of NADOs and stakeholders as too lenient and a sign of tolerance. In 2019 and 2020, these processes came to a halt and/or were reversed due to Russia's ongoing non-compliance with the Code. As a result, Russia continued to be prevented from hosting international events, and it was repeatedly contested whether Russian athletes could participate under the Russian flag.[61]

The governing organizations themselves – IOC and WADA – were not subject to any form of liability for their failures to create a more effective system and for the fact that the anti-doping regime had allowed such a large-scale doping operation for years.[62] The investigations into the scandal discovered that WADA was ignoring repeated reports of doping. The two whistle-blowers mentioned above, who triggered the scandal, had filed a large number of reports to WADA before appearing in the German documentary, but WADA did not act on the information, instead passing the reports to the IAAF for verification.

Neither the IOC nor WADA were of the opinion that they needed to take responsibility for these failures. True, the rules that governed the legal framework of the system did not oblige them to do so. Yet there have not been instances of "moral accountability,"[63] in which individuals would resign to take the blame for the discovered failure.[64] This contrasts with some prior examples where sports officials, for instance, Iranian weightlifting official Abdullah Falahatinejad, had resigned to demonstrate "moral accountability."[65]

[60] CAS fist overturned in 2018 the ban on twenty-eight Russian athletes who were banned from Rio 2016. See: S. Ingle, IOC Dismayed after Doping Bans on 28 Russian Athletes Overturned by CAS, *The Guardian* (February 1, 2018), www.theguardian.com/sport/2018/feb/01/russian-doping-scandal-athletes-bans-overturned-courts-of-arbitration-for-sport-athletics. Later, in 2020, CAS overturned the life bans for three Russian athletes for their doping in the Winter Olympics in Sochi 2014. See N. Gillen, CAS Overturn Life Bans of Three Russian Athletes Convicted on Evidence of Grigory Rodchenkov, *Inside the Games* (September 24, 2020), www.insidethegames.biz/articles/1098790/cas-overturns-biathletes-life-bans.

[61] WADA, WADA Provisionally Suspends Approved Status of Moscow Laboratory (January 22, 2020), www.wada-ama.org/en/media/news/2020-01/wada-provisionally-suspends-approved-status-of-moscow laboratory.

[62] Read et al., *supra* note 27, at 238.

[63] D. F. Thompson, Moral Responsibility of Public Officials: The Problem of Many Hands (1980) 74 *American Political Science Review* 905.

[64] The investigation showed, for instance, that, prior to the release of the documentary on the ART television, WADA had received more than 200 emails form the two Russian runners–whistle-blowers but had not acted on those emails accordingly to launch raise the alarm and launch an investigation. See S. Ingle, Athletes "Have Lost Faith" in IOC and WADA over Russia Failures, *The Guardian* (June 14, 2016).

[65] Associated Press, Iranian Official Resigns in Wake of Doping Scandal (November 13, 2006), www.espn.co.uk/olympics/news/story?id=2659618.

In terms of proactive liability measures, over the last five years, the regime adopted stricter sanctions for athletes for future doping discoveries. At the level of enforcement, a whole range of measures was introduced, from the adoption of stricter certification codes and audit standards for laboratories, through the provision of training to doping enforcement officers, to the introduction of private anti-doping organisations, thanks to which the prospects of athletes being doped without being discovered have significantly reduced.[66]

At the level of governing organizations, no performance or procedure-related changes have been introduced to institute sanctions for IOC and WADA members for the regime's ineffectiveness. Their transparency has increased to an extent, as discussed earlier, but their liability has not. For the principle of accountability to be realized, increased transparency in itself will not suffice if there are no consequences for the observed breaches or failures.[67]

Overall, the observed developments in the five years after the scandal indicate that the liability response has been limited and certainly much less present than the transparency response. In terms of sanctioning, there has been a mixed reaction, which sent similarly mixed messages and did not conclusively demonstrate the IOC's immediate resolve to impose adequate sanctions against the doping scheme's perpetrators. In terms of the proactive aspect of liability, considerable progress has been made at the lowest level of the hierarchy, namely in the operational aspect, but not as much in the ad hoc and systemic liability among the governing organizations.

11.5.3 *Controllability*

Controllability refers to whether actors within a system are subject to control by other actors.[68] Several levels of controllability can be distinguished in our case. One is the way in which WADA controls the actors operating at the lowest level of the system such as the NADOs, domestic laboratories, and sporting federations. As a group, they constitute the weakest link within the regulatory system, whose failures or complicity enabled the doping scheme to continue for a longer period.

Over the observed five years, controllability from WADA downwards has significantly improved.[69] WADA has adopted a number of governance changes that have tightened sanctioning and monitoring standards. It introduced a system of graded sanctions and adopted rules to clarify the sanctioning framework, specifying

66 WADA, Progress of the Anti-doping System in Light of the Russian Doping Crisis (2018), www.wada-ama.org/sites/default/files/20180920_progress_of_anti-doping_system_exco.pdf.

67 Koppell, *supra* note 9.

68 Ibid.

69 A full review of the WADA's measures that are listed in the current paragraph can be found at WADA, *supra* note 60.

responsibilities of signatories.[70] The result is that sporting federations can no longer use their discretion to interpret Code ambiguities in ways that would enable doped athletes to avoid (major) sanctions.

WADA has also adopted new certification standards for laboratories.[71] Further, as mentioned, WADA has introduced external audit visits to local NADOs, as a method of verifying the information received through the CC. In practice, though, representatives of local NADOs find WADA audits a rigid "one-size-fits-all" instrument that does not encourage the staff in local anti-doping communities to tailor their approaches to the local context.[72] An Independent Testing Authority (ITA) has been formed too, following a joint decision by WADA and the IOC, to manage anti-doping programs for international sporting federations, organizers of international competitions, and other organizations requiring support.[73] ITA is supposed to reduce commercial conflicts of interests among those preparing testing strategies and carrying out athlete testing in the field.

Controllability is not always, and in every aspect, a positive feature that contributes to stronger accountability of a regime. At the higher, governing level of a regime, stronger inter-organizational controllability could be a negative occurrence, if it comes at the expense of the autonomy of its key organizations. In our specific case, WADA's autonomy vis-à-vis IOC has remained low throughout the observed period, and this has not played into the efforts to strengthen WADA's position vis-à-vis the sporting community whose conduct it is supposed to regulate. The fact that IOC is reluctant to grant WADA fuller autonomy – and thus leadership in the anti-doping regime – encourages sporting organizations, particularly the richest ones, to drag their heels in observing the Code.[74]

In 2016, the IOC indicated that it is ready to reduce its presence in WADA and thus make it more independent,[75] but, to date, the IOC continues to retain significant appointment and funding powers over WADA. It has enabled the adoption of provisions that define that WADA should have an independent president and vice-president, appointed without the IOC's nomination, but, even so, IOC has remained the most powerful stakeholder in its internal work, where, de facto, IOC representatives have stronger impact on WADA's decisions than the government representatives.

[70] Read et al., *supra* note 27, at 242.

[71] WADA, *supra* note 60.

[72] E. Zubizarreta and J. Demeslay, Power Relationships between the WADA and NADOs and Their Effects on Anti-Doping (2021) 8 *Performance Enhancement & Health* 1, at 8–9.

[73] IOC, International Testing Agency (ITA) Moves Closer to Being Operational (January 23, 2018), www.olympic.org/news/international-testing-agency-ita-moves-closer-to-being-operational. ITA, About Us, https://ita.sport/about-us.

[74] Houlihan and Hanstad, *supra* note 24, at 209.

[75] R. Axon, IOC Seeks to Give WADA More Independence in Anti-Doping Efforts, *USA Today Sports* (October 8, 2016), https://eu.usatoday.com/story/sports/olympics/2016/10/08/ioc-wada-anti-doping-summit/91783618.

11.5.4 *Responsibility*

Responsibility is a broad notion that can mean various things in the context of accountability, including adherence to rules, adherence to professional standards, or adherence to internal standards of behavior and performance.[76] Translating the principle of responsibility into observable implications in our case study is not a straightforward endeavor, not least because some of the interpretations of responsibility overlap with other dimensions of accountability, such as transparency, controllability, or liability.

If responsibility is contextualized as the adoption of professional and wider integrity standards, then, again, WADA has demonstrated significant activity in its response to the crisis, and the IOC slightly less so. As mentioned in the discussion of the various aspects of accountability above, WADA has instituted a range of integrity and certification standards related both to the work of the "lower tier" actors whose work it monitors and to its internal standards. These have served to remove a number of embedded conflicts of interest that had existed in the network of local anti-doping organizations and sports federations and to enhance the procedural decision-making and performance integrity of WADA itself. CAS restructured itself, too, creating a separate specialized unit to deal with anti-doping cases. This was in line with the principle of specialization and autonomization, a measure that removed some conflicts of interest embedded within the institution when deciding on cases.

Responsibility can also be understood as increasing external monitoring capacities over an actor. In the last five years, we could observe significant increases in the prospects of a wider stakeholders' community to follow WADA's work and sometime make interventions, in event of misconduct. WADA has made a number of changes that have led to increased effectiveness and transparency in the monitoring of its internal wrongdoings. It has enhanced the system for discovering violations within its own organization, by setting up an external ombudsman, to deal with complaints in relation to the failure to act or abuse of powers by its officials, and has set up an internal whistle-blower unit.[77]

11.5.5 *Responsiveness*

Responsiveness refers to two aspects: whether a regime attends to the demands of its constituencies/stakeholders and whether it attends to their needs as implied by the proclaimed mission.[78] It is worth noting that the anti-doping regime's audiences are diverse. Some stakeholder groups were louder in imposing their demands than

[76] Koppell, *supra* note 9, at 98.
[77] Read et al., *supra* note 27, at 242.
[78] Koppell, *supra* note 9, at 99 .

others (e.g., the Western-bloc headed by the American NADO – USADA),[79] and the solutions that they required of the IOC and WADA might not have all been shared by other athletes, anti-doping organizations and other stakeholders. But there were common directions of change that were widely considered as being shared by the sporting and anti-doping stakeholder communities: more robust sanctioning, governance reforms to strengthen the regime's capacity to remove conflicts of interest and monitor compliance, and greater independence for WADA.

The expectations of more robust sanctioning were partially met. As mentioned, the IOC showed a protracted and patchy response in banning the Russian Olympic team, Russian federations' hosting of international sporting events, and the suspension and reintroduction of the Moscow lab. This response was severely criticized in the years following the 2016 Rio Olympics by athletes, representatives of national anti-doping agencies, and WADA.

Yet, over time, as the pressure from those groups increased, the IOC attended to some of their expectations of adopting a total ban on the Russian team (for the 2018 Winter Olympics). At the same time, it allowed the reinstatement of the Moscow lab as well as some of the Russian federations under looser criteria than was being demanded. Similarly, the IOC did not grant the level of independence to WADA that some of the loudest stakeholders required. Conversely, WADA undertook a range of reform measures that were praised by the broader stakeholder communities as steps in the right direction, that is, toward removing some of the long-standing conflicts of interest within the system and toward ensuring stronger compliance monitoring.

In terms of improving systems to gauge and attend to stakeholders' needs, both WADA and the IOC increased opportunities for athletes' representation, whether through newly formed dedicated commissions run by athletes' representatives or through increases in quotas to these representatives who sit on their governing bodies.[80] However, athletes and other stakeholders have found this to be insufficient. Recently, a growing number of voices from the athlete community could be heard complaining about "voice suppression" tactics both in the IOC and WADA, the result of which has arguably been a marginalization of athletes' influence on institutional decision-making.[81] Thus, limited progress has been made. Formal institutional co-optation of athletes into the IOC and WADA has not been matched by a notable increase in their influence over the decision-making in these organizations.

[79] See, for example, Houlihan and Hanstad, *supra* note 24, at 209.

[80] L. Jørgensen, Global Athlete: "We are Noticed," Play the Game (November 20, 2019), www.playthegame.org/news/news-articles/2019/0634_global-athlete-we-are-noticed.

[81] Ibid. L. Morgan, Exclusive: WADA and IOC Athlete Representatives Clash over Participants at Global Athlete Forum, *Inside the Games* (June 6, 2018), www.insidethegames.biz/articles/1065917/exclusive-wada-and-ioc-athlete-representatives-clash-over-participants-at-global-athlete-forum.

11.6 DISCUSSION

Reflecting on the regime's response across the five accountability dimensions, several observations can be made.

First, the anti-doping regime has, overall, demonstrated in the five years after the scandal some degree of accountability in its response to the Russian doping scandal, certainly more than it was mandated to do by the formal legal framework. Accountability can, therefore, be pursued as a virtue even when accountability as a mechanism does not exist.[82]

Second, the levels of demonstrated accountability vary across its different dimensions. It is not possible to compare with precision whether the extent of accountability is greater, and how much, in one dimension rather than another, so any attempt to "weigh them" up against each other would be a rough approximation. Still, it seems safe to say that the regime's response in the transparency and controllability dimensions has been stronger than in the other three dimensions. Liability was partially demonstrated in both the reactive and proactive aspect. We have also seen only partial responsiveness to stakeholders' demands and needs, although the level of responsiveness was somewhat greater in WADA than the IOC.

What does this variation across these five conceptions of accountability tells us regarding a regime's resilience? It could be the case that increasing transparency is the easiest response to a legitimacy crisis. It could also be that the immediate response is first demonstrated as a virtue, and thereafter it can set in motion a process of further institutionalization, that is, the establishment of accountability as a mechanism.[83] "Giving in" to other aspects of accountability might be less opportune, that is, more threatening to a regime's or an organization's power; increasing transparency could be seen as the least "sacrificing" accountability measure. A strong transparency response is also in line with commonly observed post-scandal organizational behavior where, often, one of the first responses that an affected organization takes is to increase its transparency, with the aim of restoring the stakeholders' trust.

Further, we could see that, following the scandal, some degree of institutionalization of the regime's accountability framework has occurred. Five years after the crisis, the anti-doping regime has formalized certain accountability parameters, both at the enforcement and governing level. That was not always the case in the previous history of the regime. During the first fifteen years, from WADA's creation in 1999 to 2015, the regime did not take measures that would lead to the institutionalization of its accountability framework, despite occasional calls for this and intermittent voices of discontent with the regime's performance.[84]

82 Bovens, *supra* note 5.

83 Ibid.

84 See, for example, Read et al., *supra* note 27, at 234.

Why has the regime's accountability response differed this time then? It is possible that the severity of the crisis played a role. Unlike prior calls for a stronger accountability response, the Russian doping scandal has the features of a 'focusing event," which, as observed in the literature on policy dynamics, can precipitate major change after long-standing inertia and long periods of stasis.[85] The noninstitutionalized accountability framework has set in motion a strong "negative feedback" dynamic, which for a long time helped the regime deflect pressures for change and resist major reform. If we look into the institutionalization of the regime's accountability framework over a wider period of twenty years, the model it has developed conforms to the punctuated-equilibrium model of institutional change,[86] rather than an incremental one. This suggests that systems with noninstitutionalized accountability frameworks might "push" regimes toward rarer yet more intense episodes of institutionalization. In systems that have some form of institutionalization from their outset, it is likely that changes to the system will be more frequent and probably less comprehensive, as its governing actors will be more responsive to demands for change.

Third, the extent of undertaken accountability response was strongest at the lowest, operational level, and it decreased as one moves up the hierarchy. At the top, WADA regime's gave strong accountability responses in some respects – fewer than it forced at the lowest operational level, and the IOC showed accountability response in even fewer aspects than WADA.

The institutionalization of the accountability framework varies across the regime's tiers. As one moves up the hierarchy of the accountability framework system, the degree of institutionalization decreases. As Table 11.2 indicates, this institutionalization is stronger at the bottom, the enforcement tier of the system, than at the upper tier, the governing tier. The differences between WADA and the IOC could be indicative too.

This suggests that the observed model is one of "nested institutionalization." What does this model indicate? Two observations can be made. First, that the limits to how extensive one's accountability response will be were probably conditioned by the regime's initial noninstitutionalized framework. Its "void accountability" did not oblige the governing organizations to be fully responsive to wider expectations. This afforded them the "luxury" to attend to calls for accountability only to a certain point. Second, the extent to which the IOC resisted an extensive accountability response, as opposed to WADA, was probably mediated by the power dynamic between them. The legal organizational framework gave the IOC a comfortable "starting position." As mentioned, before the crisis, the IOC enjoyed the position of the regime's supreme authority, under a constellation where its stakeholders did not

85 F. R. Baumgartner and B. D. Jones, *Agendas and Instability in American Politics*, 2nd ed. (2010).

86 Ibid.

TABLE 11.2. *Observed accountability responses within the anti-doping system between 2015 and 2020, across the five dimensions of accountability*

	Transparency	Liability	Controllability	Responsibility	Responsiveness
IOC	✓	x	x	✓	x
WADA	✓	x	x (no autonomy from IOC) ✓ (overall operational level)	✓	✓
Operational level	✓	✓	✓	✓	N/A

Note: The bigger the "tick signs" in a cell – the greater the extent to which the given aspect of accountability has been demonstrated by the actor in question.

have "exit" possibilities. From a political economy perspective, this means that the cost of limited accountability response is nonexistent or lower than in other transnational regimes.

Of course, the observed period of five years, while long enough to cover more than a full Olympic cycle, could at the same time be viewed as only a snapshot of a longer transformative period. Thus, one could argue that the regime's accountability development is still "in flux" and that the framework that has emerged so far is not yet consolidated. It is difficult to predict whether the extant accountability process will "accelerate," "slow," or "halt" in the coming period. Still, an interesting question that could be raised is whether WADA's ongoing progress in accountability institutionalization will have any implications for the internal regime's power play. Will WADA's stronger accountability response give it an opportunity to profile itself as an "accountability champion" within the anti-doping community – specifically when juxtaposed to the IOC – and, if so, will this have any implications for the regime's future transformation? As WADA potentially increases its legitimacy within the system,[87] this could build momentum to force the IOC to change its own accountability structure, too. Currently, the IOC still enjoys supreme authority in the system, primarily because of the present institutional design according to which its members and leadership cannot be changed externally or be subjected to external accountability forums. This might keep eroding its reputation within the system and increase pressures to institutionalize its own accountability, but at the same time the IOC will still have a strong institutional basis to keep its position of superior authority. In any case, it will be interesting to see how their respective pursuit of accountability will shape future development of power-play between the IOC and WADA.

[87] Read at al., *supra* note 27.

11.7 CONCLUSION

In this chapter, we analyzed, from an accountability perspective, the response of the global sports anti-doping regime to the Russian doping scandal. We have asked two questions. First, could legitimacy pressures force the pursuit of "accountability as a virtue" even when formal "accountability as a mechanism" is nonexistent? Second, can legitimacy pressure lead to an institutionalization of a regime's accountability framework?

The analysis yielded three main findings, which contribute to our understanding of the drivers of the evolution and resilience of transnational private regulation organizations amidst a crisis:

First, in the face of major legitimacy pressure, which in our case occurred-following a "system shock," there will be a pursuit of accountability as a virtue despite the nonexistent accountability mechanism. Put differently, the normative can overcome the formal-legal (design).

Second, noninstitutionalized frameworks can evolve into institutionalized ones; and partially institutionalized frameworks can evolve into more fully institutionalized frameworks. There are limits to the "negative feedback" potential that a noninstitutionalized framework will have in retaining the status quo. Strong legitimacy pressures can catalyze institutionalization, even in the most unfavorable structural environment.

Third, although legitimacy pressure can be a catalyst of a regime's institutionalization of accountability, at the same time this will be limited by the regime's prior structure. Legitimacy can "bend" even the most "resistant" structure, but the more resistant the structure is, the less range this bending will have. The extent of accountability demonstration will be shaped by power struggles, and where the prior structure accords one governing actor the position of supreme authority, the accountability institutionalization will be most pronounced in the "lower tiers" of the system.

12

"Keynesian" Shipping Containers?

Maritime Transnational Regulation before the Advent of "Neoliberalism"

Daniel R. Quiroga-Villamarín

Containers are the material representations of the rhizomatic movement of global capital that characterizes the post-West. They are a concrete symbol of the transnational imaginary they embody.[1]

At present [1992] we are living through a curious combination of the technology of the late twentieth century, the free trade of the nineteenth, and the rebirth of the sort of interstitial centres characteristic of world trade in the Middle Ages.[2]

12.1 INTRODUCTION

Future observers will not hesitate in concluding that our age has been profoundly marked by the anxieties of the adjective "global."[3] In law, history, ethnography, and other diverse fields of knowledge and practice, much ink has been spilled on what exactly does it mean to have a global perspective.[4] For better or worse, the relentless onslaught of what is understood as "globalization" rang the death knell of methodological nationalism across the social sciences: The nation-state has slowly, but surely, lost its privileged place as primal unit of the international system.[5]

[1] S. Hirsch, Inhabiting the Icon: Shipping Containers and the New Imagination of Western Space (2013) 48:1–2 *Western American Literature* 17.

[2] E. Hobsbawm, *Nations and Nationalism since 1780: Programme, Myth, Reality* (1992), at 182.

[3] M. Lang, Globalization and Its History (2006) 78:4 *The Journal of Modern History* 899.

[4] In law, see G. Teubner, Global Bukowina: Legal Pluralism in the World Society, in *Global Law without a State* (G. Teubner ed., 1997), 3–28. S. Merry, Global Legal Pluralism and the Temporality of Soft Law (2014) 46:1 *The Journal of Legal Pluralism and Unofficial Law* 108. In history, see S. Conrad, *What Is Global History?* (2016); T. Duve, *Global Legal History* (2017). In ethnography, see E. Darian-Smith, *Laws and Societies in Global Contexts: Contemporary Approaches* (2013); E. Darian-Smith and P. McCarty, *The Global Turn: Theories, Research Designs, and Methods for Global Studies* (2017).

[5] A. Wimmer and N. Glick Schiller, Methodological Nationalism and Beyond: Nation-State Building, Migration and the Social Sciences (2002) 2:4 *Global Networks* 301; G. Vasilev,

In this vein, the (international) legal field has witnessed the emergence of an ever-growing body of literature that questions the traditional assumptions regarding the (state-centric) sources and processes that govern lawmaking in the international sphere. Thus, it appears that a classical approach concerned mainly with state consent can no longer explain – if it ever did – the complex regulatory dynamics of informality, normative pluralism, and fragmentation that occur in contemporary global governance.[6] Transnational law, a term coined by Jessup in the past century, seems to be more analytically precise than international law to categorize the way regulation at the world scale occurs nowadays.[7] In this spirit, international lawyers and their fellow interdisciplinary travelers have opened the "black box" of the state – daring to "disaggregate" its inner contents and de-reify its "univocity."[8] This, in turn has diminished its relative importance vis-à-vis other actors in the international sphere, such as international organizations and even private actors.

Implicit in this narrative, however, lies an ambiguous assumption about the role of time in the transformations that occur in (international) law and society. This assumption revolves a seemingly banal question: what is globalization and when did it exactly occur? Was it in the nineties, as most early theorists of globalization tend to argue? Or, as historians suggested, was there a deeper *longue durée* in the genealogy of the processes of world-making?[9] But even if this was the case, when did this earlier and broader globalization occur?[10] If not the nineties, were then the seventies the pivotal decade where the "shock of the global" was first felt?[11] But what to make then of the pioneer global connections of the nineteenth century and its so-called first globalization?[12] And what shall we do if, as postcolonial scholars have argued, these different interpretations about the origins of globalizations have been dazzled by the

Methodological Nationalism and the Politics of History-Writing: How Imaginary Scholarship Perpetuates the Nation (2019) 25: 2 *Nations and Nationalism* 499.

6 See, inter alia, N. Krisch, *Beyond Constitutionalism: The Pluralist Structure of Postnational Law* (2010); P. Berman, *Global Legal Pluralism: A Jurisprudence of Law beyond Borders* (2012); J. Pauwelyn, R. Wessel, and J. Wouters, (eds.), *Informal International Lawmaking* (2012); R. Liivoja and J. Petman, *International Law-Making: Essays in Honour of Jan Klabbers* (2014); T. Schultz, *Transnational Legality: Stateless Law and International Arbitration* (2014).

7 P. Jessup, *Transnational Law* (1956). See further P. Zumbansen, *The Many Lives of Transnational Law: Critical Engagements with Jessup's Bold Proposal* (2020).

8 S. Strange, *The Retreat of the State: The Diffusion of Power in the World Economy* (1996); A. Slaughter, *A New World Order* (2005); J. Scott, *Seeing Like a State: How Certain Schemes to Improve the Human Condition Have Failed* (2008).

9 For an introduction, see J. Osterhammel, Globalizations, in *The Oxford Handbook of World History* (J. Bentley ed., 2012), 89–104. See also B. Gills and W. Thompson (eds.), *Globalization and Global History* (2006); Conrad, *supra* note 4, at 97, 110–114.

10 For an overview of the historiography, see J. N. Pieterse, Periodizing Globalization: Histories of Globalization (2012) 6:2 *New Global Studies*.

11 N. Ferguson et al. (eds.), *The Shock of the Global: The 1970s in Perspective* (2010); D. Hellema, *The Global 1970s: Radicalism, Reform, and Crisis* (2019).

12 E. Hobsbawm, *The Age of Empire, 1875–1914* (1989); C. Bayly, *The Birth of the Modern World, 1780–1914: Global Connections and Comparisons* (2004).

spell of Eurocentrism, and instead one must go back to the Early Modern or even the Medieval periods to think about non-Western global connections?[13] Perhaps, as my decolonial Latin American colleagues have suggested, one could trace the start of globalization all the way back to the Caribbean encounters that happened in 1492.[14]

In this chapter, I do not aim to provide a definitive and comprehensive answer of how international legal scholars should engage with the "origins" of globalization or of "transnational law."[15] Indeed, as Bloch reminds us, often the search for origins can mislead historians and laypeople alike into confusing causes and effects.[16] Instead, my much more modest contribution is to highlight that, for better or worse, international lawyers have overwhelmingly come to adopt one (out of many) interpretations about the beginnings of globalization: the so-called neoliberal late eighties.[17] While it is undeniable that the end of the cold war has brought unprecedented qualitative and quantitative changes in the way global integration occurs, it might also be a disservice to focus too much on the novelty of it all.[18] Or, to paraphrase Bloch again, one must not exaggerate the advantages of the present.[19] In fact, for a long time the state has often relied –willingly or not – on hybrid and private authorities to "govern in different sites, in relation to different objectives."[20] Historians, to paraphrase Tuori, have long shown that the only accurate use of the adjective "Westphalian" is related to dogs, not states or world-systems.[21]

For this reason, in this chapter I invite the discipline to also interrogate the plethora of instances of private regulation and non-state lawmaking that predated the arrival of neoliberal globalization at the end of the twentieth century. To do so, I reconstruct the process through which private and public actors from the North

[13] S. Gunaratne, Globalization: A Non-Western Perspective: The Bias of Social Science/ Communication Oligopoly (2008) 2:1 *Communication, Culture & Critique* 60.

[14] E. Dussel, Origen de La Filosofía Política Moderna: Las Casas, Victoria y Suárez (1514–1617) (2005) 33:2 *Caribbean Studies* 35; W. Mignolo and A. Escobar (eds.), *Globalization and the Decolonial Option* (2013).

[15] On the impossibility (and perhaps unfeasibility) of such definition, see P. Zumbansen, Transnational Law: Theories & Applications, in *Oxford Handbook of Transnational Law* (P. Zumbansen ed., 2021), at 5.

[16] M. Bloch, *The Historian's Craft*, trans. P Putnam (1992), at 24ff.

[17] M. Koskenniemi, International Law as "Global Governance," in *Searching for Contemporary Legal Thought* (J. Desautels-Stein and C. Tomlins eds., 2017), 199–218.

[18] L. Winner, *The Whale and the Reactor: A Search for Limits in an Age of High Technology*, 2nd ed. (2020).

[19] Bloch, *supra* note 16, at 47.

[20] N. Rose, P. O'Malley, and M. Valverde, Governmentality (December 2006) 2:1 *Annual Review of Law and Social Science* 83, at 86. See also S. Sassen, *Territory, Authority, Rights: From Medieval to Global Assemblages* (2008).

[21] K. Tuori, The Beginnings of State Jurisdiction in International Law until 1648, in *The Oxford Handbook of Jurisdiction in International Law* (S. Allen et al. eds., 2019), 24–39. See *supra* note 6, at 27. See also B. Teschke, *The Myth of 1648: Class, Geopolitics, and the Making of Modern International Relations* (2003).

Atlantic competed within (and beyond) the International Organization for Standardization (ISO) to set the global standards for containerized maritime shipping in the mid-twentieth century. I argue that in this "Keynesian" epoch, the lines between the private and the public were as blurry as they seem in our contemporary regulatory dilemmas. To be sure, I do not claim there was anything distinctively "Kenyesian" about shipping containers. My use of the adjective is meant to describe how they emerged in a period that the Western legal imagination has often associated with the dominance of a broad Keynesian compromise in macroeconomic management during the so-called *Les Trentes Glorieuses* (1945–1975), which was later upended by the general crisis of the seventies and the rise of "neoliberalism."[22] This framing, I suggest, casts a shade of doubt on the narratives that center the novelty of private lawmaking. It highlights, instead, that we have much to learn from the long histories of "pre-neoliberal" non-state transnational regulation – of which maritime shipping is but merely one example. After the introduction already presented to the reader, I turn to the relative hegemony of the 'globalization as a product of the nineties' thesis in contemporary studies of transnational law-making and private governance (Section 12.2). Then, I turn to the concrete case of shipping containers as an example of "pre-neoliberal" transnational standardization (Section 12.3). Finally, I close with some concluding remarks on the importance of material "nuts and bolts" standards in global governance, at a time in which most attention seems to turn to the allure of immaterial, digital, or service-based standards (Section 12.4).

12.2 VISIONS OF GLOBALIZATION IN THE SCHOLARSHIP ON PRIVATE LAWMAKING

Despite the "almost infinite variety" of transnational law and its corresponding analyses,[23] there is a common trope in most of the recent scholarly interventions: a repetition of key words that denote the emergence of something new or the transformation of a previous state of affairs. As Steinitz puts it, regardless of the differences between different theories or approaches, one can detect an underlying sense of "increased urgency" in academic narratives.[24] Transnational legal norms or actors "have grown in prominence,"[25] are "increasingly frequent,"[26] or stem from an

[22] E. Hobsbawm, *Age of Extremes: The Short Twentieth Century* (1994), at 257–286, 403–432.

[23] Jessup, *supra* note 7, at 4.

[24] M. Steinitz, Transnational Legal Process Theories, in *The Oxford Handbook of International Adjudication*, (C. Romano, K. J. Alter, and Y. Shany eds., 2013), at 340.

[25] P. Delimatsis, Global Standard-Setting 2.0: How the WTO Spotlights ISO and Impacts the Transnational Standard-Setting Process (2018) 28 *Duke Journal of Comparative & International Law* 273.

[26] E. Partiti, Polycentricity and Polyphony in International Law: Interpreting the Corporate Responsibility to Respect Human Rights (2021) 70:1 *International and Comparative Law Quarterly* 133, at 134.

"evolving complex society."[27] Instances of private lawmaking emerge out of the "progressive" interlinking of commerce or on the heels of certain rising technologies of communication or transport.[28] For instance, Berman links both the rise of human rights norms (which he pinpoints to a post–world war II constellation) and the end of the cold war in an overarching narrative arc of the erosion of traditional law throughout the twentieth century.[29] Graz, in turn, suggest the late eighties were the moment in which governance finally escaped from the narrow corridors of corporate management to become a global trend – a view that is shared by Delimatsis' helpful introduction to this edited volume ("The Resilience of Private Authority in Times of Crisis," Chapter 1).[30] To cite one last example, Zumbansen notes that "while the globalization of human and institutional, material and immaterial affairs is widely accepted to have prompted, inter alia, significant challenges for inherited conceptual frameworks of societal ordering, the contours of what will replace them remain nebulous at best."[31]

But the rather ambiguous notion of globalization itself is hardly problematized in a historical fashion.[32] While interventions recognize that the phenomena of transnational and private governance is not entirely new, scholars tend to suggest we are standing on the verge of a threshold.[33] Perhaps the most explicit elaboration of this radical transformation has been offered by Pauwelyn, Wessel, and Wouters, in their oft-cited conclusion that the post–cold war formal lawmaking enthusiasm of the nineties has bled into a more complicated landscape of informal regulation in our post-national age.[34] This framing dovetails neatly with the contested history of the body of knowledge and practices that we often understand under the label of

[27] P. Zumbansen, Defining the Space of Transnational Law: Legal Theory, Global Governance and Legal Pluralism, in *Beyond Territoriality: Transnational Legal Authority in an Age of Globalization* (G. Handl, J. Zekoll, and P. Zumbansen eds., 2012), at 55.

[28] U. Sieber, Legal Order in a Global World: The Development of a Fragmented System of National, International, and Private Norms (2010) 14:1 *Max Planck Yearbook of United Nations Law* 1.

[29] P. Berman, From International Law to Law and Globalization (2004) 43 *Columbia Journal Transnational Law* 485, at 555.

[30] J. Graz, *The Power of Standards: Hybrid Authority and the Globalisation of Services* (2019), at 31. On the rise of a new era of "Private Ordering 2.0," see P. Delimatsis, "The Resilience of Private Authority in Times of Crisis" in this volume (Chapter 1).

[31] P. Zumbansen, Introduction: Transnational Law, with and beyond Jessup, in *The Many Lives of Transnational Law: Critical Engagements with Jessup's Bold Proposal* (P. Zumbansen ed., 2020), at 21.

[32] F. Garcia, Globalization's Law: Transnational, Global or Both? (2016) *Global Community: Yearbook of International Law and Jurisprudence* 31.

[33] A. Cutler, V. Haufler, and T. Porter (eds.), *Private Authority and International Affairs* (1999), at 4.

[34] J. Pauwelyn, R. Wessel, and J. Wouters, When Structures Become Shackles: Stagnation and Dynamics in International Lawmaking (2014) 25:3 *European Journal of International Law* 733; N. Rajkovic, The Visual Conquest of International Law: Brute Boundaries, the Map, and the Legacy of Cartogenesis (2018) 31:2 *Leiden Journal of International Law* 267, at 276.

"neoliberalism."[35] While Slobodian and other global historians have shown the long roots of this school of thought in the early twentieth century, few would deny that its heyday would come in the late eighties and in specially in the aftermath of the cold war.[36] Indeed, wouldn't it make sense to date the rise of private rule-making precisely at the crossroads of this paradigm shift in the ways states and markets (and their relations) were understood in Western political thought?[37]

In this chapter, I do not want to create a straw person argument. It is undeniable that there is much truth to this framing. At the same time, following Winner and other proponents of the history of science and its cousin science and technology studies (STS), I want to take a step back before assuming the novelty of our neoliberal world.[38] Instead of seeing technology as a game changer per se, Winner would push us to see how seemingly unprecedented forms material and ideological techniques draw from the legacy of previous institutional arrangements.[39] While it is tempting to feel that our age has long surpassed the dilemmas of the previous century, a closer look into the historical record shows that many of the techniques of governance that we now associate with the emergence of private authority in the last decades have indeed long roots in the previous forms of regulatory imaginaries. Logistics, as we will see with more detail, was long a science closely related to military and public power before it became the realm of transnational private lawmaking.[40] Technical standards created by private transnational bodies, despite their recent salience, were an integral part of the nineteenth-century project of "governing the world."[41] As Tzouvala (drawing from the work of the historian Pedersen) recently noted, international legal scholarship on the use of standards, indicators, and "international best practices" can learn much from the seemingly unrelated context of the interwar colonial mandates system of the League of Nations.[42] While the power of multinational corporations and their supply chains might seem unprecedented, our colleagues working on imperial history would be quick to point out that "company-states" have been a fundamental force in the

[35] G. Gerstle, The Rise and Fall of America's Neoliberal Order (2018) 28 *Transactions of the Royal Historical Society* 241.

[36] Q. Slobodian, *Globalists: The End of Empire and the Birth of Neoliberalism* (2018); J. Klabbers, Book Review "Globalists: The End of Empire and the Birth of Neoliberalism" (2020) 31:1 *European Journal of International Law* 369. See also D. Leshem, *The Origins of Neoliberalism: Modeling the Economy from Jesus to Foucault* (2017); J. Whyte, *The Morals of the Market: Human Rights and the Rise of Neoliberalism* (2019).

[37] S. Strange, *States and Markets* (2015). See also A. Cutler, *Private Power and Global Authority: Transnational Merchant Law in the Global Political Economy* (2003).

[38] Winner, *supra* note 18.

[39] L. Winner, History of Technology Contextualized: Technology's Storytellers (1986) 231:4739 *Science* 750.

[40] D. Cowen, *The Deadly Life of Logistics: Mapping Violence in Global Trade* (2014).

[41] M. Mazower, *Governing the World: The History of an Idea, 1815 to the Present* (2013), at 65–93.

[42] N. Tzouvala, *Capitalism as Civilisation: A History of International Law* (2020), at 106–107. See also S. Pedersen, *The Guardians: The League of Nations and the Crisis of Empire* (2015).

making of the modern world.[43] While Delmitatsis convincingly argues that enormous transformations have occurred in the domain of privately led normative constellations in the last decades, in this chapter, I take his caveat that one must not forget that not all of this means that non-state regulatory orders are –themselves – a "recent phenomena."

Indeed, as Zumbansen himself noted,

> it is important to mention that a growing segment of transnational law scholarship points to the fact that the questions raised by transnational law resonate on many levels with those already raised by critical legal scholars and, in particular, legal sociologists and legal anthropologists at earlier times in the context of domestic [and colonial] law.[44]

For these reasons, my aim in this chapter is to push transnational legal scholars to look for traces of our contemporary fascinations in previous times and places, especially those in which the silhouette of territorial state is less visible: cases of colonial administration and the high seas.[45] I suggest that we might be able to understand better the resilience of private authority and lawmaking if we place their normative activity in the a broader chronological and spatial framework of analysis.[46] In what follows, I provide a modest example of the role of private and non-public actors in the creation of maritime shipping standards in the mid-twentieth century, long before the advent of neoliberalism (broadly understood). I suggest this is only but an initial sketch of a history that remains to be written about the domestication of land and sea by private (or privatized) visions of world ordering in the second half of the twentieth century.[47] To do so, I draw from the rich literature on

[43] J. Barreto, Cerberus: Rethinking Grotius and the Westphalian System, in M. Koskenniemi, W. Rech, and M. Jiménez *International Law and Empire: Historical Explorations* (2017); A. Phillips and J. Sharman, *Outsourcing Empire: How Company-States Made the Modern World* (2020).

[44] Zumbansen, *supra* note 31, at 27.

[45] On the later, see R. Mawani, *Across Oceans of Law: The Komagata Maru and Jurisdiction in the Time of Empire* (2018); L. Khalili, Keynote Address, Millennium 2020 Online Conference, October 22, 2020, www.millennium2020.co.uk/recordings?fbclid=IwAR0jaXc3NCLuMj-Vf3cgKXtvEnF_ZrIvOkoZC6k_VBiNsidj5aJvH_5xidM. On the former, see L. Benton, *Law and Colonial Cultures: Legal Regimes in World History, 1400–1900* (2002), at 127–166. This follows Delimatsis' invitation ("The Resilience of Private Authority in Times of Crisis," Chapter 1) to engage with forms of private regulation that become borderless.

[46] Following the pathbreaking work done by scholars of International Organizations. See S. Block-Lieb and T. Charles Halliday, *Global Lawmakers: International Organizations in the Crafting of World Markets* (2017), at 228.

[47] For a more extensive discussion, see D. R. Quiroga-Villamarín, Normalising Global Commerce: Containerisation, Materiality, and Transnational Regulation (1956–68) (2021) 8:3 *London Review of International Law* 457. The following section draws from this article, which in turn is a revised version of a chapter of my MA dissertation, Containing Globalization: A Material History of Transnational Regulation through Shipping Containers, submitted in 2020 at the IHEID.

containerization that has emerged in neighboring disciplines to augment our understandings of transnational regulation.[48]

12.3 KEYNESIAN STANDARDIZATION? CONTAINER STANDARDIZATION BEFORE THE HEYDAY OF NEOLIBERALISM

To begin, a word or two on the world of pre-containerized shipping is in order, so the reader can better grasp the sociotechnical transition that occurred in just a couple of decades. Indeed, if one looks today at what George has called our "mechanized, inhuman docks,"[49] it is difficult to imagine these places as bustling *entrepôts* of human interaction. For instance, as its Port Authority itself recognizes and celebrates, Hamburg has been "transformed dramatically" since the first container ship arrived on their docks on May 31, 1968.[50] Before that, in crowded and dense spaces, the movement of cargo and the conditions of labor were negotiated at every twist and turn. For this reason, Sekula argues that the European ports of the interwar era should be remembered as unstable melting pots of "overlapping cosmopolitanisms, both bourgeois and proletarian."[51] Appalling work conditions converted these docks into spaces of contention, in which disputes between labor and capital slowed down the operations of an already lethargic industry. Tight relationships between kin and a particular understanding of the nature of the dangers of this industry gave rise to a distinct "maritime masculinity" working class culture.[52]

For our present discussion, what matters is that all goods were transported as break-bulk cargo, which can be "characterized by its multiplicity and diversity [as] cargo arrive[d] in any number of shapes, sizes, and configurations."[53] This, of course, required "swarms of workers [that] clambered up gangplanks with loads on

[48] See, for an overview of the literature, F. Broeze, *The Globalisation of the Oceans: Containerisation from the 1950s to the Present* (2000); B. Cudahy, *Box Boats: How Container Ships Changed the World* (2006); T. Birtchnell, S. Savitzky, and J. Urry (eds.), *Cargomobilities: Moving Materials in a Global Age*, Changing Mobilities (2015); L. Hoovestal, *Globalization Contained: The Economic and Strategic Consequences of the Container* (2016); A. Klose, *The Container Principle: How a Box Changes the Way We Think* (2015); M. Levinson, *The Box: How the Shipping Container Made the World Smaller and the World Economy Bigger*, 2nd ed. (2016). For a different perspective, see A. Sekula and N. Burch, The Forgotten Space: Notes for a Film (2011) 69 *New Left Review* 263; A. Sekula, *Fish Story*, 3rd ed. (2018).

[49] R. George, *Deep Sea and Foreign Going: Inside Shipping, the Invisible Industry That Brings You 90% of Everything* (2013), at 29.

[50] Port of Hamburg, Anniversary "50 years of Containers in Hamburg" in the World Wide Web (May 15, 2018), www.hafen-hamburg.de/en/news/anniversary-50-years-of-containers-in-hamburg-in-the-world-wide-web—35793.

[51] A. Sekula (ed.), *Fish Story*, 2nd English ed. (2002), at 133.

[52] D. Williams, Recent Trends in Maritime and Port History, in *Struggling for Leadership: Antwerp-Rotterdam Port Competition between 1870–2000*, Contributions to Economics (R. Loyen, E. Buyst, and G. Devos eds., 2003), 11–26.

[53] Cudahy, *supra* note 48, at 9.

their backs or toiled deep in the holds of ships, stowing boxes and barrels in every available corner."[54] For this reason, maritime shipping demanded a copious amount of workers, both when it comes to sailors and stevedores (also called dockers in the United Kingdom, wharfies in Australia, or longshoremen in the United States). What is more, the packing, loading, and delivery of cargo took quite some time, which entailed that vessels could spend more time at port than at the high sea. This "colorful chaos of the old time pier," in which workers, cargo, and crewmates of all places swelled in spatially dense locales seems almost foreign in comparison with today's automatized ports.[55] The rise of containerized maritime trade – a revolution that occurred across several decades and regions of the globe – can only be understood in the backdrop of the crisis and collapse of this previous regulatory imagination of world ports.

In sum, this fragmented system of break-bulk cargo did not allow for standardized practices, which in turn implied that cargo loads, working conditions, and ship sizes were negotiated at every loading, departure, and arrival. In fact, laborers did not even have a fixed or guaranteed schedule of work. Across the North Atlantic, the turns of employment were adjudicated each dawn following a rather irregular practice called the "pick-up," "shape-up," or "scramble." Thus, even in one country, ports worked under very different conditions. One example of this is the variety of jurisdictional approaches, regulations, and strategies pursued by organized labor in one coast of the United States compared to the other.[56]

Another important issue was the tight connection between the (private) merchant navy and the (public) military-industrial complex. One must note that the concept of the "merchant navy" itself was only coined amidst the interwar fears of the return of a total war.[57] With the rise of oil and diesel power, naval strategy demanded "maritime time, previously unpredictable, [to be submitted] to a new metronomic industrial regularity."[58] With the cold war looming over the horizon, North Atlantic elites realized that it was important to maintain a robust and reliable national private fleet that could be temporarily enlisted in the support of the war effort if needed.[59] In other words, maritime policy was strongly connected with the fears and anxieties of national security concerns, and private actors were expected to act taking into account this national interest rather than the pure maximization of profit. Of course, there were exceptions to this trend, especially in the industry of oil tanking, where some rogue companies were avoiding these national regulations by listing their ships

54 Levinson, *supra* note 48, at 20.

55 Ibid., at 7.

56 Ibid., at 135–169.

57 J. McDermott, Total War and the Merchant State: Aspects of British Economic Warfare Against Germany, 1914–16 (1986) 21:1 *Canadian Journal of History* 61.

58 Sekula, *supra* note 51, at 108.

59 Cowen, *supra* note 40, at 4. See also A. Tooze, *The Deluge: The Great War and the Remaking of the Global Order, 1916–1931* (2015), at 35.

in the registry of another (laxer) state: a practice we now call "flags of convenience." Sekula and Khalili have shown that these unorthodox practices later became a template for containerships in the late eighties.[60] However, in the fifties and sixties, public and private actors in the shipping field still saw their *métier* as an extension of national maritime war policy.

In exchange, North Atlantic states provided generous subsidies and enacted protectionist regulations to strengthen their domestic seafaring industries. In the United States, for example, the 1916 Shipping Act, the 1920 Jones Act, and the Marine Act of 1936 "combined a New Deal interest in invigorating the nation's dormant industrial base with a concern for future [military] international engagements."[61] While they required companies to use domestic captains, crews, and ships for all domestic trade, they rewarded their loyalty with discounted prices on wartime ships and public assistance for the creation of new models. Even if these measures did not apply for international trade, a similar mindset prevailed on the high seas. As Broeze reminds us, a transnational network of commodity and bulk conference maintained the stability of prices in transatlantic shipping.[62] While Hoovestal assumes that containerization has, from its very beginnings, implied a (neo)liberal challenge to state sovereignty and its regulatory overreach.[63] I argue that this reading fails to capture the enormous dependence of early (and even contemporary) containerized trade on state subsidies, international trusts, and other non-market mechanisms.

It was in this context of a union between maritime trade and war policy and the irregularity of break-bulk cargo that the owner of a US trucking company first thought of linking sea and land in a single transport chain. While some companies had tried loading automobiles and trailers into ships (a technique that is now called roll-on & roll-off: ro/ro), the owner of this North Carolina trucking company, the magnate Malcolm McLean, wanted to maximize the amount of cargo per ship. He suggested removing the chassis of the truck and leaving only a box filled to the brim with goods on the ship's deck. After acquiring a peripheral steamship firm (renamed Sea-Land), McLean had to remove himself from the chair of his previous hauling company, to avoid contravening the regulations of the US Interstate Chamber of Commerce.[64] In what has been called an "unprecedented piece of financial and legal engineering," he pursued a leveraged buyout with a loan delivered by the

60 Sekula, *supra* note 51, at 134. See also L. Khalili, Tankers, Tycoons, and the Making of Modern Regimes of Law, Labour, and Finance, Aga Khan Program Lecture, April 13, 2020, www.gsd.harvard.edu/event/laleh-khalili-tankers-tycoons-and-the-making-of-modern-regimes-of-law-labour-and-finance/.

61 Cudahy, *supra* note 48, at 3.

62 Broeze, *supra* note 48, at 72.

63 Hoovestal, *supra* note 48, at 3. Compare with Cudahy, *supra* note 48, at 174. See further M. Mazzucato, *The Entrepreneurial State: Debunking Public vs. Private Sector Myths* (2015).

64 Cudahy, *supra* note 48, at 24.

National City Bank (now Citibank) to buy a bigger shipping firm: Waterman.[65] Then, he bought (through a subsidized government program) a couple of old World War II–era oil tankers, which he adapted to make the pioneer vessels of containerization. Instead of seeing McLean as a lone private entrepreneur, I argue that one must note his dependence on public subsidies and other elements of the regulatory landscape of the mid-fifties.

In his quest, McLean enlisted the help of an engineer named Keith Tantlinger from Brown industries (based in Spokane, Washington) to design the first modern shipping containers. These novel boxes could be stacked up to two when placed on a ship, travel by train, or fit in a chassis pulled by a truck, Tantlinger suggested a length of thirty-three feet just because the available space aboard the refitted oil tankers was divisible by thirty-three, making these new boxes at least seven times bigger than all previous experiments. The first container-carrying ship left port in New York in 1956, signaling the start of containerized trade on the US east coast. On the west coast, a rival company called Matson sailed its first hybrid ship in 1958, which was quickly followed by its first fully containerized ship in 1960. For Broeze, this was the threshold of a new decade in which "the fundamentals of the new system were determined, on the basis of which containerization during the 1970s could spread all over major trade routes of the world."[66]

Before this global expansion could take flight, the "early days of containerization … were plagued by the kind of format war familiar to historians of science: differences in widths, interlocking methods, and internal as well as external specifications generated turbulence."[67] In 1957, McLean had used a slightly bigger model of thirty-five-foot long containers, as this was the maximum length of trucks allowed by the state of Pennsylvania. Over on the west coast, Matson instead opted to carry out an "extensive engineering analysis" that revealed that twenty-four feet was the best length for the narrow Hawaiian roadways, which their business model wanted to conquer. Moreover, after the Korean War, the US Army had been using ten-foot "Conex" boxes. With the purpose of calming the standards wars raging between overlapping regulatory authorities and competing companies, the US Maritime Administration (MarAD) created a panel in 1958 tasked with the creation of universal sizes for containers. The same year, the American Standards Association (ASA) (renamed to the American National Standards Institute [ANSI] in 1969), a private nonprofit organization, also created a task force with the same aim. Then the National Defense Transportation Association also demanded a seat at the table. The stage was set for a competition between different visions of (self-) regulation by private and public actors. I suggest we see this confrontation as an early case of what Delimatsis identifies as instances of "voluntary economic

[65] Levinson, *supra* note 48, at 60.
[66] Broeze, *supra* note 48, at 28.
[67] C. Mutlu, Containers, in *Making Things International* (M. Salter ed., 2015), at 69.

activism." Each transport operator sought to cloak their private – and even often patented – standards with a stamp of public approval, thus setting the industry-wide norms of conduct. While the old system of maritime trade was not, yet, in crisis, private and public actors quickly understood that the potential of standardized containerized trade could create a "critical juncture" to reshape the rules of the game.[68]

In this context, MarAD created two expert commissions (on dimensions, construction, and fittings) tasked with endorsing "the principle of standardization of container sizes for the United States Merchant Marine."[69] This was not a minor issue, because only the ships that accommodated standardized containers could be allocated public "differential subsidie[s], mortgage insurance or other form of Government aid."[70] This can be seen as a pioneer case of "free riding of private ordering": non-state actors benefit from state legitimacy and even public subsidies without assuming the political costs of their outward role as standard-makers. These norms, as Delimatsis argues, function "in the shadow of the state" but still have a very heavy weight in the sliding scale of bindingness due to their function as gatekeepers to the market or to public aid.[71]

Due to the importance of these standards, it quickly became clear that creating a single universal size would not be easy, these committees instead tried to make a "modular family" of containers. In their proceedings, they argued that they "would have to be guided mainly by domestic requirements with the hope that foreign practice would gradually conform to our standards."[72] Hence, they settled on a width of eight feet, as this was the average dimension in US regulations (whereas some European railroads and highways had a limitation of seven feet). The question of length, however, proved more controversial: as we have seen, the shipping companies of the east coast tended to prefer longer containers (thirty-five feet) whereas west coast firms would have preferred a length of twenty-four feet. As a compromise, MarAD suggested a modular family based on multiples of eight: eight feet, sixteen feet, twenty-four feet, thirty-two feet, and forty feet.[73]

On the other hand, also in 1958, ASA had created a Materials Handling Sectional Committee (MH-5). This committee was composed of several subcommittees, one

[68] See P. Delimatsis, "The Resilience of Private Authority in Times of Crisis" in this volume (Chapter 1).

[69] Congress of the United States, Committee on Standardization of Van Container Dimensions, Minutes of 18 November 1958, in *Standardization of Containers: Hearings before the Subcommittee on Merchant Marine and Fisheries of the Committee on Commerce of the Senate* (1967), at 253.

[70] Ibid., 254.

[71] P. Delimatsis, "The Resilience of Private Authority in Times of Crisis" in this volume (Chapter 1).

[72] Congress of the United States, *supra* note 69, 254.

[73] Ibid., 255.

of them tasked with "van" containers.[74] This body suggested instead a modular family of twelve feet, seventeen feet, twenty feet, twenty-four feet, thirty-five feet, and forty feet. Against them both, the National Defense Transportation Association (which represented firms handling military cargo, without participation from "civil" shipping or trucking companies) instead pushed for the adoption of a system comprising lengths of multiples of ten feet (to facilitate integration with the Army's Conex format).[75] In the midst of this dispute, the chairperson of ASA's MH-5 surprisingly agreed with the military cargo companies' standards and argued for the elimination of the twenty-four foot and thirty-five foot sizes and to instead adopt a modular family of ten feet, twenty feet, thirty feet, and forty feet.[76] In "three critical meetings" that occurred in late 1959, this proposal was eventually ratified.[77] This left the two early proponents, Sea-Land and Matson, with abnormal sizes compared to the agreed upon standards. While they would try to overturn these sizes throughout the sixties (eventually raising their complaints against the ASA all the way up to the US Congress), their ultimate defeat meant that standardization helped latecomers "gain at the expense of the pioneers."[78]

This struggle in the United States ultimately proved to be only a dress rehearsal for a later global dispute that began when, in 1961, the ISO created its own committee for the standardization of containers (chaired by the ASA).[79] As Vince Gray (who worked in the US Merchant Marine Academy, the ASA, the US Navy, the US delegation to ISO, and ISO itself) reminds us, when ASA brought their case before the ISO for the creation of an ISO committee on container standards, they did so because they wanted to globalize their national formula.[80] The assigned committee, Technical Committee 104, would have its inaugural meeting in New York (1961),

[74] ASA-MH5 Van Container Subcommittee Meeting – February 25, 1959, cited in Congress of the United States, *Ocean Cruise Vessels: Hearings before the Subcommittee on Merchant Marine and Fisheries of the Committee on Commerce of the Senate* (1967), at 63.

[75] Congress of the United States, Minutes of the September 11 1959 Meeting of the NDTA Special Subcommittee on Containerization and Standardization, in *Standardization of Containers* (1967), at 329.

[76] Levinson, *supra* note 48, at 181.

[77] Congress of the United States, *supra* note 69, at 63–65.

[78] Levinson, *supra* note 48, at 182.

[79] On the ISO and its role in Global Governance, see K. Hallström, *Organizing International Standardization: ISO and the IASC in Quest of Authority* (2004); W. Higgins and K. Hallström, Standardization, Globalization and Rationalities of Government (2007) 14:5 *Organization* 685; K. Hallström and W. Higgins, International Organization For Standardization, in *Handbook of Transnational Economic Governance Regimes* (C. Tietje and A. Brouder eds., 2009), 201–211; J. Koppell, International Standards Organization, in *Handbook of Transnational Governance: Institutions and Innovations* (T. Hale and D. Held eds., 2011), 289–295; P. Delimatsis (ed.), *The Law, Economics and Politics of International Standardisation* (2015); Graz, *supra* note 30. See further S. Bijlmakers, "The International Organization for Standardization: A Seventy-Five-Year Journey Toward Organizational Resilience" in this volume (Chapter 13).

[80] Cited in International Organization for Standardization (ISO), *Friendship among Equals: Recollections from ISO's First Fifty Years* (1997), at 40.

followed by other meetings in France (1964), Germany (1964), The Netherlands (1965), London (1967), and the USSR (1967), and it would adopt its first global standard, ISO 668, in 1968. In 2020, this standard has just been updated for the seventh time, and it has now been joined by a wide variety of ISO standards on shipping containers.[81] It would be too simplistic, however, to tell this story as if it were simply a US imposition on the rest of the world.[82] Klose aptly noted that Kurt Eckelmann (the Hamburg-based shipping magnate who chaired the ISO's subcommittee on container sizes) pushed for the ASA standards due to the profound divisions among the European delegations (and the absence of the global south at the negotiation table).[83]

For this reason, it would be more precise to narrate the ISO negotiation process as a long dispute not only between national preferences but also among the different transportation philosophies of shipping, trucking, and train executives from all around the North Atlantic region. Length and sizes were not the only thorny questions at hand. While Sea-Land had initially threatened to sue the firms that followed their interlocking designs, McLean and Tantlinger eventually permitted royalty-free use of their corner castings and twist locks.[84] At the end of the process, the 1967 draft forwarded by the ISO to its member bodies for review included three accepted series of sizes, of which only Series 1 became a universal industry standard.[85] According to this model, boxes should comply with a uniform height and width of eight feet (or 2,435 millimeters) and could have lengths of forty feet (12.192 meters), thirty feet (9.144 meters), twenty feet (6.096 meters), or ten feet (3.048 m).[86] These new sizes eventually became the "universal yardstick of the brave new world of containerisation."[87] Ever since, the acronym TEU (twenty-foot equivalent unit) became a cornerstone of the new universal language of the maritime trade. The later global (and perhaps neoliberal) development of the containerization only became possible due to these seemingly banal normalized series of material practices and discursive knowledge that entrench a particular socio-technical imaginary of world commercial integration.[88]

81 See, e.g., details on the ISO website, www.iso.org, ISO 668, Series 1 Freight Containers.

82 Cited in ISO, *supra* note 80, at 42.

83 Klose, *supra* note 48, at 51.

84 Levinson, *supra* note 48, at 186–187.

85 ISO, *supra* note 80, at 42.

86 Congress of the United States, *supra* note 69, at 314–315.

87 Broeze, *supra* note 48, at 15.

88 M. Foucault, *Abnormal: Lectures at the Collège de France* 1974–1975, trans. G Burchell (2003), at 50. On the notion of socio-technical imaginaries, see S. Jasanoff and S. Kim, Containing the Atom: Sociotechnical Imaginaries and Nuclear Power in the United States and South Korea (2009) 47:2 *Minerva* 119; S. Jasanoff, Future Imperfect: Science, Technology, and the Imaginations of Modernity, in *Dreamscapes of Modernity: Sociotechnical Imaginaries and the Fabrication of Power* (S. Jasanoff and S. Kim eds., 2015), 1–33; S. Jasanoff, Subjects of Reason: Goods, Markets and Competing Imaginaries of Global Governance (2016) 4:3 *London Review of International Law* 361.

12.4 CONCLUDING REMARKS: MATERIAL STANDARDS IN GLOBAL GOVERNANCE

In their pathbreaking history of global standards, Yates and Murphy argue that we could periodize the creation of transnational engineering norms in at least three waves.[89] While they recognize the undeniable importance of the "third wave" that emerged in the late eighties,[90] they insist on the pioneer efforts of the late nineteenth century and the historical relevance of the processes that led to the creation of standards for a global market in the sixties and seventies.[91] In my view, international legal scholars have tended to focus mostly on the (undeniably important) actors and events of this third wave, paying little heed to the longer history of technical standardization.[92] In a way, this is entirely understandable – the third wave standards seem to deal with cutting-edge issues of social regulation that intersect with certain traditional legal concerns, like corporate social responsibility or environmental protection.[93] Most importantly, the rise of the service economy has led scholars to focus their attention on the immaterial and digital "containers" that underpin global commerce today, instead of the sturdy old boxes that remind us more of the technological feats of yesteryear.[94]

Instead, I conclude this chapter with a plea for the interrogation of "old twentieth century" technological devices, especially their material implications. As I have explored more elsewhere, in the last decades across the social sciences and the humanities there have been important calls to reengage with the materiality of the social world, in the wake of the critique of the fascination of our intellectual age with discourse.[95] Slowly but surely, even our discipline has come up to speed with this "new materialist" perspective that comes from feminist social theory and the history of science, leading to new studies of the material practices, objects, and infrastructures of global governance.[96] But, as I have argued in the past, one of the

[89] J. Yates and C. Murphy, *Engineering Rules: Global Standard Setting since 1880* (2019).

[90] Ibid, at 239–323.

[91] Ibid., at, respectively, 17–126, 158–189.

[92] For a brief overview, see A. B. Villarreal, *International Standards and the Agreement on Technical Barriers to Trade* (2018), at 8.

[93] J. Clapp, The Privatization of Global Environmental Governance: ISO 14000 and the Developing World (1998) 4:3 *Global Governance* 295; S. Bijlmakers and G. Van Calster, You'd Be Surprised How Much It Costs to Look This Cheap! A Case Study of ISO 26000 on Social Responsibility, in *The Law, Economics and Politics of International Standardisation* (P. Delimatsis ed., 2015), 275–310.

[94] Graz, *supra* note 29, at 55.

[95] D. Quiroga-Villamarín, Domains of Objects, Rituals of Truth: Mapping Intersections between International Legal History and the New Materialisms (2020) 8:2 *International Politics Reviews* 129.

[96] L. Eslava and S. Pahuja, Between Resistance and Reform: TWAIL and the Universality of International Law (2011) 3:1 *Trade, Law and Development* 103; M. Chiam et al., History, Anthropology and the Archive of International Law (2017) 5:1 *London Review of International Law* 3; J. Hohmann, The Treaty 8 Typewriter: Tracing the Roles of Material Things in

limitations of these first waves of new materialist interventions has been their fidelity to "traditional" state and consent-centered understandings of regulation. As Pottage has argued in the case of new materialists approaches to domestic law, often our work has been "too indulgent of the lawyer's sense of the law."[97] Perhaps we have been caught under Article 38's specter of sources,[98] in our studies of legal documents, rituals, and courts.

For this reason, the materiality of standards (and the standardization of materiality) remains a relatively unexplored and promising area for further cross-fertilization between new materialist approaches and a transnational law perspective. This chapter, with its incipient exploration of the little-known history of material standards in the history of maritime commerce is only but a snapshot of the many instances the relation between (private) expertise and physical and technical infrastructures colluded to create socio-technical imaginaries of world ordering. If we are, indeed, living in an era of "Private Ordering 2.0," perhaps it might be helpful to unearth the blueprints of previous hybrid regulatory constellations that preceded the age of the "territorial" and "public" nation-state. In hindsight, such an age might appear as a rather short interlude in a longer span of time marked by "private" and "extraterritorial" forms of global ordering.[99]

Imagining, Realising, and Resisting Colonial Worlds (2017) 5:3 *London Review of International Law* 371; D. Joyce and J. Hohmann, Introduction, in *International Law's Objects*, (J. Hohmann and D. Joyce eds., 2018), 1–11; B. Kingsbury, Infrastructure and InfraReg: On Rousing the International Law "Wizards of Is" (2019) 8:2 *Cambridge International Law Journal* 171; J. Hohmann and D. Joyce, Material Pasts and Futures: International Law's Objects (July 1, 2019) 7:2 *London Review of International Law* 283. See also D. Quiroga-Villamarín, Book Review: International Law's Objects (2021) 21:1 *Melbourne Journal of International Law* 236.

97 A. Pottage, The Materiality of What? (2012) 39:1 *Journal of Law and Society* 167, at 170.

98 Of the Statute of the International Court of Justice. See further R. Parfitt, The Spectre of Sources (2014) 25:1 *European Journal of International Law* 297.

99 D. R. Quiroga-Villamarín, *Vicarius Christi*: Extraterritoriality, Pastoral Power, and the Critique of Secular International Law (2021) 34:3 *Leiden Journal of International Law* 629, at 641–642. See also N. Krisch, Framing Entangled Legalities beyond the State, in *Entangled Legalities Beyond the State* (N. Krisch ed., 2021), at 7–11.

PART V

Resilience in Technical Standardization

13

The International Organization for Standardization

A Seventy-Five-Year Journey toward Organizational Resilience

Stephanie Bijlmakers[*]

13.1 INTRODUCTION

The International Organization for Standardization (ISO) has grown to become one of the world's most influential standards development organization (SDO) since its creation in 1946 (formally in 1947). A main source of its influence resides in its epistemic authority and standard-setting capacity, reflected, among others, in the increasing number of International Standards and standard-like instruments it has developed over the years, totaling 22,913 by 2020.[1] These standards cover a wide spectrum of issues in the economic, environmental, and social spheres. These issues range from terms and definitions and the dimensions and physical interoperability of goods, to product and service quality and safety requirements, management standards, conformity assessment practices, social responsibility, and climate change.[2] ISO standards and deliverables have an important role in the global economy; their use can improve the efficiency of production, the dissemination of innovation and best practices, and facilitate trade and market access. ISO standards are voluntary in that individuals or organizations have no legal

* This research has received funding from the European Research Council (ERC) under the Horizon 2020 research and innovation program (Grant Agreement No ERC-2016-CoG 725798 - REVEAL). I am thankful for the comments by Panagiotis Delimatsis, Enrico Partiti, M. Konrad Borowicz, and participants at the ERC conference on "The Evolution of Transnational Private Rule-Makers" in November 2020, and the research support from Zuno Verghese, Shravan Subramanyam and Paul Forrester. Any errors are of the author's alone.

1 ISO, About Us: ISO in Figures, www.iso.org/iso-in-figures.html. Also see C. Ruwet, Towards a Democratization of Standards Development? Internal Dynamics of ISO in the Context of Globalization (2011) 5:2 *New Global Studies* 9, www-degruyter-com.tilburguniversity.idm.oclc.org/document/doi/10.2202/1940-0004.1140/pdf?stream=true.

2 A. Bryden, Standards are boring? Think twice . . ., *ParisTech Review*, June 21, 2010, http://www.paristechreview.com/about-us/.

obligations to use or adhere to them.[3] Nonetheless, ISO standards are influential in shaping global markets and the behavior of companies and organizations, including their management of environmental and social impacts, thereby affecting the conditions under which people live. ISO does not develop its standards with the intention to establish regulation, nor does it perceive its organization to engage in any rule-making activity.[4] However, public authorities use and reference ISO standards in legislation and regulation and rely on them in support of public policy decisions and actions or as an alternative for regulation.[5]

ISO's history and evolution has been well-documented in the literature. This chapter builds on this literature to illuminate how many changes within ISO's organizational system and its standard-setting activities are a response to trends, changes and related challenges within the environment in which ISO operates. ISO's evolution can be explained in relation to its ability to respond and adjust to meet these challenges, in order to ensure its continued relevance. While it is possible to examine ISO's growth over the almost seventy-five years of its existence, this chapter posits that it is especially during crisis moments that ISO has undergone rapid transformation and change. During such decisive moments, the viability of the organization is threatened. The organization itself may be affected and its legitimacy and capacity to realize its goals questioned. Such organizational crises "require an urgent response by the organization under conditions of considerable uncertainty as to the precise causes and probable consequences of the situation at hand."[6]

Kuipers and Wolbers distinguish between three types of crises: a crisis whose cause and problems both originate from within an organization, upsetting its primary process or performance; a crisis to an organization that is caused by an exogenous event or development but implicates the organization, having caused or allowed it to occur; and a crisis about the organization, or an institutional crisis, in the form of a perceived performance deficit becoming "so deeply problematic that the organization itself is subject to intense scrutiny and criticism." According to the authors, "even the most tangible crises in organizations do not only prompt a functional response (putting out the fire, informing those directly affected), but have a political dimension too (regarding the legitimacy of the organization, and accountability for the problems and its functional response to the crisis)."[7]

This chapter adds to the existing literature an empirical account of how ISO has responded and transformed in connection to such critical moments throughout its history. ISO has experienced various and different types of crises compelling it to

3 OECD/ISO, International Regulatory Co-operation and International Organizations: The Case of the International Organization for Standardization (2016), at 36, www.oecd.org/gov/regulatory-policy/ISO_Full-Report.pdf.

4 Interviewee. ISO, Policy, https://policy.iso.org/home.html.

5 ISO/IEC, Using and Referencing ISO and IEC Standards to Support Public Policy (2015), www.iso.org/files/live/sites/isoorg/files/store/en/PUB100358.pdf.

6 S. Kuipers and J. Wolbers, Organizational and Institutional Crisis Management, in *Oxford Research Encyclopaedia of Politics* (2021), doi.org/10.1093/acrefore/9780190228637.013.1611.

7 Ibid.

change. ISO's continued existence and relevance despite and because of these challenges demonstrate its resilience as an organization. An analysis of ISO's resilience is also justified at this moment, in light of the recent COVID-19 pandemic. ISO is considered to have demonstrated "agility, flexibility and solidarity" during this crisis.[8] It seized opportunities to promote and rapidly disseminate existing ISO standards[9] and initiated the development of new standards in support of the global effort in dealing with this pandemic. ISO promoted the International Standard ISO 22301 (updated in 2019) Security and resilience – Business continuity management systems as a dynamic tool that can assist businesses and other organizations in navigating through it.[10]

This chapter builds on the theoretical framework provided by Delimatsis[11] and tests some of its claims against the empirical findings. This framework captures how crisis moments present both challenges and opportunities for private or hybrid standard-setting organizations, such as ISO, to grow more resilient and more influential as an organization. When an organization experiences a crisis, its adaptability is put to the test. Such crisis moments create a need and incentives to respond and adopt strategies that activate internal processes of change to restore the equilibrium. Opportunities arise to accumulate knowledge and develop the capacity to expect the unexpected and absorb it. Resilience is viewed as "the capacity to absorb stress and reorganize after the occurrence of a disturbance that upsets the equilibrium."[12]

This empirical study is based on eleven semi-structured interviews with officials currently or formerly working for ISO. Next to the empirical data collected from the interviews, this study is based on research of primary sources (ISO official documents, minutes of meetings, brochures, etc.) and secondary sources (mainly but not exclusively empirical studies about ISO).[13]

Section 13.2 explains the origins of ISO and its rise to prominence. Section 13.3 provides an illustrative example of ISO's responses and adaptations to one of its first crisis moments, originating from the needs of its new member national standardizing bodies (NSBs) from developing countries, including ISO's creation of its Committee on Developing Country Matters (DEVCO) in 1961. Section 13.4 identifies ISO's most essential qualities, how ISO acquired or leveraged these qualities in face of crises, and their cultivation over time. Finally, the chapter concludes and reflects on ISO's future (Section 13.5).

The empirical research points to several (external) events being of special importance in driving transformative change of the ISO system. This chapter identifies key

8 ISO, Strengthening Standardization More Important Than Ever in Times of Crisis, www.iso.org/news/ref2571.html.

9 ISO, Covid-19 Response: Freely Available ISO Standards, www.iso.org/covid19.

10 B. Lewis, Never Too Late to Get Ready, ISO, March 30, 2020, www.iso.org/news/ref2494.html.

11 See P. Delimatsis, "The Resilience of Private Authority in Times of Crisis" in this volume (Chapter 1).

12 Ibid.

13 Ibid.

crisis moments during which ISO was compelled to change, their drivers, and some of the resilience strategies enacted by ISO during these episodes. Discussing these events and their implications for ISO in detail goes beyond the scope of this chapter. The author therefore views merit in further empirical research on ISO's organizational responses and adaptations to these crisis events and the internal dynamics behind decision-making and ISO's enactment of resilience strategies.

The chapter finds confirmation in the empirical data for the claim that ISO's core standard-setting capacity and flexibility, and specifically ISO's ability to promulgate voluntary standards rapidly and to ensure their quality and diffusion on a global scale, is a key dynamic property of ISO. This property is essential for ISO to achieve its strategic goals and mission. It confers resilience onto ISO in the face of adversity and enables it to establish or expand its (relative) influence within and across various domains of standard-setting. The research also points to ISO's institutional structure and its complexity and its continued adherence to certain governance principles founding this structure, along with its business model, as key strengths of the ISO system. These qualities render ISO stronger and more influential today, as it seeks to contribute to the realization of the United Nation's (UN) 2030 global agenda for sustainable development and meeting the many global challenges under the seventeen Sustainable Development Goals (SDGs), thereby also ensuring its continued relevance.

13.2 ISO'S ORIGINS AND ITS GROWTH IN STRENGTH AND INFLUENCE

ISO was created in 1946, in response to a need for international standards that could support the economic recovery after World War II and facilitate industrial growth worldwide. At the initiative of the UN Standards Coordinating Committee (UNSCC), under the direction of Charles Le Maistre, sixty-five delegations representing twenty-five countries gathered at the London Conference in 1946. The first Statute and Rules of Procedure for ISO were drafted at this conference. ISO formally came into existence on February 23, 1947, after their formal ratification by the necessary fifteen countries. ISO succeeded the International Federation of the National Standardizing Associations (ISA); this main prewar standard-setting organization with a generic mandate had ceased to exist during World War II.[14] ISO adopted many of ISA's statutes and standard development procedures. ISO's standard-setting work began in 1947 with the creation of sixty-nine technical committees. These committees were concerned with the development of technical

[14] Creating a new international standardization institution was preferred over reactivating ISA in order to avoid any prejudices that the involvement of ISA's old membership from "enemy countries" might cause to future standard-setting work. J. Yates and C. N. Murphy, Coordinating International Standards: The Formation of ISO, at 24, https://web.mit.edu/iandeseminar/Papers/Fall2006/Yates.pdf.

standards. ISO's approach to standard development was to harmonize existing "national standards," to then recommend the re-implementation of the international standard nationally. The purpose of these international standards, referred to as "Recommendations" then, was to enable "industry to operate smoothly by having technical standards to refer to in order to harmonize terminology or ensure interoperability, exchange information, test performance etc."[15]

ISO was legally established as a nonprofit association under Swiss law, with its main seat in Geneva. It was structured as a federation of NSBs, one representing each country in the world. ISO's membership was made up of a heterogenous group of NSBs, whose statute (public/hybrid or private) and membership composition varied, depending on the country context. Decision-making within ISO was based on the principle of "one country, one vote." ISO was given three official languages: English, French, and Russian. The ISO Constitution defined the organization's institutional structure, consisting of a General Assembly (GA), a Council, a president, a vice-president, a secretary-general, and a treasurer. Members would meet once a year in ISO's General Assembly (GA), its plenary organ. The secretary-general would oversee the secretariat, its executive organ, which coordinates the system and runs its day-to-day operations. The International Electrotechnical Commission (IEC) was formally integrated within the ISO structure by its constitution, treating it as an autonomous "technical division" within ISO.[16]

ISO experienced rapid growth in output from the 1960s onwards. An important transition facilitating this growth was ISO's change of approach to standard development. That is, from harmonizing national standards, ISO moved to the direct development of international standards at ISO level.[17] ISO's renaming of the output of its technical work from "Recommendations" to "International Standards" in 1971 exemplified this change.[18] ISO, as a developer of these International Standards, became directly involved in the international community by supporting international organizations in their efforts to facilitate trade by way of harmonizing technical regulations, in which reference could be made to ISO standards.[19] This involvement increased as international trade grew and markets opened throughout the 1960s and 1970s.[20] ISO's standard-setting activities accelerated in the 1980s after ISO began its development of product quality–related standards for an increasingly

[15] Interviewee.

[16] C. N. Murphy and J. Yates, *The International Organization for Standardization (ISO): Global Governance through Voluntary Consensus* (2009), at 17.

[17] An important impulse behind this shift was the work of ISO's TC 104 – Freight containers and its publication of ISO Standard 668. This standard encompassed the ISO Series 1 container, a standard for a middle-sized container that ISO TC 104 had developed from scratch. See ISO, *Friendship among Equals: Recollections from ISO's First Fifty Years* (1997), at 41. Also see Section 12.3 in this volume.

[18] Also see OECD/ISO, *supra* note 3, at 11–12.

[19] ISO, *supra* note 17, at 60.

[20] Interviewee.

globalizing market. The scope of ISO's standard-setting activities further broadened after that, to management and organizational issues, service standards, and conformity assessment practices. ISO standards now cover practically all technical and economic activities.[21]

13.3 MEETING THE NEEDS OF DEVELOPING COUNTRIES AND DEVCO'S CREATION

One of the first critical episodes ISO encountered after its creation was between 1950 and 1960, resulting in ISO expanding its membership from developing countries and adapting to accommodate their evolving needs and requirements. The so-called new countries had recently gained their autonomy or independence from their colonial rulers. They were aware that adherence to international standards was a quid pro quo to access international trade and supply chains.[22] These developing countries were less interested in the "threads, bolts and nuts" that ISO standards had addressed previously and preferred ISO to develop standards on topics for which they required a solution.[23] ISO recognized that most countries in the world were developing countries and that these countries should have a say and actively participate in ISO in order for ISO to meet global needs and create globally relevant standards.[24] Against this background, and to the end of being able to identify and respond to the specific needs and requirements of developing countries in the fields of standardization and related areas, ISO created its Committee on Developing Country Matters (DEVCO) in 1961. A main objective of DEVCO was to provide a forum for discussion about all aspects of standardization and related activities in developing countries and the exchange and sharing of experiences among developed and developing countries.[25]

Further organizational changes followed to meet this challenge of ensuring active involvement of ISO's membership from developing countries. In 1964 and 1992, ISO created the new membership categories of "correspondent" and "subscriber" to facilitate their access in the ISO system. This status enabled developing countries to be informed about international standardization without having to incur the full costs of membership.[26] Changes were made to ISO's governance structure to ensure that the ISO Council would have a fair representation of the various sizes of the

[21] A. Bryden, Sustainable Development, Emerging Technologies, Can International Standards Make a Difference, *ParisTech Review*, May 29, 2014, www.paristechreview.com/2014/05/29/sustainable-development-standards.

[22] Interviewee.

[23] See, ISO, *supra* note 17, at 51.

[24] Interviewee. Also see, ISO, ISO/DEVCO Committee on Developing Country Matters, www.iso.org/committee/55004.html.

[25] Council Resolution 44/1975 (DEVCO Terms of reference)

[26] ISO, About Us, www.iso.org/about-us.html#6. Also see, ISO, Capacity Building, www.iso.org/capacity-building.html.

economy. For instance, in 1980, the ISO Council passed a resolution recommending to member states that "when they make nominations to fill seats of Council … they should bear in mind that six members should be member bodies from developing countries."[27] In 1985, ISO created the ISO Programme for Developing Countries (DEVPRO), to provide training on topics related to standardization, sponsorship to attend technical meetings, and manuals on technical matters related to standardization, free for use by developing country members.[28]

The adoption of the WTO Agreement on Technical Barriers to Trade (the TBT Agreement) in 1994 created new impetus behind this effort.[29] Many of ISO's members from developing countries belong to or operate under the policy direction of the public service of their countries, for instance, the Ministry of Trade and Industry. Most importantly, the TBT Agreement sets the requirement for WTO members that when having identified a need to regulate to fulfil certain public policy objectives, their technical regulation must be based on international standards, or the relevant parts thereof – if these standards exist or their completion is imminent (Article 2.4).[30] This harmonization of the development of technical regulations by use of international standards serves the TBT Agreement's objective of ensuring that national regulations, standards, and conformity assessment procedures do not create unnecessary obstacles to international trade. The TBT Agreement also establishes criteria for the development of standards by NSBs through the TBT Code of Good Practice for the Preparation, Adoption and Application of Standards (the TBT Standards Code) in Annex 3 to this agreement, related to balanced representation of interests, coordination to avoid overlap, and the availability of the standards to the public.

ISO has responded to the TBT Agreement's adoption by actively promoting the implementation of its provisions, of which certain aspects are of special relevance to developing countries.[31] As an observer to the WTO Committee on Technical Barriers to Trade (the TBT Committee), ISO has been "aware and attentive" to

[27] See ISO, *supra* note 17, at 46.

[28] S. Gujadhur, International Trade Centre, Commonwealth Secretariat, Influencing and Meeting International Standards: Challenges for Developing Countries (2005), www.intracen.org/uploadedFiles/intracenorg/Content/Exporters/Exporting_Better/Quality_Management/Redesign/ENGInfluencingVol2.pdf.

[29] The adoption of the WTO TBT Agreement was a critical moment for ISO for various reasons. For a study of ISO's responses to this event, see P. Delimatsis and S. Bijlmakers, How Standard Setting Bodies Have Grown Resilient by Overcoming Adversity in Times of Crisis: A Theoretical Perspective (on file with the author).

[30] Article 2.5 establishes the presumption that a domestic regulation is compatible with the TBT Agreement insofar as it is in accordance with relevant international standards and pursues a public policy objective.

[31] See WTO Committee on Trade and Development, Special and Differential Treatment Provisions in WTO Agreements and Decisions, March 2, 2021, WT/COMTD/W/258, at 41–53, https://docs.wto.org/dol2fe/Pages/SS/directdoc.aspx?filename=q:/WT/COMTD/W258.pdf&Open=True.

the issues that arise within the WTO in relation to standard development.[32,33] An important development was the adoption by the TBT Committee of the six WTO principles that guide the development of international standards,[34] of which principle 6 requires WTO members to facilitate the effective participation of developing countries in international standardization. ISO has pledged alignment of its standard development processes to these principles. A response by ISO that can be linked to this change was ISO's creation of a TMB task force to facilitate the participation of developing countries in ISO's work.[35] ISO updated its Directives in 2003 to introduce provisions on "twinning," that is cooperation between a developed and developing country, for instance, in leading a working group or a technical committee,[36] a concept that was expanded to "partnering" in 2007.[37]

In September 2004, the ISO Council endorsed ISO's first Action Plan for developing countries (2005–2010).[38] ISO's Developing Countries Task Force (DCTF), created in 2002, had issued a report on developing a program of action to increase the immediate involvement of developing countries in ISO's standard-setting work. A high-level ad hoc group was established in 2003 to study this task force's recommendations relating to ISO governance, which resulted in ISO con-

[32] WTO Committee on Technical Barriers to Trade, Assistance to ISO Developing Country Members, Statement by Rob Steele, ISO Secretary-General, July 2, 2010, G/TBT/GEN/101.

[33] P. Delimatsis, "Relevant International Standards" and "Recognised Standardization Bodies" under the TBT Agreement, in *The Law, Economics and Politics of International Standardization* (P. Delimatsis ed., 2015), at 114.

[34] In 2002, the TBT Committee decided that the development of international standards should comply with the six WTO principles (transparency, openness, impartiality and consensus, relevance and effectiveness, coherence, and developing country interests), in order to ensure the quality of these standards and the effective application of the TBT Agreement. The TBT Committee adopted this decision during its second triennial review. See Annex 4, Decision of the Committee on Principles for the Development of International Standards, Guides and Recommendations with relation to Articles 2, 5 and Annex 3 of the Agreement, contained in the Second Triennial Review of the TBT Agreement, https://docs.wto.org/dol2fe/Pages/FE_Search/FE_S_S009-DP.aspx?language=E&CatalogueIdList=231,4879&CurrentCatalogueIdIndex=1.

[35] TMB resolution 36/2001, www.open-std.org/jtc1/SC22/WG20/docs/n848-TMB%20Resolutions.pdf.

[36] WTO, TBT Committee, Developments within the International Organization for Standardization (ISO) that are Related to the Second Triennial Review of the TBT Agreement: Communication from ISO, G/TBT/W/158, May 18, 2001, https://docs.wto.org/dol2fe/Pages/SS/directdoc.aspx?filename=Q:/G/TBT/W158.pdf&Open=True.

[37] See WTO, Committee on Technical Barriers to Trade, Summary Report of the TBT Workshop on the Role of International Standards in Economic Development (2009), https://docs.wto.org/dol2fe/Pages/FE_Search/FE_S_S009-DP.aspx?language=E&CatalogueIdList=131032,85352,50747,98991,93791,86196,86668,97091,68966,90563&CurrentCatalogueIdIndex=6&FullTextHash=&HasEnglishRecord=True&HasFrenchRecord=True&HasSpanishRecord=True. Also see, ISO, Action Plan for Developing Countries (2004) 2(11) ISO Focus.

[38] ISO, ISO Action Plan for Developing Countries 2005–2010, www.iso.org/files/live/sites/isoorg/files/archive/pdf/en/actionplan_2005.pdf.

verting DEVPRO into a five-year Action Plan.[39] ISO's first Action Plan covered the entire spectrum of ISO's activities of interest to developing countries and structured these activities with five clear objectives.[40] This Action Plan was intended to more effectively link ISO's organizational structure for developing countries to ISO's strategy. It implemented those elements of the ISO Strategic Plan 2005–2010 relating to developing countries. This ISO Strategic Plan set out ISO's view that support for developing countries is essential to realizing its global vision of contributing to a more efficient and sustainable world economy.

The first five-year ISO Action Plan for developing countries was in place from 2006 to 2010. Subsequently, a new Action Plan came into force every five years. These Action Plans are designed in consultation with ISO members from developing countries, to ensure the relevance and alignment of its programs with their needs.[41] DEVCO monitors the Action Plan's implementation. DEVCO's terms of reference were reviewed to include this monitoring function, and ISO created the DEVCO Chair's Advisory Group (CAG) to assist DEVCO in fulfilling this function.[42] A key focus of the latest ISO Action Plan for developing countries (2021–2025) is the UN 2030 Agenda and the seventeen SDGs. ISO's strategic plan for 2030 aligns ISO's ambitions for 2030 with the SDGs, viewing standards as instruments, and their development as an opportunity for ISO, to contribute to their delivery and achieve a sustainable future. The Strategy is meant to ensure ISO's position within a rapidly changing global context and the potential of standard-setting in realizing ISO's vision for 2030, that is "making lives easier, safer and better."[43]

13.4 ISO'S KEY TRAITS OF RESILIENCE

Section 13.3 provided an illustrative example of how a crisis episode created a need and incentives for ISO to respond and adapt in order to ensure the responsiveness of its International Standards to the needs of developing countries, their global relevance and uptake, and ISO's continued relevance as an organization. ISO's creation of DEVCO and other subsequent organizational changes strengthened ISO's capacity and its position as a standard-setting organization in the face of future crisis events. As will be further illustrated, the adoption of the TBT Agreement, and its interpretation by the WTO Appellate Body, was a change in ISO's (regulatory) context that had a significant impact on ISO. This event created opportunities for

[39] ISO Council Resolution 27/2003.

[40] See WTO, Committee on Trade and Development, Special and Differential Treatment Provisions in WTO Agreements and Decisions, March 2, 2021, WT/COMTD/W/258, at 47, https://docs.wto.org/dol2fe/Pages/SS/directdoc.aspx?filename=q:/WT/COMTD/W258.pdf&Open=True.

[41] ISO, ISO Action Plan for Developing Countries 2011–2015, www.iso.org/files/live/sites/isoorg/files/archive/pdf/en/iso_action_plan_developingcountries-2011-2015.pdf.

[42] ISO Council Resolution 26/2003.

[43] ISO, Strategy 2030, www.iso.org/strategy2030.html.

ISO to assert its competence and legitimacy as a developer of "relevant" international standards in contribution to the realization of the objectives of the WTO agreement, for its International Standards to obtain relevance and a legal status within the WTO regime, and to consolidate ISO's (dominant) position in the standard-setting community.[44]

The empirical research points to ISO having witnessed various such crisis moments throughout its history and related challenges driving transformative change within its system. Such crisis moments seem to have never affected ISO to such a problematic degree that the organization's continued survival was truly at stake:

> ISO has not had a significant institutional crisis, I'm happy to say, in the sense that over the years, internationally, ISO has been recognized as a very useful organization and has managed to adjust to the evolution of the international scene. Of course, there have been some adjustments and tensions.[45]

The findings suggest that ISO successfully recovered and reorganized after experiencing a crisis moment. ISO's ability to realize such internal organizational change attests to its resilience. As Section 13.3 showed, ISO has retained and acquired new capacities in face of crises that have rendered ISO stronger in the face of future threats, though issues remain.[46] This section identifies key strengths of ISO, draws linkages to crisis moments during which ISO acquired or built these capacities, and reflects on their cultivation over time.

13.4.1 *Standard-Setting Capacity and Flexibility*

The research provides empirical evidence for the claim that ISO's core standard-setting activities and its flexibility are essential properties that have rendered ISO stronger in the face of adversity. ISO's flexibility in the fulfillment of its standard-setting functions is apparent from certain shifts in ISO's work over the years. The change in ISO's approach to standard-setting from the harmonization of national standards to the development of International Standards in the late 1960s is a case in point.[47] ISO has also demonstrated an ability to enter into new domains of standard-setting by promulgating voluntary standards rapidly and to interpret its standard-setting procedures flexibly in face of changing stakeholder expectations about the ISO system. As will be illustrated, this evolution of topics has followed wider trends

[44] According to Wood, competence can be understood as a jurisdictional attribute, meaning "an actor's authority to declare and apply norms for particular actors or activities in a particular arena." S. Wood, Exploring the Relationship between Administrative Norms and Competence in Transnational Governance: ISO, ISEAL and Sustainability Standards (2016) 21 *Tilburg Law Review* 193, at 215, 197, 206.

[45] Interviewee.

[46] See Section 13.4.4.

[47] See Section 13.2.

in society.[48] ISO's ability to develop standards rapidly[49] was strengthened during an important episode in the 1980s when the organization was under pressure to self-organize to improve the efficiency of its standard development process.[50]

ISO's flexibility in standard-setting is evident from its shift in focus in the 1960s from technical standardization to the development of product standards, which relate to the performance, safety, and health aspects of products.[51] ISO's decision to promote consumer participation in its work was a consequence of its entry into this domain of standards.[52] The products that were covered by these products standards were used by consumers (not industry) and impacted on their welfare.[53] Impetus to reconsider ISO's structure to facilitate consumer participation came at a time when the consumer movement in the United States, under the leadership of Ralph Nader, had gained traction in the 1970s–1980s and demands increased for consumers to have a greater say in ISO's policymaking and its standard-setting work. Against this background, ISO made a proposal that led to the decision of the ISO in 1977 to establish the ISO Committee on Consumer Policy (COPOLCO), which held its first meeting in 1978.[54]

ISO's publication of its first quality management system standards in 1987 marked another shift, away from performance standards toward process standards. ISO 9001 was adopted against the background of a proliferation of quality standards and big purchasers, including government wanting "zero defects" in the manufacturing of weaponry or nuclear power plants, imposing many different quality standards to avoid quality problems.[55]

Rapid developments in the global high technology sector created opportunities for ISO to meet a demand for rapid standardization in the 1980s. ISO experienced competitive pressure from a proliferation of consortia and other types of standard-setting organizations developing "open standards" and "proprietary standards" for a

[48] According to an interviewee, ISO's evolution of topics is reflected in the numbering of the list of ISO technical committees, which represents the chronology of the creation of these committees. See ISO, Who Develops Standards: Technical Committees, www.iso.org/technical-committees.html.

[49] Also see, OECD/ISO, *supra* note 3, at 45–46.

[50] Interviewee.

[51] ISO, *supra* note 17, at 46.

[52] B. J. Farquhar, Draft Report of Background Research on ISO and IEC for Consumers International Project "Decision-making in the Global Market," March 13, 2004, at 7, https://docbox.etsi.org/STF/Archive/STF285_HF_MobileEservices/STF285%20Work%20area/UG/Inputs%20to%20consider/ConsumerDecisionMaking_ISO_IEC_31052004.pdf.

[53] For instance, "food products, sports and recreation equipment, the sizing of clothes and shoes, and the care-labelling of textiles." See ISO, *supra* note 17, at 46.

[54] D. Kissinger, A Journey through COPOLCO's First 25 years, ISO Bulletin, August 2003.

[55] ISO adopted its first quality management system standard in 1987, titled ISO 9000: 1987, Quality Management and Quality Assurance. This standard was renamed ISO 9001 after an update and sequentially complemented by a number of standards with numbers above 9001 (ISO 9000 series). J. Yates and C. Murphy, *Engineering Rules: Global Standard Setting Since 1880* (2019), at 294.

global high-tech sector. ISO was criticized for its process of developing ISO standards being "too bureaucratic and slow"[56] and not responding to market needs. There were concerns that unless ISO improved its performance, international standards would be developed through other organizations, especially in these industry consortia, which could develop standards "in a faster and cheaper way."[57] ISO standards could become less relevant to the need of industry and the world economy in general.[58]

According to an interviewee, there were around 7,300 projects running in 1996. Many of these projects had been registered twenty, fifteen, or twelve years before. There were three projects with a lifespan of thirty years in the work programs of ISO committees. ISO had introduced a harmonized stage code system in 1993 for use to describe the process and indicate where in the process an item had reached. "I saw that there were projects that stayed for 5, 6, 7, 10, 15 years in the same stage. So, there was absolutely, in my opinion, no management of the technical program." Addressing these problems posed challenges for the ISO; the experts participating in its technical work are volunteers, and ISO could not "dictate the speed of development or the making available of resources for ISO work." "There was also no higher-level monitoring system across all the committees, the technical fields and so on to see all these problems."[59]

ISO created the Technical Management Board (TMB) in 1986, which after its first meeting in 1994, systematically addressed ISO's problems. ISO put in place a new management structure to speed up the process for the preparation of standards. It stressed the need, in a decentralized organization like ISO, to strengthen the self-responsibility of the committee.[60] ISO introduced certain disciplines for project management: work programs of ten years and older were cancelled, unless a plan was developed to produce a Draft International Standard (DIS) within one year. ISO introduced clear rules for standard development, such as that requiring a work-item to reach a certain stage by a declared target date. When a committee failed to meet this target date, and could not justify this delay, the respective work-item would be cancelled.[61]

56 Murphy and Yates, *supra* note 16, at 101.

57 Ruwet, *supra* note 1.

58 Interviewee. An additional impulse for change came from the European Commission; while having adopted international standardization as the primary aim of European standardization, it threatened to defect from ISO standards in case ISO would not develop an important standard quickly and legislate an alternative standard, which many were likely to follow. Murphy and Yates, *supra* note 16, at 97.

59 Interviewee.

60 ISO, Confirmed Minutes of the First Meeting of the Technical Management Board, Geneva, April 18–19, 1994, ISO/TMB 24, June 1994, https://isotc.iso.org/livelink/livelink/fetch/-15620806/15620808/15623592/15768435/15849525/TMB_24_-_Confirmed_minutes_of_the_1st_meeting_of_the_Technical_Management_Board%2C_18–19_April_1994.pdf?nodeid=15768968&vernum=-2.

61 TMB Communiqué, March 1997, No. 1. Also see, ISO Bulletin, November 1998. See, ISO/IEC Directives Part 1, Clause 2.1.6.

The adoption of ISO 14000 Environmental Management System (EMS) was another important milestone in ISO's history. Various trends coalesced that pushed this project onto ISO's agenda in advance of the UN's 1992 Earth Summit.[62] According to an interviewee, "environmental issues were becoming important to the point that there was a need to have a reference document internationally recognized to deal with how a company may be organized to achieve and demonstrate that it is working properly in relation to the environment."[63] An important driver behind the development of the ISO 14000 series was the interests and need of industry, ISO's traditional constituency, for a common international EMS standard and their preference for ISO to take a lead in its development, owing to their influence in ISO.[64] Importantly, developments in the General Agreement on Tariffs and Trade (GATT) negotiations indicated that States, which were unable to monitor and enforce compliance with the many environmental regulations, were willing to accept an approach of compliance with an EMS.[65] Industry believed that having a common international EMS standard could justify such an approach to legislation, which would bring "regulatory relief" to companies.[66]

Around the turn of the century, ISO reoriented the strategic goals behind its standard-setting toward addressing the complex challenges posed by globalization and sustainable development.[67] ISO viewed global relevance for its voluntary standards as tools in supporting societal actors in meeting these challenges.[68] ISO 14000 was one of the first standards that marked ISO's entry into the public policy arena. ISO further broadened the scope of its work from 2000 onwards, entering many other new areas of standard-setting, including "tourism, water distribution and sewage, financial services, IT services or health services."[69] This expansion in ISO's work program was a response "to current and new stakeholder needs" and was seen as essential for ISO "to maintain itself as a highly relevant international standards developer."[70] Further institutional changes followed this shift in support of the

[62] V. Haufler, Negotiating International Standards for Environmental Management System: The ISO 14000 Standards (1999), www.researchgate.net/publication/237466208_Negotiating_International_Standards_for_Environmental_Management_Systems_The_ISO_14000_Standards.

[63] Interviewee.

[64] Haufler, *supra* note 62.

[65] Murphy and Yates, *supra* note 16, at 78.

[66] J. Clapp, The Privatization of Global Environmental Governance (1998) 4 *Global Governance*, 304, www-jstor-org.tilburguniversity.idm.oclc.org/stable/27800201?seq=1#metadata_info_tab_contents.

[67] ISO Strategic Plan 2005–2010.

[68] ISO, Annual Report: Platform for Performance (2014), www.iso.org/files/live/sites/isoorg/files/about%20ISO/annual_reports/en/annual_report_2004.pdf.

[69] Bryden, *supra* note 2.

[70] ISO, Additional Guidance from the TMB on Stakeholder Engagement (2008), https://studylib.net/doc/18738260/additional-guidance-from-the-tmb-on-stakeholder-engagement.

delivery of these standards and to ensure the protection of public interests within the ISO system.[71]

With ISO's decision to develop standards in support of sustainable development, whose content is of public interest, also came changing expectations about the ISO system and quests to legitimize its authority by ensuring the involvement of a broader group of stakeholders in its standard development procedures. This trend already took off with ISO's development of the ISO 14000 standards series.[72] The potential policy implications of ISO 14001, addressing environmental aspects of organizations' activities, raised its importance to NGOs. ISO was criticized for the underrepresentation of environmental NGOs in the TC 207 process, especially in the early stages.[73] This resulted in varying and increasing efforts by NSBs to engage environmental NGOs at the national level.[74] ISO approved "ISO Long-Range Strategies 1999-2001," expressing its commitment to "balanced representation," including to ensuring "more effective representation of consumers and of other social forces', and its concern about the 'transparency of [ISO] activities."[75]

ISO experimented with a novel construct and an approach to direct stakeholder involvement in its technical work at the ISO level in its development of ISO 26000.[76] This out of the box project demonstrated ISO's ability to interpret and apply its ISO/IEC Directives and rules for standard development flexibly; ISO 26000 was developed within a Working Group (not a technical committee), through an intense multi-stakeholder process that engaged subject matter experts from six

[71] ISO's formal status under Swiss law changed to "quasi-governmental international organization" in 2006, defined as "in-between an intergovernmental organization and a classic NGO." Also see OECD/ISO, *supra* note 3, at 67. The adoption of the ISO code of ethics can be viewed as a response to ISO's transition into this domain of sustainable development. See Section 13.4.3.

[72] Discussion Paper ISO/TC 2017 NGO Contact Group, Ecologia, June 17, 2000, www.ecologia.org/ems/iso14000/ngoinvolve/st_n418.html

[73] Clapp, *supra* note 66.

[74] For instance, in 1994, the United States invited NGOs to participate in the US Technical Advisory Group (TAG), which subsequently cooperated with the NGO network and the NGO Initiative Working Group to enhance their capacity and representation in TC 207 meetings. Ibid., at 9

[75] ISO, ISO's Long-Range Strategies 1999–2001 – Raising Standards of the World, www.jtc1sc34.org/repository/0032T.pdf.

[76] Wood, *supra* note 44, at 215. ISO's involvement in this field of social responsibility was questioned from the start. ISO created a multi-stakeholder Strategic Advisory Group (SAG) to decide whether ISO should proceed with an ISO initiative on CSR, and if so, the type of deliverable ISO should develop. This SAG recommended the development of a non-certifiable "guidance standard" type deliverable and for ISO to not get involved in SR standardization unless it could ensure the meaningful participation of the full range of interested parties. See ISO, ISO Strategic Advisory Group on Social Responsibility, Recommendations to the ISO Technical Management Board, at 1, ISO/TMB AG CSR N32, (April 30, 2004), http://isotc.iso.org/livelink/livelink/fetch/-8929321/8929339/8929348/3935837/3974906/ISOSRAdvisoryGroup_-_Recommendations%20to%20the%20ISO%20TechnicalManagementBoard.pdf?nodeid=4274012&vernum=-2.

stakeholder groups, acting in their own capacity (not as representatives of their NSBs or governments). ISO also signed Memoranda of Understanding with the ILO, GRI, and SAI to coordinate its work with these organizations and to facilitate their participation and expert input into the process.[77] ISO opening up its standard-setting process to include a broader range of stakeholders can be viewed as a resilience strategy. ISO has not applied a similar process and multi-stakeholder approach in its standard-setting work since. This was despite NGOs considering this approach a "major improvement"[78] and calling for ISO to broaden it to cover all ISO TC work in similar areas of fundamental interest.[79]

In 2008, that is, before the publication of ISO 26000 in November 2010, the TMB decided to form a mechanism in the form of a Process Evaluation Group (PEG) to investigate the responsiveness of ISO's standard development processes to changing dynamics. The experience of ISO 26000 informed this investigation.[80] The PEG's investigations resulted in the publication of two ISO brochures: Guidance for Liaisons[81] and Guidance for NSBs.[82] These brochures confirm and uphold the commitment of the ISO system "to participation via national standards bodies, as well as through the consideration of the input received from liaison organizations." ISO sought to "safeguard the outcomes of the ISO system and to promote the existing value, strength and authority of International Standards and the processes by which they are produced." ISO also alleged that "the existing ISO model works well, is well defined and is accepted by stakeholders."

ISO's approach to stakeholder involvement in its standard-setting work has thus remained unchanged in essence; ISO ensures stakeholder representation via two streams, that is, through NSBs and organizations in liaison with ISO committees.[83] "ISO/IEC Directives are reviewed each year and small incremental changes have been made to the standard-setting process to improve stakeholder engagement and

77 ISO's efforts to meet certain standards of transparency and inclusiveness in this process also enhanced ISO's competitive position vis-à-vis both public and private standard developers in the field of social responsibility. Ruwet, *supra* note 1.

78 ANEC, ECOS, Pacific Institute, ISO TC 207 "Environmental Management" Gives NGOs the Cold Shoulder: NGO Proposals for Improved Procedures Slammed Down after Five Years of Negotiations, www.ecostandard.org/wp-content/uploads/anec_ecos_pacific_institute_communique_on_iso_tc_207.pdf.

79 ISO did draw lessons from this experience, however. According to an interviewee, "ISO 26000 has resulted in a much more careful set up of different stakeholders, looking at the balance between stakeholders, also looking at developed/developing countries, and gender issues." Also see OECD/ISO, *supra* note 3, at 47.

80 ISO acknowledged that it had not succeeded in ensuring a "full and equitable balance" of stakeholder participation in the development process of ISO 26 000. See, ISO 26000: 2010 V.

81 ISO, Guidance for ISO Liaison Organizations: Engaging Stakeholders and Building Consensus (2010), www.iso.org/iso/guidance_liaison-organizations.pdf.

82 ISO, Guidance for ISO National Standards Bodies, Engaging Stakeholders and Building Consensus (2019), www.iso.org/files/live/sites/isoorg/files/store/en/PUB100269.pdf.

83 Individual liaisons between NGOs and committees are approved on a case-by-case basis, and certain qualification criteria apply. See ISO/IEC Directive part 1, Clause 1.17.

to ensure that the process keeps meeting the needs of those involved."[84] ISO's standard development relies on the input from these stakeholders that view ISO as carriers through which they can influence how industry operates and bring in their own competence and experience. The involvement of diverse stakeholder interests also creates conditions of legitimacy,[85] enables ISO to foster acceptance, and facilitates the widespread diffusion of its standards and deliverables.

13.4.2 *Coordination of Activities through Partnerships*

ISO has demonstrated an ability to establish connections and coordinate its work with other organizations in support of the realization of its goals. ISO's recognition of having consultative status in the UN, and its cultivation of this recognition since the 1970s, is said to have been key to ISO's strong position in international standardization. "As early as the 1970s, the ISO Council decided 'that ISO should continue to overcome problems of conflict of competence with other international organizations through direct contacts with the latter.'"[86] Over time, ISO has sought to partner as much as possible, which is reflected by the different types of relationships ISO has entered into with other organizations.[87] ISO's involvement in the SDGs resulted in ISO renewing existing and creating new partnerships, including with the UN.[88]

An illustrative example of a crisis moment that ISO managed through cooperation was the EU's adoption of a "new approach" to EU legislation in 1985.[89] This new approach meant that EU Directives would set essential requirements that products and services placed on the community market must meet and rely on voluntary, consensus-based European standards to provide the technical specifications to implement and verify conformity with these requirements. Products manufactured in compliance with these standards are presumed to be in conformity with essential requirements of EU legislation. European standards are defined as technical specifications adopted by a European Standards Organization (ESOs).[90] This approach recognized the role of European standardization in supporting public policy objectives and, in particular, the creation of the Single European Market. It

84 Interviewee.

85 See J. Wouters, "Corporations and the Making of Public Standards in International Law: The Case of China in the ITU" in this volume (Chapter 3).

86 OECD/ISO, *supra* note 3.

87 See ISO, Structure and Governance, www.iso.org/structure.html.

88 See ISO, Our Common Roadmap, www.iso.org/news/ref2325.html.

89 The New Approach was updated and refined in the "New Legislative Framework" from 2008.

90 European Committee for Standardization (CEN), European Committee for Electrotechnical Standardization (CENELEC), European Telecommunication Standards Institute (ETSI). European Commission, Directorate-General for Enterprise (Brussels), *Guide to the Implementation of Directives Based on the New Approach and the Global Approach*(2000), at 27.

called for "a considerable expansion of European standardization activities, diverting a significant amount of interest and resources away from international standardization work."[91] This posed challenges to ISO in that the key European players in ISO at that time (Germany, France, the United Kingdom, and Italy) withdrew their resources and focused on European standardization instead. This gave rise to the question of how ISO could continue to be relevant while at the same time being so dependent on key standard-setting bodies from Europe.[92]

ISO responded by signing the Vienna Agreement with the European Committee for Standardization (CEN), its European equivalent, which was formally approved in 1991 (and revised in 2001) and issuing common guidelines for its implementation.[93] The Vienna Agreement governs technical cooperation between ISO and CEN, with the aim to avoid duplication and increase the efficiency of standardization at the international and European level. It recognizes the primacy of international standards and offers the opportunity for a joint development of standards, the exchange of information and mutual representation at meetings, and the recognition of the same standard as an ISO and European standard. Either CEN or ISO can take the lead in developing a standard, which will then be presented for approval by both organizations. A Joint ISO-CEN Coordinating Group of the Technical Boards consisting of representatives of both organizations was created to monitor application of the Agreement and to advise the boards of both ISO and CEN on issues relating to the agreement.[94]

13.4.3 *Alignment of Principles with Strategic Goals*

ISO has demonstrated an ability to align its principles of governance[95] with the strategic goals and priorities of the organization, which ISO has adjusted over the

[91] These ESOs could develop and adopt European standards, referred to as "harmonized standards," at the request of the European Commission. EU members must transpose the European standard into a national law and withdraw conflicting national standards. ISO, International Standards and "Private Standards" (2010), at 3, https://web.archive.org/web/20121101111235if_/http://www.iso.org/iso/private_standards.pdf.

[92] Interviewee.

[93] These guidelines were revised in 1996 and 1998 to incorporate improvements.

[94] In a parallel development, CENELEC signed an agreement with the IEC, the Dresden Agreement (revised by the Frankfurt Agreement in 2016), which establishes that new electrical standards projects should be planned jointly and conducted by the IEC at the international level, if possible, and the parallel voting on international standards in order to achieve one standard that is valid for Europe and internationally.

[95] ISO embodies certain principles of governance (inter alia, to ensure a degree of openness and transparency in the ISO system) ISO, Directives and Policies, www.iso.org/directives-andpolicies.html.

years in response to changes in its external environment.[96,97] This alignment has affected the evolution and resilience of the organisation, as the following crisis moment illuminates.

ISO's adoption of the TBT Agreement in 1994 created both risks and opportunities for ISO to grow in strength and influence. More specifically, it created opportunities for ISO to demonstrate its relevance (and legitimacy) in contributing to freer trade by reducing barriers to trade and realizing the goals of the WTO. The TBT Agreement did not expressly recognize ISO, or any other standard-setting organization, as a developer of "relevant international standards" for the purpose of Article 2(4). Amidst debate about whose standards could be utilized for this purpose, ISO was among the organizations most likely to qualify.[98] ISO had risen to authority and acquired credibility and a dominant position in standardization at the time of the TBT Agreement's adoption.[99] Also, there was synergy between ISO's governance model and the terms in the TBT Agreement, which had adopted these terms from ISO/IEC Guide 2: 1991,[100] with some modification (Annex 1).[101] Moreover, the purpose of ISO standards to facilitate international trade aligns with that of the TBT Agreement.[102]

The adoption of the TBT Agreement created incentives on the part of ISO to respond and adapt to ensure its continued relevance and to build and maintain its legitimacy within the WTO regime.[103] This meant meeting the evolving requirements of the TBT Agreement, as interpreted by the WTO Appellate Body. ISO confirming adherence of its standard development process with the six WTO principles, shortly after the TBT Committee's adoption of these principles in 2002,

96 ISO adopts strategic goals and priorities in order to realize its mission and vision. While ISO's mission remains the same at its core, that is, to develop standards in support of global trade, it has expanded in scope over the years. According to ISO's strategy for 2030, ISO develops standards to "drive inclusive and equitable economic growth, advance innovation and promote health and safety to achieve a sustainable future." ISO, Strategy 2030, www.iso.org/publication/PUB100364.html.

97 ISO, Drivers of Change, www.iso.org/strategy2030/drivers-of-change.html.

98 See Farquhar, *supra* note 52, at 5-7.

99 Wood, *supra* note 44. F. Fontanelli, ISO and CODEX Standards and International Trade Law: What Gets Said Is Not What's Heard (2011) 60:4 *The International and Comparative Law Quarterly* 908.

100 The TBT Agreement indicates that the terms used in its texts have the same meaning as the terms given in ISO/IEC Guide 2: 1991. This Guide 2 was replaced by a new version in 1996 and revised and updated once more in 2004.

101 The TBT Agreement does not apply to services, and it covers documents that are not based on a consensus, unlike is the case for ISO/IEC Guide 2: 1991. Moreover, the TBT Agreement defines standards as voluntary and technical regulations as mandatory documents. TBT Agreement, Annex 1.2, explanatory note.

102 Fontanelli, *supra* note 100, 909.

103 For ISO, as a private standard-setting organization, building and maintaining its legitimacy is important in the pursuit of its goals. See Section 9.2 in this volume. Also see P. Delimatsis, Global Standard-Setting 2.0: How the WTO Spotlights ISO and Impacts the Transnational Standard-Setting Process (2018) 28:2 *Duke Journal of Comparative and International Law* 273.

was an important response. ISO also claimed that ISO and its NSB members adhered to the disciplines of the TBT Standards Code.[104] ISO has taken various reform initiatives in response to developments in the WTO, which have enabled the further recognition and implementation of the WTO principles in its governance structure and technical standard-setting work, with a special focus on enhancing the effective participation by developing countries and engaging a broad range of stakeholder interests.[105]

ISO further aligning its governance principles with the WTO principles and disciplines, for the purpose of facilitating international trade, can be interpreted as a resilience strategy.[106] For instance, in 2003, ISO approved a definition of global relevance and a set of principles and implementing guidance to ensure the global relevance of its technical work and publications.[107] This was in response to the TBT Committee's decision that an international standard should meet a set of seven criteria in order to meet the WTO principle of "relevance."

ISO's alignment of its own principles of governance with the WTO principles has affected stakeholder perceptions of ISO and has led to increased social sensitivity and scrutiny of ISO's performance against these principles. As illustrated above, ISO standards are influential in shaping economic activity and take on de facto or de jure binding effects when referenced, and rendered mandatory, under national regulation and international regulation.[108] This increasing influence of ISO standards, also in relation to the state, has raised concerns among NGOs. According to an interviewee, critical studies by NGOs and academics scrutinizing ISO procedures against its standards[109] have caused ISO to reflect and "to become more principle oriented,

[104] Since this code was modeled after ISO/IEC Guide 59:1994 (revised in 2019) on recommended practices for standardization by national bodies, ISO's adherence to this code did not come as a surprise. See TBT Committee, Factual Comparison between the Annex 3 of the WTO/TBT Agreement – Code of Good Practice for the Preparation, Adoption and Application of Standards and the ISO.IEC Guide 59 – Code of Good Practice for Standardization, G/TBT/W/132, 29 March 2000, https://docs.wto.org/dol2fe/Pages/SS/directdoc.aspx?filename=Q:/G/TBT/W132.pdf&Open=True.

[105] Farquhar, *supra* note 52. For a detailed analyses of ISO's responses to the TBT Agreement, see P. Delimatsis and S. Bijlmakers, How Standard Setting Bodies Have Grown Resilient by Overcoming Adversity in Times of Crisis: A Theoretical Perspective (on file with the author).

[106] ISO Council Resolution 9/2001. Also see ISO, Foreword – Supplementary Information, www.iso.org/foreword-supplementary-information.html.

[107] ISO defines global relevance as the "required characteristic of an International Standard that it can be used/implemented as broadly as possible by affected industries and other stakeholders in markets around the world." ISO/IEC Directives, Part 1, Consolidated ISO Supplement – Procedures Specific to ISO (Eleventh edition, 2020) Annex SM (normative) Global relevance of ISO technical work and publications. SM.3 Principles, www.iso.org/sites/directives/current/consolidated/index.xhtml#_idTextAnchor004. Also see ISO, ISO/TMB Implementation Guidance Global Relevance of ISO Technical Work and Publications (2004), www.iso.org/files/live/sites/isoorg/files/developing_standards/docs/en/iso_tmb_implementation_guidance_global_relevance.pdf.

[108] ISO/IEC, *supra* note 5.

[109] OECD/ISO, *supra* note 3, at 1. Delimatsis, *supra* note 103.

and to implement these principles in practice to the extent they can or are willing."[110] Illustrative is ISO's adoption of the ISO code of ethics in 2004. This code expresses the commitment of ISO members and each of ISO's organizational entities to ensuring fair and responsive application of a set of principles ("due process, transparency, openness, impartiality and voluntary nature of standardization"), which mirror the WTO principles.[111]

ISO has relied on adherence to the WTO principles to instil confidence by public regulators that when using ISO International Standards in support of their policy decisions and actions, [112] they are not creating unnecessary barriers to trade.[113] ISO emphasizes in its communication to public regulators that they can be confident they meet their obligations under the TBT Agreement when using ISO standards as a basis for their technical regulation and that the standards they use are globally relevant.[114] The reliance by public regulators on ISO standards to avoid technical barriers to trade has further increased the significance of ISO's work.[115]

Adherence to the WTO principles has enabled ISO to distinguish itself from other standard-setting organizations. It has aided ISO to consolidate its position as a dominant global standard-setter in areas of standardization in which it is the sole standardization body and to expand its influence in specific domains in which more organizations develop substitutive standards and are thus more competitive, such as sustainability standards. In 2014, ISO issued a brochure in which it differentiates its ISO International Standards from "private international standards" developed by other standard-setters.[116] ISO relies on the argument that ISO standards and those of its members are developed through processes that use the WTO principles and disciplines and therefore are "superior" to "private" standards by other organizations that are not developed according to these principles.[117]

[110] Interviewee.

[111] ISO, ISO Code of Ethics, www.iso.org/publication/PUB100011.html.

[112] The ISO brochure, Using and Referencing IOS and IEC Standards to Support Public Policy, is an important tool aiding this effort. The brochure explains the advantages and benefits of using ISO standards, providing various reasons for why ISO believes that ISO standards have earned the public policy maker's trust and reliance. ISO/IEC, *supra* note 5. Also see, OECD/ISO, *supra* note 3, at 15–16.

[113] Also see, ISO/IEC Directives, Part 1, Consolidated ISO Supplement – Procedures Specific to ISO (Eleventh edition, 2020) Annex SO (normative) Principles for developing ISO and IEC Standards related to or supporting public policy initiatives. SO.3 Implementation, www.iso.org/sites/directives/current/consolidated/index.xhtml#_idTextAnchor004

[114] ISO/IEC, *supra* note 5, at 5.

[115] See Farquhar, *supra* note 52, at 3.

[116] According to Stepan Wood, the interactions between ISO and the ISEAL alliance are illustrative of how "organizations in regulatory regimes respond to multiple legitimacy claims and how they seek to build legitimacy and 'regulatory share' in complex and dynamic situations." Wood, *supra* note 44, at 199.

[117] ISO, *supra* note 92.

13.4.4 *Institutional Setup, Complexity, and Governance Principles*

ISO's institutional structure was established at its creation, and while it retains its core, it has grown more complex.[118] ISO has adapted its statutes in response to (geopolitical) changes and challenges in its environment.[119] ISO created policy committees to provide forums to include the perspectives of developing countries (DEVCO) and consumers (COPOLCO) into ISO's decision-making. ISO created CASCO to provide guidance on conformity assessment.[120] In addition, ISO created a President's Committee to advise the Council on matters decided by the Council, four Council standing committees, and Advisory Groups to advise ISO on matters relating to commercial policy and information technology. The mechanisms ISO built into the system in order to give application to its governance principles further adds to its complexity. ISO's institutional structure and its complexity is an important feature that ISO can harness in its crisis responses.[121]

ISO has never revisited the governance model that was chosen for the organization at its creation. ISO has continued to adhere to certain core governance principles founding its institution. Adherence to these governance principles is meant to ensure, inter alia, neutrality in ISO's institutional setting, thereby protecting against the risk of abuse of dominant positions.[122] More specifically, ISO's institutional structure, and in particular ISO's adherence to the national delegation principle and its one-country-one-vote modality, serves to protect against the risk of undue influence of individual NSBs within the organization and capture by certain country interests. Moreover, the requirement that ISO standards reflect a consensus between all parties affected by the standard, and that the standard development process seeks to balance the interests of these parties, serves to prevent a single interest from dominating the standardization process. It follows from ISO's definition of a consensus that its members can reach an agreement on standards despite opposition by a particular interest (e.g., dominant firms, leading states, or states acting together, like those belonging to the EU).[123] ISO's continued adherence to its

[118] ISO, About Us: Structure and Governance, www.iso.org/structure.html.

[119] Also see, OECD/ISO, *supra* note 3, at 21.

[120] See Caltronix, The History of ANAB (ANSI-ASQ National Accreditation Board), www.caltronixinc.com/article.cfm?ArticleNumber=3.

[121] For instance, DEVCO played an important role in ISO's navigation through the recent COVID-19 pandemic as it provided solutions to develop standards in support of a COVID-19 response and recovery plan, thereby strengthening ISO's position in times of change, turning crisis into an opportunity. ISO notes how "the progress made in strengthening DEVCO's policy development role is key to accelerating that change and enhancing developing country participation in ISO governance and technical work." ISO, *supra* note 8.

[122] See J. Wouters, "Corporations and the Making of Public Standards in International Law: The Case of China in the ITU" in this volume (Chapter 3).

[123] ISO defines a consensus as a "general agreement, characterized by the absence of *sustained opposition* to *substantial issues* by *any important part of the concerned interests* and by a process that involves seeking to take into account the views of all parties concerned and to recognize

governance model and its underlying principles is an important strength, and ISO derives legitimacy from it.[124]

Whether ISO achieves neutrality in its decision-making and standard-setting work in practice is subject of discussion. ISO was and still is perceived as a business-driven organization.[125] The degree of influence of NSBs in standard development varies depending on their membership rights, roles, capabilities, and preferences. The barriers facing developing countries to effective representation and participation in ISO's technical standard work, and to influencing the content of ISO standards, are well documented.[126] NGOs have criticized how decision-making in ISO is unbalanced in practice and dominated by private industry interests (especially in industrialized countries). As illustrated above in connection to the development of ISO 14000 and ISO 26000, ISO has adapted to internal dynamics and pressures, inter alia, by creating multi-stakeholder committees to advise on ISO's involvement in new areas of standard-setting, by interpreting ISO standard-setting rules flexibly and investing resources to create opportunities for more balanced stakeholder representation and participation. Nonetheless, issues of (un)equal access and influence remain and result in NGOs and other stakeholders to deny ISO legitimacy.[127]

ISO's ability to withstand pressure from within its membership to make changes to its institutional setup and governance principles attests to its resilience. An illustrative example is how ISO has resisted challenges by the United States, an influential member with a long tradition in standardization, at several occasions, in what can be interpreted as attempts by the United States to exert a dominant

any conflicting arguments." See ISO/IEC Directives (ISO/IEC Dir 1), Part, Edition 10.0, 2013-10, clause 2.5.6.

ISO's definition of "sustained opposition" entails views "maintained by *an important part of the concerned interest* and which are incompatible with the committee consensus." See ISO/IEC Directives, Part 1, Consolidated ISO Supplement – Procedures Specific to ISO, 4th ed., 2013, clause 2.5.6.

[124] Yates and Murphy, *supra* note 55, at 299.

[125] M. Morikawa and J. Morrison, Who Develops ISO Standards? A Survey of Participation in ISO's International Standards Development Process, Pacific Institute (2004), https://pacinst.org/wp-content/uploads/2013/02/iso_participation_study2.pdf.

[126] For instance, developing countries could not effectively participate in the TC 207 committee process "due to their limited membership role, their small delegate representations at negotiation meetings, and their failure to provide secretariat support to the ISO." Also the lack of access to information on the ISO 14000 series was identified as a problem especially for these stakeholders. "Developing countries were neither adequately represented in the negotiations of the ISO 14000 series, nor were they key players in the administrative bodies of ISO that ultimately decided what standards to finalize and promulgate. The negotiation process was dominated by countries of the developed world, principally the United States. U.S. revisions to the standards diluted any impact that the standards could have on environmental protection." A. Mikulich, ISO 14000–14001, The Developing World's Perspective (2003) 17:1 *Tulane Environmental Law Journal* 120.

[127] ISO's competence is taken for granted by other stakeholders, which confer (cognitive) legitimacy onto the organization despite its procedural shortcomings. According to Wood, this is because of ISO's "pervasiveness and accumulated social capital." Wood, *supra* note 44, at 228.

influence within ISO.[128] For instance, the United States has challenged the representation of EU countries within ISO. A concern by the United States has been that the EU countries benefit from the one-country-one-vote modality, and that the EU has gained economic advantage by dominating the ISO process. According to an interviewee, after the creation of the EU internal market in 1993, the EU was perceived as an economic block. Since the EU had been formed as such, with its ESOs – CEN was viewed as a counterpart of ISO in terms of scope – the United States argued that the EU should be represented as such, that is, through CEN, and not the individual member countries. This attempt failed "because of the realization that the individual EU members were an asset for the organization." The one-country-one-vote modality and the representation of EU countries within ISO remain unchanged.

It seems that giving into these pressures and departing from its governance model can pose a risk (of capture) to the organization and have implications for ISO's attractiveness as a forum for standard development, especially in the view of NSBs and governments.[129]

13.4.5 *Business Model*

Another key property that aids ISO in its navigation through crisis episodes is its business model, which ensures that the ISO system can access and leverage resources to achieve its objectives and recover its costs. ISO International Standards are not available for free in the public domain and ISO asserts and maintains copyright in International Standards.[130] It follows from ISO's business model that the activities of the ISO secretariat are funded through the membership fees paid by NSBs ("which give them the right to participate in the International Standardization process, to use, nationally adopt and sell the International Standards produced") and the sale of International Standards. ISO members bear the costs of running the secretariats of the technical committees. The expenses of experts working on the technical committees are borne by their employers or themselves. ISO views the financing of its system through the sale of its standards as fair: "the user who wants to benefit from a standard pays to use it." ISO also claims to be

[128] According to an interviewee, the United States tabled a proposal to change the official languages of the organization – English, French, and Russian. The proposal was to adopt English as a single official language or to opt for English, Spanish, and Chinese as the official languages for ISO. This proposal received pushback from the French-speaking countries and was rejected eventually. Another United States proposal to change the headquarters of the organization suffered a similar faith. ISO's language policy has not been revisited; ISO's official languages remain English, French, and Russian.

[129] See O. Kanevskaia and J. Baron, "Global Rivalry over Leadership in ICT Standardization: SDO Governance amid Changing Patterns of Participation" in this volume (Chapter 14).

[130] ISO/IEC, *supra* note 5.

"constantly looking for new ways to improve access to standards, while ensuring that the costs of developing them can be recovered."[131]

An event within ISO's history that implicated ISO's business model and strengthened its resources (and its authority) was the adoption of ISO 9001. The publication of ISO 9001, and especially the opportunities that the extra source of revenues from the sale of this standard created, resulted in ISO reflecting on how to further finance standardization and expand the scope of the organization. ISO came to rely more on the sale of standards and less on membership fees to generate an income for the organization. The sale of this standard also supported further evolutions within both ISO and its NSB members. According to an interviewee, the publication of the ISO 9000 series resulted in NSBs expanding their activities "both in terms of standards development, because this was bringing additional resources to support finance, and then expand also the scope of the activities, going into at some point training activities, training, consulting services. Some became actually fully independent organizations, which was quite an interesting evolution."[132]

ISO's model of financing has created both challenges and opportunities for ISO. According to ISO, it keeps participation costs down and allows for the broadest possible stakeholder participation. As is well known, however, developing countries have fewer resources and technical capabilities than developed countries to exert influence, especially at the technical standard-setting level. In fact, developed countries remain most active in leading technical committees and subcommittees in practice. Chairpersons and secretaries may be required to act in a "purely international capacity," and experts participating in standard-setting, at least at working group level, in a personal capacity.[133] However, in practice, these individuals have had difficulty making decisions independently from the interests of their employer (who funds their participation in the process) or the NSB (who appoints them).[134] ISO's claim that, because of its financing model, its International Standards are developed in a neutral environment without undue influence from individual sponsors[135] is debatable.

According to an interviewee, the revenues obtained from the sale of standards enables ISO to develop standards, to better promote ISO's work, and have a broader scope. ISO's pricing policy has had implications for the relevance of its standards

[131] Ibid., at 34–35.

[132] Interviewee. Also see, Yates and Murphy, *supra* note 55, at 298–300.

[133] ISO Directive Part 1, clause 1.12.1.

[134] E. Shamir-Borer, *The Evolution of Administrative Law-Type Principles, Mechanisms and Practices in the International Organization for Standardization (ISO)*, at 66–67, www.iilj.org/wp-content/uploads/2016/11/Shamir-Borer-The-Evolution-of-Administrative-Law-Type-Principles-Mechanisms-and-Practices-in-the-International-Organization-for-Standardization.pdf.

[135] ISO/IEC, *supra* note 5, at 34.

(and its claim for authority), especially in the ICT domain.[136] Upon its entry into the domain of sustainability, ISO has been challenged by criticism that charging money for ISO standards whose content is of public interest is inappropriate and creates barriers to acquisition, and pressure to make them available in the public domain, free of charge.[137] ISO's pricing policy can be a particular concern to States that reference International Standards in their legislation. ISO's adjustments to its pricing policy in relation to certain standards in specific contexts, to the extent needed to ensure stakeholder support and realize its mission, demonstrate its flexibility. More generally, however, ISO has demonstrated resistance to pressure to adjust its financing model.[138] ISO's responses and ability to retain its business model despite these pressures attests to its resilience.

13.5 CONCLUSION

This chapter examined how ISO has evolved and grown more resilient, and influential, over the course of its seventy-five-year existence, in relation to crisis. An assumption is that ISO's evolution and resilience can be explained in relation to the continuously evolving environment in which it operates. It finds that the ISO system is flexible and adaptable to account for changes and to meet related challenges within its environment, in order to ensure its continued relevance. This chapter focused on ISO's responses and adaptation during crisis moments when its resilience was put to the test. It finds that ISO has experienced multiple and different types of crisis events; however, developments have never cumulated to a point where ISO was subject to an (institutional) crisis of such problematic scale that its continued existence was truly in jeopardy.

The chapter provides empirical evidence for the theoretical proposition that ISO's core standard-setting activities and its flexibility are key dynamic properties that render ISO stronger in the face of crisis. ISO has demonstrated a capacity to expand quickly to include new members from across the world, and in doing so, also the potential global reach and use of its standards. It has also demonstrated an ability to identify and enter into new areas of standardization and to rapidly promulgate and

[136] Why Should ISO Make All Standards Publicly Available, see https://docs.google.com/document/d/12Gmy2s4Nmkw6VDv2B6b5K1DLYhPrTUqSntrlmYzJpNw/edit#.

[137] For instance, discussion about ISO's pricing policy arose in the context of ISO 26000. Some argued that charging for ISO 26000 is ill-suited because it uses and copyrights the content of authoritative intergovernmental documents that are publicly available. See G. Guertler, Best Prices for ISO 26000, ISO 26000, An Estimation (December 2011), www.26k-estimation.com/html/best_prices_for_iso_26000.html.

[138] While the ISO Council agreed to make ISO/DIS 26000 freely available on the ISO website, for ISO 26000 it decided that "the current pricing policy should be applied with no deviation." ISO, ISO Council Resolution – No Free Availability of ISO 26000, September 25, 2009, ISO/TMB/WG SR, https://isotc.iso.org/livelink/livelink/fetch/-8929321/8929339/8929348/3935837/3974906/4034859/8680335/2009-09-25_Cover_letter%2C_ISO_Council_Resolution_-_No_free_availability_of_ISO_26000.pdf?nodeid=8419078&vernum=-2.

disseminate voluntary standards while ensuring their underlying potential and quality. ISO's ability to align its principles of governance and the value and impact of its standards with the strategic objectives behind its standard-setting work, and trade facilitation in particular, is an important trait. ISO has proven able to interpret its rules and procedures flexibly to meet changing expectations in stakeholder involvement and to experiment and draw lessons from previous experiences. ISO's institutional structure in conjunction with its complexity, and its continued adherence to the governance principles founding it, confers strength onto ISO. ISO's ability to safeguard these principles, and its continuing adherence to its business model, despite and because of criticism and pressure, attests to its resilience. Most importantly, this study showed how ISO has built these qualities by overcoming adversity during crisis moments, and how these qualities shape ISO as an organization and its resilience today.

Overall, the interviewees point to the aforementioned qualities of ISO as strengths, giving optimism for ISO's future. These qualities render it stronger and more influential today, as it seeks to ensure its continued relevance in contributing to the delivery of the UN 2030 global agenda for sustainable development and meeting the many global challenges that appear in the seventeen SDGs as part of this agenda. The interviewees highlighted opportunities offered by the SDGs to promote ISO's existing portfolio and to expand into new domains of standard development to resolve these global challenges, which facilitates further growth. New challenges abound as ISO might lose in influence to other organizations that, mainly because of their specialized expertise, can act more efficiently and swiftly in identifying and responding to the needs of users in the domain of sustainability standards. In this light, future research could examine how ISO has grown resilient through competition with other actors, claiming authority through its standard-setting activities, and offering the most attractive institutional setting for the development of standards.

14

Global Rivalry over Leadership in ICT Standardization

SDO Governance amid Changing Patterns of Participation

Justus Baron and Olia Kanevskaia

14.1 INTRODUCTION

Recent years have witnessed geopolitical tensions resulting from China's rapid ascension to technological power. The increasing technological influence of Chinese companies is particularly apparent in the development of global technology standards in information and communication technologies (ICT). ICT standards codify specifications for interoperability among various technological components and prescribe methods applied in electronic devises;[1] notable examples include wireless LAN specifications, internet protocols, and cellular networks such 4G/ LTE and, more recently, 5G.

Influence over the development of ICT standards is potentially highly valuable to commercial stakeholders – inclusion into a standard may increase the value of certain patented technologies;[2] and standard specifications may provide certain firms' products with a competitive advantage. Competition for leadership in ICT standards development has thus long been characterized by rivalry between large commercial stakeholders. At the same time, and with the significantly increasing participation of Chinese companies in many standards development organizations (SDO), there is a growing geopolitical dimension to this commercial competition.

Particularly in the United States, the important role of Chinese companies, most notably Huawei, in ICT standards development has fueled a variety of policy initiatives intended to curb the influence of Chinese actors and bolster the position

[1] Based on the definition by M. A. Lemley, Intellectual Property Rights and Standard-Setting Organizations (2002) 90 *California Law Review* 1889, at 1889.

[2] See, among many others, J. Lerner and J. Tirole, Standard-Essential Patents' (2015) 123 *Journal of Political Economy* 547.

of US stakeholders in international standardization. To illustrate, US government officials have testified that the increasing number of SDO leadership positions held by Huawei affiliates may enable the adoption of standards that disadvantage the market position of US companies.[3] The growing representation of Chinese companies in SDOs was also discussed in the proposals for the recent US Innovation and Competition Act.[4] More recently, the National Institute of Standards and Technology (NIST) has been tasked to study and provide recommendations with respect to the effect of China's standardization policies on, and the engagement of Chinese stakeholders in, international SDOs, especially those developing standards for emerging technologies.[5]

These policy initiatives furthermore take place in the context of allegations that Huawei and other Chinese technology companies may present risks to US national security interests. In this light, some Western countries, including the United States, adopted a number of restrictive measures, ranging from the bans on (telecommunications) equipment supplied by Chinese manufacturers and that pose a threat to national security,[6] to Huawei's listing on the US Export Administration Regulation (EAR) entity list, prohibiting it from supplying components for essential communications infrastructure.[7] Also these tensions have not gone unnoticed in SDOs, not least because restrictions on the exchange of technical information with entities on

[3] See, among others, the testimony of Christopher Krebs, Director of Cybersecurity and Infrastructure Security Agency, during the hearing of the Committee on the Judiciary, 5G: National Security Concerns, Intellectual Property Issues, and the Impact on Competition and Innovation (May 14, 2019), www.judiciary.senate.gov/imo/media/doc/Krebs%20Responses%20to%20QFRs.pdf; the statement of Jonathan E. Hillman, Senior Fellow, Simon Chair in Political Economy, and Director, Reconnecting Asia Project, CSIS, before the US-China Economic and Security Review Commission (January 25, 2018), www.uscc.gov/sites/default/files/Jonathan%20Hillman%20Written%20Testimony%203.13.20.pdf, providing examples of International Telecommunications Union (ITU), Food and Agriculture Organization (FAO) and the International Civil Aviation Organization (ICAO).

[4] 117th Congress, United States Innovation and Competition Act of 2021, S.1260 (adopted June 8, 2021).

[5] Study on People's Republic of China (PRC) Policies and Influence in the Development of International Standards for Emerging Technologies, Federal Register, notice of NIST published on November 4, 2021, www.federalregister.gov/documents/2021/11/04/2021-24090/study-on-peoples-republic-of-china-prc-policies-and-influence-in-the-development-of-international.

[6] See H.R. 4747, 115th Congress (2018); Federal Acquisition Regulation; FAR Case 2018-017, Prohibition on Contracting for Certain Telecommunications and Video Surveillance Services or Equipment (August 7, 2019), at 48 C.F.R. pts. 1, 3, 12, 13, 39, and 52 (prohibiting federal agencies to purchase Chinese telecommunications equipment) and, more recently, Federal Communications Commission, Report and Order, Order, and Further Notice of Proposed Rulemaking (November 11, 2022) FCC 22-84, ET Docket No. 21-232.

[7] 85 Fed. Reg. 42665 Federal Acquisition Regulation: Prohibition on Contracting with Entities Using Certain Telecommunications and Video Surveillance Services or Equipment (July 14, 2020), at 48 C.F.R. pts. 1, 3, 12, 13, 39, and 52.

the EAR entity list may preclude Huawei's affiliates from taking part in certain activities of the standardization process.[8]

It has long been recognized that ICT standards can have significant political implications and can be used as tools of national or regional industrial policy.[9] Leadership in the development of international ICT standards may thus provide opportunities for "regulatory export," a strategy of promoting the international diffusion of domestic regulations. It is thus not surprising that policymakers view the possibility of Chinese stakeholders acquiring significant influence over ICT standards development as a particular cause for concern.

In this chapter, we argue that the tensions that result from China's, and in particular, Huawei's increasing representation in standardization processes, as well as the policy reactions that they generated, create "a moment of stress"[10] for the normal functioning of SDOs. In addition to causing frictions in the daily business of SDOs, these dynamics challenge seemingly well-established governance principles of the standardization ecosystem.

Scholarly commentary has highlighted institutional features of SDOs, such as the openness and transparency of technical deliberations, the representation of a wide diversity of interests, and the fact that technical decisions are reached by consensus,[11] which seem to counter the suggestion that certain Chinese stakeholders may exercise undue influence within these SDOs to negatively affect US national security interests. Nevertheless, the recent tensions around increasing Chinese participation in SDOs expose fragilities in the existing norms of SDO governance. All this calls for an empirical analysis of SDOs' governance processes to better assess these organizations' aptitude to adapt to the present situation of institutional crisis.

This chapter aims to advance the understanding of the current power dynamics in SDOs by explaining the rules, processes, and traditions of four global SDOs, namely: the International Telecommunication Union (ITU), 3rd Generation Partnership Project (3GPP), Institute of Electrical and Electronics Engineers (IEEE), and the Internet Engineering Task Force (IETF). The reasons for selecting these SDOs are the following: firstly, they span across the spectrum of SDO governance models, ranging from an intergovernmental agency to an informal

[8] E.g., IEEE, Compliance with US Trade Restrictions Should Have Minimal Impact on IEEE Members Around the World (May 29, 2019), www.ieee.org/about/news/2019/compliance-with-us-trade-restrictions.html?utm_source=twitter&utm_campaign=huawei&utm_medium=social; 3GPP, Statement regarding Engagement with Companies Added to the U.S. Export Administration Regulations (EAR) Entity List in 3GPP activities (June 3, 2019) (both statements have been subsequently revoked or reversed following the adverse reaction of the SDOs membership).

[9] See, e.g., M. Cantero Gamito, Europeanization through Standardization: ICT and Telecommunications (2018) 37 *Yearbook of European Law* 395.

[10] See, generally, P. Delimatsis, "The Resilience of Private Authority in Times of Crisis" in this volume (Chapter 1), defining the events of crisis.

[11] See O. Kanevskaia, *The Law and Practice of Global ICT Standardization* (2023); J. Yates and C. N. Murphy, *Engineering Rules: Global Standard Setting since 1880* (2019).

group of internet experts. Secondly, they have recently sparked off the debates regarding the increasing role of Huawei, and Huawei's affiliates, in their standardization decisions. In particular, our analysis focuses on the rules for leadership appointments and expected conducts of individuals holding critical positions in SDOs. In a broader sense, this chapter contributes to the debate on the neutrality, independence, and trustworthiness of SDOs in the light of the global commercial and geopolitical rivalry in the ICT sector.

14.2 THE RISE OF CHINA AND HUAWEI AS GLOBAL TECHNOLOGY LEADERS

Over the past few years, participation by Chinese individuals and organizations in international ICT standards development has significantly increased.[12] Two factors have contributed to this evolution: first, the fast growth of the Chinese ICT industry and, second, structural and institutional changes in China' national industrial and technology policy,[13] often categorized as an evolving process of "techno-nationalism."[14] Chinese industrial policy had long sought to reduce dependence of China's companies on foreign technologies through the development of indigenous alternatives to Western standards, for example, for 3G (TD-SCDMA) and 4G (TD-LTE) technology.[15,16] Current Chinese standardization policy by contrast incentivizes Chinese stakeholders to participate in the development of international technology

[12] See, e.g., J. L. Contreras, Divergent Patterns of Engagement in Internet Standardization: Japan, Korea and China (2014) 38 *Telecommunications Policy* 914.

[13] See J. Xia, China's Telecommunications Evolution, Institutions, and Policy Issues on the Eve of 5G: A Two-Decade Retrospect and Prospect (2017) 41 *Telecommunications Policy* 931; D. Breznitz and M. Murphree, The Rise of China in Technology Standards: New Norms in Old Institutions (2013), www.uscc.gov/sites/default/files/Research/RiseofChinainTechnologyStandards.pdf, discussing China's rapid industrial development and success in innovation technology.

[14] M. Kim, H. Lee, and J. Kwak, The Changing Patterns of China's International Standardization in ICT under Techno-nationalism: A Reflection through 5G Standardization' (2020) 54 *International Journal of Information Management* 1021. For further explanations of the term "techno-nationalism," see M. Kohno, Ideas and Foreign Policy: The Emergence of Techno-nationalism in US Policies toward Japan (1995) *National Competitiveness in a Global Economy* 199, S. Ostry and R. Nelson, *Techno-nationalism and Techno-globalism: Conflict and Co-operation* (1995).

[15] In particular, when it comes to the supply of technologies that are essential for the implementation of ICT standards for which Chinese firms had to pay royalties; see D. Breznitz and M. Murphree, *Run of the Read Queen; Government, Innovation Globalization and Economic Growth in China* (2011). See also, among others, Kim et al., *supra* note 15; M. Murphree and D. Breznitz, Indigenous Digital Technology Standards for Development: The Case of China (2018) 1 *Journal of International Business Policy* 234; X. Liu and P. Cheng, National Strategy of Indigenous Innovation and its Implication to China (2014) 3 *Asian Journal of Innovation and Policy* 117; D. Ernst, Indigenous Innovation and Globalization: The Challenge for China's Standardization Strategy (2011), www.eastwestcenter.org/sites/default/files/private/ernstindigenousinnovation.pdf.

[16] Liu and Chen, *supra* note 16.

standards:[17] the recent "China Standards 2035" initiative, for instance, encourages Chinese stakeholders to lead the development of global standards for critical telecommunications technologies as well as for emerging technologies, such as artificial intelligence.[18]

It is against this backdrop that the aforementioned claims of China's increasing influence in SDO processes arise. However, for any further discussion regarding the resilience of these processes, it is important to assess these concerns in light of empirical evidence.

14.2.1 *Empirical Evidence on Chinese and Huawei's Participation in SDOs*

Our data suggests that the increasing Chinese participation in international SDOs is reflected in a general increase in the share of Chinese individuals among attendees of international SDOs, such as 3GPP, IEEE-SA 802.11, and IETF.[19] Nevertheless, individuals from Western countries continue to represent a significant majority of the attendees in each of these SDOs (Figure 14.1).

Earlier studies demonstrated that increasing Chinese participation in SDOs has translated into an increasing share of Chinese stakeholders in SDO leadership positions, most notably in the intergovernmental ITU,[20] where it has also introduced a large number of standardization proposals.[21] In the past decade, the number of Chinese stakeholders holding secretariat positions in the International Organization for Standardization (ISO) and the International Electrotechnical Commission (IEC) technical committees has increased by nearly 70 percent.[22] However, the recent number of leadership positions held by Chinese stakeholders in the technical bodies of ISO and IEC seems not have increased dramatically or even

[17] Kim et al., *supra* note 15, at 4–5.

[18] See the NIST notice, *supra* note 5

[19] For methodology and detailed explanation of the empirical findings, see J. Baron and O. Kanevskaia , Global Competition for Leadership Positions in Standards Development Organizations, https://papers.ssrn.com/sol3/papers.cfm?abstract_id=3818143; and J. Baron, Participation in the Standards Organizations Developing the Internet of Things: Recent Trends and Implications, in *Shaping the Future through Standardization* (K. Jakobs ed., 2019) 117–147.

[20] M. Cantero Gamito, From Private Regulation to Power Politics: the Rise of China in AI Private Governance through Standardisation, https://papers.ssrn.com/sol3/papers.cfm?abstract_id=3794761.

[21] See J. Wouters, "Corporations and the Making of Public Standards in International Law: The Case of China in the ITU" in this volume (Chapter 3).

[22] ANSI, Comments on the Request for Information on the Study on People's Republic of China (PRC) Policies and influence in the Development of International Standards for Emerging Technologies (December 6, 2021), at 3, citing the report by the US-China Business Council 'China in International Standard Setting' (February 2020), www.uschina.org/sites/default/files/china_in_international_standards_setting.pdf.

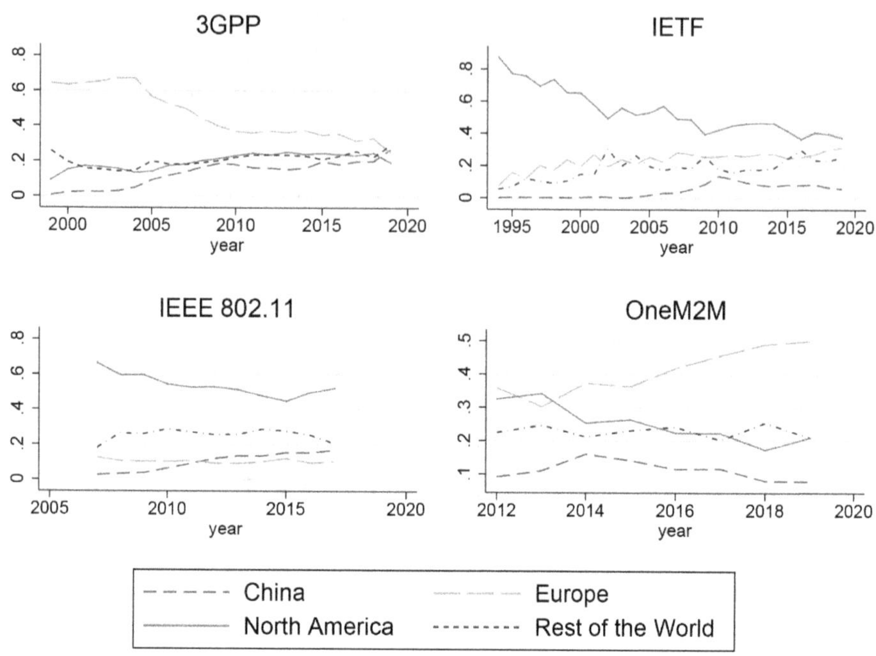

FIGURE 14.1. Trends in SDO meeting attendance

declined, despite the fact that China has undertaken new chair positions and secretariats in these SDOs.[23]

A similar observation can be made from our data: at 3GPP, IETF, and IEEE 802.11, the share of Chinese individuals among SDO working group chairs significantly trails the share of Chinese among attendees, demonstrating no disproportionate representation of Chinese individuals in the leadership of these three SDOs (Figure 14.2).

One must note, however, that most policy discussions focus specifically on Huawei. In this regard, our empirical evidence suggests that while individuals from Europe and North America are affiliated with many different organizations, the affiliations of SDO participants from China are significantly more concentrated, with Huawei holding a disproportionate share. As a consequence, Huawei was, in the most recent years, the single affiliation with the largest number of attendees in each of these SDOs. Similar to other large companies, Huawei affiliates are generally over-represented in working group chair positions (Figure 14.3).

Furthermore, in different SDOs, Huawei-affiliated individuals have been appointed to particularly influential roles. In ITU, this included the chair of important committees, such as ITU-T SG16 on AI-enabled multimedia applications

[23] Ibid. "By the end of 2020, China had undertaken the chairmanship and vice chairmanship of 75 ISO and IEC technical bodies (compared to 73 by 2019 as listed in the 2019 report) and 75 secretariats (88 by 2019)."

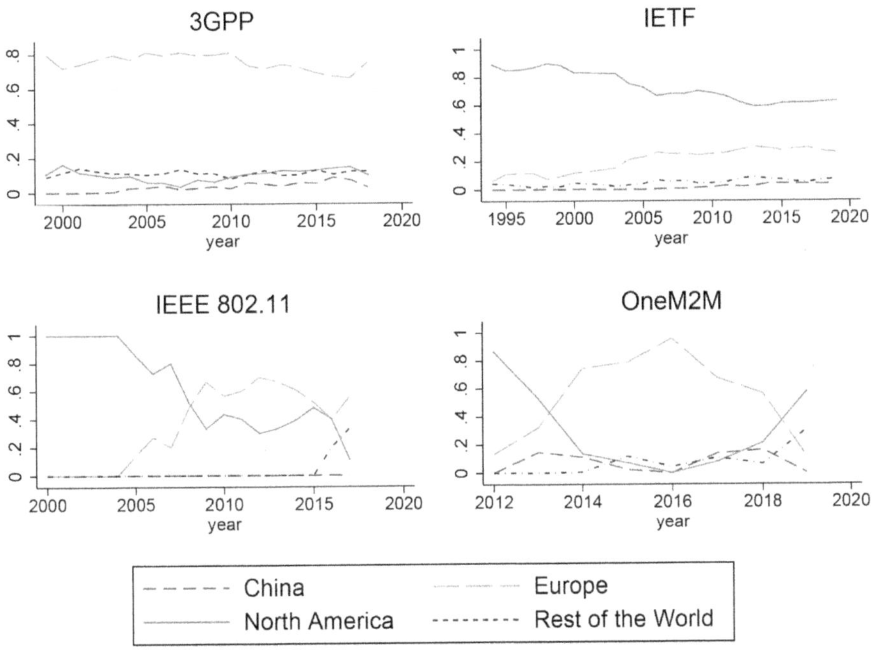

FIGURE 14.2. Trends in chairs appointments of SDO meeting

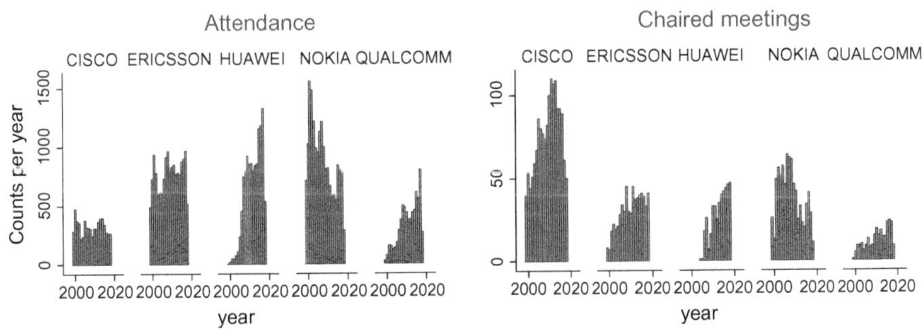

FIGURE 14.3. Meeting attendance and chair appointments of five largest stakeholders in 3GPP, IEEE, OneM2M, and IETF

and ITU-T Focus Groups on AI standardization.[24] Individuals affiliated with Huawei or associated companies have also been nominated for the IETF chair election in 2021.[25]

The empirical evidence also suggests that Huawei is not unique in holding large numbers of leadership roles in these SDOs. At 3GPP, Ericsson, Nokia, and

[24] Focus Groups support standardization work of the SG in a specific domain and are comprised of non-ITU members; however, such FG may go "beyond their terms of references" and leading them may be one of the many strategies to steer the activities of a SG.

[25] M. Ermert, Diversity at Any Price? IETF Looking for New Chair (December 16, 2020), www.centr.org/news/blog/ietf109-new-chair.html.

Qualcomm also hold larger number of leadership positions; while at IETF, Cisco continues to hold a leading position both in terms of attendance records and chair positions. Empirically, what sets Huawei apart from its main competitors is the breadth of Huawei's engagement – Huawei's lead in attendance records in the three SDOs marks the first time that one company leads attendance counts in each of these SDOs. Furthermore, the observable data point to future increases in Huawei's position in SDO leadership: as Huawei affiliates attend SDO meetings more assiduously than affiliates of any other company, and Huawei recruited far larger numbers of individuals with previous SDO participation experience than any other company,[26] Huawei is growing a workforce with significant SDO experience. Having this experience is the most important predictor of future appointments to SDO chair positions.

14.2.2 *Huawei's Rise as a Moment of Stress for SDO Governance*

The observable pattern of Huawei's increasing influence in ICT SDOs alone does not constitute an institutional crisis. Several concerns and/or allegations have been raised, which suggest that Huawei's rise represents a challenge to the (current) normal functioning of international SDOs.

First, governmental support of Chinese companies, arguably enabling them to gain competitive advantages in SDOs, is accused of interfering with the competitive process.[27] Second, the increasing role of Chinese stakeholders, coupled with generally lower standards of patent protection in China, is often presented as a threat to the protection of Western companies' patent rights.[28] Third, Huawei and other Chinese stakeholders are seen as promoting certain governance models for the development of ICT standards. To illustrate, Huawei-driven attempts at the ITU to reform the Internet with the "New IP" protocol have been presented as a challenge not only to IETF's traditional prerogative over the development of

[26] This pattern is in line with Huawei's general strategy of acquiring significant technical know-how through targeted recruitments of foreign technical experts; see K. J. Schaefer, Catching up by Hiring: The Case of Huawei (2020) 51 *Journal of International Business Studies* 1500. E. Gifford, M. Holgersson, M. McKelvey, and S. Bagchi-Sen, Tapping into Western Technologies by Chinese Multinationals: Geely's Purchase of Volvo Cars and Huawei's Hiring of Ericsson Employees in Sweden, in *Innovation Spaces in Asia: Enterpreneurs, Multinational Enterprises and Policy* (M. McKelvey and S. Bagchi-Sen eds., 2015), at 231.

[27] Xia, *supra* note14; H. Farrel and A. Newman, Weaponized Globalization: Huawei and the Emerging Battle over 5G Networks (2019) 14 *Global Asia* 8, www.globalasia.org/v14no3/cover/weaponized-globalization-huawei-and-the-emerging-battle-over-5g-networks_henry-farrellabraham-newman; Schaefer, *supra* note 23, on how governmental support to Huawei enabled it to expand its sales and build a foreign customer base.

[28] See, e.g., P. K. Yu, *The Sweet and Sour Story of Chinese Intellectual Property Rights* (2004), www.peteryu.com/sweetsour.pdf.

internet protocols but more generally to a nongovernmental, de-centralized, multi-stakeholder model of standards development and internet governance.[29]

In addition to these specific issues, concerns about China's and Huawei's influence in SDOs unfold against the background of a broader discussion on China's role in the global economic order. ICT standardization, for example, in the field of Artificial Intelligence, carries complex ethical implications;[30] and some ICT standards, including 5G, define the performance and resilience of a critical communications infrastructure.[31] In this context, several policy discussions around China's and/or Huawei's leading role in ICT standards development, and the telecommunications infrastructure more generally, focus on potential risks to national security interests, human rights, or political values; as exemplified by multiple cybersecurity incidents allegedly linked to Huawei[32] and unease about the leading role of Chinese stakeholders in the development of international facial recognition standards.[33]

The US policy response to these (perceived) threats to the SDO ecosystem can equally be seen as menacing the normal functioning of SDOs. The exclusion of certain entities from relevant standardization activities and adjacent forms of technology exchange represents a departure from the general principle of openness of the standards development process. Ultimately, it also risks splintering the technical and governance structure of international ICT standardization. Furthermore, at least some of the measures contemplated in the United States in order to counter Chinese influence in international SDOs can themselves be perceived as interference of a national government with the normal competitive process in private international SDOs.

[29] S. Hoffmann, D. Lazanski, and E. Taylor, Standardising the Splinternet: How China's Technical Standards Could Fragment the Internet (2020) 5 *Journal of Cyber Policy* 239, at 244.

[30] D. Lewis, D. Filip, L. Hogan, and P. J. Wall, Global Challenges in the Standardization of Ethics for Trustworthy AI (2020) 8:2 *Journal of ICT Standardization* 123.

[31] B. Lee-Makiyama and F. Forsthuber, Open RAN: The Technology, Its Politics and Europe's Response (October 2020) ECIPE Policy Brief No 8/2020, https://ecipe.org/publications/open-ran-europes-response/ (explaining that 5G security issues are different than of its predecessors). See also J. Wouters, "Corporations and the Making of Public Standards in International Law: The Case of China in the ITU" in this volume (Chapter 3).

[32] FCC 19-121 in the Matter of Protecting Against National Security Threats to the Communications Supply Chain Through FCC Programs (WC Docket No. 18-89), Huawei Designation (PS Docket No. 19-131), ZTE Designation (PS Docket No. 19-352) release November 26, 2019; European Parliament, 2019/2575 (RSP) Resolution, Security threats connected with the rising Chinese technological presence in the EU and possible action on the EU level to reduce them; K. Kaska, H. Beckvard, and T. Minárik, Huawei, 5G and China as a Security Threat, Report of the NATO Cooperative Cyber Defense Center of Excellence (2019), https://ccdcoe.org/library/publications/huawei-5g-and-china-as-a-security-threat/; Farrell and Newman, *supra* note 24. Whereas these incidents should be seen in isolation from Huawei gaining global technological power, they present a broader picture of possible concerns that may arise from Huawei's participation in SDOs.

[33] A. Gross, M. Madhumita, and Y. Yang. Chinese Tech Groups Shaping UN Facial Recognition Standards (2019), www.ft.com/content/c3555a3c-0d3e-11ea-b2d6-9bf4d1957a67.

14.2.3 *Fragility of Existing Norms of SDO Governance*

The recent tensions around China's and Huawei's increasing participation in the leadership of SDOs developing international ICT standards constitute a "moment of stress" for SDO governance, as both the rising influence of Huawei (and some other Chinese stakeholders) itself as well as the policy response (especially in the United States) to this ascension can be seen as challenging certain institutional norms and governance principles of SDOs.

ICT standardization is characterized by rivalry between different commercial stakeholders with vested interests in influencing the outcomes of standardization processes; it also involves considerable R&D investments. In this highly competitive setting, most SDOs emerge as nongovernmental, nonprofit, voluntary professional and/or industry associations that provide an infrastructure for neutral and nonpartisan deliberation processes. The primary aim of this particular institutional organization of the deliberative process is to promote technical objectivity in standardization decisions.

It is an accepted (and often expected) feature of SDOs that most or all individual participants of the standards development process vigorously pursue different interests. By contrast, it is a violation of institutional norms of standardization if the SDO itself or its agents or representatives side with individual SDO stakeholders or constituencies.[34] From this vantage point, the resilience of the existing SDO ecosystem to the present "moment of stress" hinges on whether the rival commercial and political interests of Chinese and Western stakeholders fuel particularly vigorous competition within the nonpartisan standards development process or whether there is competition for opportunities to influence (and bias) the nature of the deliberative process.

Nevertheless, the supposedly well-established norms separating the partisan activity of SDO participation from the neutrality of the institutional setting are inherently fragile. There have been numerous episodes in which individual SDO chairs have been accused of favoring their company's proposals or otherwise biasing the standardization process.[35] At several occasions, SDOs made decisions opposed by significant stakeholder constituencies, illustrated by the W3C Encrypted Media Extensions (EME) recommendations.[36] The notion of a competitive standards development process taking place within a nonpartisan process is also belied by the hyper-partisan nature of some SDO governance discussions, as illustrated by the

34 See M. I. Marpet, An Ethical Issue in Voluntary-Consensus-Standards Development: A Decision-Science View (1998) 17 *Journal of Business Ethics* 1701.

35 E.g., *American Society of Mechanical Engineers* v. *Hydrolevel Corporation*, 456 US 556 (1982) and, later, *TruePosition, Inc.* v. *LM Ericsson Tel. Co.* (January 6, 2012), No. 11-4574, 2012 WL 33075 [2012].

36 H. Halpin, The Crisis of Standardizing DRM: The Case of w3c Encrypted Media Extension (2017) *International Conference on Security, Privacy, and Applied Cryptography Engineering* 10.

latest update of IEEE's patent policy and the still ongoing controversy that it has generated.[37]

While appealing, the optimistic representation of the standards development process as a highly competitive process within a neutral institutional framework is thus overly simplistic. For a more thorough assessment of SDOs' resilience to the present "moment of stress," it is important to have a closer empirical look at SDOs' institutional architecture and the drivers of their decision-making.

14.3 SDO GOVERNANCE PROCESSES

Next to a set of formal rules that define SDOs' membership, voting rights, and obligations of SDO participants, the conduct of business within SDO committees hinges upon informal practices and expectations rooted in cultural historical traditions, which determine the hierarchy of operational rules and their interpretation. Furthermore, SDOs usually comprise many committees, which in turn are made up of specialized groups, each of these subcommittees having their own internal ways of working. In this regard, while there are different ways in which SDOs and their standards can be legitimized as instances of private rule-making,[38] it can also be argued that different SDO models present different legitimization techniques.

14.3.1 *Models of SDO governance*

SDO governance is heterogenous.[39] While SDOs appear to share some fundamental governance features, those are further concretized in their operational frameworks in a way that serves their membership and is entrenched in their cultural traditions. Generally, a distinction can be made between four models of SDO governance, often combined in reality.

In the first model, SDOs comprise national committees established at the country level and according to the national rules ("national representation"). This modus operandi is exemplified by the three international SDOs, namely the ISO, IEC, and ITU. National committees participating in these SDOs represent national consensus, as opposed to the interest of a particular stakeholder group. However, SDOs may have different understandings of what the "national consensus" entails: in ITU, for instance, it refers to the interests of States, whereas ISO and IEC are preliminary

37 P. Delimatsis, O. Kanevskaia, and Z. Verghese, Strategic Behavior in Standard Development Organizations in Times of Crisis (2021) 29:2 *Texas Intellectual Property Law Journal* 127.

38 See the analysis of different facets of legitimacy in standardization in M. Eliantonio and C. Cauffman (eds.) *The Legitimacy of Standardization as a Regulatory Technique: A Cross-disciplinary and Multi-level Analysis* (2020).

39 O. Kanevskaia, *supra* note 12; J. Baron et al., *Making the Rules: The Governance of Standard Development Organizations and their Policies on Intellectual Property Rights, Report of the EU Joint Research Center* (2019), http://publications.jrc.ec.europa.eu/repository/bitstream/JRC115004/sdo_governance_final_electronic_version.pdf.

concerned with consensus among domestic industry actors.[40] SDOs that are based on national representation derive their legitimacy from recognition by governmental authorities, either explicit or by the indirect means of co-regulation[41] or, as it is the case with ITU, from participation of the public sector, that is, ministries and governmental agencies, in their standardization processes.[42] Furthermore, since the national committees are treated equally in terms of membership rights and obligations, such as voting for standards' approval, this type of SDO also enjoys legitimacy from the perspective of the international standardization system.

The second governance model represents a global partnership of regional SDOs, such as the 3GPP and OneM2M. The rules and processes of these SDOs strive to strike a balance between the interests of private actors ("balance of commercial stakeholders"). Stakeholders participate in these partnerships by virtue of their organizational membership in regional SDOs. Adherence to the requirements of commercial and regional balance is the legitimizing force behind their standards, immunizing them, at least in theory, from undue commercial influence. This type of SDO furthermore enjoys increased legitimacy from the perspective of commercial stakeholders, since the voting rights are typically allocated according to stakeholders' size and financial contribution to the SDO.[43]

In contrast to the two entity-based governance models, SDOs designed according to the third governance model represent associations of professionals rooted in the traditions of democracy ("democracy of experts"). Individuals participating in these SDOs typically follow the norms of conduct of their profession but may also participate through their affiliation and represent the interests of their employer. An example of such an SDO is the Standards Association of the Institute of the Electrical and Electronics Engineers (IEEE-SA). Standards developed in these SDOs are largely legitimized by their inclusive processes, which seek to provide equal opportunities for all members to voice their opinion, for instance, through the democratic election of SDO leadership. To enhance their legitimacy, such SDOs may also seek formal accreditation of their processes or standards by an organization in the highest hierarchical position, such as the American National Standards Institute (ANSI) or JTC1, which transposes public law requirements imposed on these national and global standards bodies to these private-sector associations.

The fourth and last model is even more centered on individuals and represents "informal groups of likeminded experts": IETF, which started as a loosely organized

40 This concept was adopted at the IEC meeting in London in 1906. J. Yates and C. N. Murphy, *Engineering Rules: Global Standard Setting since 1880* (2019).

41 For instance, ISO is recognized in the TBT and SPS Agreements of the World Trade Organization.

42 Note, however, that companies may also participate in ITU as sector members, but their rights and obligations slightly differ from Member States.

43 See, by analogy, Annex 4 of ETSI Rules and Procedures (May 20, 2021) (ETSI provides secretariat to both 3GPP and OneM2M and its procedures are also transposed in these partnerships' operational frameworks).

group of internet researchers and to this day operates without formal membership requirements, is a vivid example of this governance model. Although some of these consortia have pledged the alignment of their processes with public law principles for standardization governance,[44] they usually do not seek formal recognition or accreditation at the higher hierarchical level.[45] Their legitimacy is exclusively derived from meritocracy and free participation of all interested individuals, regardless of their affiliation: more often than not, such SDOs would require individuals to refrain from representing the position of their employer as a vital requirement to the independence of the SDO.

14.3.2 *Integrity of SDO Processes of Different Governance Models*

The governance models discussed above generally demonstrate two different approaches to ICT standardization. Under the first approach, standardization decisions should reflect a consensus of those affected by the standard; standardization processes should therefore be open to the relevant stakeholders and seek a balance of the different stakeholder groups and assure sufficient representation of different types of interests. SDOs adhering to these principles may give greater weight to stakeholders with a larger stake in the standard, assess consensus within different categories of interests, and/or encourage participation of representatives of specific underrepresented interest categories. Under the second approach, standardization decisions should reflect a technical consensus among subject matter experts. SDOs operating following this approach seek to be open to any interested individual expert, expect their participants to take technical decisions on merit, and often discourage individuals to represent the interests of a particular stakeholder. Such approach is traditionally maintained in internet governance,[46] which is also illustrated by the IETF's requirement for experts to participate in the individual capacity rather than represent their employer.

While impartiality and independence of SDOs has gained attention in the recent scholarly and political discussions,[47] an element that has been neglected in these

[44] See the IAB reply to the European ICT questionnaire, Impact assessment study on the "standardization package." Request for information from forums and consortiums, www.iab.org/wp-content/IAB-uploads/2011/03/2010-02-05-IAB-Response-Euro-ICT-Questionnaire.pdf; WTO TBT Standards Code criteria applied to W3C, (July 12, 2009), www.w3.org/2009/07wto-std-crit.html.

[45] J. Baron et al., Balance Requirements for Standards Development Organizations. A Historical, Legal and Institutional Assessment' (January 2021), https://papers.ssrn.com/sol3/papers.cfm?abstract_id=3806876.

[46] See P. J. Weiser, Internet Governance, Standard- Setting, and Self-Regulation (2001) 28 *Northern Kentucky Law Review* 822.

[47] See, for instance, Report on the 802.11ax dominance complaint (Investigation), (November 9, 2016), https://mentor.ieee.org/802.11/dcn/16/11-16-1519, which was covered by A. Harcourt, G. Christou, and S. Simpson, *Global Standard Setting in Internet Governance* (2020), as well as abovementioned discussion on DRMs approval in W3C and IEEE patent policy change.

debates is the interplay of different motives and incentives shaping individuals' conduct in SDO committees. Irrespective of governance models, stakeholders participate in SDO processes by sending individual employees to attend their meetings. Furthermore, since SDOs have limited staff, their administrative and management functions – including editors and working group chairs, as well as the members of appeals boards, policy committees, and other governance bodies – are filled by volunteers who are often affiliated with private companies. Hence, the impartiality of the standardization process depends on the decisions of individuals employed by organizations with direct stakes in the SDOs' decisions.

The individual dimension of SDO participation is quintessential, since it provides insights on decision-making within the standards body and its committees, revealing some fundamental accountability questions that are not always evident on the surface, including the following: who are the main decision-makers, how are they appointed, and what are their obligations towards the membership. The role of individuals is especially critical in a highly competitive environment, such as ICT standardization: experts sitting on the committees may wear different hats and have contradictory commitments to their employer, peers, or profession. Against this backdrop, understanding how individuals are selected to SDO leadership is an important facet through which the integrity and independence of different SDO governance models can be examined.

14.4 FORMAL RULES OF SDO LEADERSHIP SELECTION

By far the most important and common leadership function in SDOs is the role of a working group chair. Individuals holding these positions have weighty responsibility but also considerable power: they coordinate the work of the respective working group, serve as the first stage of appeal or investigation processes into the breaches of SDOs' procedural rules, and make pivotal decisions such as whether consensus has been achieved or the voting should be conducted. In some cases, chairs may delay or even stall their working groups' discussion.[48] A position of a chair may thus be highly advantageous for companies actively participating in standards development and exert a significant influence on the outcome of standardization decisions; at the same time, since chairs serve as tie-breakers, they are critical to balancing the interests and ensuring impartiality of SDO processes.[49] Furthermore, pursuant to the established jurisprudence, decisions of chairs are attributable to an SDO and may thus entail legal responsibility for the organization,[50] which will also affect SDO membership.

48 See examples in Harcourt et al., *supra* note 48.

49 Marpet, *supra* note 35, discussing chairs' obligation to balance the rights of members and ability of the group to perform its function.

50 See the relevant jurisprudence, *supra* note 36.

Each SDO has its own rules for election or appointment of its leadership that are entrenched in historical traditions and have evolved due to the membership expansion and the emerging jurisprudence.[51] This section reviews the rules of the four prominent ICT SDOs that apply to the conduct of working groups' chairs, including their appointment, tenure, and resignation, in the light of the overall institutional rules and traditions of these organizations.

14.4.1 *ITU*

Formally, holding leadership positions in ITU Study Groups[52] does not confer the individuals with any influence over standards development. This however contradicts the fact that chairs are tasked with maintaining the order in their committees, authorizing the voting as a "last resort" where consensus by the means of "sound out" cannot be achieved, ruling on motions, and suspending meetings.[53] While seeking the balance is not explicitly listed as a chair's responsibility, they are required to protect the rights of each member's representative.

Officials for ITU Study Groups, including chairs and vice-chairs, are appointed the Sector Assembly (e.g., the WTSA for the ITU Standardization Sector). Each member state's and Sector member's delegation nominates their candidate(s) for chairs and vice-chairs by consensus; the list of nominees, including their resumes and qualifications, is then circulated among the Sector membership and is made available on the ITU website.[54] When appointing the officials, the Sector Assembly should take into account individuals' personal competences, equitable geographical distribution, and the need to promote more efficient participation by the developing countries;[55] the individuals' professional knowledge and expertise, managerial skills, candidates' and their administration's commitment to fulfill the duties of the Study Group officials, as well as individual's prior experiences as rapporteurs or editors and continuous participation in Study or Advisory groups, also counts.[56] Members are discouraged from nominating candidates who failed to participate in at least half of all meetings in the prior study period. In case the nominees' qualifications are equal, preference is given to members with lowest number of chairs. Members cannot nominate candidates for chairs and vice-chairs for the same Study Group to

[51] An example is the requirement for chairs to follow the SDOs' antitrust training, e.g., https://standards.ieee.org/faqs/ldrship.html.

[52] Those are ITU committees where technical work is carried out.

[53] ITU General Rules on Conferences, Assemblies and Meetings (2019), Articles 59–61.

[54] In 2020, China had a long list of candidates for chairmen and vice-chairmen for the WTSA-20, see www.itu.int/en/ITU-T/wtsa20/candidates/Pages/ms.aspx.

[55] ITU Convention (2018) No 189 and Article 20.

[56] See ITU-T Resolution 35 on Appointment and maximum term of office for chairmen and vice chairmen of study groups of the Telecommunication Standardization Sector and of the Telecommunication Standardization Advisory Group (Hammamet, 2016). See also the letter from Chaesub Lee (February 4, 2021), www.itu.int/md/T17-TSB-CIR-0202/en.

safeguard geographical distribution; moreover, the appointment of vice-chairs is limited to three candidates from each region, but the ultimate number of vice-chairs appointed per Study Group depends on equitable distribution as well as the workload.

To allow introducing new ideas on a periodic basis and to provide opportunities to different States, Study Group chairs are appointed for a limited time and with a maximum tenure of two terms.[57] For the sake of continuity, this term does not count for another appointment, meaning that a Study Group's chairman can be appointed as the group's vice-chairman and vice-versa.[58] However, no individual can hold more than one vice chairmanship.

14.4.2 *3GPP*

Working Group chairs of 3GPP are responsible for the management of their committees, and their compliance with the prescribed processes, and are required to maintain impartiality and act in the interests of 3GPP when performing their leadership tasks.[59] Working Group officials are tasked with formulating the questions put forward for voting as well as with maintaining impartiality in the Working Group.[60] Furthermore, chairs determine when consensus is reached and may impose voting or temporary arrangements in case consensus is not achieved.[61] At the beginning of each meeting, the chair is required to make a statement of antitrust compliance and call for IPRs;[62] for a short period of time in 2019, the chair was also required to make a statement of compliance with the US EARs.[63]

The Working Group officials are elected by the members of the respective Working Group every two years.[64] Candidates for (vice)-chairmanship should provide a letter of support from the 3GPP member, which should also assure the candidate's compliance with antitrust rules if elected for the office.[65] In an endeavor to maintain balance, a Working Group's chair and vice-chair, as well as their successive officials, cannot be from the same region, organizations, partner, or group of companies, unless no other individual is available to hold the office.[66] If more

[57] See ITU-T Resolution 35 and Resolution 208 (Dubai, 2018) on the Appointment and maximum term of office for chairmen and vice-chairmen of Sector advisory groups, study groups and other groups.

[58] Ibid.

[59] 3GPP Working Procedures (April 29, 2021), Article 23.

[60] Ibid., Articles 23 and 25.

[61] Ibid., Articles 19 and 25.

[62] Statement of Antitrust Compliance, www.3gpp.org/about-3gpp/legal-matters/21-3gpp-calendar/1616-statement-of-antitrust-compliance.

[63] Statement regarding Engagement with Companies Added to the U.S. Export Administration Regulation (EAR) Entity List in 3GPP Activities, www.3gpp.org/about-3gpp/legal-matters.

[64] 3GPP Working Procedures (April 29, 2021), Article 22.

[65] Ibid., Article 22.1 and 22.2.

[66] Ibid., Article 14.

than one candidate is nominated for the chair position, the election of Working Groups' officials occurs through secret balloting, with a threshold of 71 percent of Working Groups members voting and present; if the processes is unsuccessful, it is followed by a second ballot between the candidates obtaining the highest amount of votes.[67] Individuals can be reelected as Working Group chairs for the second term, and exceptionally, their tenure in the office can last even longer; there are no restrictions for the election of chairs whose tenure is due to expire as vice-chairs and vice-versa.[68]

An incumbent chairman or vice-chairman who changes their affiliation, for instance, due to taking up new employment, is required to present a new letter of support from their new employer. If affiliation is changed due to the individual's hiring by another company, and not their company's merger or acquisition, the Working Group should also agree by consensus that the individual can remain in their role as a (vice-)chair.[69] When a chair is believed not to effectively perform their duties, their dismissal can be requested by 30 percent of a Working Group in a secret ballot, with 71 percent of votes considered as recommending the dismissal. Furthermore, if a Working Group member doubts the chair's impartiality and believes the chair does not act in the interest of 3GPP, they should object to the chair's decision and request that the objection is recorded, prior to taking the issue to the PCG.[70] (Vice-)chairs can be dismissed through a secret vote of the Working Groups when they fail to effectively perform their duties.[71]

14.4.3 *IEEE-SA*

IEEE-SA Working Group chairs provide leadership and guidance and serve as a contact point for questions or comments regarding standardization activity. Their main task is to move the Working Group forward while ensuring that every voice has been heard and that the rules and procedures of the working groups are respected.[72] In carrying out their activities, chairs need to be objective, refrain from making motions and strive to balance the interests in their Working Group. The chair is also in power to determine the Working Group's participants and is (almost) the only official who holds control over distributing the draft standard.[73]

IEEE Study Groups officials, including chairs and mentors, are appointed by the Sponsor committee – a body that provides oversight for the working groups'

67 Ibid., Article 28.
68 Ibid., Article 22.
69 Ibid.
70 Ibid., Article 29.
71 Ibid., Article 24.
72 Managing the Working Group, https://standards.ieee.org/develop/mobilizing-working-group/managewg.html.
73 Sharing Draft IEEE Standards, https://standards.ieee.org/faqs/copyrights/working-group-and-activity-chairs.html#5-1.

activities. Once assigned, the Study Group chair can further appoint the secretary who is charged with record keeping and contacting Study Group members; yet it remains the task of the chair to distribute the call for participation in a Study Group.[74] IEEE Working Groups chairs are either appointed by a standards committee or elected by the respective Working Group; in the latter case, the official should be confirmed by the sponsor.[75] Procedures for officials' election, as well as the definition of what constitutes a consensus, are further specified in the Working Group's charters; for instance, chairs of the IEEE-SA 802.11 Working Group, responsible for the development of WLAN specifications, including Wi-Fi, are elected biannually from the nominated individuals, following a debate in the biannual working group, upon receiving a simple majority of cast votes.[76]

While there is no specification of the qualities and skills crucial for the chairs (presumably because those are left to Study and Working groups), it is required that the Working Groups' chairs hold the membership of both IEEE and IEEE-SA, which implies that by the virtue of individual IEEE membership, they should be familiar to and with the SDO. There is no overarching requirement for a maximum term of office: chairs may either serve limited terms or undergo a regular vote confirmation.[77]

14.4.4 *IETF*

IETF Working Group chairs are the formal contact point of their Working Group and IETF governance bodies and other SDOs. Chairs preside over the Working Group meetings, manage its activities and publications, accept or reject participants' input, and decide whether a draft recommendation is to be published as an official Working Group draft;[78] they also moderate mailing lists, prepare face-to-face sessions, and serve as a first stage of conflict resolution. They have a wide discretion in administering Working Group activities and may also make decisions on behalf of their Working Group, where they may be assisted by the area directors – individuals in charge of a particular domain of IETF activities.[79] Chairs are also responsible for deciding when and whether consensus between the group members is reached,[80] which can be particularly challenging in the absence of formal voting and when most of the meetings occur through the mailing list. Crucially, chairs should

[74] IEEE-SA Study Group Guidelines, https://standards.ieee.org/content/dam/ieee-standards/standards/web/documents/other/corpchan/studygrp.pdf.
[75] How are Working Groups Governed?, https://standards.ieee.org/develop/mobilizing-working-group/governedwg.html.
[76] IEEE 802.11 Wireless Local Area Networks Operations Manual (July 13, 2018) Article 3.4.
[77] See How are Working Groups Governed?, *supra* note 76.
[78] See The Tao of IETF (November 8, 2018), www.ietf.org/about/participate/tao/.
[79] BCP 25, IETF Working Group Guidelines and Procedures (September 1998), https://tools.ietf.org/html/bcp25.
[80] See Working Groups, www.ietf.org/wg/.

balance "progress and fairness" and ensure that the Working Groups move forward while the process remains fair and open.[81]

IETF Working Group chairs are assigned by the area directors who in turn are selected by the nominating committee (NomCom), whose members are randomly selected from a pool of volunteers and approved by the Internet Architecture Board (IAB).[82] While both technical and communication skills of a chair candidate matter, individuals who have been around in IETF for a long time and have been actively participating in its meetings are more likely to get appointed as chairs, especially if they gained "favorable prominence"[83] by having previously contributed to the documents or volunteered to review them.

IETF chairs' neutrality and impartiality has been challenged on a number of occasions, including allegations of abuse of power and breaching fairness and neutrality of IETF processes by favoring solutions preferred by the chairs' affiliation.[84] Interestingly, at least in these instances, the IETF appeal bodies did not find any evidence of conflict of interest stemming from the individuals' affiliation,[85] illustrating two important elements of IETF leadership: first, the high level of trust in independent and unbiased judgment of chairs and, second, the chairs' wide prerogative for moving forward the discussions in the working groups.

14.4.5 *Takeaways from Analyzing the Rules for Leadership Appointment*

Even though the four studied SDOs are rooted in different historical traditions, we can observe some similarities and differences in their rules for leadership appointment. The distinction between entity-based and individual-based governance models is particularly striking: as illustrated with the examples of ITU and 3GPP, entity-based SDOs devote particular attention to the balance in their leadership composition with such aspects as regional and commercial diversity and non-transferability of chairs' positions.[86] Likewise, the employers' formal and explicit support plays a significant role when selecting or appointing the chairs in these two organizations. Contrarily, the rules for leadership appointment in individual-based

[81] The Tao of IETF, Article 4.1.

[82] BCP 25.

[83] RFC 4144, How to Gain Prominence and Influence in Standards Organizations (September 2005), https://tools.ietf.org/html/rfc4144.

[84] See www6.ietf.org/iesg/appeal/anderson-2007-12-26.txt; www6.ietf.org/iesg/appeal/gellens-2007-06-22.pdf; and https://www6.ietf.org/iesg/appeal/masotta-2013-11-14.txt.

[85] See www6.ietf.org/iesg/appeal/response-to-anderson-2007-12-26.txt; https://www6.ietf.org/iesg/appeal/gellens- 2007-06-22.pdf.

[86] That said, possible theoretical claims that the requirement of balance in SDO leadership obviate regional dominance do not always find confirmation in the data on SDO leadership: at least in case of 3GPP, being an affiliate of an EU company appears to increase an individual's chances to be selected to the chair position, casting doubts about the practical effectiveness of this requirement. See Baron and Kanevskaia, *supra* note 19.

SDOs such as IEEE and IETF rely on the culture of meritocracy, rather than on balance of interests, and do not require any type of support from the officials' employers or affiliations.

At the same time, surveying procedural rules demonstrates the importance of experience and expertise in all four SDOs. This is apparent from the conditions that candidate-chairs have to fulfill regarding, for example, meeting attendance, knowledge and experience in the organization, and compliance with SDOs' antitrust policies. In both entity and individual-based organizations, chairs are always required to participate in an individual capacity and have a fiduciary duty to the SDO (although admittedly, whether or not the chairs indeed respect fiduciary duty is difficult to verify).

14.5 LEGAL AND INSTITUTIONAL DIMENSIONS OF SDO LEADERSHIP

The institutional analysis suggests different approaches to legitimacy of SDO leadership, which correspond to the contrast between "commercial balance" and "meritocracy" of entity- and individual-based SDOs respectively. Yet, despite the identified procedural differences, including such nuances as opportunities for reelection and the duration of tenure, both types of SDOs approach leadership in a similar way in the sense that they have certain behavioral and reputational expectations for individuals holding leadership positions, requiring them to set their personal preferences, or employers' agenda, aside in the interest of the SDO. These nuances undoubtedly contribute to the checks and balances that different SDO models have in place, depending on these SDOs' governance structure, culture, and membership.

The fact that the requirements of expertise and experience appear to be the main determinants for leadership appointments, regardless the SDO's institutional setup, demonstrates a strong culture of individual independence and meritocracy. The "community of professionals" mobilized through this culture functions outside the SDOs' organizational hierarchy or State-driven processes, evidencing the phenomenon of "voluntary economic activism."[87]

While these observations do not allow us to conclude which SDO type is better equipped in dealing with the situation of distress, they help in reflecting on the SDOs adaptive capacities. They also indicate that despite the presence of checks and balances in their governance models, SDOs are not immune to crises caused by the capture of their processes. To strengthen SDO resilience, revisiting leadership rules in terms of neutrality and independence is in order.

[87] See, in this regard, the definition of P. Delimatsis, "The Resilience of Private Authority in Times of Crisis" in this volume (Chapter 1).

Furthermore, and without any pretense of exhaustiveness, our descriptive analysis of SDO leadership rules, interpreted through the previous empirical studies on participation in SDOs suggesting the increase of participation of Chinese companies in ITU[88] and the unchallenged supremacy of Western companies in 3GPP, IEEE, and IETF,[89] allows us to make some observations regarding the integrity of different SDO governance models but also their relevance for global standardization activities. It is commonly assumed that standards developed through intergovernmental bodies, such as ITU, enjoy increased legitimacy, which also facilitates their global dissemination. However, the role of ITU appears to be limited for the industry, and Western countries where standardization traditions are entrenched in the private sector prefer to streamline their standardization efforts in the industry-led SDOs rather than intergovernmental ITU.[90] Conversely, ITU is a preferred standards development platform for standardization newcomers and, in particular, Chinese companies, which arguably use ITU processes as an opportunity to promote their technologies in non-Western countries: for instance, ITU standards are adopted as regulatory policy in Africa and Asia,[91] while Huawei's technologies are actively used in the development of smart cities on the African continent.[92]

It is not entirely clear what served as a catalyst for this fragmentation. On the one hand, the global openness of ITU may have been the reason for Western States to resort to private organizations whose cultural traditions they are more comfortable with. On the other hand, the preference of Western industry for institutions with particular properties and their lack of interest in ITU may have created openings for emerging standardization stakeholders, which were quick to fill the vacant spots with their own standardization efforts. Most likely, these two phenomena are jointly determined. Regardless of their source, they indicate a serious lack of "openness" in terms of inclusiveness and geographical representativeness in SDO leadership.

Two perspectives emerge from this suggestion. The first one is the perspective of Western stakeholders, characterized by the growing distrust in ITU and concerns that its greater openness may allow for strategic national interests to prevail over commercial ones. These concerns go beyond ITU and are particularly relevant for the "national representation" governance model, since equal voting rights per national committee may not always correspond to the level of contribution to, or use of, their standards. Indeed, equal voting rights seem to facilitate achieving fairness and impartiality; in reality, however, precisely for this reason, this type of SDO is also extremely prone to lobbying and "packing the vote" strategies by the

88 Cantero Gamito, *supra* note 21.

89 Baron and Kanevskaia, *supra* note 19.

90 Hoffmann et al., *supra* note 30, at 246, mentioning the recent drop of industry membership in ITU-T.

91 Cantero Gamito, *supra* note 20, at 2.

92 Gross et al., *supra* note 34.

stronger stakeholders. Leadership of this type of SDO should be subjected to additional safeguards that ensure not only its diversity but also integrity and impartiality.

The second perspective is the one of non-Western stakeholders, and in particular Chinese actors whose participation in ICT standardization has surged only recently. From this potential viewpoint, industry-driven SDOs such as 3GPP, IEEE, and IETF exhibit bias toward Western stakeholders and a significant lack of diversity and global interest representation in their leadership. As this lack of diversity may render Western-driven SDOs increasingly less attractive for Asian stakeholders, these SDOs may also lose important technical contributions, which in turn may also affect standards implementation on the non-Western markets; the latter is especially worrisome given the current climate of techno-nationalism in countries such as China. In due course, this development may not only contribute to further fragmentation of ICT standards but also put into question the legitimacy of the global standardization ecosystem as well as these SDOs role as global standard-setters.

14.6 CONCLUSION

Huawei's increasing influence in the global technological sector has generated various scholarly and policy discussions. With regard to standards development, the narrative shared by some Western policymakers and commercial actors is that through acquiring leadership positions in SDOs, Chinese stakeholders, particularly Huawei, may pave the way for SDO processes to become partisan towards China's commercial and political strategic interests. However persistent, these concerns should be viewed in the light of the empirical evidence of Chinese and Huawei's participation in SDOs and their representation in the critical positions in these institutions.

In this regard, the empirically observed pattern demonstrated that, currently, SDO leadership is still largely dominated by Western stakeholders. At the same time, the meeting attendance by individuals affiliated with Chinese stakeholders, and in particular Huawei, has been dramatically increasing. Hence, while concerns of Chinese stakeholders taking over SDO leadership are still premature, there is undisputable evidence of China's and Huawei's strategy to increase their presence in these SDOs. The question is then whether SDO processes can be trusted to address the arising concerns of a single group of stakeholders controlling their decision-making and whether SDO institutional framework will hold to the standards of neutrality and impartiality.

Our contribution addresses this question by discussing different SDO governance models, focusing in particular on the roles of individuals holding critical positions in four prominent SDOs. We demonstrate that, despite the strong institutional traditions of meritocracy and neutrality and the existent checks and balances of the different institutional frameworks, SDO leadership relies on the system where private interests are actively pursued through the incentives of individuals holding critical positions and is thus inherently fragile. To trust this institutional setup, we need to carefully consider how individuals that represent these institutions are selected and which institutional mechanisms are available to constrain their power over SDO decision-making. Despite the common, and rather optimistic belief, neutrality in standardization processes should not be taken for granted: further institutional and empirical analyses are at order to assess the resilience of SDOs to different types of crises.

15

The International Electrotechnical Commission

A 115-Year Journey of Challenges, Change, and Resilience

Tim Büthe and Abdel fattah Alshadafan[*]

15.1 INTRODUCTION

Within a few years after it was established in 1906, the International Electrotechnical Commission (IEC) became the institutional focal point for the governance of electro-technologies and has for 115 years retained this preeminence – exhibiting striking resilience. As of the end of 2021, the IEC had developed 11,200 international technical standards and standard-like documents,[1] specifying design, performance, labeling, and other aspects of millions of electrical and electronic components and products. These standards are widely used across the globe for consumer products (with implications for consumer safety, consumer choice, and market share)[2] and – even more so – in business-to-business transactions.[3] In a wide range of industries,

[*] The authors thank Panos Delimatsis, Henk de Vries, Oliver Gray, and Enrico Partiti for comments on a previous draft and Stephanie Bijlmakers for sharing several drafts of her ISO chapter. Access to all hyperlinks was last checked on June 20, 2022.

[1] IEC, Understanding Standards: IEC Publications at a Glance, www.iec.ch/understanding-standards#publications.

[2] See, e.g., A. F. Alshadafan, Energy Efficiency Standards: The Struggle for Legitimacy (January–June 2020) 18:1 *International Journal of Standardization Research* 1–23; T. Büthe, The Power of Norms; the Norms of Power: Who Governs International Electrical and Electronic Technology?, in *Who Governs the Globe?* (D. Avant, M. Finnemore, and S. K. Sell eds., 2010), 292–332, esp. 292–294; K. Imagawa, Y. Mizukami, and S. Miyazaki, Regulatory Convergence of Medical Devices: A Case Study Using ISO and IEC Standards (2018) 15:7 *Expert Review of Medical Devices* 497; K. Kazlovich et al., Open Ventilator Evaluation Framework: A Synthesized Database of Regulatory Requirements and Technical Standards for Emergency Use Ventilators from Australia, Canada, UK, and US (2022) 11 *HardwareX* 2–13; S. Moon and H. Lee, Exploring Standard Dynamics in Electronics Industry: Focusing on Influencing Factors and Revision of IEC Standards (August 2022) 69:4 *IEEE Transactions on Engineering Management* 1365–1377; T. S. Ustun and S. M. S. Hussain, IEC 61850 Modeling of UPFC and XMPP Communication for Power Management in Microgrids (2020) 8 *IEEE Access* 141696–141704.

[3] See, e.g., S. Moon, K. Chin, and H. Lee, IEC Standard Revision Dynamics: Symbiosis between Standard and Technology (2018) *Portland International Conference on Management*

they affect the functioning of markets, including market access and the distribution of costs and benefits, through interoperability, substitutability, etc. IEC standards thus ultimately govern technologies ranging from magnetics; electro-acoustics; batteries, and energy production, storage, and distribution; to information and communication technologies and various aspects of the digital economy, including artificial intelligence–supported applications and virtual/extended reality.

IEC technology governance thus is an example of private authority. The IEC exercises this authority as a nongovernmental transnational organization, along with its national member bodies (of which the most prominent ones are also mostly nongovernmental) and the overwhelmingly private-sector experts who populate its technical committees and carry out most of the technology governance functions in practice. This chapter examines the resilience of IEC private ordering.[4]

Notwithstanding the often high commercial stakes and the substantive societal importance of its standards, the IEC has attracted much less attention than its companion international standard-setting body, the International Organization for Standardization (ISO), examined in this volume in the chapter by Stephanie Biljmakers.[5] One reason why the IEC has received less public and scholarly attention is that it has deliberately steered clear of getting involved in efforts to govern broad issues such as general quality management, environmental impact assessment and management, and corporate social responsibility, which the ISO addresses through its 9000-, 14000- and 26000-series of standards, respectively. These issues are of great economic and societal importance and have created much, sometimes controversial, visibility for the ISO. The public interest in these issues has prompted ISO to set up multi-stakeholder processes that have been extensively scrutinized by scholars and practitioners alike[6] but remain atypical of the technical

of Engineering and Technology (PICMET) 848–1751; J. C. Webb, T. Neighbours, and H. Karandikar, IEC versus IEEE/ANSI MV Switchgear: Matching the Standard to the Application, 2020 IEEE/IAS 56th Industrial and Commercial Power Systems Technical Conference (I&CPS, 2020), at 1–9; M. Voytchev, R. Behrens, R. Radev, Latest Updates for the IEC Standards for Active and Passive Dosemeters (2020) 166 *Radiation Physics and Chemistry* 108–509.

4 On the notion of transnational orders, see B. D. Richman, Firms, Courts, and Reputation Mechanisms: Towards a Positive Theory of Private Ordering (2004) 104:8 *Columbia Law Review* 2328–2367; T. Halliday and G. Shaffer (eds.), *Transnational Legal Orders* (2015).

5 See S. Bijlmakers, "The International Organization for Standardization: A Seventy-Five-Year Journey Toward Organizational Resilience" in this volume (Chapter 13).

6 See, in particular, J. Clapp, The Privatization of Global Environmental Covernance: ISO 14000 and the Developing World (1998) 4:3 *Global Governance* 295–316; K. T. Hallström, Organizing the Process of Standardization, in *A World of Standards* (N. Brunsson and B. Jacobsson eds., 2000), 85–99; K. T. Hallström and M. Boström, *Transnational Multi-Stakeholder Standardization* (2010); P. Gibbon and L. F. Henriksen, On the Pre-history of ISO 9000: The Making of a Neo-liberal Standard and C. N. Murphy and J. A. Yates, ISO 26000, Alternative Standards, and the 'Social Movement of Engineers' Involved with Standard Setting, both in *Governing Through Standards* (S. Ponte, P. Gibbon, and J. Vestergaard eds., 2011), 130–158, 159–183; P. Catska and Ch. J. Corbett, Diffusion, Impact and Governance of

standard-setting processes in ISO and IEC (as well as the many organizations that mimic the ISO-IEC blueprint).[7]

IEC standards tend to be more strictly technical and relatively narrowly focused on issues specific to electro-technologies. Most scholarship about the IEC has accordingly been standard-specific.[8] And with very few exceptions,[9] previous work has paid little attention to the IEC's institutional resilience.

This dearth of analytical attention is unfortunate since the IEC has, over the course of its 115-year history, experienced a series of challenges to its centrality as the preeminent international body for the governance of electro-technology and a key node in the increasingly global network of electrical and electronics engineering, which make studying the IEC insightful for understanding institutional resilience. The IEC has adapted to technological changes, the rise of the consumer movement, power shifts in the world economy, and other challenges with remarkable agility, building and exhibiting resilience, often by heading off challenges before they became existential crises. Examining the pursuit of resilience in the specific case of the IEC is valuable not just because it is even more purely representative of

ISO 9000, ISO 14000, and Other Management Standards (2015) 7:3–4 *Foundations and Trends in Technology, Information and Operations Management* 161–379; R. Hahn and C. Weidtmann, Transnational Governance, Deliberate Democracy, and the Legitimacy of ISO 26000: Analyzing the Case of a Global Multistakeholder Process (2016) 55:1 *Business and Society* 90–129.

7 See T. Büthe and W. Mattli, Private Regulators in Global Product Markets, in *The New Global Rulers: The Privatization of Regulation in the World Economy* (2011), 126–161. The deliberateness of the IEC decision to steer clear of contentious issues of broad public significance was conveyed to the authors in not-for-attribution interviews with current and former members of the IEC Standardization Management Board; it may be considered part of its resilience strategy (avoiding risks to the IEC's legitimacy by getting directly involved in public controversies).

8 In addition to the work noted above (*supra* notes 2 and 3), see, e.g., M. Ianoz, H. Kunz, and D. Moehr, Standardization Activities in the Field of EMC, in *Proceedings from the 3rd International Symposium on Electromagnetic Compatibility, 21–24 May 2002* (L. Zhang and Y. Wen eds., 2002), 23–26; M. Felser and T. Sauter, Standardization of Industrial Ethernet: The Next Battlefield?, in *International Workshop on Factory Communication Systems: Proceedings* (2004), 413–420; A. Schreiner-Karoussou, Review of Image Quality Standards to Control Digital X-Ray Systems (2005) 117:3 *Radiation Protection Dosimetry* 23–25. Note, however, that electro-technology has long been understood to include electronics and hence in principle any and all issues related to gathering, storing, processing/analyzing, and otherwise using data. In the digital age of industry 4.0, it is therefore ever less obvious what issues are outside the purview of IEC standard-setting. General (brief) overviews of the IEC and its role in global technology governance are provided by J. Buck, International Electrotechnical Commission, in *Handbook of Transnational Economic Governance Regimes* (C. Tietje and A. Brouder eds., 2010), 573–584; O. Kanevskaia, International Electrotechnical Commission (IEC), in *Elgar Encyclopedia of International Economic Law* (T. Cottier and K. Nadakavukaren Schefer , 2017), 149–150.

9 T. Büthe, Engineering Uncontestedness? The Origins and Institutional Development of the International Electrotechnical Commission (IEC) (2010) 12:3 *Business and Politics* 1–62; H.-W. Liu, International Standards in Flux: A Balkanized ICT Standard-Setting Paradigm and Its Implications for the WTO (2014) 17:3 *Journal of International Economic Law* 551–600; Alshadafan, *supra* note 2.

institutionalized technical standard-setting than the ISO, but also because it offers some distinctive insights, in part due to its longer history. We therefore provide this analysis of IEC resilience as a complement to the analysis of ISO resilience by Stephanie Bijlmakers.[10]

Our analysis of IEC resilience builds on Panagiotis Delimatsis' notion of resilience as the ability to "absorb stress and reorganize after the occurrence of a disturbance that upsets" the status quo equilibrium.[11] A private regulatory body – or more generally an inter- or transnational organization – is resilient to the extent that it does not just nominally survive an exogenous (or possibly endogenous) sudden shock or gradual yet serious challenging internal or environmental changes but "absorb[s] stress," adapts, reorganizes, or in other ways responds to the "stress" on the system so as to "emerge" from the episode "resembling its former state and functionality."[12]

A conceptualization of resilience as persistence through adaptability, however, raises the – theoretically and empirically challenging – question of at what point adaptability entails so much change that it is no longer a means of resilience but rather an indication of the lack thereof, as illustrated by the long-standing conceptual and empirical debate over escape clauses in trade agreements.[13] Similarly, when EU political leaders temporarily set aside state aid rules to allow member states to subsidize their domestic firms to help businesses stay afloat and prevent mass unemployment in light of, first, the COVID-19 pandemic and subsequently the Russian invasion of Ukraine, is this indicative of the resilience of the state aid rules or indicative of how brittle European political leaders' commitment to the ordo-liberal regime of controlling economic nationalist subsidies really is?[14] In Section

[10] See S. Bijlmakers, "The International Organization for Standardization: A Seventy-Five-Year Journey Toward Organizational Resilience" in this volume (Chapter 13).

[11] See P. Delimatsis, "The Resilience of Private Authority in Times of Crisis" in this volume (Chapter 1).

[12] Ibid.

[13] A. O. Sykes, Protectionism as a "Safeguard": A Positive Analysis of the GATT "Escape Clause" with Normative Speculations (Winter 1991) 58:1 *University of Chicago Law Review* 255–305; B. P. Rosendorff and H. V. Milner, The Optimal Design of International Trade Institutions: Uncertainty and Escape (Autumn 2001) 55:4 *International Organization* 829–857; K. Bagwell, K. and R. W. Staiger, Enforcement, Private Political Pressure, and the General Agreement on Tariffs and Trade/World Trade Organization Escape Clause (June 2005) 34:2 *Journal of Legal Studies* 471–513; K. J. Pelc, Seeking Escape: The Use of Escape Clauses in International Trade Agreements (June 2009) 53(2) *International Studies Quarterly* 349; W. Phelan, *In Place of Inter-State Relations: The European Union's Rejection of WTO-Style Trade Sanctions and Trade Remedies* (2014).

[14] See, e.g., S. Meunier and J. Mickus, Sizing up the Competition: Explaining Reform of European Union Competition Policy in the Covid-19 Era (2020) 42:8 *Journal of European Integration* 1077; I. Agnolucci, Will COVID-19 Make or Break EU State Aid Control? An Analysis of Commission Decisions Authorising Pandemic State Aid Measures (January 2022) 13:1 *Journal of European Competition Law & Practice* 3–16. For a pre-crisis account of the evolution of the regime, see T. Büthe, Historical Institutionalism and Institutional Development in the EU: The Development of Supranational Authority over Government

15.2, we therefore briefly introduce the IEC as a private regulatory body, focusing on four fundamental, defining characteristics or "attributes" of IEC-based technology governance, which would have to remain largely intact for any adaptation of this private regulatory body under changing circumstances to be considered indicative of resilience.

In Section 15.3, we then sketch the theoretical framework guiding our empirical analyses, before we identify and discuss four key challenges to the IEC's preeminence and legitimacy over the course of its 115-year history in Sections 15.4–15.7, where we examine how the IEC has responded to those challenges. In Section 15.8, we discuss whether the experience of previous challenges has increased the private rule-making body's resilience over time.

15.2 THE INTERNATIONAL ELECTROTECHNICAL COMMISSION: ESSENTIAL ATTRIBUTES

Advances in electrical engineering in the late nineteenth century motivated prominent electrical engineers from across the then-developed world to seek common terms and measurements. In creating common metrics and nomenclatures, they sought to facilitate scientific and commercial exchange, reduce safety risks in the development and operation of electrical machinery, and foster the development of electrical engineering as a new field of science and engineering without borders. The developments in electro-technology and other considerations, which prompted them to institutionalize their information exchange and standardization efforts by founding the IEC in 1906, have been examined in some detail elsewhere.[15] Rather than recap the early history of the IEC, we highlight here four essential or "fundamental attributes"[16] of the IEC. These fundamental attributes would need to remain intact in the face of stress-induced adaptation for persistence to constitute "resilience" as defined above.

The first essential attribute of the IEC is being the institutional focal point for inter- or transnational electro-technology governance – or at least being able to make a defensible claim to being such a focal point and have that claim be widely believed. Being such a focal point implies, above all, providing the institutional structure and having the technical and administrative ability for developing high-quality technical standards in its area of expertise. It also implies that those standards, once they have been developed, will be widely used across the globe, not just where

Subsidies (State Aid), in *Historical Institutionalism and International Relations: Explaining Institutional Development in World Politics* (T. Rixen, L. A. Viola, and M. Zürn eds., 2015), 37–67.

[15] Büthe, *supra* note 2, at 297–302; Büthe, *supra* note 9, esp. 16–20; J. A. Yates and C. N. Murphy, *Engineering Rules: Global Standard Setting since 1880* (2019), esp. 63–80.

[16] See P. Delimatsis, "The Resilience of Private Authority in Times of Crisis" in this volume (Chapter 1).

their implementation might be required by public laws and government regulations but also voluntarily because they are considered useful by producers and users of the products and services governed by those standards.[17] If a standards-developing organization (SDO) is widely believed to have these qualities, it will lead to a widespread expectation that this SDO will (maybe even should) be the place where stakeholders will address further standard-setting needs related to the organization's area of expertise.

As highlighted by Büthe and Mattli's typology of global regulation,[18] having such a single focal institution for technical standard-setting in a given jurisdiction or market avoids the (often drawn-out and resource-intensive) process of multiple standards competing in "standards wars" for market share *after* two or more conflicting standards have been fully developed – though at the cost of shifting the underlying conflicts of interest to the standard-setting stage.[19] It creates incentives to invest in institutionalized joint standards development before a particular technical solution gets finalized and adopted as an international standard – subject to the structure, rules, and procedures of the standards-developing organization.

A second essential attribute of the IEC is maintaining internationally broad-based input legitimacy for its role as a global governor through inclusiveness toward all legitimate stakeholders based on a structure of nominally equal national representation.[20] The creation of the International Electrotechnical Commission was preceded in the late nineteenth century by the establishment of domestic electrotechnical "societies" – professional associations of physicists and early electrical engineers – within virtually all the "advanced," industrializing countries at the time.

[17] For a discussion of the many economic, socio-political, and legal incentives to implement such "voluntary" technical standards (or at least claim compliance) even when it is not required, see T. Büthe, Private Regulation in the Global Economy: A (P)Review (October 2010) 12:3 *Business and Politics* 1, esp. 15–20; T. Büthe, Global Private Politics: A Research Agenda (October 2010) 12:3 *Business and Politics* 1, esp. 8–11; and H. Schepel, *The Constitution of Private Governance: Product Standards in the Regulation of Integrating Markets* (2005).

[18] Büthe and Mattli, *supra* note 7, at 18–41.

[19] On standards wars, see, e.g., C. Shapiro and H. R. Varian, The Art of Standards Wars (Winter 1999) 41:2 *California Management Review* 8–32; A. Augereau, S. Greenstein, and M. Rysman, Coordination versus Differentiation in a Standards War: 56k Modems (Winter 2006) 37:4 *Rand Journal of Economics* 887–909; A. A. Quark, *Global Rivalries: Standards Wars and the Transnational Cotton Trade* (2013); G. Llanes and J. Poblete, Technology Choice and Coalition Formation in Standards Wars (June 2020) 68:2 *Journal of Industrial Economics* 270–297. The classic analysis of the efficiency of cooperative development of technical standards vs. standards wars remains J. Farrell and G. Saloner, Coordination through Committees and Markets (Summer 1988) 19:2 *Rand Journal of Economics* 235–252.

[20] On legitimacy and participation in global governance institutions, see J. Pauwelyn et al., eds. *Rethinking Participation in Global Governance: Challenges and Reforms in Financial and Health Institutions* (2022); esp. M. DeMenno and T. Büthe, Voice and Influence in Global Governance: An Analytical Framework, in Pauwelyn et al. (eds.), 31–70; regarding the notion of global governors and their various possible sources of authority, see D. D. Avant, M. Finnemore, and S. K. Sell, Who Governs the Globe?, in *Who Governs the Globe?* (D. Avant, M. Finnemore, and S. K. Sell eds., 2010), at 9–14.

The highly transnationally connected individuals who started the IEC were mostly the leading figures within those domestic bodies.[21] And while they initially largely acted on their own (and often with a personal commercial stake in the matter as commercially successful scientist-entrepreneurs), they laid a claim to acting on behalf of those national bodies. The IEC then later asserted these bodies to be representatives of all legitimate stakeholders in those countries. The IEC's structure reflects this historical legacy to this day, and it is central to its claim of legitimacy based on inclusiveness toward all legitimate stakeholders via internationally broad representation. This claim to internationally broad representation means concretely that participation in IEC governance is organized by country and requires each participating country to have a domestic Electrotechnical Committee, which, upon becoming the country's IEC member body, is recognized as the country's "National Committee" in the IEC.

A third essential attribute of the IEC is its status as a nongovernmental (and therefore transnational) organization. The electrotechnical societies that were the IEC's founding member bodies were mostly nongovernmental bodies.[22] Over time, many of them have been recognized by their respective governments as private bodies with a public purpose; quite a few are also partially government-funded and/ or regulated by governments; and a number of the national committees, especially from the Global South, are even government entities. The IEC, however, considers itself a strictly nongovernmental body – a defining feature that was consciously and emphatically selected already in the very beginning[23] – and governments as such have no direct role in IEC governance.[24]

The IEC's nongovernmental status has numerous important consequences. Among them is that the IEC does not have guaranteed public financial support but instead depends for its financial viability on buy-in from its – mostly commercial – stakeholders. Those stakeholders provide the IEC with expertise through their participation in standard-setting as well as financial resources, directly, by literally buying the documents that contain the technical specifications of IEC standards, as well as indirectly, via the National Electrotechnical Committees that comprise the IEC and pay membership fees. At the same time, the IEC's nongovernmental

[21] Büthe, *supra* note 2, at 297–301; D. Cahan, Helmholtz in Gilded-Age America: The International Electrical Congress of 1893 and the Relations of Science and Technology (2010) 67:1 *Annals of Science* 1–38; E. Warburg, Werner Siemens und die Physikalisch-Technische Reichsanstalt (1916) 4:50 *Naturwissenschaften* 793–797; Yates and Murphy, *supra* note 15, at 64–67.

[22] Even in cases such as Hungary, for which the delegate at the 1906 meeting officially represented the Ministry of Commerce, the body that became the IEC member body for Hungary was the nongovernmental Elektrotechnischer Verein.

[23] Report of Preliminary Meeting, London: International Elecrotechnical Commission, 1906, at 10.

[24] Büthe, *supra* note 2, at 312–314.

character constrains the usability of traditional power resources of states[25] but also means that the legitimacy of global technology governance may be much more easily challenged than the legitimacy of a traditional (inter-state) international organization.

The fourth "fundamental attribute" of IEC governance is maintaining a balance between decentralized, bottom-up agenda-setting and decision-making, on the one hand, and centralized coordination and oversight, on the other, to ensure coherence and consistency as well as maintain the IEC's ability to act in pursuit of its organizational self-interest. As discussed below (Section 15.3.2), the pursuit of this balance has been a key driver of the IEC's structure and procedures and an essential source of both its technical authority (enabling it to become the focal institution for international electrotechnical standard-setting) and its legitimacy.

15.3 EXPLAINING RESILIENCE

15.3.1 *Theoretical Sketch*

A fully developed theory of organizational resilience is beyond the scope of this chapter. Yet an explicit sketch of the theoretical ideas underpinning our empirical analysis is warranted before we turn to examining specific challenges faced by the IEC over the course of its 115-year history. Building on Büthe's proto-theory of preeminence in global private governance,[26] we posit that, for a substantively important international organization or transnational governance body, resilience – in the sense of its ability to survive shocks and environmental changes, such that it still resembles its former state and functionality as defined by its essential attributes – requires such a body to have three characteristics:

(1) **Capacity and capability for autonomous agency.** To be resilient, a global governance body needs to be set up in such a way that it is able to pursue its organizational self-interest even in cases when the body's interests are distinctive from the interests of the national-level or sub-national units that comprise the inter- or transnational body. Such capacity for agency implies a structure where the leadership and staff support does not just rotate among these "members" but has some permanence and genuinely identifies with, or has allegiance toward, the global governance body. It also requires the leadership to be authorized and incentivized to speak and act on behalf of the organization with some degree of autonomy.

[25] W. Mattli and T. Büthe, Setting International Standards: Technological Rationality or Primacy of Power? (October 2003) 56:1 *World Politics* 1–42.

[26] Büthe, *supra* note 9, at 9ff., esp. 10–12.

Following Cafaggi and Pistor's work on regulatory regimes, Lavenex, Serrano and Büthe have recently introduced into the analysis of global governance bodies Nussbaum and Sen's distinction between capacity and capability. The latter is defined as "the ability to recognize and articulate" the organization's self-interest, even when it is not just the lowest common denominator (or some other function) of the constitutive units' self-interest but might even diverge from them. Capability thus also implies an ability to develop original, alternative proposals for how best to pursue the organization's own interests.[27] Having capability implies that the transnational body must have some permanent staff with the requisite analytical skill set, as well as financial resources that are at least in part independent of its members.

(2) **Embeddedness among stakeholders.** There is no global governance in a Hobbesian state of nature. Governance authority at the inter- or transnational level must be built and actively maintained since such authority is usually and traditionally situated at the local or national level – or at most at the level of regional common markets.[28] To be resilient, retain authority, and remain a focal point for developing standards or to govern other aspects of technology in the face of challenges, a global governance body needs to be at least sufficiently embedded among its members (and possibly other stakeholders) to ensure the continued relevance of the organization's work to those stakeholders. Particularly important in this respect is the ability to recognize and meet the needs of stakeholders who might be in a position to participate in, or even set up, alternative inter- or transnational governance arrangements – sufficiently so that it reduces the incentive of those stakeholders to explore alternatives. At the same time, meeting the particular needs of those stakeholders must not to so far that the global governance body loses the required autonomy or legitimacy in the eyes of the organization's other stakeholders.[29]

(3) **Ambition.** The combination of capacity and capability should in principle assure the active and strategic pursuit of the organization's survival

[27] S. Lavenex, O. Serrano, and T. Büthe, Power Transitions and the Rise of the Regulatory State: Global Market Governance in Flux. Introduction to a Special Issue (July 2021) 15:3 *Regulation and Governance* 445–471, at 450. See also F. Cafaggi and K. Pistor, Regulatory Capabilities: A Normative Framework for Assessing the Distributional Effects of Regulation (June 2015) 9:2 *Regulation and Governance* 95–107.

[28] P. Genschel and R. Werle, From National Hierarchies to International Standardization: Modal Change in the Governance of Telecommunications (July–September 1993) 13:3 *Journal of Public Policy* 203–225; S. Schmidt and R. Werle, *Coordinating Technology: Studies in the International Standardization of Telecommunications* (1998); M. Egan, *Constructing a European Market: Standards, Regulation, and Governance* (2001).

[29] On the notion of embeddedness, which informs this discussion, see J. Ruggie, International Regimes, Transactions, and Change: Embedded Liberalism in the Postwar Economic Order (Spring 1982) 36:2 *International Organization* 379–415; and P. B. Evans, *Embedded Autonomy: States and Industrial Transformation* (1995).

with its essential attributes intact – that is, its resilience – because the continued existence and substantive relevance can be assumed to be an essential first-order preference of any organization.[30] In practice, however, the actual active and strategic pursuit of the organization's self-interest is also a function of the skill of the organization's leadership and its ambition to ensure the organization's continued existence and importance. Institutional factors, such as career incentives and rewards for senior leaders' skillful pursuit of resilience, can increase the likelihood that the global body will exhibit such ambition and develop the skills to pursue resilience, but the idiosyncratic qualities of the individuals who fill those leaderships conditions also matter.[31]

15.3.2 *Does the IEC Meet the Requirements for the Pursuit of Resilience? Applying the Analytical Framework to the Specific Case*

Operationalizing the required characteristics for the specific case of the IEC suggests that the IEC meets (and for a long time has met) the criteria set up abstractly above, which should empower it to pursue resilience. We first discuss how the IEC assures embeddedness, which is critical to the IEC's technical expertise and authority, as well as key to the commercial usefulness of its standards. Given that electro-technology has changed tremendously over the course of the IEC's existence (and it continues to evolve over time), with innovations resulting in "new" areas of electro-technology not yet covered by the IEC's structure, maintaining (the ambition for) such preeminence also implies the ability to pursue organizational interests actively and strategically. It also implies a responsiveness to – and maintaining a reasonable balance between – major stakeholders who might otherwise have the credible option to try to "go it alone"[32] by developing competing standards outside of the IEC.[33] So does the IEC exhibit capacity and capability, as well as embeddedness?[34]

[30] T. Büthe, Historical Institutionalism and Institutional Development in the EU: The Development of Supranational Authority over Government Subsidies (State Aid), in *Historical Institutionalism and International Relations: Explaining Institutional Development in World Politics* (T. Rixen, L. Viola, and M. Zürn eds., 2016), 37–67.

[31] See J. A. Yates and C. N. Murphy, Charles Le Maistre: Entrepreneur in International Standardization (2008) 51 *Entreprises et Histoire* 10; and *supra* note 15.

[32] L. Gruber, *Ruling the World: Power Politics and the Rise of Supranational Institutions* (2000); J. Odell, *Negotiating the World Economy* (2000), esp. 47ff.

[33] A focus on practically "useful" IEC standards has been a characteristic of the IEC from the beginning, since many of the scientist-engineers that played a central role in founding the IEC were also highly commercially successful entrepreneurs. They therefore sought to bridge emphatically valued basic research and the creation of entrepreneurial opportunities for commercial applications.

[34] The ambition and skills of IEC leaders are harder to operationalize at the level of generality required for this preliminary discussion; they will be discussed as part of the empirical analyses in subsequent sections.

The IEC's structure and procedures ensure its embeddedness. As of the end of 2021, the IEC has 110 Technical Committees (TCs); some of them also have numerous subcommittees (SCs), for a total of 212 TCs and SCs.[35] Much of the technical work in those TCs and SCs is actually done in distinct working groups (of which there were 725), project teams (200), and maintenance teams (669 as of the end of 2021). This structure and the procedural norms and rules of the IEC allow for bottom-up agenda-setting, making it very easy for a small number of national member bodies to launch the development of a new standard for a product or electrotechnical phenomenon.[36] Consensus norms then give a right to be heard to all member bodies that have elected to be "participating members" (P-members) of the TC where a given standard is developed, reviewed, or revised. These norms – at least in theory – provide all stakeholders with opportunities to make alternative or compromise proposals for all aspects of the technical work. They are reinforced by procedural rules governing the IEC standards development process, which require large super-majorities in formal votes on the penultimate "Committee Draft for Voting" (CDV)[37] and for the adoption of the resulting "Final Draft" as an official IEC standard.

Balancing these decentralized elements of the IEC's institutional structure, the IEC has for a long time reserved a crucial (if mostly light-touch) centralized role for the IEC leadership, especially its Standardization Management Board (SMB) and the IEC Central Secretariat. Jointly, they provide coordination and oversight to ensure coherence and consistency as well as maintain the IEC's ability to act in pursuit of its organizational self-interest.

The IEC leadership consists of a president, three vice presidents (one each for standardization management, market strategy, and conformity assessment), a treasurer, and the IEC Secretary General.[38] Candidates for the part-time positions of

[35] For instance, TC23, devoted to "electrical accessories and related systems" for household, industrial, and other commercial uses (www.iec.ch/dyn/www/f?p=103:7:::::FSP_ORG_ID:1299) and has separate SC's inter alia for circuit breakers; plugs and socket-outlets; couplers for electric vehicles; switches for appliances; and devices for monitoring, measuring, controlling, managing, and optimizing the efficient use of AC and DC electrical energy (www.iec.ch/dyn/www/f?p=103:7:::::FSP_ORG_ID:10046).

[36] Büthe, *supra* note 9, esp. 32–34.

[37] Positive votes on a CDV committee draft can and negative votes must be accompanied by comments. This gives P-members a formal opportunity to object to any aspect of the proposed standard and to request changes as a condition for supporting the adoption of a revised version as an IEC standard. The TC in charge of the standard then has an opportunity to revise the standard one last time before submitting the resulting Final Draft International Standard (FDIS) to a vote of the full IEC membership. At the CDV stage, National Committees also have the option to provide comments while voting to "abstain," thus allowing the committee to proceed while reserving judgment on the resulting FDIS.

[38] The three vice presidents lead, respectively, the IEC Standardization Management Board (discussed separately below), the Market Strategy Board (tasked with early identification of important technological changes and market trends that might warrant an IEC response), and the Conformity Assessment Board (tasked with overseeing the IEC's four, commercially very

president or vice president(s) tend to come from the private sector and customarily have previously held prominent leadership positions in one of the largest IEC's national member bodies. They are elected for (once-renewable) three-year terms, and during this time, (vice)presidents are supposed to pursue the interest of the IEC, only, though they usually retain their private sector full-time (and income-providing) position.

Not as visible but at least as important for the IEC's capability and its capacity for autonomous agency are the Secretary General and the senior staff of the central secretariat of the IEC. They are longer-term, full-time employees of the IEC, which gives them a strong incentive to think and act in the institutional self-interest of the organization. The staff, which supports the work of the IEC leadership and administratively and technically handles most of the coordination between the IEC's many committees, is lean (much smaller than the ISO's) but readily provides the support to enable capacity and capability.

The SMB is critical to the IEC's agency, as it coordinates and oversees the work of the many technical committees, subcommittees, and working groups of the IEC. It ensures that these various groups do not work at cross-purposes, for example, by developing competing IEC standards for the same purpose where the purview of two or more committees might overlap. The SMB (similar to the other boards) comprises "automatically appointed members" (representatives of the largest member bodies in terms of their contributions to the IEC annual budget and staff support for technical committees), elected representatives of the remaining member bodies, and IEC senior staff ex officio. The elected members of the SMB are elected for three-year terms, renewable once, by the IEC General Assembly, usually in the annual meeting of the member body presidents and senior officers.

SMB oversight is supposed to ensure timeliness and high quality of the technical output – and that all IEC work follows the procedural rules and norms for IEC standard-setting and no one company or country might highjack any TC or larger parts of the organization. The SMB also may reorganize the technical work by merging TCs; it appoints TC secretariats and chairmanships; it adjudicates jurisdictional conflicts between the TCs; and it is responsible for relations with other organizations.[39] In doing so, the SMB ensures the ability of the IEC to act in the self-interest of the organization while keeping the IEC leadership grounded in the organization's member bodies – which we would expect to play an important role in the IEC's ability to exhibit organizational resilience.

important conformity assessment programs). These three fifteen-member boards are the primary management bodies of the organization, their tasks officially delegated to them from the overall IEC Board, the core executive body of the organization; see IEC, Management Structure, www.iec.ch/management-structure.

39 For details, see IEC, Management Structure: SMB, www.iec.ch/dyn/www/f?p=103:48:0::::FSP_ORG_ID,FSP_LANG_ID:3228,25; Büthe, *supra* note 2, at 318–320; and *supra* note 9, at 24.

15.4 IEC RESILIENCE IN THE FACE OF TECHNOLOGICAL CHANGE

One of the remarkable features of the early history of the IEC is how few committed individuals it took to launch a transnational private body that has – for 115 years and counting – played a major, increasingly global role in the development and governance of an enormous range of electro-technologies. The entrepreneurial approach and skill of key figures – above all Charles Le Maistre, the IEC's first and long-term secretary general – surely was important for bringing the IEC into existence as an organization with its consensus-oriented structure and procedures for developing "voluntary" technical standards.[40] The relative ease of its creation may also have been a function of fortuitous temporal sequence: the IEC was the first body of its kind, set up to address functional needs and serve the (largely common) interests of key political-economic stakeholders in the early years of a new field (electro-technology).[41] Rapid technological development in this field meant that standardization tended to open up a wealth of new, profitable opportunities while foreclosing few. Standardization at that time thus resembled a coordination game with large gains from coordination and relatively small distributional effects, making distributional conflicts a second-order concern.[42]

Yet, the conditions that facilitated the establishment of the IEC in 1906 also applied to a greater or lesser extent in later cases of "new" technologies. Indeed, over the decades, the development of new areas of electro-technology – such as batteries for mobile electrical devices, digital audio and video formats, electronics, and more recently artificial intelligence – have time and again created challenges to IEC preeminence. The IEC has proven remarkably resilient in the face of these technological changes.

The IEC was initially set up to agree upon a common set of terms and measurements that would be foundational for the development of electro-technologies and electrical products – anything from light bulbs to electricity-powered heavy

[40] Yates and Murphy, *supra* note 31. Regarding the role of entrepreneurial actors in global governance more generally, see also J. F. Green, *Rethinking Private Authority: Agents and Entrepreneurs in Global Environmental Governance* (2014).

[41] On the issue of temporality and sequence for institutional development in general, see T. Büthe, Taking Temporality Seriously: Modeling History and the Use of Narratives as Evidence (2002) 96:3 *American Political Science Review* 481–494. See also P. Pierson, Not Just What, but When: Timing and Sequence in Political Processes (2000) 14:1 *Studies in American Political Development* 72–92; W. Streeck and K. Thelen (eds.), *Beyond Continuity: Institutional Change in Advanced Political Economies* (2005); C. Trampusch, Sequence-Oriented Policy Analysis (2006) 16:1 *Berliner Journal für Soziologie* 55; D. Bach and A. L. Newman, Governing Lipitor and Lipstick: Capacity, Sequencing, and Power in International Pharmaceutical and Cosmetics Regulation (2010) 17:1 *Review of International Political Economy* 665–695; E. Posner, Sequence as Explanation (2010) 17:4 *Review of International Political Economy* 639–664; O. Fioretos, T. G. Falleti, and A. Sheingate (eds.), *Oxford Handbook of Historical Institutionalism* (2015); T. Rixen, L. Viola, and M. Zürn (eds.), *Historical Institutionalism and International Relations: Explaining Institutional Development in World Politics* (2016).

[42] See Büthe, *supra* note 9, at 35.

machinery.[43] Its agenda soon broadened to include the development of standards for the design and performance of actual electrical devices. Initially, the focus was on power-generating equipment, industrial machinery, and standards for use (in scientific research and) within and between private enterprises.[44] Already by 1911, the agenda had become so broad that discussing all current projects in a single (multi-day) plenary meeting was deemed impractical, prompting the IEC to delegate the technical work to more specialized committees, known today as the IEC Technical Committees.[45] Setting standards for consumer goods was added to the IEC agenda starting in the 1920s and became an important focus of multiple TCs after World War II thanks to the widespread electrification of households throughout advanced industrialized countries and the mass-market production of electrical devices for household use.[46] And as new electro-technologies were developed, the scope of IEC rule-making broadened further.

IEC standards have remained essential to the development of a wide range of electrical (and in more recent decades electronic) technologies in part because IEC standards define elements and components used as the foundation or building blocks for innovations and technological change. The units and methods for the measurement of voltage and frequency of electrical currents, established by the IEC early on, remain a good example: using other units or methods has become literally unthinkable. Another, more recent example are sensors, which have long had various industrial and household uses, and continue to become ever more important as key parts of complex smart manufacturing and a wide variety of artificial intelligence–driven or –supported systems.[47] A variety of sensors have, for instance, been integrated into smart "wearable technologies"[48] used, inter alia, in the healthcare sector. Such devices promise great improvement in patient care by tracking, recording, and (remotely) monitoring physiological processes and biomedical signals.[49] The COVID-19 pandemic brought this into focus: sensors installed in a wearable device can alert the user when changes in their metrics match those associated with COVID-19 or even track the stability and recovery of those

43 See 1904 Declaration for the establishment of the IEC; E. B. Paxton, AIEE: A Leader in Electrical Standards (1954) 25:8 *Magazine of Standards* 242–245, at 244ff.

44 W. H. Onken Jr., Work of the International Electrotechnical Commission (April 17–26, 1919) 73 *Electrical World* 856–857.

45 Yates and Murphy, *supra* note 31), at 17 note 53.

46 L. Ruppert, *Brief History of the International Electrotechnical Commission* (1956), at 6ff.; A. Raeburn, IEC Technical Committee Creation. The First Half Century, 1906–1949 (on file with the author).

47 Sensors can interpret analog or electrical stimuli, including temperature, sound, motion, smell, and pressure.

48 Wearables are a class of Internet of Things devices that act as a portable computer system attached to the user's body such as smart-watches, patches, and t-shirts.

49 S. Patel, H. Park, P. Bonato, L. Chan, and M. Rodgers, A Review of Wearable Sensors and Systems with Application in Rehabilitation (2012) 9:1 *Journal of NeuroEngineering and Rehabilitation* 21, doi: 10.1186/1743-0003-9-21.

infected.[50] The IEC plays a role in the development of all these new technologies because the sensors used are designed and manufactured according to the IEC 60747-14 "family" of standards, developed by IEC Technical Committee 47, such as the IEC 60747-14-10 for glucose sensors.[51]

Even more important is that the IEC has proven adept at adding new issues to its agenda to keep abreast of technological changes. This is partly a function of the relative ease with which a "new work item" can be added to any Technical Committee's standards development agenda. Such a proposal to develop a new standard can be put forward by any National Committee, any Technical Committee (for topics fitting its expertise), the secretary of that TC, the SMB, or the IEC leadership. The proposal is then put to a vote only among the P-members of the TC or SC specified in the proposal as the one to develop the standard. Among them, a simple majority and a commitment of at least four of them (five for larger committees) is all that is required to launch the new standards project. These procedural rules make it very easy to extend the scope of the IEC's technical authority while making it very difficult for those who do not want to see an IEC standard developed to prevent the launch of such an effort, as long as at least a small number of members share the desire to develop it.[52]

There are limits, however, to such incremental additions to existing technical committees' agenda as a response to the need for standards development, especially if this work requires distinctive expertise or involves a distinct set of stakeholders. Accordingly, the SMB added entirely new TCs to the IEC portfolio (and occasionally restructured existing TCs), including for computing and information-processing standards in the 1960s; for laser equipment in 1970s; for fiber optics (TC86), superconductivity (TC90), and wind turbines (now "wind energy generation systems", TC88) in the 1980s; for fuel cells (TC105) in the 1990; and for flat-screen panels (TC110), for nanotechnology in electrical and electronic products (TC113), and for marine energy (i.e., the conversion of tidal and other water currents into electric energy, TC114) in the 2000s. Recently established TCs include committees focused on smart grid user interfaces (TC118), wearable electronic devices and technologies (TC124), and "robotics for electricity generation, transmission and distribution systems" (TC129). Even the development of futuristic-sounding flying cars will involve IEC standardization: such urban air mobility devices will likely rely upon existing standards and standards newly developed by IEC TC100 for surround-view monitoring of the car, by ISO/IEC JTC1 for biometric interchange formats, and IEC 62668 to ensure that the electronic parts safely work together.[53]

[50] A. Ravizza, C. De Maria, L. Di Pietro, et al., Comprehensive Review on Current and Future Regulatory Requirements on Wearable Sensors in Preclinical and Clinical Testing (2019) 7 *Frontiers in Bioengineering and Biotechnology* 313.

[51] Sensors inserted under the skin can monitor diabetes and transmit the information to a device.

[52] For details, see Büthe, *supra* note 9, at 31–34.

[53] IEC, Auto Manufacturer Says Flying Cars Will Arrive in Cities by 2030, www.iec.ch/blog/auto-manufacturer-says-flying-cars-will-arrive-cities-2030; Z. Kleinman, Flying Car Completes Test

In sum, the IEC has, time and again, responded to technological change directly by extending the range of electro-technologies (by now long including in principle all kind of electronics, too) for which it claims standard-setting expertise and authority. While this has not completely prevented the creation of new, more specialized bodies for developing technical standards (see below), it has allowed the IEC to remain the preeminent forum for such activities, especially where cooperation, coordination, and interoperability with related technologies is important, as the standards for them are often already being developed or maintained at the IEC. Importantly, IEC resilience in the face of technological change was by no means coincidental but part of a conscious strategy, as occasionally documented, such as when TC111 was set up in 2004 and assigned the task to "monitor closely the corresponding regional standardization activities worldwide to become a *focal point* for discussions concerning standardization."[54]

15.5 IEC RESILIENCE VIS-À-VIS POSSIBLE COMPETITOR SDOS

Having been the first transnational body for setting electro-technology standards gave the IEC something of an incumbency advantage, making it the default focal point for subsequent initiatives to achieve coordination or even harmonization of technical standards related to any area of electro-technology.[55] From early on, however, other standards-developing organizations arose at various times, and it appears that IEC leaders quite consciously sought to head off possible challenges from potential competitor organizations by establishing more or less formal relationships with them, turning them into collaborators instead. The International Conference on Large Electric Systems and the World Power Conference, for instance, were initially set up as fora for electrotechnical standard-setting in 1921 and 1926, respectively, thus effectively threatening the IEC's preeminence for commercially very important segments of electro-technology.[56] Over time, however, their standards-developing activities were either absorbed by the IEC, or they yielded them to the IEC. Other potential competitors established a symbiotic, complementary relationship vis-à-vis the IEC, as in the case of the International Federation of National Standardizing Associations (ISA), founded in 1926 and also

Flight between Airports, BBC News June 30, 2021, www.bbc.com/news/technology-57651843; I. Bogost, When Cars Fly, *The Atlantic*, May 2016, www.theatlantic.com/magazine/archive/2016/05/when-cars-fly/476382.

[54] Original official scope of the work of TC111 in 2004, today online at TC 111 Scope, www.iec.ch/dyn/www/f?p=103:7:1100173035120 38::::FSP_ORG_ID,FSP_LANG_ID:1314,25 (emphasis added).

[55] Büthe, *supra* note 9.

[56] The empirical record of the individual motivations of the key actors and the internal deliberations within these bodies is slim (for the most comprehensive treatment, see Yates and Murphy, *supra* note 15) but appears that the pursuit of the IEC's organizational self-interest by Le Maistre and other early IEC leaders was quite conscious.

headed by Le Maistre, who ensured that its portfolio was defined as standardization outside of the field of electro-technology.

IEC resilience was also helped by fortuitous elements of its institutional design, which allowed it to survive the hiatus of World War II largely unscathed – in contrast to many other inter- and transnational organizations. The statutes of the ISA, for instance, required the organization to hold a general meeting at the latest every three years and tied the terms of office of anyone who could claim to act on behalf of the organization to that meeting schedule. Having held a meeting in 1939 just prior to the beginning of the war, the ISA could go until 1942, but then the ISA arguably ceased to exist; it thus became a collateral organizational casualty of the war. The IEC's more minimalist rules, by contrast, allowed its secretary general to continue to serve in that role until the next meeting after the war (at which Le Maistre was confirmed once more).[57]

After World War II, the establishment of the ISO as a standards-developing organization for all industries put the IEC's preeminence or independence at risk. Yet, here again the IEC, led by Le Maistre (who continued as IEC secretary general until 1952), intervened to make certain that the ISO agenda would not clash with the IEC's. The IEC then proceeded to establish quite quickly institutional mechanisms for a division of labor between IEC and its "sister organization" and to ensure that, for any issue at the intersection of the IEC's and ISO's respective areas of specialization, they would not develop competing standards but coordinate. This cooperation has been maintained for more than seven decades – albeit with a growing set of work items assigned to various subcommittees of the rather unwieldy "Joint Technical Committee 1," which the two standards bodies manage and staff jointly.

The most serious challenge to the IEC's institutional preeminence in recent decades arose from a group of IEC "insiders" in the process of the EU Common Market initiative in the 1980s. After the failure of its attempts to achieve regulatory harmonization through inter- or transgovernmental negotiations,[58] the EU sought to overcome divergent, markets-fragmenting regulatory requirements, standards, and norms by delegating the development of technical standards to transnational, non-governmental standard-setting bodies.[59] Seeking to balance the attainment of common technical standards with the achievement of legitimate public policy objectives as defined by Europe's political (governmental) authorities through

[57] J. A. Yates and C. N. Murphy, Coordinating International Standards: The Formation of the ISO, Unpublished manuscript (on file with the authors), MIT 2006; Yates and Murphy, *supra* note 15.

[58] A. Dashwood, Hastening Slowly: The Community's Path Toward Harmonization, in *Policy-Making in the European Community* (H. Wallace, W. Wallace, and C. Webb eds., 1983) 177–208.

[59] J. Pelkmans, The New Approach to Technical Harmonization and Standards (1987) 25:3 *Journal of Common Market Studies* 249–269; K. Schreiber, The New Approach to Technical Harmonization and Standards, in *The State of the European Community* (L. Hurwitz and C. Lequesne eds., 1991) 97–112; Egan, *supra* note 28.

democratic processes, they set up a system where European policymakers specify the overarching objectives through legislative processes, then delegate finding a "consensus" technical solution for achieving those objectives (subject to international trade law and EU stipulations against discrimination, anti-competitive conduct, etc.) to the then-nascent European-level standard-setting bodies, CEN and CENELEC (corresponding to ISO and IEC, respectively). This arrangement constituted a dangerous challenge to the IEC's preeminence, given the prominent role of numerous EU countries' IEC member bodies in IEC-based electrotechnology governance.

The IEC responded to this challenge (heading it off for the most part, though not without compromising some of its autonomy) by striking the 1991 Lugano Agreement and then the 1996 Dresden Agreement with CENELEC, which sets out detailed procedures for cooperation between the two transnational SDOs.[60] For new standards, for instance, it specifies joint decisions by the pertinent TCs of both organization about whether IEC or CENELEC shall take the lead in developing the standard. If IEC takes the lead, it commits to writing a standard that allows for achieving the EU objectives, as well as completing the work on the time line necessary to meet the EU legislative mandate. If CENELEC takes the lead, it keeps the corresponding IEC committee informed, but the technical work then takes place in CENELEC, where non-European IEC member bodies do not have any automatic status. Either way, voting on the final draft standard takes place in parallel in both organizations. If adopted by both, then the often-European-made standard becomes an international standard without further technical discussion at the IEC.[61]

Notwithstanding the IEC's propensity to swiftly pick up on (market demand for transnational private governance of) new technological developments, some firms have sidestepped the IEC to develop standards for new technologies in so-called standards consortia – ad hoc groups of firms set up (sometime formally as joint ventures) to develop a technical standard for a particular use and usually with exclusive intellectual property rights claims regarding the standard and the technical expertise contained therein.[62] There are precedents for developing standards collaboratively in small, exclusive groups of firms,[63] but standards consortia became a

[60] See Egan, *supra* note 28; G. Eickhoff and B. Hartlieb, Einfluss auf Normen-Inhalte: Europäischer und internationaler Fokus, in *Normen und Wettbewerb* (T. Bahke, U. Blum, and G. Eickhoff, 2002) 172–188.

[61] See Mattli and Büthe, *supra* note 25, at 28.

[62] See T. Büthe and J.-M. Witte, Product Standards in Transatlantic Trade and Investment: Domestic and International Practices and Institutions, AICGS Policy Report no. 13, Washington, DC, American Institute for Contemporary German Studies (2004), at 32ff.; R. Werle, Institutional Aspects of Standardization: Jurisdictional Conflicts and the Choice of Standardization Organizations 8:3 (2001) *Journal of European Public Policy* 392–410.

[63] See, e.g., C. F. Cargill, *Information Technology Standardization: Theory, Process, and Organization* (1989).

distinct method of standard-setting only in the late 1980s and early 1990s, especially in the fast-changing information and telecommunications sector, where the long time required for IEC standards development (five to eight years in the 1980s) was considered particularly problematic.[64] The IEC responded to this challenge by taking various measures to accelerate the technical work in the TCs, SCs, and working groups, shortening the average time required, from the launch of a proposal for a new standard to the vote on the final draft, to less than three years by the early 2000s.

The IEC also has incorporated into its portfolio numerous standards initially developed by standards consortia (thus committing the holders of standards-essential patents to license those patents to any user on "fair, reasonable, and non-discriminatory" [FRAND] terms while usually also greatly enhancing the value of those patents). To give just two examples with particular importance to the entertainment industry: the audio CD standard, maintained since 1987 as IEC standard 60908, was originally developed by a Sony-Philips consortium in 1979/80.[65] And the Blu-ray optical disc standard, maintained since 2011 by ISO/IEC JTC1/SC23 as ISO/IEC 30193, was originally developed in 2000 by the Sony-Philips-Panasonic-led consortium in a fierce race with the Toshiba-led consortium, which had developed the competing High Definition DVD standard.[66] In all three cases (and many more like it), the IEC succeeded in gaining authority and in some sense restoring its pre-eminence, though at the cost of recognizing and arguably sanctifying standards developed without IEC input and without regard to the procedures and norms of IEC standardization.

Another challenge to the IEC's authority arose from governments in the context of the multilateral international trade regime of GATT and WTO. In the 1960s and 1970s, cross-national differences in technical standards (as such or when subsequently used as a basis for government regulations) were increasingly recognized as important non-tariff barriers to trade.[67] By the 1990s, their trade-inhibiting effect for manufactured goods was estimated to far exceed the effect of the remaining tariffs for such goods between advanced industrialized countries, resulting in a strong push to incorporate the previously optional GATT Agreement on Technical Barriers to

[64] R. Hawkins, The Rise of Consortia in the Information and Communication Technology Industries: Emerging Implications for Policy (1999) 23 *Telecommunications Policy* 159–173; S. Bolin (ed.), *The Standards Edge* (2002); J. Baron, Y. Ménière, and T. Pohlmann, Standards, Consortia, and Innovation (September 2014) 36 *International Journal of Industrial Organization* 22–35.

[65] See Büthe and Mattli, *supra* note 7, at 46ff.

[66] See S. Greenstein, Format Wars All Over Again (2006) 26:1 *IEEE Micro* 7, 140; Ibid., at 27ff., 34ff.

[67] R. E. Baldwin, *Nontariff Distortions of International Trade* (1971); M. Emerson (ed.), *The Economics of 1992: The E.C. Commission's Assessment of the Economic Effects of Completing the Internal Market* (1988); J. Grieco, *Cooperation among Nations: Europe, America, and Non-Tariff Barriers to Trade* (1990).

Trade into the WTO Treaty, of which it became an integral part, binding on all WTO member states. The resulting international trade law obligation to use "international standards" as the "technical basis" for regulatory measures (whenever international standards exist that can achieve the stated regulatory purposes, such as consumer health and safety) promised to be very profitable for competitive producers and to yield substantial macroeconomic gains.[68]

For the IEC, the new prominence of international standards in international trade law created unprecedented visibility (beyond the niche world of standards experts), but it also created two risks: first, it created the risk that the IEC's preeminence might be diluted through provisions in the intergovernmental agreement for the recognition of alternative transnational bodies for electrotechnical standard-setting. Second, it created the risk of overt politicization and government attempts to interfere in the work of the IEC. Working jointly with ISO, the IEC addressed these risks, first, by actively lobbying (successfully) for the incorporation of the ISO-IEC joint Code of Good Practices for the Preparation, Adoption and Application of Standards, which was written into the TBT-Agreement as Annex 3, which also gave ISO and IEC, via their joint "Information Center," an official role in the implementation of the agreement. They also successfully lobbied against any mention of other "international standards" bodies (except for the more specialized, intergovernmental ITU) in the Agreement. The exclusive recognition of IEC, ISO, and ITU does not, strictly speaking, give these organization exclusive rights, but it raised their status and made it clear that they met the requirement for WTO recognition as an international standard-setter.[69] IEC responded to the second risk by being even more protective of its nongovernmental status. In the end, the entry into force of the WTO Treaty with its TBT provisions thus confirmed and may have even strengthened the resilient IEC and its preeminence.

The most recent risk to the IEC from an SDO competitor arises from China's efforts to enhance its role in global technology governance, especially technical standardization through its Regional Comprehensive Economic Partnership and, more generally, through its Belt and Road Initiative (BRI). The BRI is an extremely broad – comprehensive, though not necessarily cohesively planned, and in parts still rather vague – initiative, sparked by Chinese President Xi Jinping in 2013, to connect China-centered continental East Asia more closely with East and South Asia, Oceania, Central Asia, Europe, the Middle East, and Africa via land and maritime

[68] K. Blind et al., Volkswirtschaftlicher Nutzen and A. Töpfer et al., Unternehmerischer Nutzen, in *Gesamtwirtschaftlicher Nutzen der Normung* (B. Hartlieb ed., 2000), 23–34; 9–22; WTO, World Trade Report 2005: Exploring the Links Between Trade, Standards, and the WTO (2005), esp. 57ff.; H. de Vries, Standards for Business: How Companies Benefit from Participation in International Standards Setting, in *International Standardization as a Strategic Tool* (2006), 131–141.

[69] T. Büthe, Agent Selection in the International Delegation of Regulatory Authority: Food Safety, Health Regulations, and Free Trade under the WTO, unpublished manuscript (on file with the authors), Duke University and University of California, Berkeley, February 2009.

networks.[70] These networks go by now far beyond the trade and transport networks of the Han Dynasty's "silk road," which is said to have inspired the BRI. It includes foreign direct investments, all kinds of development cooperation, and various forms of international, trans-governmental, and transnational exchanges (though the latter appear often high centrally directed from the Chinese side).

Most of the BRI is not about technical standards at all, but many observers have reported that China has been using BRI-created or -intensified interdependence as leverage to get other countries to accept Chinese national technical standards as de facto international standards – facilitated by the hub-and-spokes bilateral rather than multilateral structure of BRI governance, which guarantees China a dominant position vis-à-vis each of its BRI partners.[71] A recent example has been the pandemic-induced demand for digital tools to fight COVID-19 to get BRI partners to adopt technologies based on Chinese standards that diverge from international ones.[72] Chinese officials have attributed such efforts (as well as occasional talk of possibly setting up BRI-based institutions for international joint development of technical standards) to the inability of Chinese – or, generally, developing and transition economy countries' – technical experts to get a fair hearing with the IEC. We therefore postpone discussion of this issue to Section 15.6.3.

15.6 IEC RESILIENCE AND THE GLOBAL SOUTH: ECONOMIC GLOBALIZATION, INTERNATIONAL POLITICS, AND TRANSNATIONAL PRIVATE REGULATION

15.6.1 *A Growing Yet Still Marginal Role for Most Stakeholders from the Global South*

From the beginning, participants in IEC standard-setting have paid their own way, which created a bias in favor of commercially successful stakeholders from rich countries. By the time World War I put the IEC on hold (eight years after it had been founded in 1906), the IEC had member bodies from only seventeen countries.

[70] See, e.g., Y. Huang, Understanding China's Belt & Road Initiative: Motivation, Framework and Assessment (September 2016) 40 *China Economic Review* 314; European Bank for Reconstruction and Development, China's Belt and Road Initiative, www.ebrd.com/what-we-do/belt-and-road/overview.html.

[71] See, e.g., T. N. Rühlig, *Technical Standardisation, China and the Future International Order: A European Perspective* (2020); R. Arcesati, Chinese Tech Standards Put the Screws on European Companies, Mercator Institute for China Studies *Kurzanalyse*, January 29, 2019, www.merics.org/de/blog/chinese-tech-standards-put-screws-european-companies; M. Ziegelmeir, *The Politics of High-Speed Rail: Understanding the Role of Intellectual Property Rights and Technology Standards for China's Overseas Rail Investments* (2020); J. C. Byrnes, Is This Belt One Size Fits All? China's Belt and Road Initiative (2020) 8 *Penn State Journal of Law & International Affairs* 723.

[72] K. Iwasaki, Covid-19 Brings New Developments in China's Digital Silk Road (October 2020) 3:9 *Japan Research Institute Research Journal* 1–12.

Most of them were European: Austria, Belgium, Denmark, France, Germany, Italy, the Netherlands, Norway, Russia, Spain, Sweden, Switzerland, and the United Kingdom. Canada and United States also were among the founding members. Argentina (at the time one of the richest, most technologically advanced countries) and the quickly rising Japan were the only countries beyond the Northern transatlantic area to have national electrotechnical societies that joined the IEC before World War I.

In the beginning, this exclusionary focus was generally overtly considered desirable – as it was expected to facilitate agreement through similarities in engineering expertise, professional norms, and general needs and interests in international standards.[73] And the IEC became only marginally more diverse during the interwar years, adding mostly further European members and only five member bodies from countries beyond Europe: Australia (1927), India (1929), Egypt (1930), China (1936), and South Africa (1938). After the end of World War II, IEC membership continued to grow further but only at a very modest pace throughout the decades of the Cold War compared to other international and transnational organizations with a similarly universalist claim to global governance.[74] By the end of the Cold War in 1990, the IEC had grown to have member bodies from forty-four countries, including twenty non-OECD countries (eleven of them from the Global South).

The de facto role of stakeholders from non-OECD countries and especially the Global South in IEC-based global governance, however, remained more marginal as the membership roster might suggest: IEC National Committees from the non-OECD countries generally held participating membership in only a few IEC Technical Committees and Subcommittees; their actual participation in the process of developing new IEC standards was even rarer; and secretariats and chair positions were virtually all held by the technologically most advanced countries with the largest domestic markets (Sweden, Switzerland, and the Netherland were outliers as "small" countries regularly holding more than one of those positions).

The limited membership roster and the even more limited actual participation in standards development became a problem for the IEC in the post–Cold War period. It threatened the IEC's persistence as the focal institution for the global governance

[73] Assessment based on the founding documents and exchanges between IEC participants of the early meetings; see also C. Ainsworth, Standardization Abroad 35:12 (December 1964) *Magazine of Standards* 364–367; Büthe, *supra* note 2, at 301ff.; Yates and Murphy *supra* note 15, at 67–71.

[74] It is noteworthy, not least in light of the reaction to Russia's invasion of Ukraine in 2022, that the fluctuating tensions of the Cold War appear to have had relatively little effect on the IEC. Russia itself, as well as Romania, Serbia, and Hungary, which had become members in 1911, 1927, 1936, and 1949, respectively, all retained their full membership throughout the Cold War (and Bulgaria even joined anew in 1958), although a review of the minutes of technical committee meetings shows that the active participation of non-USSR Eastern European technical experts notably declined when the USSR tightened its control over Eastern bloc countries in the 1950s.

of electro-technology in the post–Cold War years for four reasons. (1) Intensified economic globalization in the 1990s integrated ever more countries of the Global South into truly global markets and value chains, from which they often ended up excluded or unable to reap the full benefits without adopting international standards (including IEC standards) domestically.[75] The WTO-enhanced role of IEC standards in governing market access gave many countries quite suddenly a much greater stake in IEC standards, leading them (and some observers) to make their marginalization in IEC governance an issue. (2) The explosive growth in preferential trade agreements (PTAs) in the 1990s, covering a growing range of issues, including regulatory issues and technical non-tariff barriers to trade,[76] created a risk for the IEC that standards other than IEC standards might get written into PTAs as the technical basis for trade integration – especially in the growing number of South-South PTAs – unless at least one and ideally both countries had a stake in ensuring the continued centrality of IEC standards.[77] (3) The shift from the bipolar to a multipolar international system reduced the willingness of many countries, especially in the Global South, to be deferential to a small group of Northern countries on issues such as market governance, all the more so in light of simultaneous widespread demands for more democratic participation, both domestically within many countries and in global governance.[78] This resulted in rising expectations that global governance bodies provide at least for "voice opportunities" for the Global

[75] S. M. Stephenson, Standards, Conformity Assessment and Developing Countries, World Bank Policy Research Working Paper no. 1826 (May 1997); K. Maskus, O. Tsunehiro, and J. S. Wilson, The Cost of Compliance with Product Standards for Firms in Developing Countries, World Bank Policy Research Paper no. 3590 (May 2005); J. P. Singh, The Evolution of National Interest: New Issues and North-South Negotiations During the Uruguay Round, in *Negotiating Trade: Developing Countries in the WTO and NAFTA* (J. S. Odell ed., 2006), 41–84; J. Lee, G. Gereffi, and J. Beauvais, Global Value Chains and Agrifood Standards: Challenges and Possibilities for Smallholders in Developing Countries (December 13, 2010) *Proceedings of the US National Academy of Sciences*, doi.org/10.1073/pnas.0913714108; T. Dietz et al., The Voluntary Coffee Standard Index (VOCSI) (August 2018) 150 *Ecological Economics* 72.

[76] A. Estevadeordal, K. Suominen, and R. Teh (eds.), *Regional Rules in the Global Trading System* (2009); A. Dür and M. Elsig (eds.), *Trade Cooperation: The Purpose, Design and Effects of Preferential Trade Agreements* (2015).

[77] See R. Hartlem et al., Internationalization of Cable Standards: An Overview of the Variety of Methods and Motivations of Standards Developing Organizations around the World (1997) 17:11 *IEEE Power Engineering Review* 19–20; Büthe, *supra* note 9, 38ff.

[78] See, e.g., J. Steffek, C. Kissling, and P. Nanz (eds.), *Civil Society Participation in European and Global Governance: A Cure for the Democratic Deficit?* (2008); J. Tallberg, et al., *The Opening up of International Organization: Transnational Access in Global Governance* (2013); R. B. Stewart, Accountability, Participation, and the Problem of Disregard in Global Regulatory Governance (April 2014) 108:2 *American Journal of International Law* 211–270; A. Grigorescu, *Democratic International Organizations? Normative Pressures and Decision-Making Rules* (2015). See also R. W. Grant and R. O. Keohane, Accountability and Abuses of Power in World Politics (February 2005) 99:1 *American Political Science Review* 29–43.

South and arguably also influence over outcomes.[79] Global governance institutions that failed to live up to these expectations were increasingly subjected to legitimacy challenges.[80] (4) The economic and political transition after the end of the Cold War resulted in several countries becoming new major powers, especially China, India, and Brazil. Until the 1980s and in some areas even the 1990s, they had been "rule-takers" in global economic affairs; but from the 1990s or 2000s onward, they have increasingly demanded greater voice and real influence in the governance of the world economy.[81]

The IEC responded to these challenges with several initiatives to grow and diversify its membership, as well as some efforts to increase opportunities for substantively meaningful participation by countries from the Global South. IEC leaders worked with several Global South countries' electro-technical organizations to transform their informal relationships with the IEC into official associate (or even full) memberships. These efforts were complemented by the introduction of the Affiliate Country Program in 2001, through which developing countries can (to a limited but substantively meaningful extent) participate in IEC standard-setting without the financial burden of membership. In addition to gaining access to up to 200 standards documents free of charge (which they can then sell to interested users in their respective countries, providing them with resources they can use to strengthen domestic electro-technical standards bodies), the program gives participants access to IEC meetings and IEC trainings.

In some sense, these efforts have been tremendously successful. The IEC today has sixty-two full members plus twenty-six associate members (which pay lower fees in exchange for more limited participation rights) and eighty-six affiliate countries (which have certain voice opportunities but no voting rights).[82] The IEC membership has thus become much more global and diverse, enhancing its input legitimacy, at least formally. P-membership in the IEC Technical Committees and Subcommittees, too, has increased for many non-OECD countries, including countries from the Global South (see Figure 15.1).

As Figure 15.1 shows, however, for most developing countries, the increase is very small, and most of the long-dominant larger OECD countries have actually increased their P-memberships to the same extent or even to a proportionally larger extent. A similar pattern emerges with regard to committee chairs and secretariats, as depicted in Figure 15.2 for the (more powerful) committee secretariats: only four

79 For a discussion of the difference, see Pauwelyn et al. and esp. DeMenno and Büthe, *supra* note 20.

80 For a recent review of the literature, see A. Berman et al., Introduction: Rethinking Stakeholder Participation in Global Governance, in Pauwelyn et al., *supra* note 20, at 3–30.

81 For a review, see the introduction to the recent special issue of *Regulation & Governance* by Lavenex et al., *supra* note 27.

82 See IEC, National Committees, www.iec.ch/national-committees; and Affiliate Country Program, www.iec.ch/acp.

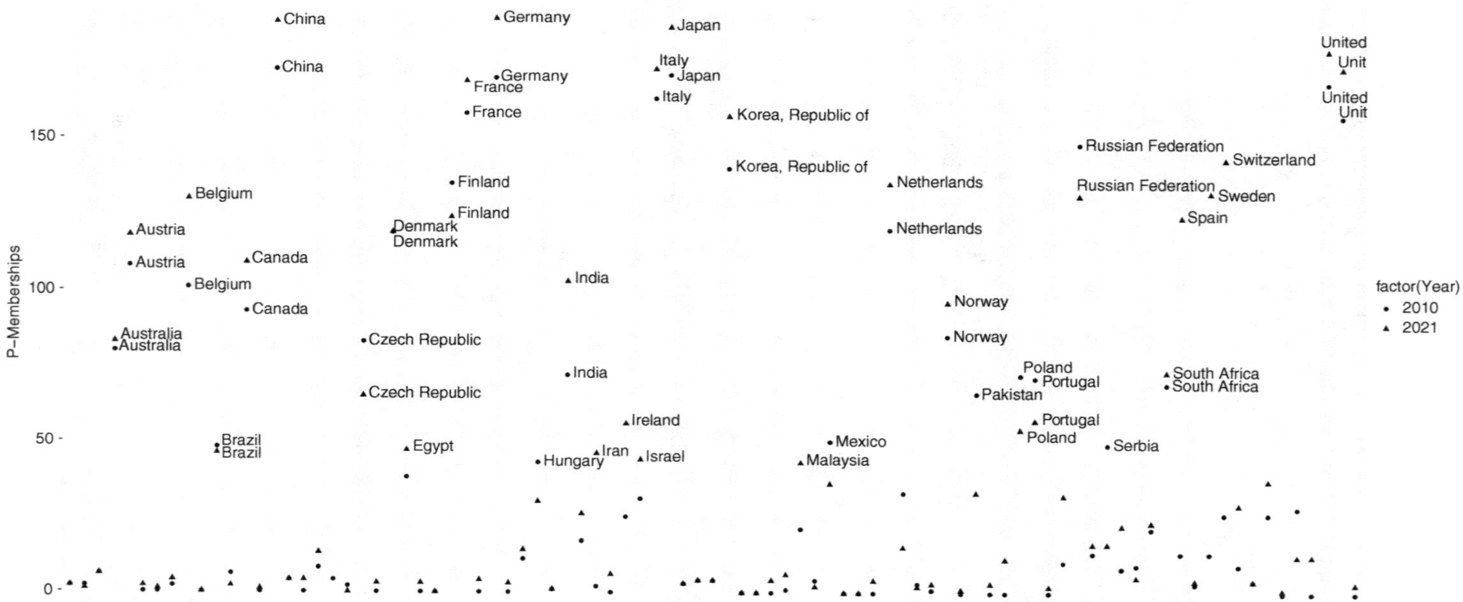

FIGURE 15.1. IEC P-Memberships 2021 vs. 2010.
Source: Authors' original work based on publicly available data from the IEC website October 2010 and January 2022

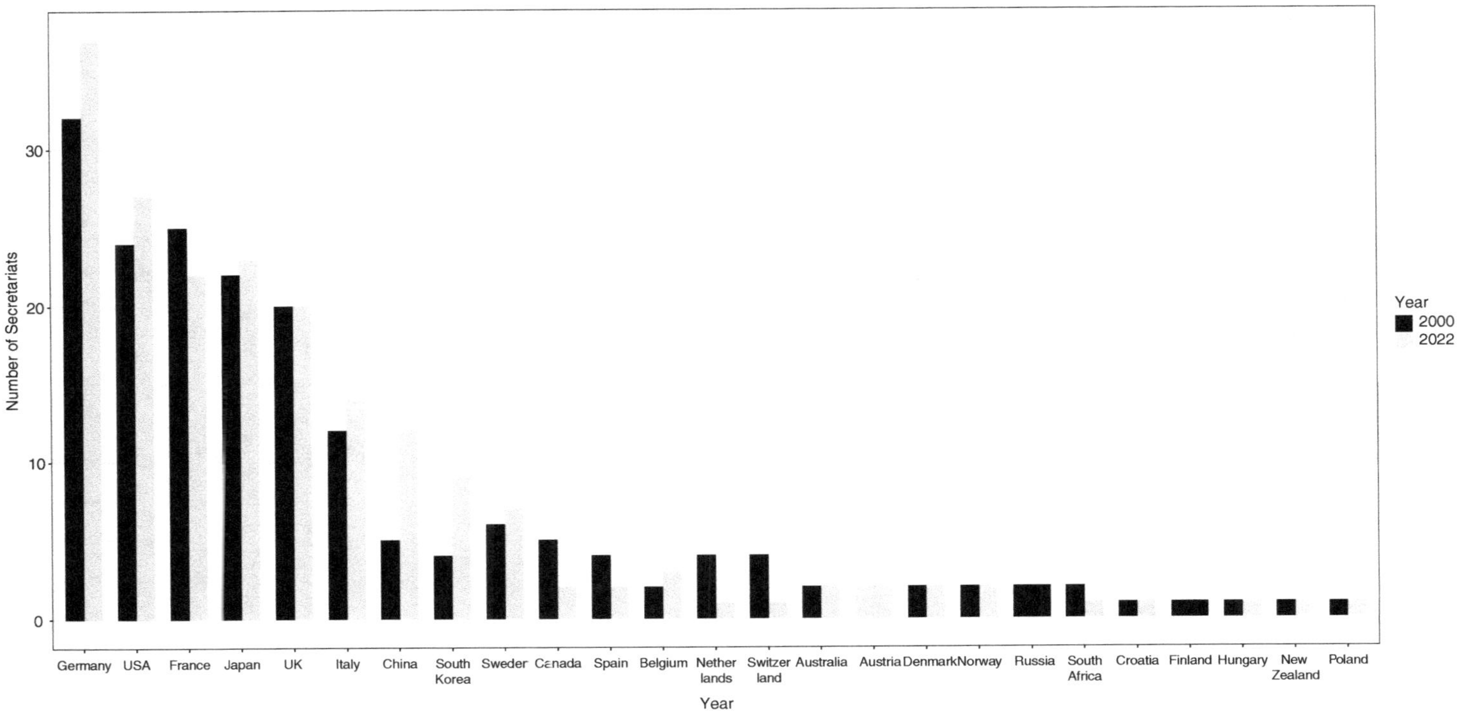

FIGURE 15.2. IEC TC Secretariats 2021 vs. 2000.
Source: Authors' original work based on publicly available data from the IEC for January 1, 2000 and January 1, 2022

non-OECD countries hold any committee secretariats today. Russia, which used to hold one such secretariat in 2000, holds none anymore; the number of South Africa's secretariats has shrunk from two to one; and EU members Croatia and Poland each hold one (unchanged even when considering the longer twenty-year time span for which this data is available). The striking exception to this overall pattern is China, which has significantly increased both its P-memberships and the number of secretariats held (from five to twelve).

Complementary qualitative evidence supports this interpretation of the quantitative evidence summarized in the figures: with the exception of Chinese participants, experts from the Global South report in interviews that they are still facing challenges in participating in IEC standard-setting. Participants from affiliate countries, in particular, report insufficient advance awareness of IEC work to be able to make substantive contributions to the development or revision of standards, and several of them indicated that much more training and advance preparation would be needed for them to be able to understand how the IEC works as an SDO (despite the IEC offering some training opportunities on just these issues already).[83] Our evidence aligns with a recent internal survey conducted by the IEC.[84] Additionally, our data show that, since the introduction of the affiliate program, only 59 comments on standards proposals have been submitted by more than one hundred affiliate-participants over the period 2004–2020, during which thousands of IEC standards were developed or revised.

15.6.2 *The Rise of China as a Special Challenge for the IEC*

Recent decades have not only seen a greater role of the Global South in the world economy. Distinctly – even when compared to the other "rising" BRICS powers – China has risen to the status of an economic superpower, demanding a greater voice and real influence in global economic governance, including in the governance of technology.

Communist/mainland China's standardization regime emerged in the early 1950s. Under strong influence from the Soviet Union, it was characterized by top-down state control and widely considered ineffective in supporting Chinese industrial and technological development.[85] Beginning in the 1980s and accelerating in

[83] Not-for-attribution telephone and online interviews, mostly conducted by Abdel Alshadafan, July 2020–January 2022.

[84] www.iec.ch/blog/affiliate-country-programme-survey-results. What we observe, moreover, matches the experience of developing countries in international standardization more generally, see P. C. Mavroidis and R. Wolfe, Private Standards and the WTO: Reclusive No More (January 2017) 16:1 *World Trade Review* 1.

[85] W. Ping, W. Yiyi, and J. Hill, Standardization Strategy of China, Achievements and Challenges, 2010, EAST-WEST Center Working Paper no. 107 (January 2010); R. Suttmeier and C. A. O. Cong, China's Technical Community: Market Reforms and the Changing Policy Cultures of Science, in *Chinese Intellectuals Between State and Market* (M. Goldman and E.

the 1990s, China introduced a series of reforms, which made technical standards, including international standard-setting, a central element of China's national development policies, initially with the primary aim of reducing dependence on foreign technologies and the respective intellectual property rights.[86] These reforms included massive state funding to boost engineering education, structural changes in the Chinese domestic standards-developing institutions, specialized training courses for technical standards development, as well as numerous incentives to encourage Chinese stakeholders to increase their participation at the international level, resulting in increased Chinese presence across a broad range of inter- and transnational SDOs.[87]

Having superseded the United States as the largest patent applicant in the world, China is now capable of developing domestically sophisticated alternative technical standards to many international ones. This can already be observed in its pursuit to establish, among other others, a homemade satellite navigation system (as an alternative to GPS) and a Cross-Border Interbank Payment System (as an alternative to SWIFT).[88] These developments have posed a major challenge to the IEC as the focal institution for electrotechnical standard-setting, for at least three reasons. First, China internationalizing its technical standards outside the IEC's institutional framework directly undermines the IEC preeminence and status as the focal institution for electrotechnical standard-setting. Second, China has occasionally hinted at establishing competing international bodies to allow stakeholders that are traditionally marginalized at the IEC to have better representation. This might prompt such stakeholders to leave the IEC to join the China-led institutions. Finally, China-centered competing institutions threaten established powers' ability to keep tabs on newly developed standards and technologies. This is important, not least because they are particularly skeptical of Chinese activity in the area of digitalization and data protection.[89]

Gu eds., 2004), 138–157; Y. Zhou and X. Liu, Evolution of Chinese State Policies on Innovation, in *China as an Innovation Nation* (Y. Zhou et al. eds., 2016), 33–67.

86 M. Murphree and D. Breznitz, Innovation in China: Fragmentation, Structured Uncertainty and Technology Standards (2013) *Cardozo Law Review De Novo* 196.

87 D. Breznitz and M. Murphree, The Rise of China in Technology Standards: New Norms in Old Institutions. Research Report Prepared on Behalf of the U.S.-China Economic and Security Review Commission (2013); M. C. Gamito, From Private Regulation to Power Politics: The Rise of China in AI Private Governance Through Standardisation (2021), https://ssrn.com/abstract=3794761; S. Hoffmann, D. Lazanski, and E. Taylor, Standardising the Splinternet: How China's Technical Standards Could Fragment the Internet (2020) 5(2) *Journal of Cyber Policy* 239.

88 N. Godehardt, *Wie China Weltpolitik Formt: Die Logik von Pekings Außenpolitik unter Xi Jinping* (2020).

89 B. Bartsch and A. Laudien, *Survey: Europe's View of China and the US-Chinese Conflict* (2020).

15.6.3 *IEC Responses to the Rise of China*

China has repeatedly emphasized that it has no desire to overthrow the current standardization regime and that it only seeks to ensure that its interests are taken into account similarly to those of the other major, technologically most advanced countries.[90] The IEC's response has taken these Chinese assurances seriously and has attempted to accommodate China to a greater extent, so as to give it a greater stake in the continued functioning and preeminence of the IEC – in sense of what we have defined as resilience in the introduction.

Concretely, the IEC has facilitated China becoming one of the most active and prominent member countries. Since 2011, China has been recognized as one of the leading members, entitled to an automatically appointed seat on the SMB and the other IEC decision-making bodies. China also holds two IEC "ambassador" positions (responsible for representing the IEC interest in IoT and cyber security). And in 2019, the IEC elected Yinbiao Shu, chairman of one of China's five largest state-owned electricity generation enterprises, as its next president; his three-year term started on January 1, 2020.

Already a P-Member of most TCs, China has increased its formal participation even further with P-memberships in now 90 percent of the IEC TCs. At least as importantly, the volume and quality of Chinese delegates' contributions to the technical discussions at the committee and working group level has notably increased. China has also substantially increased the number of TC secretariats held by its delegates. Working with some of the traditionally leading member bodies (especially Germany's DIN/DKE), IEC has also attempted to address what are widely seen as key reasons for Chinese experts' arguably often limited success in IEC committees, including language skills and lack of understanding the norms and procedures of IEC committee work.[91] Interviews with a former secretary general (CEO) of the IEC confirmed that these changes were a conscious response to the rise of China, seeking to elevate its status in the IEC in accordance with its increased status in the world economy.

[90] Y. Kuang, China in Global Technology Governance: Experimentation, Achievements, and Uncertainties, in *China: Champion of (Which) Globalisation?* (A. Amighini ed., 2018), 81–100.

[91] An interviewee highlighted, for instance, incidents whereby Chinese delegates attempted to push their position by asking high level IEC decision-makers to intervene. This created concerns within the IEC, that such behavior might trigger clashes with other member countries. The IEC offered special training sessions to familiarize some Chinese nationals with the relevant internal procedures and practices and explain that without the approval of the other member countries (achieved via negotiating, compromising, lobbying), China's proposals would not be successful. Regarding the China–Germany link, see D. Fuchs and S. Eaton, Diffusion of Practice: The Curious Case of the Sino-German Technical Standardization Partnership, https://ssrn.com/abstract=3723303.

15.7 UNRESOLVED CHALLENGES

15.7.1 *Democratic versus Expertise-Based Legitimacy: The Rise and Resurgence of the Consumer Movement*

The IEC has always maintained that it welcomes the input and seeks balanced participation from all who have a legitimate stake in the development of electrotechnology.[92] The IEC Code of Conduct for Technical Work also requires the national member bodies to represent all interests at the national levels. In practice, however, stakeholder representation has been (with rare exceptions) limited to technical experts whose participation is funded by private sector employers with an immediate commercial stake in the issue at hand.

This predominance of private sector experts is consistent with the IEC's reliance, from the start, on the expertise-based authority of the IEC, its national member bodies, and the individual participants in its technical committees for the legitimacy of IEC governance.[93] The IEC's expertise-based authority has in recent decades been supplemented by delegated authority, especially since WTO member states designated ISO and IEC standards (in the WTO's TBT-Agreement) as a way to achieve legitimate public policy objectives without setting up unnecessary technical barriers to trade through divergent national standards.[94] The consumer movement, however, increasingly calls into question the IEC's reliance on little more than expertise-based and delegated authority.

The IEC started to develop standards specifically for consumer products – and explicitly acknowledged consumer safety and welfare as objectives of IEC regulatory governance – starting with the lamp socket standards it developed in the 1920s.[95] But the question of whether consumers needed to be incorporated into the standard-setting process to safeguard the IEC's centrality and legitimacy was only brought to the fore by the rise of the consumer movement in the late 1960s and the 1970s,[96] as well as the broader shift toward post-materialist values across most advanced capitalist democracies.[97] To be sure, consumer interests are far from assured voice or

[92] Yates and Murphy, *supra*, note 15, at 73.

[93] Avant et al., *supra* note 20, esp. 12ff.; Büthe, *supra* note 2, at 296, 302ff., 305.

[94] Büthe, *supra* note 2, at 304ff.

[95] A. Raeburn, IEC Technical Committee Creation: The First Half-Century (1906–1949), www.iec.ch/history/first-50-years.

[96] L. Cohen, A *Consumers' Republic: The Politics of Mass Consumption in Postwar America* (2003); M. Hilton, Social Activism in an Age of Consumption: The Organized Consumer Movement (May 2007) 32:2 *Social History* 121.

[97] See, e.g., R. Inglehart, *The Silent Revolution: Changing Values and Political Styles among Western Publics* (1977); and *Culture Shift in Advanced Industrialized Society* (1990); R. Inglehart and C. Welzel, *Modernization, Cultural Change and Democracy* (2005).

influence over policy – even in democratic political systems,[98] which might be due to organized opposition from producer interests[99] or difficulties in discerning consumer preferences.[100] Research on the political consequences of post-materialism also yields mixed findings regarding the relationship between post-materialism and political consumerism or, more generally, willingness and forms of political participation. Yet the dearth of consumer representation (and more generally the representation of noncommercial interests) in IEC technology governance[101] has consequences for the contents of IEC standards and increasingly has come to be seen as a threat to the IEC's legitimacy.[102]

In response, IEC (and ISO) in 2019 created the ISO/IEC Guide 59, which mirrored the "Six Principles for the Development of International Standards, Guides and Recommendations," articulated in 2000 by the WTO TBT Committee as part of its Code of Good Practice: transparency, openness, impartiality and consensus, relevance and effectiveness, coherence, and ensuring de facto opportunities for participation by stakeholders from developing countries.[103] ISO/IEC Guide 76:2020 also calls for taking consumers' inputs in consideration in developing service standards.[104]

To implement the Guides, the IEC sought to facilitate noncommercial stakeholders' participation in standard-setting, for instance, by allowing "liaison organizations" participation (differentiating between three types with different participation rights).[105] Moreover, the IEC has increased its use of digital tools to boost participation. Beginning in 2001 already, it required all comments to be submitted online and started to introduce electronic voting on technical work. More recently, the IEC introduced to its website a tool to allow the public to submit comments online, and it has continued to increase opportunities for remote access to documents and standard-setting activities – including through the "online authoring tool," introduced to enable participants to work on a given document simultaneously. All of

98 T. Betz and A. Pond, The Absence of Consumer Interests in Trade Policy (April 2019) 81:2 *Journal of Politics* 585. Regarding voice and influence in global governance more generally, see M. DeMenno and T. Büthe, Voice and Influence in Global Governance: An Analytical Framework in *Rethinking Participation* (J. Pauwelyn et al. eds., 2022).

99 See, e.g., S. Eckert, *Corporate Power and Regulation: Consumers and the Enviroment in the European Union* (2019).

100 D. Vogel, When Consumers Oppose Consumer Protection: The Politics of Regulatory Backlash (October–December 1990) 10:4 *Journal of Public Policy* 449.

101 B. Farquhar, Consumer Representation in International Standards (January/February 2006) 16:1 *Consumer Policy Review* 26; C. Hauert, Where Are You? Consumers' Associations in Standardization (2010) 8:1 *International Journal of IT Standards and Standardization Research* 11.

102 Alshadafan, *supra* note 2.

103 See www.wto.org/english/tratop_e/tbt_e/principles_standards_tbt_e.htm; also P. Delimatsis, Global Standard-Setting 2.0: How the WTO Spotlights ISO and Impacts the Transnational Standard-Setting Process (2018) 28 *Duke Journal of Comparative and International Law* 273, at 311.

104 www.iso.org/obp/ui/#iso:std:iso-iec:guide:76:ed-2:v1:en

105 www.iec.ch/global-partnerships

these steps aim to lower the costs of participation (which had been frequently noted as an important impediment for noncommercial stakeholders).

Regrettably, however, the limited publicly available information – as well as interviews with IEC insiders with access to performance data for the IEC-internal systems – suggest that all of these efforts have yielded little actual participation by consumers so far. The public commenting tool, for instance, has registered a small number of records only.

15.7.2 *Gender Equality in IEC Standard-Setting*

The IEC has also been repeatedly criticized for the lack of women participants in its work.[106] Recently, the IEC admitted the existence of the problem, having examined it through an internal survey.[107]

The IEC has, so far, responded to this, above all, by promising to take corrective action. It also joined the United Nations Economic Commission for Europe, supposedly to ensure representation of women in TCs. Additionally, the IEC has partnered with the ISO under the stewardship of the Joint Strategic Advisory Group to develop guidance to help TCs ensure they are developing gender-responsive standards. These efforts, however, have only recently begun, and it remains to be seen whether they are effective, given the continued strong gender imbalance in most engineering fields.

15.8 CONCLUSION: LEARNING RESILIENCE?

Over the course of its 115 year history, the IEC has exhibited remarkable resilience in the face of numerous and diverse challenges to its preeminence – challenges that have arisen from technological change, the emergence of alternative institutions for developing electrical and electronics standards, and geopolitical upheavals and related power shifts in the world economy, including two world wars, decolonization, the end of the Cold War and the arrival of new, rising powers in the world economy. In this chapter, we have provided a sketch of this resilience and examined its drivers (as well as its limitations).

We started by identifying (in Section 15.2) four essential attributes of the IEC, which, we suggested, would have to remain intact in the face of otherwise

[106] See, e.g., M. Parkouda, *When One Size Does Not Protect All: Understanding Why Gender Matters for Standardization* (2020); P. Heß, SDG 5 and the Gender Gap in Standardization: Empirical Evidence from Germany (2020) 12:20 *Sustainability* art.8699. For compelling examples of the – likely unconscious yet consequential – biases that result from such underrepresentation, see T. Betz, D. Fortunato, D. Z. O'Brien, Women's Descriptive Representation and Gendered Import Tax Discrimination (2021) 115:1 *American Political Science Review* 307–315.

[107] www.iec.ch/blog/disappointing-results-gender-survey-technical-committees.

extraordinary adaptability to head off challenges to its predominance and legitimacy, if we are to consider the IEC's continued existence indicative of genuine resilience. We then sketched a theory of resilience, extending Büthe's proto-theory of organizational preeminence in light of Delimatsis' analytical framework for this book. The empirical account of IEC resilience in light of a variety of challenges that it has encountered over the course of more than a century show time and again the central importance of the IEC's autonomous agency in pursuit of its organizational self-interest – while largely maintaining the inclusive, participatory governance structures and procedures on which its legitimacy is in large part based.

At the same time, the IEC cannot be said to have (yet) successfully addressed all challenges to its preeminence, raising questions about the extent to which resilience can be "learned." To be sure, some changes made by the IEC in response to earlier challenges, such as its creation of the Standards Management Board (originally set up in the 1920s as the Committee on Action to coordinate the work of its then-fifteen Technical Committees), have lastingly enhanced its ability to combine autonomous agency with legitimacy-enhancing embeddedness of the IEC leadership in the community of member bodies. Yet the ultimate test of resilience arises from having to respond to shocks that are different from prior ones, necessarily limiting the extent to which past resilience might predict future resilience.

Epilogue

An Evolutionary Theory of Transnational Private Regulation: Investigating Causes and Effects of Crises

Fabrizio Cafaggi[*]

The rich and stimulating contributions in this book focus on transnational private rule-making and investigate the resilience of private regulators in various sectors, primarily in the field of finance and technical standardization. Within this conceptual framework, special attention has been devoted to the impact of crises on transnational private regulation (TPR) and whether organizational resilience may provide a good conceptual tool to describe the modes of evolution of TPR: its birth, development, consolidation, dissolution.

My analysis first provides a short overview of TPR and then focuses on the impact of crises.

I.1 WHO ARE THE TRANSNATIONAL PRIVATE REGULATORS?

TPR is a form of regulation that encompasses standard setting, monitoring compliance, and enforcement. Unlike conventional self-regulation, where regulation is produced by regulated entities, in TPR, regulators and regulated do not coincide. It differs from the more conventional forms of self-regulation since it includes in the regulatory process not only the regulators and the regulated but also the potential beneficiaries of and those harmed by the regulatory process.[1] Inclusion may take different forms from loyalty (membership) to voice (participatory rights to standard-setting processes for those who are not members of the organization). Increasingly, voice has been provided also to those potentially harmed by transnational regulatory regimes, deepening the differences between transnational self-regulation and private

[*] This short essay has benefited of comments by Panos Delimatsis and M. Konrad Borowicz to whom I would like to express my gratitude. The responsibility remains my own.

[1] See F. Cafaggi, New Foundations of Transnational Private Regulation (2011) 38:1 *Journal of Law and Society*; The Many Features of Transnational Rule Making: Unexplored Relationship between Custom, *jura mercatorum* and Global Private Regulation (2015) 36 *University of Pennsylvania Journal of International Law* 875.

regulation.[2] However, the voice of the disregarded is still limited and the participatory instruments are not always effective.[3]

It is important to consider both the governance structure and the participants in the regulatory process.[4] Often regimes arise out of confrontation between firms and NGOs with some degree of participation by public actors, including international organizations (IOs) and individual states. These features permit the internalization of regulatory externalities, usually left out in self-regulatory regimes. However, whereas the costs of regulatory regimes might be internalized, distributional issues between insiders and outsiders of the regulatory regime often remain unsettled. But even when, as it is the case in the financial sector, private regulation is primarily industry regulation, different forms of accountability have developed to move away from conventional self-regulatory regimes for more integrated standard-setting processes. Governance is relevant but the regulation of standard-setting processes may provide opportunities to increase legitimacy without modifying the single stakeholder governance structure of the private regulator.

TPR differs also from soft law.[5] TPR is produced by private actors, at times in collaboration with public actors, with instruments typically private like codes, guidelines, principles, etc. These instruments only bind those who sign on. Soft law, instead, is produced by public bodies according to the procedures defined for rule-making but it does not have binding effects on the addressees[6].

One common dimension to soft law and private regulation is the role of persuasion. Unlike hard law standards where coercion is the rule, soft law and private regulation are mainly based on persuasion. Steering instead of prohibiting is the main objective. In TPR, consent is at the core of legitimacy and accountability. Clearly the regulatory share of the private regulator affects the role of consent and may transform in practice persuasion into coercion. This is the case where the only available standard is produced by private actors as is often the case in the banking

2 See R. Stewart, Remedying Disregard in Global Regulatory Governance: Accountability, Participation, and Responsiveness (2017) *American Journal of International Law* 211.

3 For example, ISO invested resources and efforts to ensure broad and balanced stakeholder engagement in the development of ISO 26000 and to strengthen its cooperation with other organizations developing standards in this domain. This can be viewed as an important strategy to justify its involvement in the domain of social responsibility and to ensure the legitimacy and uptake of its standards. However, ISO later acknowledged that a full and equitable balance of stakeholders affected by the standard was not achieved: “it was constrained by various factors, including the availability of resources and the need for English language skills.” ISO, International Guidance Standard on Social Responsibility (2010), vi.

4 See M. Dowdle, *Transnational Law: A Framework for Analysis* (2022), at 205, distinguishing between technocratic and pluralistic governance models. This distinction can play a significant role when analyzing organizational resilience.

5 See J. Pauwelyn, R. Wessel, J. Wouters (eds.), *Informal International Law Making* (2013).

6 This is not to say that soft law does not have legal effects but these effects differ from those stemming from signing codes that impose obligations on the signatories. On the distinction between soft law and private regulation, see F. Cafaggi (ed.), *Reframing Self-reguation in European Private Law* (2006); and Cafaggi, *supra* note 1.

sector for payments or other instruments like the Society for Worldwide Interbank Financial Telecommunication (SWIFT).[7] Hence, consent is relevant, but to understand its real function, it needs to be correlated to the distribution of regulatory power. The more dispersed the power the more relevant is consent for legitimacy and accountability of TPR.

Transnational private regulatory processes do not reflect a single governance framework concerning standard setting, monitoring, and enforcement. Two basic governance models are in place: one based on structural separation and the other on functional separation. In the former, each function is performed by an independent organization. In the latter, all functions are performed by the same organization, but internal functional separation is warranted by having both procedural and substantive safeguards that ensure independence of each division. There is a clear trade-off between independence and coordination. Separation among regulatory functions warrants higher independence but entails greater coordination costs. Organizational resilience may vary depending on which governance model is adopted.

In certain instances, standard setting is performed by one body whereas monitoring is performed by another body. This is the case when, for example, sustainability standards are defined by one organization (ISEAL) whereas their compliance is monitored by another organization (Transparency International). The alternative model is one that incorporates all the regulatory functions within a single body with functional rather than structural separations. Integrated models ensure stronger coordination but present higher conflicts of interest and lower degree of impartiality. Models characterized by functional separation, instead, bear higher coordination costs but warrant more protection to those potentially harmed by failure to apply the regulation or by its misapplication.

I.2 HOW IS THE TRANSNATIONAL REGULATORY SPACE COMPOSED AND ORGANIZED?

The transnational regulatory space is densely populated by multiple players who engage in different types of relationships.[8] The concentration varies significantly. There are areas (like finance and banking) where power is highly concentrated and areas (like food safety and sustainability) where it is fragmented. The space of choice concerning standards by potentially regulated entities is correlated to consent and to the legitimacy and effectiveness of private standards. The wider the choice, determined by low concentration of power and regulatory pluralism, the higher the likelihood that the regulated and the beneficiaries participate in the regulatory

7 See S. Scott and M. Zachariadis, *Society for Worldwide Interbank Financial Telecommunication* (2014).

8 See J Black, Legitimacy and Competition for Regulatory Shares, LSE Law, Society and Economy Working Papers 14 (2009).

process. The more limited the choice, when power concentration is high, the more likely is that participation is low and governance hierarchical.

The density of the regulatory space and the objectives of regulation affect the relationships among private regulators. TPR is ever more characterized by a combination of cooperative and competitive relationships among private regulators and between public and private regulators. There are different forms of cooperative relationships among private regulators ranging from informal collaboration to agreements or forms of organizational integration.[9] These collaborative forms may have different weights, depending on whether they focus only on standard setting or encompass the entire regulatory process. The focus on compliance with transnational private standards has generated new and original forms of collaboration between private regulators given also the relatively minor role played by courts. One significant element that contributes to the differentiation of forms of regulatory collaboration is the use of hard or soft law on the public side.

Competitive relationships among private regulators give rise to regulatory competition. Unlike the public domain, where the public regulator is usually a monopolist, in TPR the coexistence of regulators is the rule; often this coexistence produces competition for regulated entities to increase their share in the regulatory market. The extraterritorial reach of TPR determines competition over global shares of regulated entities.

The evolution of private regulatory models depends on multiple factors and differs across sectors. Among the determinants of changes in TPR, the following stand out: (1) power shifts within the marketplace among regulated entities, (2) regulatory failures, (3) increase or decrease of regulatory competition within the sector, (4) rules imposed or recommended by international organizations. Changes require realignment between values, objectives, and regulatory instruments.

The evolution of TPR is responsive to the change of regulatory needs and to the distribution of power among the different constituencies participating in the organization. These changes may depend on the shifting balance of power among the regulated (market players) or between the regulated (firms, banks) and the beneficiaries (consumers, customers). The example of food safety provides a clear illustration of the evolution of forms and instruments of regulation and the rise of certification with the change of powers from producers to retailers that occurred at the end of the last century.[10] The emergence of GFSI, a benchmarking institution for food certification, was the response to the change of market power along the

[9] See F. Cafaggi, Convergences and Divergences: Comparing Contractual and Organizational Models in International Regulatory Cooperation, in *Convergences and Divergences in Private Law in Asia* (G. Low ed., 2022).

[10] See G. Gereffi, The Organisation of Buyer-Driven Global Commodity Chains: How U.S. Retailers Shape Overseas Production Networks, in *Commodity Clains and Global Capitalism* (G. Gereffi and M. Korzeniewicz eds., 1994).

supply chains and of excessive private regulatory competition concerning safety standards.

The creation of GFSI did not eliminate competition but provided a constructive framework for competition among certificate scheme owners. Nevertheless, what is even more relevant is that an organization born as a membership body of retailers in opposition to producers has later become a foundation composed by both and by service providers. This transformation of the governance is the result of a change in the regulatory space. It highlights the link between the organization of regulatory space and the transformation of relationships among private regulators.[11]

1.3 WHAT IS THE RELATIONSHIP BETWEEN TRANSNATIONAL PRIVATE AND PUBLIC REGULATORS?

TPR operates in a framework of institutional complementarity between private regulators, States, and international organizations.[12] Institutional complementarity encompasses both cooperative and competitive relationships between private and public actors that can evolve over time.[13] Cooperative relationships may be compatible with common or separate standard setting where both concur to the definition of rules of conduct by the regulated. Transnational regulatory cooperation increases legitimacy and contributes to regulatory effectiveness.[14] In the past twenty years, memoranda of understanding, consultation agreements, or mutual participation in the governance structures have developed to favor regulatory cooperation.[15]

It is important to underline that the relationships between transnational private regulators and public bodies might also be competitive, where public and private actors compete for regulatory shares. Competition occurs especially when public standards are not mandatory as is the case for soft law instruments. Competition in the short run often leads to collaboration in the longer run.

[11] See T. Havinga and P. Verbruggen, "The Evolution of the Global Food Safety Initiative: The Dynamics of the Legitimacy of a Transnational Private Rule-Maker" in this volume (Chapter 9).

[12] See Cafaggi, *supra* note 1.

[13] See B. Eberlein, K. Abbott, J. Black, E. Meidinger, and S. Wood, Transanational Business Governance Interactions: Conceptualizations and Framework for Analysis (2014) 8:1 *Regulation and Governance*; B Cashore, J Steen Knudsen, J Moon, and H. van der Ven, Private Authority and Public Policy Interactions in Global Spheres: Governance Spheres for Problem Solving (2021) 15:4 *Regulation and Governance*, doi.org/10.1111/rego.12395 (distinguishing three forms, and subtypes, of public/private interactions: "complementary," "competitive," "coexistent").

[14] See OECD, International Regulatory Cooperation (2013); F. Cafaggi, A. Renda, and R. Schmidt, *Transnational Private Regulation, International Regulatory Co-operation: Case Studies, Vol. 3: Transnational Private Regulation and Water Management* (2013).

[15] See Agreement on technical cooperation between International Organization for Standardization and European Committee for Standardization (Vienna Agreement) (1991); Memorandum of Understanding between the International Organization for Standardization and the International Labor Organization.

Food offers a good illustration. Not only have GFSI internal constituencies changed, moving toward a more collaborative structure, but it has also evolved over time developing collaboration with states and public entities.[16] As a result, it has generated more products like the Global Food Security Index.

Historically, regulatory failures within the public domain have triggered important changes in the private domain. The well-known example of environmental protection and the birth of private actors in forestry after the crisis in 1994 is illustrative of one dynamic leading to the emergence of private organizations as a result of public failures.[17] The opposite dynamics occurred in relation to the payment system with the failure of the self-regulatory regime in EU and the adoption of the first payments Directive.[18] These are examples of how shortcomings in the public domain have sparked the birth of new private organizations or determined the decline of existing private organizations when political or regulatory failures have occurred.

Changes can also stem from excessive private regulatory competition and fragmentation. Excessive fragmentation and competition among private regulators have been a major driver of change of both the governance and the standard-setting activity. Food safety standards, as well as sustainability standards, provide examples of how regulatory competition may lead to a credibility and legitimacy gap and therefore instigate governance changes increasing procedural accountability and stakeholder participation.[19] Competition has also brought about aggregation and cooperation among private regulators triggering forms of meta-regulation.[20] The creation of GFSI in the area of food and of ISEAL in the area of sustainability provide good illustrations of these changes. Their creation has deeply affected the organizations participating in the meta-organization but also of those that did not enter the regime either because they did not want to or because they were excluded. Regulatory competition has also influenced the content and the scope of standards.

[16] P. Verbruggen and T. Havinga, Transnational Business Governance Interactions in Food Safety Regulation: Exploring the Promises and Risks of Enrolment, in *Transnational Business Governance Interactions: Empowering Marginalized Actors and Enhancing Regulatory Quality* (S. Wood et al. eds., 2019), 28–51.

[17] On the origins and development of FSC, see C. Overdevest and J. Zeitlin, Assembling and Experimentalist Regime: Transnational Governance Interactions in the Forest Sector (2014) 8:1 *Regulation and Governance* 22.

[18] Directive 2007/64/EC of the European Parliament and of the Council of 13 November 2007 on payment services in the internal market. On the evolution of the payment system, see A. Janczuck, Governing Global Payments Markets: The International Payments Framework-A New Actor on the Scene, in *The Governance and Regulation of International Finance* (G. Miller and F. Cafaggi eds., 2013), at 117.

[19] See A. Marx and J. Wouters, Competition and Cooperation in the Market of Voluntary Sustainability Standards, in *The Law, Economics and Politics of International Standardization* (P Delimatsis ed., 2015), at 215.

[20] See C. Scott, Regulating Everything: From Mega- to Meta-Regulation, UCD Geary Institute Discussion Paper Series WP 24 (2008).

The turn to the consumer protection and to sustainability by ISO has also been driven by external competitive pressure.[21]

So far primarily endogenous changes have been described. But exogenous factors have also played a role in the transformation of TPR. Often changes of private regulators' organizational models have been stimulated by rules recommended or imposed by IOs. This is part of the phenomenon that has successfully been labeled orchestration.[22] Prominent in orchestration has been the role of WTO.[23] WTO standards and rules have affected both the process and the content of transnational private standards.[24] These are, instead, exogenous-driven changes that do not present the features of a crisis but may transform the identity and mission of the private regulator.

Changes have come not only from IOs but also from the interaction between transnational private regulators and States. A form of regulatory interaction is clearly identifiable between ISO and the individual States.[25] Similarly, a very illustrative example of reciprocal influence is the relationship between International Swap and Derivatives Association (ISDA) and States in relation to bankruptcy where reciprocal influence has occurred over time.[26] These are examples of a broader phenomenon of institutional complementarity between transnational private regulators and public organizations including both States and international organizations.[27] The dynamics of institutional complementarity have been investigated through the lenses of interactions leading to, among other things, enhanced regulatory capacity.[28]

None of these changes, no matter how radical they might be, can be compared to those produced by systemic crises. Both the causes and the effects differ. But it is important to compare and to contrast dynamics of changes in ordinary times and

[21] See S. Bijlmakers, "The International Organization for Standardization: A Seventy-Five-Year Journey Toward Organizational Resilience" in this volume (Chapter 13).

[22] See K. Abbott, P. Genschel, D. Snidal, and B. Zangl (eds.), *International Organizations as Orchestrators* (2013).

[23] See W. Mattli and T. Büthe, *The New Global Rulers: The Privatization of Regulation in the World Economy* (2013); and P. Delimatsis, Global Standard-Setting 2.0: How the WTO Spotlights ISO and Impacts in the Transnational Standard-setting Process (2018) 28 *Duke Journal of Comparative and International Law* 273.

[24] See *supra* note 23.

[25] See P. Delimatsis, "Relevant International Standards" and "Recognised Standardization Bodies" under the TBT Agreement, in *The Law, Economics and Politics of International Standardization* (P. Delimatsis ed., 2015); S. Wood, Interactive Strategies for Advancing Marginalized Actors in Transnational Governance Contests: Labour and the Making of ISO 26000, in *Transnational Business Governance Interactions: Enhancing Regulatory Capacity, Ratcheting up Standards, and Empowering Marginalized Actors* (S. Wood, R. Schmidt, E. Meidinger, B. Eberlein, and K. W. Abbott eds., 2019).

[26] See M. K. Borowicz, Contracts as Regulation (2021) 17:1 *Capital Markets Law Journal*; C. Scott and J. Biggins, Public–Private Relations in a Transnational Private Regulatory Regime: ISDA, the State and OTC Derivatives Market Reform (2012) 13:3 *European Organisation Business Law Review* 309.

[27] See Cafaggi, *supra* note 1.

[28] See Wood et al., *supra* note 25.

dynamics of changes in times of crisis. Both dimensions of change and time of occurrence differ. During crises, changes are wider and sudden, often not always unanticipated. In ordinary times, changes are more incremental, to a greater extent foreseeable and they spread over time.

1.4 TPR AND CRISES RESPONSES: FROM ORGANIZATIONAL TO RELATIONAL RESILIENCE?

In Section 16.3, three dimensions were analyzed: (1) the structure of the regulatory process in transnational private regulation, (2) the organization of the regulatory space and the combination of competitive and cooperative relationships among regulators, and (3) the complementarity between public and private transnational regulation, its forms, and effects.How do crises impact on these three dimensions? How do changes and dynamics occurring in ordinary times differ from those originating from crises? Clearly the specific features of TPR call for a specific account of crises' impact and resolutions.

The relationship between crises and regulatory changes is at the core of many chapters in the book. A rich set of questions emerge. What are the characterizing elements of crises? How does one distinguish between a crisis and other types of radical or incremental institutional changes in regulatory processes? Is the impact of the crisis on regulatory processes permanent or temporary? Are the institutional consequences of a crisis reversible or irreversible? What factors should be considered to assess the impact of a crisis and evaluate its intensity and reversibility on transnational private regulation? Does transnational private regulation feature specific aspects in relation to crisis responses compared to public regulation? How can the impact and the role of organizational resilience in determining the consequences over TPR be measured?

The book's editors suggest that "rarity, irregularity and low likelihood are key traits of crisis events, calling for swift crisis management to allow for recovery. Crises constitute critical junctures which may result in distinct trajectories of change: chain reaction leading to collapse and extinction; transformation for the better; or recovery and rebirth under a renewed framework and context.[29] In that sense, crises are testbeds for effective crisis management and its potential for recovery and readjustment."[30]

The editors opt for a process rather than one-off-event definition of crisis. They suggest that both exogenous and endogenous factors determine both the characteristics and the responses to the crisis. A crisis is characterized by radical and

[29] See P. Delimatsis, "The Resilience of Private Authority in Times of Crisis" in this volume (Chapter 1).

[30] See also A. Carmeli and J. Schaubroeck, Organisational Crisis-Preparedness: The Importance of Learning from Failures (2008) 41 *Long Range Planning* 177, at 179.

unanticipated changes in the regulatory process. In the more radical scenario, it determines the dissolution of regimes and the emergence of new ones.

Crises should be distinguished from regulatory failures. Crises are characterized by sudden occurrence and unanticipated systemic effects. They involve a whole sector or even more than one sector. Once we distinguish between crises and regulatory failures and, within crises, we separate organizational from relational resilience, the next question is whether a unified theory of impact crisis can be proposed, or whether crises differ from one another and from sector to sector so that a single and unified impact theory cannot be plausibly offered.

Crises are characterized by unexpected and often sudden modifications of institutional conditions, determined by factors beyond the control of those institutions. The legal aspects of crises also differ depending on whether fundamental rights are at stake. This is one of the many differences between the financial crisis of 2008 and the sanitary crisis of 2020. Within crises, distinctions should be drawn depending on whether the driving factors of the crisis are endogenous or exogenous to the organization. The editors focus primarily on exogenous driven crises. A complementary inquiry into exogenous factors can help examine the impact of crises on TPR.

Clearly, it is the combination of the pre-existing institutional architecture and the specific factors determining the crisis, which influence the impact and the solution of the problems generated by the crisis, determining how private regulatory authority is redistributed among existing actors and, even more importantly, between existing and new players.

The broader question is "if" and "how" the crises impact on TPR and on the relationship between States, international organizations, and private regulators. More specifically, on which dimensions of TPR do crises have an impact? The recent COVID-19 crisis suggests that when fundamental rights are at stake changes have to be based on clear institutional architectures compliant with the rule of law. But a fully fledged theory of the relationship between crises and the rule of law has not yet been provided. The relevance of fundamental rights protection in crisis management will be shortly examined later.

To define the impact of crises on regulatory processes it is useful to distinguish between short- and long-terms effects. The short-term effects usually determine an increasing role of States and public actors. There is no evidence that during crises wider delegation of regulatory powers to private actors, including standard setting, takes place. On the contrary, emergencies often increase the power of public bodies to control regulatory processes, including those usually delegated to private regulators. This is particularly true when private regulation impinges on fundamental rights, as, for example, the area of data protection, information technologies, and freedom of expression. The COVID crisis however showed that the necessity to ensure compliance with sanitary obligations and the use of soft law has increased the role of private entities in monitoring compliance not only with soft but, at times, even with hard law.

Private standards are de jure voluntary, but the space of choice by regulated entities is determined by the concentration of regulatory power in the hands of regulators. The higher the concentration of regulatory power the more limited is the choice of regulated and the role of consent. Voluntary standards need time to be applied in order to persuade regulated entities to join in and comply. The conventional belief is that emergencies typical of crises can be incompatible with voluntary standards if persuasion rather than coercion is the basis for their adoption.

However, somewhat counterintuitively, the effectiveness of standard setting in times of emergency does not necessarily require hard public law. The COVID crisis has shown that nonbinding soft rules may be more effective than hard binding rules, especially when scientific uncertainty is pervasive and fundamental rights are at stake.[31] If persuasion and consent are the features common to both soft law and TPR then it might be possible that private standard setting might effectively operate even in emergency times. The long-term effects may simply rebalance the relationship with private actors or modify the composition of the private sphere and, at times, even increase their relevance.

A second important aspect, identified by the editors, is that of resilience. They note in the Introduction of this book that:

> resilience can also relate to a set of traits that allow an organization or system to overcome adversity either by recovering or, crucially, by reaching a new state of equilibrium. These would entail low connectivity to decrease vulnerability of a system; information flow through feedback loops; or the ability to improvise and reorient, for instance, through emergent leadership; and the learning of new behaviors and organizational patterns. As a consequence, then, resilience should be deemed as including pre-adversity organizational capabilities, capabilities of in-crisis organization and adjustment, and post-crisis resilient responses.

The contributions to the book focus on organizational resilience. The notion of resilience, according to the editors, includes not only the ability to adapt and change to respond to crisis but also resistance. It is preferable to distinguish between resilience and resistance and to correlate resilience with adaptation and change and resistance with lack of change.[32] Crises may generate both resilience and resistance and, within an organization, different interests may lead to either one. For example, the doping scandal that affected WADA prompted the organization to adopt strategies of resistance rather than resilience, as persuasively argued in by Tomic and Schmidt in their

[31] See F. Cafaggi and P. Iamiceli, Uncertainty, Administrative Decision-Making and Judicial Review: The Courts' Perspectives (2021) 14:1 *European Journal of Risk Regulation*.

[32] See P. Delimatsis, "The Resilience of Private Authority in Times of Crisis" in this volume (Chapter 1).

contribution to this book.[33] S. Tomic and R. Schmidt, "The Accountability Response of the Global Anti-doping Regime to the Russian Doping Scandal" in this volume (Chapter 11). In their account, legitimacy pressures can be a catalyst of a regime's institutionalization of accountability mechanisms, but the extent of such institutionalization will be limited by the regime's prior structure. Resilience clearly depends on the impact of change upon the preexisting distribution of power, its influence both within the organization and between the private organizations and the public actors.

In TPR, resilience associated with crises concern both the changes of individual organizations and the web of regulatory relationships within the sector. The impact of a crisis is correlated to the degree of organizational resilience and, more specifically, to the resilience of private actors within the organization (individual resilience) and between organizations (systemic resilience). The correlation between the impact of a crisis and resilience is not linear. Resilience does not necessarily increase or reduce the impact of a crisis; it affects the quality of the impact rather than its intensity. It operates differently for short- and for long-term effects of the crisis.

How does organizational resilience impact on the interactions between public and private actors in transnational regulatory processes? Crises often modify the relationship between public and private actors and redistribute power within the private domain. Usually, crises produce a concentration of regulatory power in the public hands during the time of crisis management. Thereafter, a reallocation of regulatory power between public and private occurs as a long-term effect of the crisis and the resilience of private authority emerges. As aptly illustrated by Nieves-Zárate in her contribution to this book, following the Deepwater Horizon oil spill, organizational changes introduced by the American Petroleum Institute (API) in response to demands and pressures by the US public regulator, resulted in API's standards to gain more influence in the federal regulatory framework. Within the private domain, crises redistribute power between regulated and beneficiaries and between beneficiaries and those harmed by the regulatory process.

Clearly one relevant aspect to analyse impact is represented by the geographical scope of the crisis. Whether its resolution can be delivered at local (national) level or global intervention is necessary. For example, following the global financial crisis, public policymakers in the United States aimed to address the problem of systemic risk by curbing the bankruptcy privileges of derivatives counterparties. The effectiveness of that solution required other jurisdictions to follow suit as derivatives transactions often include counterparties from multiple jurisdictions. Because it was not clear whether other jurisdictions would do it, policymakers relied on the ISDA amend the contracts commonly used in derivatives markets to achieve similar regulatory effects.[34]

[33] See M. Nieves-Zárate, "Organizational Responses of Transnational Private Regulators after Major Accidents: The Case of the American Petroleum Institute and the Deepwater Horizon Oil Spill" in this volume (Chapter 10).

[34] See Borowicz, *supra* note 26.

Often the regional level between national and global tends to be the most appropriate for measuring regulatory resilience. More specifically, the states' interests in devising collaborative versus non-collaborative solutions to the crisis play a role on the impact of crisis and its resolution. Clearly, the answer depends on the distribution of the costs of the crisis and the distribution of the costs of its resolution. Distributional effects concern the States; often crises determine uneven losses and gains across States but also across the different social constituencies. For example, the global financial crisis hit the real estate market first and then spilled over to many other areas until general taxpayers were involved. In the case of COVID-19, lockdowns harmed touristic and transport sectors first and then had a broader effect on other areas, whereas healthcare facilities and pharmaceutical industries clearly benefited from the crisis.

Resilience of public actors is driven by factors different from those affecting transnational private organizations. The allocation of powers can change within the public domain when the state of emergency is proclaimed as a consequence of the crisis. The recent crises, like that caused by the COVID-19 pandemic or by the war in Ukraine, show a shift from legislative to the executive power and an increasing role of judicial review to ensure that even in emergency times the balance of power is maintained and compliance with rule of law is warranted. Suffice to say that the role of emergency declarations to modify the relationship among powers within the State is not necessary in private organizations where the boundaries between ordinary and emergency often do not require or imply major regulatory changes. This is not to say that emergency crises do not have any impact on the operations of private regulators. Rather, it suggests that the effects of crises on the institutional balance within the organization differ depending on the public/private nature of the organization.

In private organizations, usually the effects of crises are not ex ante regulated. The occurrence of external shocks generates ad hoc reactions rather than being regulated in a systemic fashion. Hence, it is within the private autonomy that individual organizations react to crisis both in relation to their governance and their activity. This is not to say that TPR is impermeable to crises and shocks. But, unlike public organizations such as the State where emergency is the subject of specific rules that guarantee separation of powers and democratic principles, similar rules are not usually adopted in TPR – at least so far. Procedural accountability of transnational private regulators, both toward internal and external stakeholders, is certainly influenced by the emergency and given the recurrence of crises it might be important to define how private regulators should operate in time of crises.

TPR operates in a framework of complementarity with domestic and global public actors. Hence, if the focus should be on the relationship between crises and resilience, a question arises about the unit of analysis. Should resilience only be applied to the individual private regulator or should it also refer to the relationship between private regulators and public actors? In the latter case, the analysis should go beyond organizational and include relational resilience. The question is whether regulatory relationships and interactions are resilient to changes determined by crises. This is particularly important to address how complementarity between public and private actors changes during times of crises.

It is contended that organizational responses concerning individual regulators might differ from relational responses related to the sector and that internal dynamics within organizations, including States, might differ from those concerning the relationships between transnational private regulators and public actors. Institutional complementarity requires focusing on relational in addition to organizational resilience. The presence and influence of international organizations in the context of complementarity can play a significant role in promoting resilience and reducing the disruptive effects of crises. The inclusion of representatives of the International Labour Organization (ILO) within the Steering Committee of the Bangladesh Accord discussed in this book appears to have played such a role.

The issue deserves further empirical investigation, but it is fair to assume that crises modify the relationship between public and private bodies, redistributing the shares of transnational regulatory power. Hence, the core dimension of resilience becomes relational rather than organizational.

Resilience includes not only organizational changes but also relational changes concerning the consequences of the reallocation of power among regulators and of the redistribution of costs and gains from crises.

The institutional effects should be measured by analyzing not only the redistribution of power between states and private regulators but also by their modes of interaction during and after the crisis[35]. Hence, one should distinguish how crises change the interaction between public and private actors and then identify the dynamics among private actors within TPR generated by crises. Arguably, crises often tend to redistribute powers in favor of public entities and in particular States. This is especially true in relation to rule-making power, less to monitoring compliance.[36] In other words, the redistribution of regulatory power between public and private actors determined by crisis is not uniform across the regulatory process and its short-term effects differ from medium- and long-term effects. The investigation should verify how and why the regulatory arena and the allocation of regulatory shares is modified and the extent to which regulatory cooperation and interactions persist or cease to the benefit of the one (private) over the other (public).

1.5 TPR AND ITS EVOLUTION: THE WAY FORWARD

Crises have an impact on transnational regulation. They produce changes that usually differ from those brought about by regulatory failures. To determine the

[35] Eberlein et al., *supra* note 25.

[36] This is a common feature of both the financial and the COVID-19 crisis.

impact of crisis on the regulatory process, it is useful to distinguish between short- and long-term effects. The analysis shows that two intuitive conclusions may deserve greater scrutiny. Intuitively, crises should lead to the centralization of regulatory power and to a more intensive use of coercive rather than persuasive power. Centralization is determined by the need to have faster decision-making. Coercion is justified by the necessity to have more effective decision-making.

Both premises are plausible but too simplistic. There are instances where decentralization and persuasion provide faster and more effective regulatory regimes than centralization and coercion even during crises. In relation to centralization of regulatory power, the main variable is the homogeneity of the regulatory space. Centralization helps if local knowledge is not needed because there is homogeneity across regulated entities. Otherwise, when the regulatory context is heterogeneous and there are power and distributional conflicts among regulated entities, decentralization may be faster and more effective. Coercive force operates when there is general consensus about the rules by their addressees. If there are uncertainty and divergent beliefs among regulated and beneficiaries, persuasion may work better than coercion.

Hence, more empirical analysis is needed to understand when and upon which conditions the objectives of faster and more effective regulatory processes can be achieved after crises have occurred. The notion of resilience, which has become overwhelmingly relevant, may also deserve further elaboration, encompassing not only the organizational dimension but also the relational perspective that has engaged scholars in both the descriptive and normative efforts to explain the evolution of transnational regulation. Resilience is not an independent variable. Regulatory regimes can influence the degree of resilience and the ability to react to shocks and stresses.[37] Crises can affect both legitimacy and effectiveness of transnational private regulation. Resilience can contribute to make these challenges an opportunity for change rather than the cause of regimes' dissolution, but it needs to be steered by both institutional and organizational responses.

37 See FAO, The State of Food and Agriculture, Making Agrifood Systems More Resilient to Shocks and Stresses (2021).

Index

www.ingramcontent.com/pod-product-compliance
Lightning Source LLC
LaVergne TN
LVHW011702200926
848484LV00004B/1042
* 9 7 8 1 0 0 9 3 2 9 3 6 1 *